Essential Data Structures and Algorithms in Java

Apply proven problem-solving patterns to write faster and cleaner AI-native code

Joseph Su

<packt>

Essential Data Structures and Algorithms in Java

Portfolio Director: Gebin George
Relationship Lead: Srishti Seth
Project Manager: K. Loganathan
Content Engineer: Sujata Tripathi
Technical Editor: Irfa Ansari, Aysha Nadeem
Copy Editor: Sujata Tripathi
Indexer: Tejal Soni
Proofreader: Sujata Tripathi
Production Designer: Vijay Kamble
Growth Lead: Vinishka Kalra

First published: July 2026

Production reference: 1290726

Published by Packt Publishing Ltd.
Grosvenor House
11 St Paul's Square
Birmingham
B3 1RB, UK.

ISBN 978-1-83588-370-9
`www.packtpub.com`

To my wife and family, whose endless patience and unwavering support made this book possible.
Thank you for being my constant anchor and inspiration.

– Joseph Su

Contributors

About the author

Joseph Su is a veteran software engineering leader, educator, and author with over 20 years of experience building high-throughput, low-latency systems for data-intensive industries. He holds a Master of Science from the Massachusetts Institute of Technology (MIT), focusing on Bayesian AI in sensor fusion, and an M.S. in Machine Learning from Georgia Tech. Alongside engineering scalable production software, Joseph has extensive experience lecturing college and graduate-level computer science courses, specializing in data structures and algorithms, and object-oriented software and web development.

I would like to extend my sincere gratitude to the technical reviewers of this book, Sriram and Howard, for their time and invaluable feedback. I am also deeply grateful to the entire team at Packt for their continuous guidance and support throughout the writing process.

About the reviewers

Sriram Keerthy is a full-stack developer with over 21 years of experience. He has developed multiple large-scale distributed systems in Java ranging from Investment Banking applications to Ebook Catalog management and Digital Advertising services. Sriram has also conducted technical coding interviews for over 350 candidates during this time.

I thank Joseph, my colleague and the author of this book, for entrusting me with this technical reviewer opportunity. I found Packt Publishing's process well-organized and the team was accommodating to my schedule as I worked on the technical reviews alongside my time into work, academic, family and personal things.

Table of Contents

Preface **xxiii**

Free benefits with your book xxix

Part 1: Introduction **1**

Chapter 1: Data Structures and Algorithms **3**

Technical requirements 4

Data structures 5

Importance • 5

Applications • 5

File systems • 6

Data warehousing • 7

Types of data structures • 9

Linear data structures • 11

Non-linear data structures • 13

The DSA bridge to modern AI 15

The AI context • 16

Algorithmic blueprint • 16

Agentic lifecycle • 17

Input gateway • 18

Memory, context, and knowledge retrieval • 19

Reasoning • 21

Task selection and execution • 22

Routing and verification • 24

Moving to abstraction • 26

Abstract data type • 27

Java collections framework 29

Algorithms 31

Why algorithms? • 31

Algorithmic performance • 32

Algorithm analysis • 32

Algorithm 1 • 34

Algorithm 2 • 35

Complexity 36

Asymptotic analysis • 37

Big O notation • 38

Why big O matters • 38

Common big O examples • 38

Common big O time complexities • 40

Algebraic rules for big O analysis • 41

Rule 1: Focus on the dominant term • 41

Rule 2: Ignore multiplicative constants • 42

Rule 3: Ignore constant addition/subtraction • 42

Rule 4: Addition rule • 42

Rule 5: Division rule • 42

Summary 43

Part 2: Common Data Structures and Applications 45

Chapter 2: Arrays and Linked Lists 47

Arrays 48

Array operations and their efficiency • 49

Resizing arrays: Expansion and contraction • 53

Amortized analysis: Resizing an array • 55

Assessing the expansion cost • 57

Vectors • 61

Types of arrays • 61

Unordered arrays • 62

Ordered arrays • 64

Linked lists 65

Operations and efficiency • 66

Types of linked lists • 67

ConcurrentLinkedQueue • 68

LinkedHashMap • 68

Comparing arrays and linked lists 69

Flexibility, access, and operations • 69

Real-world application: High-frequency logging • 69

Summary 70

Exercises 72

Exercise 1: Token window in agentic workflows • 72

Solution • 73

Exercise 2: Remove duplicates from sorted array • 74

Exercise 3: Merge two sorted lists • 74

Exercise 4: Rotate array • 75

Exercise 5: Remove linked list nodes • 76

Exercise 6: Find the middle element of a list • 76

Exercise 7: Max subarray • 77

Exercise 8: Intersection of two arrays • 77

Chapter 3: Stacks and Queues 79

What is a stack? 80

Example 1: Browser back-button navigation • 81

Example 2: Word processor undo/redo mechanism • 83

Abstract data type (ADT): Stack • 84

Concrete implementations • 85

Array-based stack (DynamicArrayStack) • 85

List-based stack (LinkedListStack) • 86

Performance: Linked-based vs. array-based stacks • 88

Memory • 90

When to use what? • 90

A stack example • 90

Thread-safe deque • 91

Queue 93

What is a queue • 93

Example 1: Print spooler queue • 94

Example 2: Deferred processing and prioritization • 95

Abstract data type (ADT): Queue • 95

Concrete implementations • 96

Array-based queue (DynamicArrayQueue) • 97

Link-based queue (LinkedListQueue) • 99

Summary **100**

Exercises **101**

Exercise 1: Nested tool invocation in agentic workflows • 102

Solution • 102

Exercise 2: MinStack • 103

Exercise 3: Queue using two stacks • 104

Exercise 4: Daily temperatures: Next warmer day • 104

Exercise 5: Sliding window maximum • 105

Exercise 6: Reverse polish notation • 105

Exercise 7: Task scheduler • 106

Exercise 8: LRU cache • 107

Chapter 4: Maps and Hash Tables 109

What is a map? **109**

Example 1: Address books • 110

Example 2: Parking garage ticketing system • 111

Abstract data type (ADT): Map **112**

Concrete implementations **114**

Fundamentals of hashing **114**

What is a hash and hash function? • 115

Key properties of good hashing • 116

Why hashing amortizes to O(1)? • 117

Collision resolution techniques **119**

Open addressing • 119

Linear probing • 119

Quadratic probing • 119

Closed addressing • 120

Separate chaining • 120

Hashing and the core map operations **121**

Examples of hashing in practice **122**

Summary **122**

Exercises **124**

Exercise 1: HashMap-based AI agent state management • 124

Solution • 127

Exercise 2: Uniform hash function • 129

Exercise 3: Linear probing hash map • 129
Exercise 4: Quadratic probing hash map • 131
Exercise 5: Chaining hash map • 132
Exercise 6: Hash table with open addressing • 134
Exercise 7: HashMap with load factor monitoring • 135
Exercise 8: HashMap with collision statistics • 137

Chapter 5: Trees 141

What is a tree? 141
Binary trees and properties 142
Java representation • 143
Binary search trees (BST) and properties 144
Java representation • 146
General (n-ary) trees and properties 146
Java representation • 147
Abstract data type (ADT) 148
N-ary tree ADT • 148
Binary tree ADT • 149
What is a traversal? 150
Depth-first traversal 151
Recursive methods: DFS • 151
Pre-order traversal (node, left, right) • 151
In-order traversal (left, node, right) • 152
Post-order traversal (left, right, node) • 153
Iterative methods: DFS • 153
DFS traversal complexity: recursion vs. iteration • 156
Breadth-first traversal 156
Iterative methods: BFS • 157
BFS traversal complexity: recursion vs. iteration • 158
BFS vs. DFS 159
Trees in java collection framework 160
TreeMap for sorted Key-Value storage • 161
TreeSet for sorted unique elements • 162
NavigableMap interface operations • 162
NavigableSet interface range operations • 163

Custom tree sorting with comparator • 163
Summary 164
Exercises 166
Exercise 1: Knowledge base category search in AI • 166
Solution • 169
Exercise 2: Validate binary search tree • 172
Exercise 3: Pre-order from in-order implementation • 173
Exercise 4: Iterative post-order traversal with a single stack • 174
Exercise 5: Level-order traversal without a queue • 176
Exercise 6: Memory-efficient traversal • 178
Exercise 7: Maximum depth of binary tree • 178
Exercise 8: Binary tree side view • 179
Exercise 9: Lowest common ancestor of a binary tree • 180

Chapter 6: Priority Queues and Heaps 183

What is a priority queue? 183
Example 1: Seat assignment on a flight • 185
Example 2: Top K elements • 185
Abstract data type (ADT): priority queue 187
Order, priority, and efficiency • 187
Implementing priority queues using arrays 187
Unsorted array • 188
Sorted array • 189
Complexity of unsorted array vs. sorted array • 189
The heap abstraction 190
The shape property • 190
Implementations: Array- and Tree-based heap 191
Array-based heap • 191
Tree-based heap • 192
Minimum and maximum heaps • 192
Heap operations 193
Heapify-up • 195
Heapify-down • 197
Complexity analysis • 198
O(insert) • 198

O(delete) • *198*

Applications and use cases **199**

Advanced heaps **200**

Heaps in java collections framework **201**

PriorityQueue as heap • 203

ArrayDeque with custom heap logic • 203

TreeSet with heap-like functionality • 204

Summary **204**

Exercises **206**

Exercise 1: Min-Heap • 206

Solution • *207*

Exercise 2: Max-Heap • 209

Exercise 3: Find the kth largest element • 211

Exercise 4: K closest points to the origin • 211

Exercise 5: Top K frequent elements • 212

Exercise 6: Merge K sorted arrays • 213

Exercise 7: Task scheduler • 214

Exercise 8: Last stone weight • 215

Chapter 7: Graphs 217

What is a graph? **217**

Types of graphs **219**

Undirected and directed graphs • 219

Weighted graphs • 220

Graph components **223**

Vertex • 223

Edge • 225

Vertex-to-Edge • 226

Graph representation **228**

Adjacency list • 228

Adjacency matrix • 230

Performance characteristics • 232

Choosing a graph representation • 233

When to use adjacency list • *233*

When to use adjacency matrix • *233*

Abstract data type (ADT) – graph 234
What is a traversal? 235
Depth-first traversal • 236
Breadth-first traversal • 239
Trade-off analysis: DFS vs. BFS • 241
Graphs in java collections framework 242
HashSet for unweighted graphs • 242
Priority queue: Dijkstra's algorithm • 243
Deque: BFS implementation • 243
Stack: DFS implementation • 244
TreeMap: Ordered map operations • 244
ConcurrentHashMap: Parallel graph processing • 245
LinkedHashSet: Maintaining insertion order • 245
Summary 246
Exercises 248
Exercise 1: AI agent dependency resolution • 248
Problem • 248
Solution • 252
Complexity: O(n2) • 255
Exercise 2: Undirected weighted graph • 256
Exercise 3: Cycle detection in DAG • 257
Exercise 4: Counting connected regions • 258
Exercise 5: Can all courses be finished? • 260
Exercise 6: Shortest path with BFS • 261
Exercise 7: Number of connected components • 262
Exercise 8: Analyze graph connectivity • 263

Part 3: Practical Algorithms and Examples 267

Chapter 8: Dynamic Programming 269

What is dynamic programming? 270
Why DP Matters 272
Classic example: 0/1 knapsack problem • 272
Core concepts and techniques 273
Recurrence relations • 273

Classic example: Fibonacci sequence • 274

Bottom-up (iterative) approach • 275

Top-Down (recursive + memoization) approach • 275

Fibonacci recurrence: Overlapping and optimal substructure • 276

Memoization vs. tabulation • 276

Execution style • 277

Storage structure • 277

Complexity • 278

Space usage • 278

When to choose • 278

Classic DP illustrations 278

Problem: Continuous sum in an integer series • 278

Intuition • 279

Solution • 280

Observation • 281

Problem: Edit distance (levenshtein) in strings • 281

Formulation • 281

Initialization • 282

Solution • 283

Observation • 286

Problem: Cheapest flight route with At-Most K stops • 287

Intuition • 287

Solution: Bottom-Up DP • 287

Solution: Top-Down DP • 289

Problem: Building a product pipeline with DP • 293

Objectives • 293

Intuition • 293

Solution • 293

DP practicals checklist 297

Summary 298

Exercises 300

Exercise 1: Climbing stairs problem • 300

Solution • 301

Exercise 2: Maximize sum without adjacent elements • 303

Exercise 3: Coin change • 305

Exercise 4: Longest common subsequence • 306
Exercise 5: 0/1 knapsack • 307
Exercise 6: Word break • 308
Exercise 7: Longest increasing subsequence • 309
Exercise 8: Target sum • 310

Chapter 9: Recursion 313

Understanding recursion: patterns, mechanics, and pitfalls 313
Recursive patterns • 314
Designing good base cases • 314
Example: Factorial • 315
Recursion vs. iteration 316
Recursion call stack 318
The implicit call stack: How recursion works • 319
The challenge of naive recursion (overlapping subproblems) • 320
Tail recursion 322
Examples • 322
Measuring complexity 323
Analyzing merge sort • 324
Method: Recursion tree • 325
Recursive component: 2T(N/2) • 325
Non-recursive component: f(N) • 325
Recursive tree analysis of f(N) • 326
Total cost of merge sort • 326
Method: the master theorem • 326
Cost of recursive calls (aT(n/b)) • 327
Cost of non-recursive work (f(n)) • 328
Theorem summary • 329
Example 1: Merge sort • 330
Step 1: Define the recurrence relation • 330
Step 2: Identify the parameters (a, b, and f(n)) • 330
Step 3: Calculate the recursive value • 330
Step 4: Apply the master theorem • 331
Step 5: Determine the complexity • 331
Example 2: Binary search • 331

Step 1: Define the recurrence relation • 331

Step 2: Identify the parameters (a, b, and f(n)) • 331

Step 3: Calculate the recursive value • 332

Step 4: Apply the master theorem • 332

Step 5: Determine the complexity • 332

Recursion in data structures **332**

Binary tree depth-first search • 333

Quick sort depth-first search • 333

Recursive BFS on a graph • 333

Summary **334**

Exercises **335**

Exercise 1: AI prompt template expansion • 336

Example • 336

Problem • 336

Solution • 339

Exercise 2: Merge sort analysis • 341

Exercise 3: Recursion to iteration conversion • 342

Exercise 4: String permutations • 343

Exercise 5: Subset sum • 345

Exercise 6: Arithmetic expression parser • 346

Exercise 7: Binary tree traversal • 348

Exercise 8: Geometric series sum • 350

Chapter 10: Sorting 353

What is sorting? **353**

Sorting algorithm properties and trade-offs **353**

Stability in sorting • 354

In-place vs. out-of-place sorting • 355

In-place • 355

Out-of-place • 355

Time complexity • 356

Space complexity • 356

Classification of sorting algorithms **357**

$O(n^2)$ basic comparison sorts **357**

Bubble sort • 357

Selection sort • 359
Insertion sort • 360
The Ω (n log n) limit **362**
The proof sketch • 362
Selection implications • 362
Advanced comparison sorts **363**
Merge sort • 363
Algorithm walkthrough • 365
Quick sort • 366
The partition process • 367
Algorithm walkthrough • 367
Pivot selection: Mitigating the O(n2) Worst-Case • 368
Heap sort • 369
Heapification and extraction: The two-phase approach • 371
Algorithm walkthrough • 371
Non-comparison sorts **372**
Counting sort • 372
Radix sort • 375
Algorithm walkthrough • 377
When to use which sort **378**
Merge sort • 378
Quick sort • 378
Heap sort • 378
Counting sort • 378
Radix sort • 379
Hybrid comparison-based sorts **380**
Dual-pivot quicksort • 380
The Two-pivot strategy • 380
Example • 381
Timsort • 383
Example • 383
Engineered sorts in the real world **384**
Summary **386**
Exercises **388**
Exercise 1: RAG Re-ranking in AI • 388

Solution • 391

Time complexity: O(N log N) • 392

Exercise 2: Stability analysis • 392

Exercise 3: Space complexity implementation • 395

Exercise 4: Pivot selection strategies • 397

Exercise 5: Hybrid algorithm design • 400

Exercise 6: Find the K-th largest element in an array • 403

Exercise 7: Top K frequent elements • 405

Exercise 8: Merge intervals • 407

Chapter 11: Concurrency 411

Introduction to threads and concurrent execution 412

Shared state • 414

Atomic operations and hardware-level guarantees • 416

Why atomic operations are necessary • 416

Hardware-level atomicity: Compare-and-Swap (CAS) • 416

Java's atomic facilities • 416

Hardware-level guarantee • 417

Mutual exclusion • 418

Synchronization • 419

Deadlock • 419

Lock interface • 420

Condition • 423

Semaphore • 424

Lock-free data structures and memory models 426

Memory visibility • 426

Stacks and queues • 427

Arrays and lists • 431

Option A: Coarse-grained thread safety via synchronized wrappers • 431

Option B: Trade-offs of copy-on-write arrays • 432

Option C: Lock-free general-purpose deques • 433

Concurrent hash tables • 433

Lock-free striped word counter • 434

Collision resolution • 435

Safe and managed concurrency 436

BlockingQueue: Producer-consumer pattern • 436
Executors: Thread pool management • 436
ThreadLocal: Per-thread context • 437
CompletableFuture: Async composition • 437
ReadWriteLock: Read-heavy workloads • 438
CountDownLatch: Wait for N tasks • 439
Semaphore: Concurrency limitation • 439

Concurrency in java collections framework 440

ConcurrentSkipListMap: Sorted concurrent map • 440
ConcurrentSkipListSet: Sorted concurrent set • 440
CopyOnWriteArraySet: Read-heavy workloads • 441
BlockingDeque: Double-ended queue • 441
TransferQueue: With transfer operations • 442
PriorityBlockingQueue: Concurrent priority queue • 443
ConcurrentLinkedQueue: Lock-free queue • 444
ArrayBlockingQueue: Fixed-size queue • 444

Summary 445

Exercises 447

Exercise 1: Shared model registry in AI • 447
Problem • 447
Solution • 450
Exercise 2: Concurrent counter • 452
Exercise 3: Coarse-grained locking on a linked list • 453
Exercise 4: Optimistic locking on a linked list • 455
Exercise 5: The hidden bug in lazy initialization • 457
Exercise 6: The inventory race condition • 458
Exercise 7: The banking deadlock • 459
Exercise 8: The memory leak in ThreadLocal storage • 460

Chapter 12: DSA in Production 463

Foundational linear structures 463

Key applications • 463

Control flow and state management 465

Key applications • 465

Indexing and retrieval 467

Key applications • 467

Organization and hierarchy **469**

Key applications • 469

Priority and scheduling **471**

Key applications • 471

Graph theory and relational modeling **473**

Key applications • 473

Memoization and optimization **475**

Key applications • 475

Operational patterns: recursion **477**

Key applications • 477

Algorithmic ordering **478**

Key applications • 479

Concurrent system dynamics **481**

Key applications • 481

Chapter 13: Unlock Your Exclusive Benefits 483

Unlock this Book's Free Benefits in 3 Easy Steps **484**

Other Books You May Enjoy 488

Index 491

Preface

Books on Data Structures and Algorithms (DSA) typically fall into two rigid categories: those that overemphasize data structures and those that focus too deeply on abstract algorithm theory:

- **Data structure-heavy books** concentrate primarily on data organization and manipulation. They usually adopt a bottom-up approach, starting with basic concepts and building up to highly complex structures rarely utilized in modern industry, often lacking practical examples from a broader algorithmic perspective.
- **Algorithm-heavy books** take a top-down approach instead. They are often dense with theoretical formulations and mathematical models, making them too abstract to bridge with practical software engineering. While they provide high-level overviews of problem-solving techniques, they frequently overlook the lower-level mechanics of the underlying data structures.

This book, in contrast, offers a strategic, balanced mixture of **front-loaded and back-loaded concepts** in DSA, taught entirely through pragmatic software engineering examples. In an era dominated by rapid AI advancements, this dual approach is vital: front-loading foundational concepts empowers you to orchestrate and prompt code automation tools with immediate clarity, while back-loading advanced optimization techniques ensures you possess the deep analytical skills required to review and validate complex automated logic.

The evolving role of the software engineer

In the era of modern software development, the role of a Software Engineer is fundamentally changing. Engineers are moving away from simply "writing code" to "directing code generation and validating outputs." Just as calculators did not eliminate mathematicians, advanced AI automation will not replace engineers. Instead, these tools free up your cognitive capacity, allowing you to work on much harder, higher-level system problems.

By mastering the foundational concepts in this text, you will spend less time wrestling with trivial syntax and more time on high-impact engineering objectives:

- **Engineering via Algorithmic Prompting**: Specify precise abstract data types (ADTs) and Big-O bounds so automated tools generate optimal, production-ready logic on the first attempt

- **Auditing Code for Complexity**: Catch and override hidden AI performance bottlenecks (such as accidental $O(n^2)$ nested loops) with mathematically sound algorithms before code hits production
- **Designing for Structural Resilience**: Leverage foundational components like priority queues, ring buffers, and graph structures to absorb traffic backpressure and isolate systemic failures
- **Hardening Systems Against Vulnerabilities**: Spot and neutralize silent security risks that automated code generators frequently overlook, from algorithmic hash collisions to memory leaks
- **Refactoring AI Code Bloat**: Compress thousands of lines of sprawling, unmaintainable AI output into clean architectural patterns by mapping messy real-world logic onto elegant data models

Pedagogical features

This book presents a highly balanced mix of walk-throughs and hands-on exercises. To help you build solutions organically, every chapter includes:

- **Step-by-Step Instructions**: Clear, guided walkthroughs breaking down complex logic into digestible pieces
- **Graphical Illustrations**: Detailed visual aids mapping out how data moves and changes in memory
- **Learn by Doing**: Applied exercises designed to shift you immediately from passive reading to active coding

Who this book is for

This book is specifically crafted for individuals who already have exposure to programming in **Java** or who possess a foundational understanding of **object-oriented design** principles. We skip repetitive syntax tutorials, building directly upon a working knowledge of **JDK 11 (or above)** and fundamental linear memory arrangements, such as arrays and linked lists. If you want to deeply understand how to leverage, optimize, and navigate these structures within complex algorithms and modern computer science, this book is your guide.

The intentional **front-loading of core concepts** gives you more time throughout the course to digest and apply what you learn to solve real-world problems. This stands in stark contrast to many traditional books that back-load heavy concepts at the very end, helping you pace your learning trajectory much more efficiently.

What this book covers

Chapter 1, Data Structures and Algorithms, introduces foundational structures, the Java Collections Framework (JCF), and algorithmic performance concepts like Big O notation and asymptotic analysis. Readers evaluate complexity and memory trade-offs using real-world examples, including linked lists for file systems and hash maps for data warehousing, establishing the architectural metrics required to optimize system runtime and guide automated tools.

Chapter 2, Arrays and Linked Lists, provides an in-depth exploration of two primary List ADT implementations: `ArrayList` and `LinkedList`. It analyzes memory trade-offs and structural efficiencies across native arrays and linked elements using low-level primitive operations.

Chapter 3, Stacks and Queues, contrasts LIFO and FIFO linear structures across array-based and linked-list implementations using `java.util` packages and primitives. Concepts are practically anchored through industry use cases, ranging from text-editor undo mechanisms and code syntax validation to task scheduling and graph-based Breadth-First Search (BFS).

Chapter 4, Maps and Hash Tables, introduces the Map ADT and foundational hashing mechanics to achieve near-constant-time key-value data lookups. Readers learn to optimize data retrieval pipelines while navigating and mitigating hash collisions.

Chapter 5, Trees, introduces the Tree ADT, contrasting N-ary trees with Binary Search Trees (BSTs). It covers breadth and depth-first traversal strategies, teaching readers to select optimal tree layouts to execute hierarchical operations within strict `O(n)` boundaries.

Chapter 6, Priority Queues and Heaps, introduces the Priority Queue ADT and its efficient implementation via binary heaps, bypassing slow `O(n)` structural scans. It covers how heaps maintain constant-time `O(1)` lookup and logarithmic `O(log n)` restorations, applying these properties to task scheduling and live ranking pipelines.

Chapter 7, Graphs, explores graphs, $G = (V, E)$, and their structural variants to model network dependencies and routing pathways. It covers fundamental graph traversal mechanisms alongside memory representations in adjacency lists and adjacency matrices, while leveraging the Java Collection Framework to build scalable vertex-edge management and connectivity systems.

Chapter 8, Dynamic Programming, introduces the dynamic programming paradigm, demonstrating how optimal substructure and overlapping subproblems convert exponential execution trees into polynomial-time solutions. It covers state identification and recurrence formulations while contrasting top-down memoization with bottom-up tabulation to eliminate redundant calculations.

Chapter 9, Recursion, establishes recursion using precise base cases and call-stack steps to solve complex subproblems. It introduces tail recursion to mitigate memory risks and employs the Master Theorem to systematically calculate mathematical complexity.

Chapter 10, Sorting, outlines sorting fundamentals, covering comparison and non-comparison algorithms, complexity, and stability. It further details modern hybrid approaches to optimize real-world data sorting pipelines.

Chapter 11, Concurrency, introduces concurrency fundamentals, addressing race conditions, thread-safe abstractions, and lock-free structures. It teaches readers to balance synchronization overhead against algorithmic complexity to engineer scalable, multi-threaded backend architectures.

Chapter 12, DSA in Production, moves beyond theoretical analysis to explore how practical DSA patterns steer the scalability of modern production software stacks. It features comprehensive summary diagrams detailing the exact concepts, use cases, and architectural applicability of every data structure and algorithm introduced throughout this book.

To get the most out of this book

Assumed Knowledge

This book focuses purely on Data Structures and Algorithms (DSA) and is not an introductory programming text. To succeed with the concepts and implementations presented here, we assume you possess the following foundational skills:

- **Core Java syntax**: You should be comfortable writing standard Java code, including loops (for, while), conditional branching (if-else, switch), and structural scopes.
- **Object-Oriented Programming (OOP)**: You must thoroughly understand classes, objects, interfaces, inheritance, polymorphism, and access modifiers (public, private, protected).
- **Basic memory awareness**: You should understand the conceptual difference between primitive data types (like int and double) and object references, as well as how they behave when passed into methods.
- **Basic mathematical intuition**: You will need comfort with fundamental algebra, basic logarithms, and arithmetic sequences to confidently follow along with algorithmic complexity analysis.

System and Software Setup

To run and experiment with the book's examples, configure a modern Java environment on your machine:

- **JDK 11 or higher**: Required to support modern language features, standard collection library enhancements, and compiler updates.
- **Java IDE**: Use an industry-standard IDE like IntelliJ IDEA, Eclipse, or Visual Studio Code to easily trace code, debug call stacks, and benchmark.

Download the example code files

This book includes a complete downloadable code bundle containing all the example projects and files used throughout the chapters. We recommend downloading the bundle so you can follow along smoothly and experiment with the examples.

Use the bundle as a practical starting point. Modify it, extend it, and apply what you learn by creating your own variations as you progress through the chapters.

Get the code bundle

If you bought the book directly from Packt:

1. Go to packtpub.com
2. Click your profile picture and select Your Orders
3. Find this book and click **Download Code**

If you bought this book from Amazon or any other channel partner:

1. Go to packtpub.com/unlock or scan the following QR code:

1. Search for this book
2. Sign up or log in to your free Packt account
3. Upload your proof of purchase and download the code bundle locally

Usage note: You're free to use and modify this code for personal learning and non-commercial projects.

Conventions used

There are a number of text conventions used throughout this book.

`CodeInText`: Indicates code words in text, database table names, folder names, filenames, file extensions, pathnames, dummy URLs, user input, and Twitter handles. For example: "Adding a new edge can be done via `vertexSource.addEdge(vertexDestination)`, which appends the new edge to the source vertex's local neighbor list. "

A block of code is set as follows:

```
public interface Graph<V> {
    void addVertex(V v);
    void addEdge(V src, V dst);
    List<Edge<V>> neighbors(V v);
    Collection<Vertex<V>> getVertices();
}
```

Note

Warnings or important notes appear like this.

Tip

Tips and tricks appear like this.

Get in touch

Feedback from our readers is always welcome.

General feedback: If you have questions about any aspect of this book or have any general feedback, please email us at `customercare@packt.com` and mention the book's title in the subject of your message.

Errata: Although we have taken every care to ensure the accuracy of our content, mistakes do happen. If you have found a mistake in this book, we would be grateful if you reported this to us. Please visit `http://www.packt.com/submit-errata`, click **Submit Errata**, and fill in the form.

Piracy: If you come across any illegal copies of our works in any form on the internet, we would be grateful if you would provide us with the location address or website name. Please contact us at `copyright@packt.com` with a link to the material.

If you are interested in becoming an author: If there is a topic that you have expertise in and you are interested in either writing or contributing to a book, please visit `http://authors.packt.com/`.

Free benefits with your book

This book includes free benefits designed to support your learning and help you apply what you learn effectively. Activate them now for instant access (see the *How to unlock* section for instructions).

Here's a quick overview of what you can instantly unlock with your purchase:

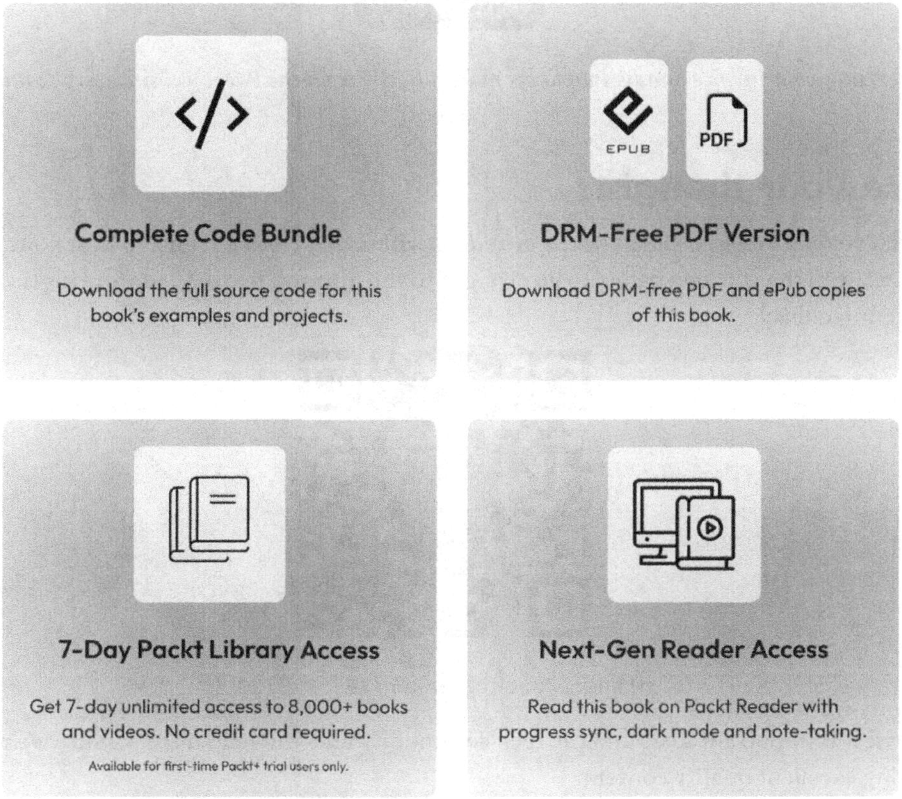

How to unlock

Scan the QR code (or go to `packtpub.com/unlock`). Search for this book by name, confirm the edition, and then follow the steps on the page.

UNLOCK NOW

Note: Have your invoice handy. Purchases made directly from the Packt website don't require an invoice.

Share your thoughts

Once you've read *Essential Data Structures and Algorithms in Java*, we'd love to hear your thoughts! Scan the QR code below to go straight to the Amazon review page for this book and share your feedback.

`https://packt.link/r/1835883710`

Your review is important to us and the tech community and will help us make sure we're delivering excellent quality content.

Part 1

Introduction

In this section, you'll establish the foundational framework of **Data Structures and Algorithms (DSA)**, demonstrating that efficient computation relies on effective data structuring and mathematically rigorous analysis. We investigate the dichotomy between linear and non-linear data structures, focusing on examples like arrays, linked lists, trees, graphs, and hash maps, while leveraging **Abstract Data Types (ADTs)** to ensure decoupling and system design flexibility.

You will master the mathematical framework of Asymptotic Analysis using Big O notation to accurately measure and compare the time and space complexity of your solutions.

Far from being purely academic, these foundational principles (i.e., structural dichotomy, ADT decupling, and asymptotic analysis) serve as the exact operational engine for modern Artificial Intelligence, allowing AI Agents and **Large Language Models (LLMs)** to plan, recall context, and execute complex workflows. By grounding yourself in these essential principles, you will develop the specialized intuition needed to evaluate performance trade-offs, select optimal data structures, and engineer scalable, intelligent software systems.

This part of the book includes the following chapter:

- *Chapter 1, Data Structures and Algorithms*

1

Data Structures and Algorithms

This book serves as a practical refresher on core Computer Science concepts. We focus on the design and efficient implementation of data structures and algorithms, providing clear, modern examples using Java (JDK17+). It is specially designed for aspiring developers and CS students who already have a solid foundation in Java OOP and are ready to elevate their problem-solving skills and write optimized code. The three main objectives of this book are:

- **Introduce Core Data Structures**: cover fundamental data structures such as arrays, linked lists, stacks, queues, trees, graphs, and hash tables
- **Teach Algorithmic Techniques**: equip readers with skills to analyze algorithms' performance characteristics and ways to optimize them through techniques like sorting, searching, and graph traversal methods
- **Foster Critical Thinking and Efficiency**: encourage readers to adopt efficient solutions using data structures such as Bloom filters or suffix trees, enabling cost savings in applications like product recommendations and search results to yield more personalized experiences for users

To achieve the above objectives, we will be following a gentle approach, introducing key concepts gradually and providing step-by-step illustrations and exercises to reinforce learning. In this chapter, we will start by delving into data structures. We will answer questions such as: What is a data structure? What is the importance of data structures, what are their characteristics and trade-offs, and why do we use them? How do we determine the right data structure to use for solving a problem in Computer Science? What would happen if we didn't have data structures in Computer Science?

By the end of this chapter, you will be able to:

- Learn what data structures are, why they are essential in organizing and managing data, and how they are used in various applications.
- Learn the purpose of certain common data structures and their general trade-offs for different tasks.
- Grasp the concept of abstraction by separating the "what" from the "how".
- Differentiate between the interface of **abstract data types** (**ADTs**), their implementation, focusing on their functionality and their operational methods, respectively.
- Understand the high-level hierarchy and core interfaces of the **Java Collections Framework** (**JCF**) (such as `List`, `Set`, `Map`, `Queue`, etc.), and their common implementations (such as `ArrayList`, `LinkedList`, `HashSet`, `TreeSet`, `HashMap`, `TreeMap`, `PriorityQueue`, etc.)

> **Note**
>
> **Download the PDF version of this book**
>
> Your purchase includes a DRM-free PDF copy of this book, the code bundle, and a range of exclusive benefits. To unlock everything, follow the *Free benefits with your book* section in the *Preface*.

Technical requirements

The examples provided in this chapter were developed using stable Java, version 17, which is recommended as the minimum version for working on these exercises. However, many exercises are also compatible with earlier versions of Java due to their independence from specific libraries and features introduced in newer versions. We encourage readers to visit `https://www.oracle.com/java/technologies/downloads/` and select the most suitable version of Java that meets their needs. The code repository is organized chapter-wise in this book's GitHub repository. To unlock the GitHub repo link, refer to the instructions in the *Download the example code files* section of the *Preface*.

Data structures

Data structures are systematic ways of organizing and arranging data to enable efficient storage, manipulation, and retrieval. Implemented in different programming languages, they play a pivotal role in fields like machine learning, big data, and AI, where they help manage large datasets and handle complex operations at scale. As a software developer, understanding data structures is essential to building efficient, performant, and maintainable computing solutions.

Importance

Different data structures have different use cases in computer science and programming. The premise behind the use of data structures is to enhance the efficiency, performance, and scalability of software and algorithms. For example, a priority queue structure is ideal for managing tasks by importance, while a hash table is useful for fast lookup operations. Without data structures, we would face significant limitations to the technology we rely on today. For instance, there would be no systematic way to structure data, leading to disorganized and inefficient memory utilization. Complex algorithms would be impossible to implement efficiently, limiting our ability to solve real-world problems.

Applications

Data structures are used in many applications. Two fundamental data structures that are often used to achieve this efficiency are linked lists and hash maps. Linked lists, which consist of nodes that contain data and pointers to other nodes, are particularly useful in file systems where files need to be stored and retrieved in a specific order. On the other hand, hash maps, which use key-value pairs to store and retrieve data quickly, are ideal for columnar databases where large amounts of data need to be analyzed and processed rapidly.

In this section, we will explore two distinct yet equally important applications that demonstrate the power of data structures.

File systems

Linked lists are used to manage file allocation and directories, to efficiently track free and occupied blocks on disk. We can also use linked lists to simulate a simple file system involving both files and directories. The concept is straightforward. In this structure, each linked list node represents either a file or a directory. Nodes are linked using the next pointer. Files are inserted before directories to collectively group all the files to support file-first listing or traversal. This file-first structure is shown in *Figure 1.1* and illustrated in the GitHub repo inside the `DirectoryManager.java` in the `Chapter01` subfolder. To unlock the GitHub repo link, refer to the instructions in the *Download the example code files* section of the *Preface*.

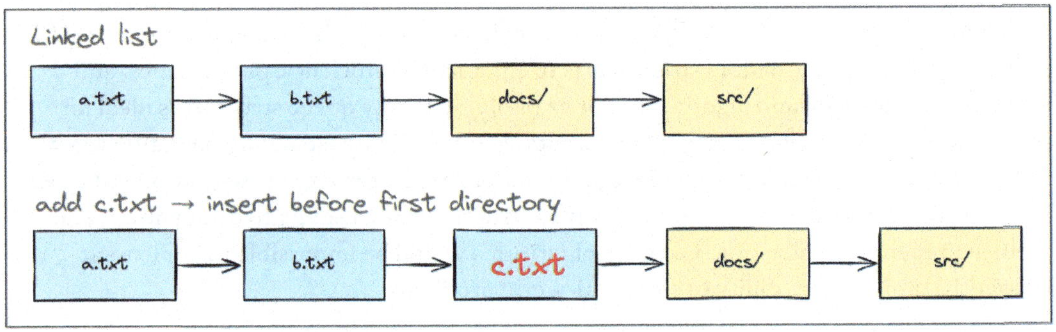

Figure 1.1: File-first insertion in a list-based file system

In a more advanced file manager, we use a left-child/right-sibling linked structure to model a directory tree. This structure supports adding entries at the root or as children, locating items via their full paths, and verifying the existence of any entry by name throughout the entire tree. This is implemented in the GitHub repo inside the `DirectoryManagerNestedVersion.java` file in the `Chapter01` subfolder. To unlock the GitHub repo link, refer to the instructions in the *Download the example code files* section of the *Preface*. While linked lists were historically used to manage file allocation (such as in FAT systems) and can simulate simple file systems, modern industry production environments use tree-based data structures (like B-Trees) and bitmaps to manage file allocation, directories, and free disk blocks efficiently at scale.

Data warehousing

In contrast to file systems that prioritize sequential organization, data warehouses require fast lookup and processing capabilities. Columnar databases, which store data by columns rather than rows, demonstrate how hash maps excel in this domain. By consistently grouping data by type within each column, the database can optimize compression algorithms to reduce data footprint in storage. Firstly, each column can be treated as a separate data unit and compressed independently, allowing for more efficient use of disk space. Secondly, compression algorithms are tailored to specific data types, resulting in improved compression ratios and reduced storage requirements. *Figure 1.2* shows the difference between row-wide and columnar storage.

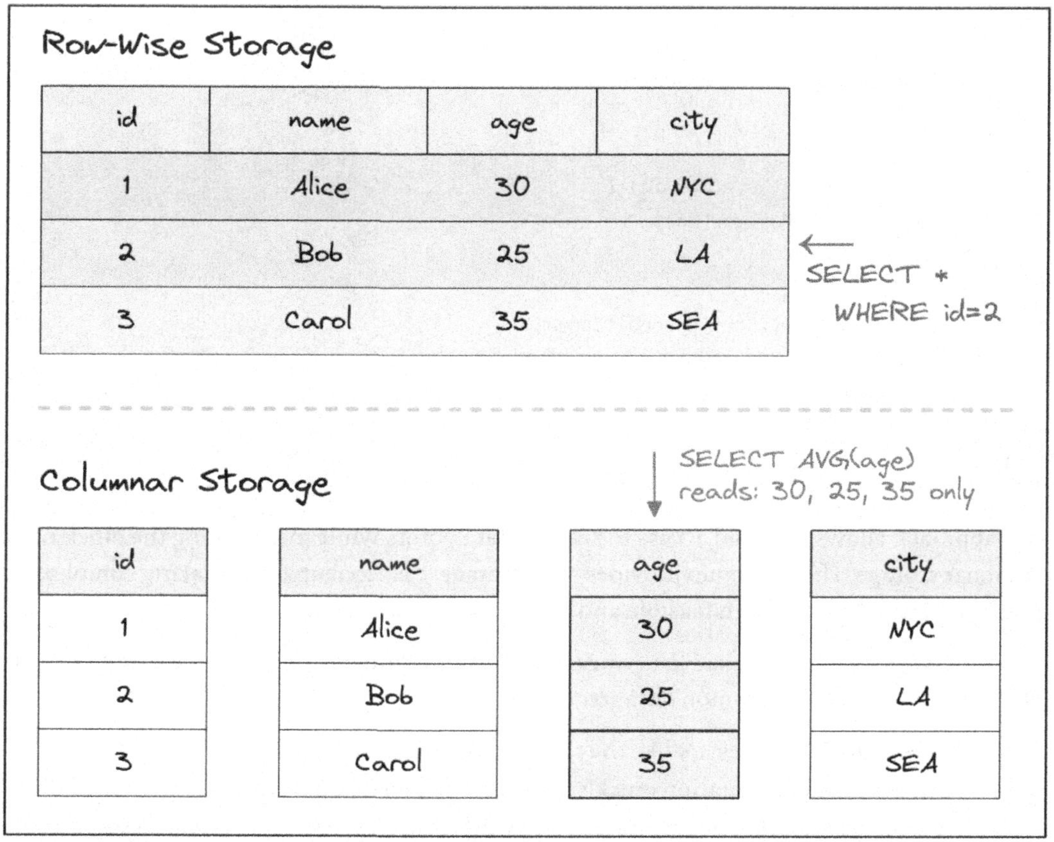

Figure 1.2: Row-wise vs columnar storage

Retrieving data from a columnar database means we access specific columns rather than rows. This approach significantly improves query performance by minimizing data transfer and reducing the amount of data that needs to be processed. For the columnar database in *Figure 1.2*, we design our query condition on the column named "age" by accessing that column only. See the `DataWarehouse.java` file in the `Chapter01` subfolder on GitHub. To unlock the GitHub repo link, refer to the instructions in the *Download the example code files* section of the *Preface*:

```
public class DataWarehouse {
    // Hash map for fast lookup by person ID
    privateMap<Integer,Person> dataMap;

    public void addData(int id, String name, int age, String city) {
        dataMap.put(id, new Person(id, name, age, city));
    }

    public Person getData(int id) {
        return dataMap.get(id);
    }

    public void query(String condition) {
        // Process only the relevant column(s)
        // Fast lookup using hash map key-value pairs
    }
}
```

This approach allows for rapid access to specific data points while maintaining the efficiency of columnar storage. The hash map provides O(1) average-case lookup time, making complex queries on large datasets both feasible and performant.

Now that we've seen how linked lists work in file systems and hash maps in data warehouses, let's explore some other common data structures:

- **B-Trees and B+ Trees** are like the table of contents in a large book. They help databases find information quickly, especially when dealing with huge amounts of data stored on disk. They're designed to work efficiently with how computers store data on hard drives.
- **Binary Search Trees** and their balanced versions (like AVL trees and Red-Black trees) act like a branching decision tree. Instead of checking every item one by one, you compare your target to the current item and instantly eliminate half of the remaining

options by moving either left or right. This geometric narrowing makes searches incredibly fast.

- **Hash Tables** and **Tries** are used by routers (the devices that direct internet traffic) to quickly find the best path for sending data packets. They help the internet work fast by storing and looking up routing information very efficiently.
- **Bloom Filters** test if something might be in a collection. For example, they can quickly tell you if an IP address has been seen before, with very little memory usage and a tiny chance of being wrong.

These data structures show how the concepts we're learning today apply to solving real problems in computer science, from databases to networking to web browsing. Each structure is chosen based on what the application needs to do most efficiently.

The above-referenced data structures and algorithms will be further explored in the latter part of this book, where their practical uses and real-world applications will be examined in greater depth.

Types of data structures

Before we dive into specific structures, it's important to understand how we categorize them. In the world of data structures, we generally divide them into two main families: Linear and Non-Linear. Linear data structures organize data sequentially in a one-dimensional fashion: think of a simple straight line or a list. This is the most common way to handle basic sequences. There are also non-linear data structures that are classified based on their interconnected organization and access patterns, allowing data to be arranged in hierarchies, networks, or branching relationships. *Figure 1.3* depicts the structural differences between linear and non-linear data structures.

In the following chapters, we will delve into the specific structures within each category, exploring their unique properties, ideal use cases, and the necessary performance trade-offs. The next sections will serve as our foundation for the detailed implementations that follow.

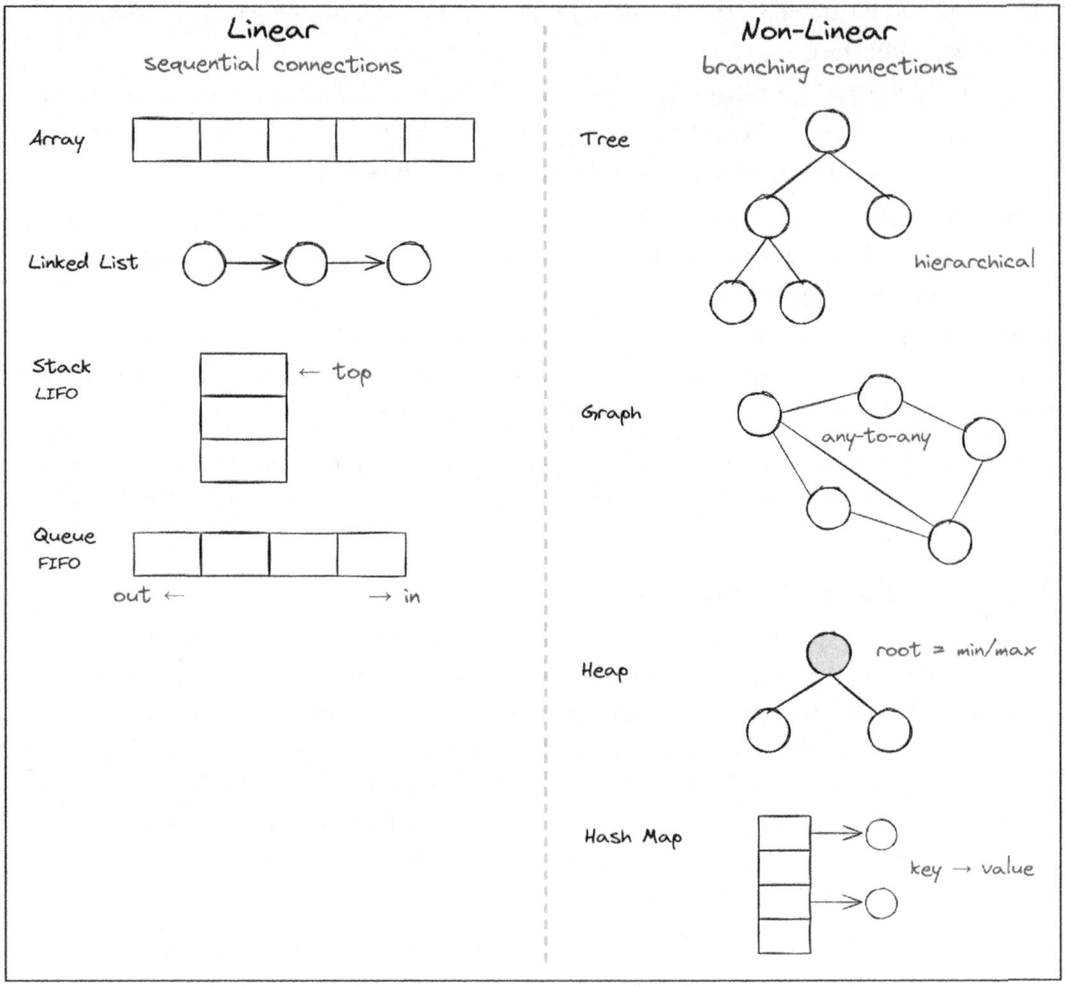

Figure 1.3: Linear vs. non-linear data structures

Linear data structures

The four common linear data structures are arrays, linked lists, stacks, and queues. Let us now understand how data is organized within each of these four linear structures.

Arrays

In digital imaging, arrays play a crucial role in representing images as collections of pixels. For instance, consider a digital camera that captures an image with a resolution of 1024x768 pixels (a total of 786,432 pixels). In this scenario, each pixel is represented by a two-dimensional array of integers, where each integer corresponds to the color values (red, green, blue) and intensity of the pixel. The array is organized in a row-by-row format, with each element storing the color information for a specific pixel position.

Linked lists

In linked lists, data is organized sequentially in nodes, with each consisting of a data element and a reference to the next node. Sometimes, each node also contains a reference to the previous node. The former is called a singly linked list, whereas the latter is a doubly linked list. *Figure 1.4* shows the `add()` and `delete()` operations in a singly linked list. The ability to dynamically add or remove elements from linked lists at both ends enables the creation of more complex data types, such as stacks and queues, which are commonly used in many algorithms and applications. For example, a web browser tracks a user's session history within a tab by employing a doubly linked list. Each visited URL is stored as a node, linked to the preceding and succeeding pages via pointers. This structure allows for highly efficient navigation: when a user clicks 'Back' or 'Forward,' the browser simply traverses the relevant pointers without re-scanning the entire list.

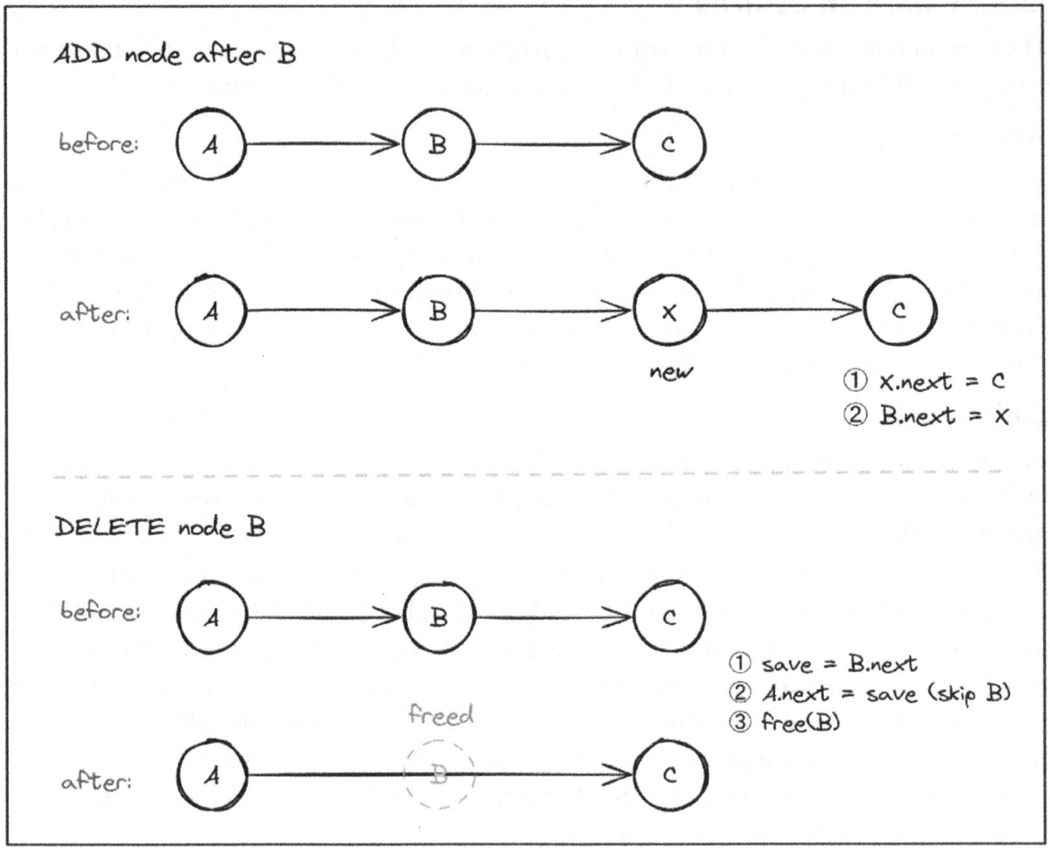

Figure 1.4: Singly linked list operations

Stack

In a stack, data access follows a **last-in first-out** (**LIFO**) pattern. This is analogous to a stack of cafeteria plates: the last plate added is the first one taken. A common example of stack is the "undo" feature in text editors. When you press the "Undo" button, the most recent change is removed, effectively creating a new top element on the undo stack, much like removing the topmost plate from the stack.

Queue

In a queue, data access follows a **first-in first-out** (**FIFO**) pattern. This is a data structure commonly found in scheduling systems. For example, in air controller software, aircraft are added to a queue and then cleared for takeoff or landing in the order they arrived. *Figure 1.5* contrasts the last-in, first-out (LIFO) method of a stack with the first-in, first-out (FIFO) approach of a queue.

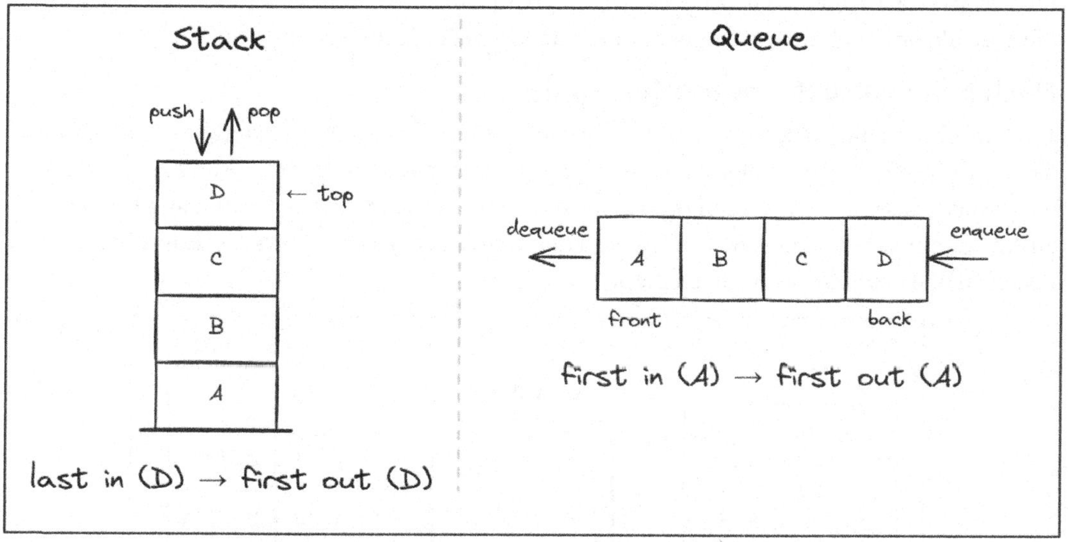

Figure 1.5: LIFO stack vs FIFO queue

We have established that linear data structures, namely Arrays, Linked Lists, Stacks, and Queues, provide the foundation for organizing sequential data. However, real-world computing rarely deals with simple sequences; it deals with relationships, hierarchies, and vast, interconnected data sets. To handle this complexity, we must move beyond linear concepts and embrace non-linear data structures. As we transition to these more advanced structures, we begin to see how data structures move from being simple containers to becoming the architectural blueprints for massive, scalable systems.

Non-linear data structures

Non-linear data structures organize data based on relationships, enabling us to model the complex connections found in the real world: from navigating the internet and managing databases to structuring knowledge. These structures are not just theoretical concepts; they are the backbone of every large-scale application. We will explore five key families next.

Hierarchical structures (tree, heap)

Tree: an HTML document structure can be visualized as a hierarchical tree, where tags such as `<h1>`, `<p>`, and others serve as nodes. The text content enclosed within these tags forms the child nodes of each parent node. This tree-like structure allows for easy navigation and organization of the document's content.

Heap: this data structure is frequently used in memory management by operating systems. When memory is allocated, it is typically organized into a contiguous block of free memory that can be efficiently divided and merged to accommodate different requests for allocation.

This heap-based approach enables the system to optimize memory usage and to facilitate rapid deallocation of unused memory blocks in logarithmic time complexity.

Hash-based structures (hash maps)

They are essential for achieving near-instantaneous lookups, such as in database indexing and network routing. For example, a hash map enables fast and flexible storage and retrieval of data by associating each piece of information with a unique identifier, known as a key. This allows for efficient lookups, insertions, and deletions of elements. *Figure 1.6* shows the insertion of 4 elements into a hash map.

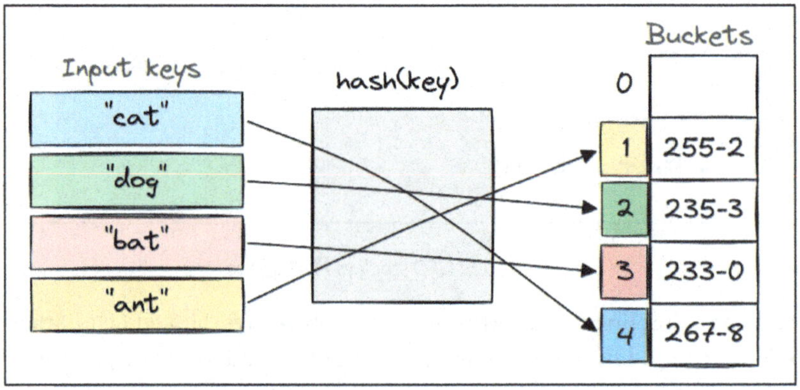

Figure 1.6: The insertion operation in a hash map

Graph-based structures (graph, adjacency list and matrix)

They are great for modeling relationships, such as social networks, road systems, and dependency tracking. For example, we use an adjacency list to represent the graph of connections among individuals. To illustrate, we create a network of 4 people, A, B, C, and D and their hypothetical connections, via an adjacency list:

```
A: [B, C]
B: [A, C, D]
C: [A, B, D]
D: [C]
```

When you want to find the connections between two individuals, say A and B, you can simply look up their adjacency lists. If they're connected, their names will appear on each other's lists. If we query "who is connected to A", the answer would be "[B, C]", indicating that B and C are connected to A.

Set-based structures (set, sorted set)

Sets are used to store unique elements without any order. This is a useful structure for tracking data elements that must be unique from each other, e.g., auto license numbers.

Hybrid structures (bloom filter, B-tree)

These structures demonstrate how we combine different methods to achieve optimal performance in scenarios like search and recommendation engines. An e-commerce ad engine uses a pre-built, read-only B-tree index to quickly fetch candidate ads matching a user's query category. The system then streams these candidates through an in-memory Bloom filter tracking the user's recently viewed history, quickly dropping ads they have already seen to prevent ad fatigue before running the final auction.

The DSA bridge to modern AI

As we explore these non-linear structures and their efficiency in practical applications, we realize DSA is not merely a tool for coding exercises; it is the foundational engine that powers the next generation of intelligent, scalable systems, including running sophisticated systems like AI agents.

Consider the complex task of instructing an AI Code Agent to refactor a software library. This seemingly simple request triggers an entire computational journey: from understanding intent to verifiable code, representing a multi-layered workflow that is governed entirely by DSA principles:

- **Memory Management**: to rapidly recall context or code snippets, the agent doesn't use a simple list; it leverages a Trie for quick prefix searching and Hash Maps for fast access to its tool registry.
- **Planning and Execution**: the agent must decide the optimal sequence of actions. This is achieved using a **Directed Acyclic Graph** (**DAG**) to map dependent sub-tasks (e.g., Parse -> Transform -> Test) and a Priority Queue to ensure it selects the most critical step next
- **Code Understanding**: to understand the structure of the code itself, the agent relies on the **Abstract Syntax Tree** (**AST**), a tree-based structure, to grasp the code's true syntax, allowing for precise refactoring

Let's dissect the AI context behind each of the above workflows next.

The AI context

In the current technological era, AI systems, particularly those that utilize Large Language Models (LLMs) and Agentic architectures, are increasingly capable of handling complex, real-world tasks. However, this apparent "intelligence" is fundamentally built upon structured logic. The LLM provides the natural language understanding and reasoning, but the *ability to execute* a plan, check credentials, or manipulate data requires a rigid, efficient computational backbone. This foundational infrastructure is where DSA become indispensable. They provide the underlying data layouts and optimized execution logic for AI agents to move from interpreting intent to achieving verifiable results.

Consider the following scenario. A developer submits a natural language prompt to an advanced AI Code Agent:

> *"Refactor the auth library to return CompletableFuture for asynchronous execution."*

While the user's prompt seems straightforward, executing it triggers a complex, multi-layered workflow powered by data structures and algorithms. These foundational components are essential for translating abstract machine intelligence into functional, verifiable code.

We will dissect this entire lifecycle, revealing how DSA function as the essential, foundational engine. Every simple user request must traverse a complex computational pathway, involving the strategic operation of multiple data structures to compute the final response.

Algorithmic blueprint

The entire process, from natural language prompt to final code, is a sophisticated, multi-stage computational journey: from understanding, planning, execution, to outcome. DSAs function as the foundational infrastructure, managing every step of the AI agent's internal logic.

Figure 1.7 illustrates the conceptual lifecycle of an AI Agent's response, mapping the process to fundamental DSA concepts. This model serves as a conceptual guide based on established computer science principles and should not be interpreted as an exact depiction of proprietary industry architectures.

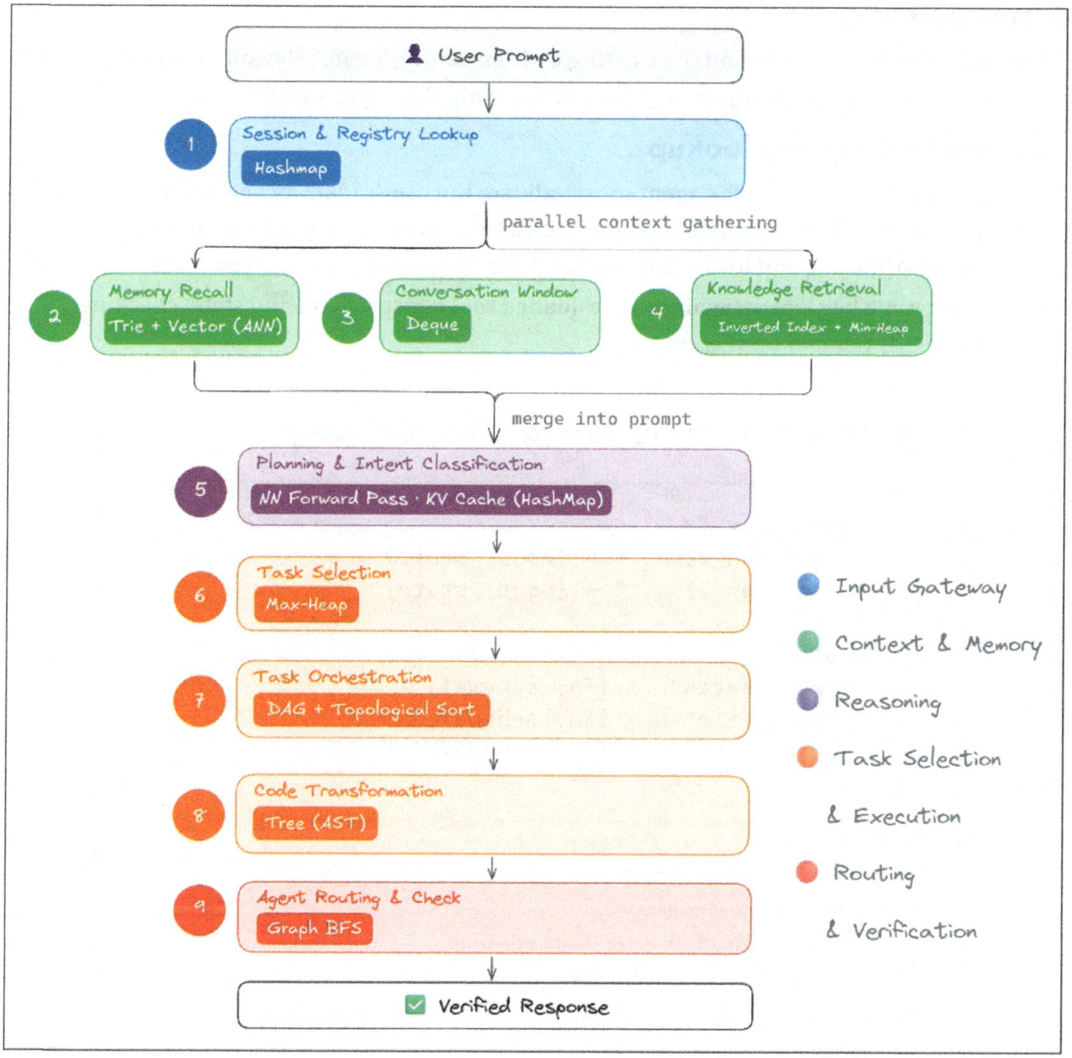

Figure 1.7: Agentic lifecycle from user prompt to verified response

Agentic lifecycle

Figure 1.7 shows the agent's operational capability through five key phases. This entire lifecycle, proceeding from the Input Gateway to Routing and Verification, is governed by the foundational computational principles of DSA underpinning the agent's operations.

Input gateway

The agent must first understand the existing code structure, locate relevant knowledge, and plan the entire change. The agent begins by structuring the request itself.

Session and registry lookup

Before processing can occur, the agent must validate the user's identity and resolve its available toolset. A Hash Map (hash table) is used to retrieve the user's session credentials by session ID in O(1) time, and to check tool availability (e.g., `web_search`, `read_file`, `exec_bash`) via constant-time key lookup against a pre-loaded tool registry, reducing state-checking overhead to O(1) per lookup (*Figure 1.8*):

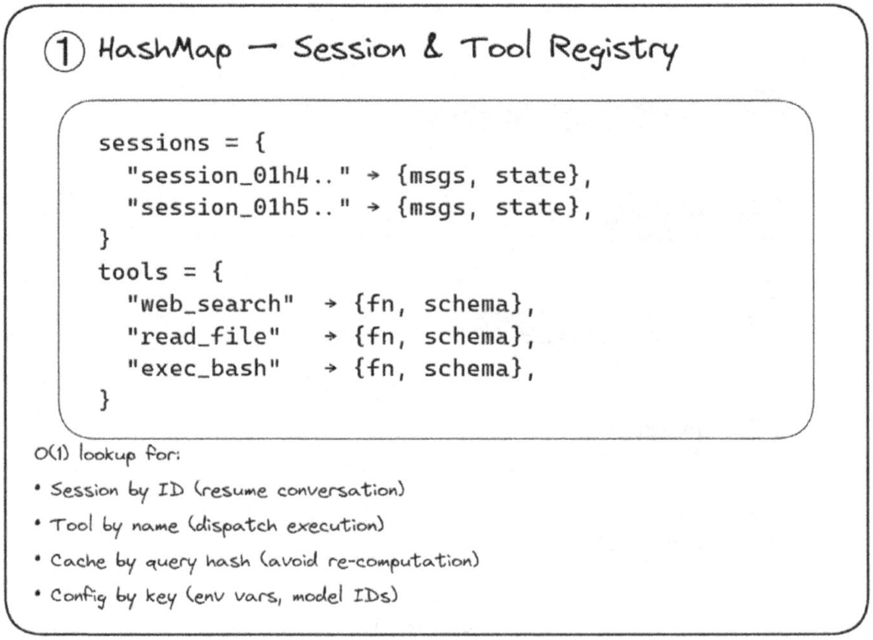

Figure 1.8: Hash Map for configuration management

Memory, context, and knowledge retrieval

By design, the agent starts to process the user's prompt by kicking off three distinct tasks (Memory, Context, and Knowledge Retrieval), concurrently or in parallel, to assemble the context needed for response generation. Here, we define:

- Memory: conversation history
- Context: current workspace files, environment, and state
- Knowledge Retrieval: retrieval-augmented generation (RAG), external documents, and tools

Memory Recall

To gather context, the agent searches its memory and historical logs. A **Trie** (prefix tree) is employed to perform rapid prefix-based search across historical keyword terms, such as querying "auth" quickly to return all related entries ("auth", "authenticate", "authorization") without scanning the full knowledge corpus. While semantic search handles contextual meaning, this Trie optimization allows for constant-time prefix matching. The agent then reviews these matches to understand the scope and conversation used (*Figure 1.9*).

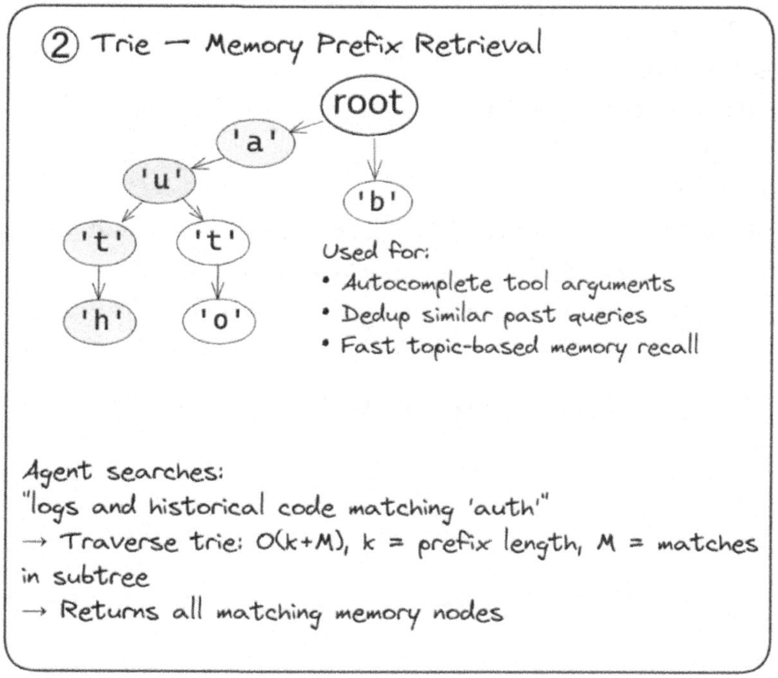

Figure 1.9: Trie for memory prefix retrieval

Conversation window

To maintain coherence with the user's immediate intent, the agent implements a **Sliding Window** mechanism over the conversation history, retaining the most recent messages within the model's context limit while older exchanges are dropped or summarized. This ensures the LLM's responses remain consistent with the ongoing conversation's tone, constraints, and prior decisions. (*Figure 1.10*).

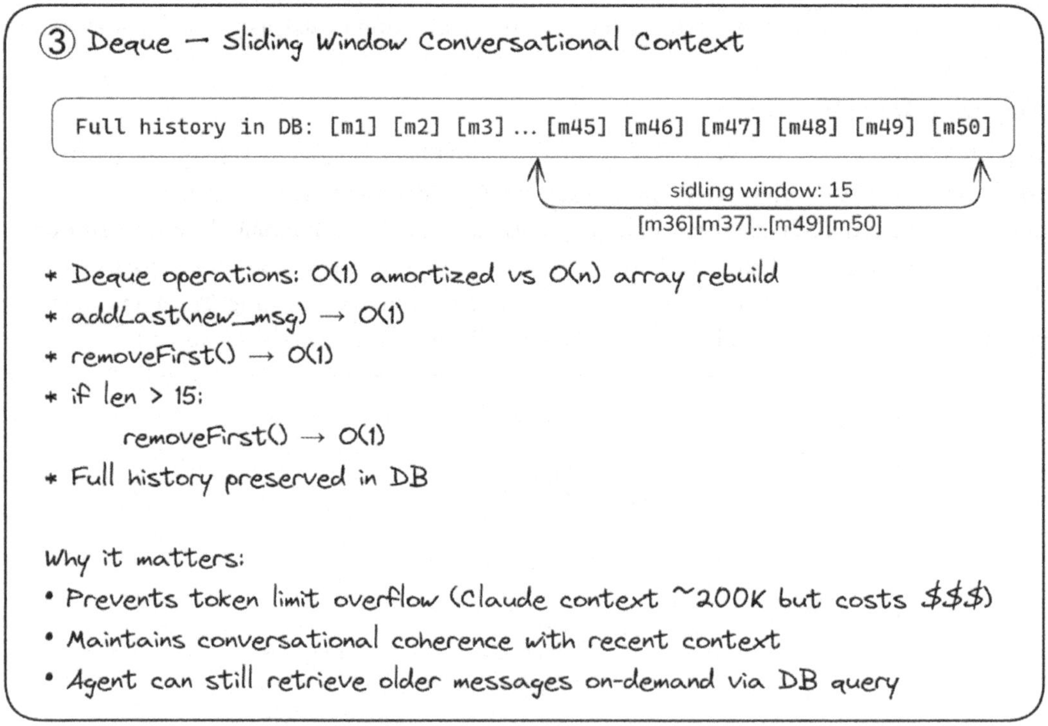

Figure 1.10: Deque sliding window for LLM context

Knowledge retrieval

To ensure the use of current industry best practices, the agent first executes an Inverted Index search using core keywords ('auth,' 'authenticator') to retrieve all matching documents. The results are then ranked by a composite score (relevance, recency, authority), and a bounded **Min-Heap** algorithm is utilized to efficiently cull this vast index, tracking the highest-scoring candidates dynamically to select only the top-k most authoritative and time-sensitive current sources without sorting the entire candidate set (*Figure 1.11*):

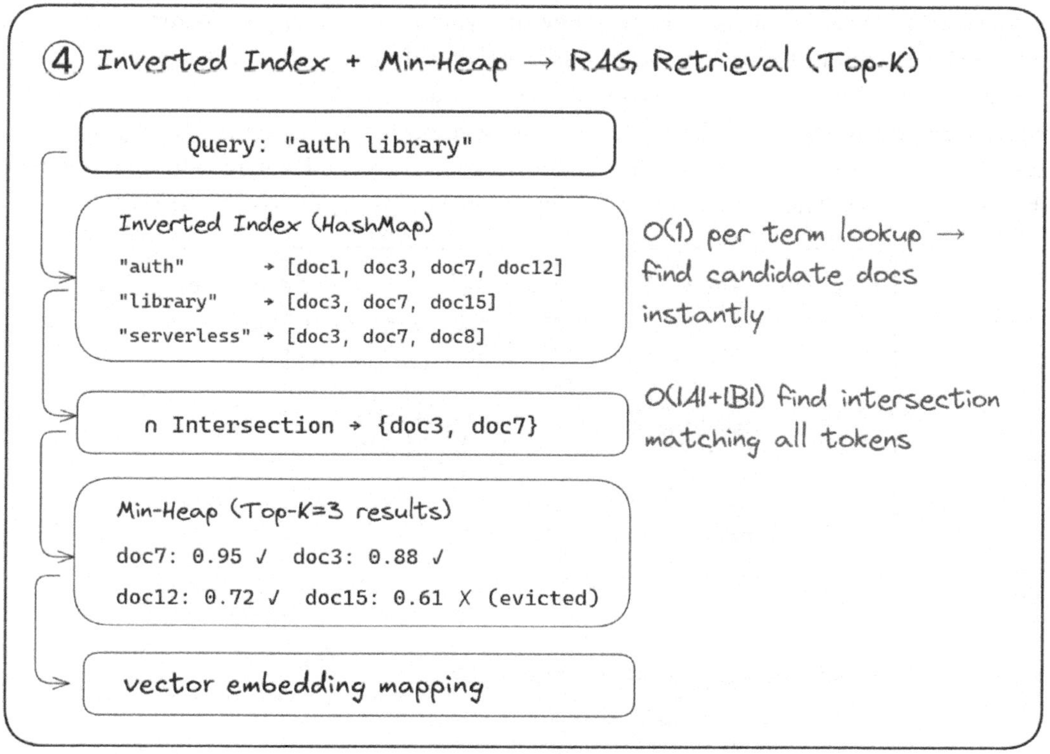

Figure 1.11: Inverted index in min-heap for RAG retrieval

Reasoning

The Reasoning phase is the agent's 'thought process.' It is here that the raw data gathered from the Context, Memory, and Knowledge streams is synthesized into a cohesive plan. At the heart of this synthesis is the LLM's inference pass. The model processes the assembled context to generate a multi-step action plan, leveraging chain-of-thought reasoning to evaluate trade-offs and select an execution strategy.

Task selection and execution

Also termed "action" in the Synergizing Reasoning and Acting (ReAct) pattern, this phase consists of deciding which tool (file read, API call, search, etc.) to invoke, constructing the parameters for that tool, and executing key tasks to fulfill the user's request.

Task prioritization

When prompting an agent to refactor software using Java `CompletableFuture`, the agent breaks the goal into a sequence of sub-tasks. It assigns an urgency or dependency score to each sub-task (e.g., 1: Scan for blocking code, 2: Rewrite syntax, 3: Run tests). By loading these tasks into a **Priority Queue**, the orchestration system ensures the agent always executes the most logically foundational task next. If a compilation error occurs, a 'fix error' task is dynamically injected into the front of the priority queue with the highest score, instantly shifting the agent's focus. The agent's orchestration engine uses this to dynamically schedule and sequence the engineering workflow based on logical dependencies, safety, and cost. (*Figure 1.12*).

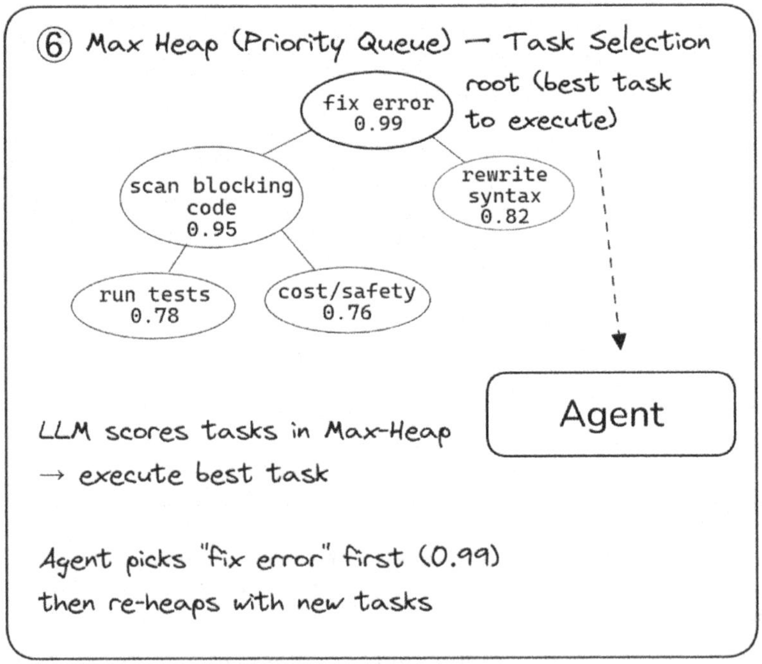

Figure 1.12: Priority queue for task selection

Task orchestration

The agent creates discrete, dependent sub-tasks, and maps them into a **Directed Acyclic Graph** (**DAG**), guaranteeing logical integrity. For example, the DAG ensures that the transformation step cannot start until the parsing step is 100% complete (Parse ⟶ Transform ⟶ Test ⟶ Commit), maintaining logical integrity and execution order (*Figure 1.13*).

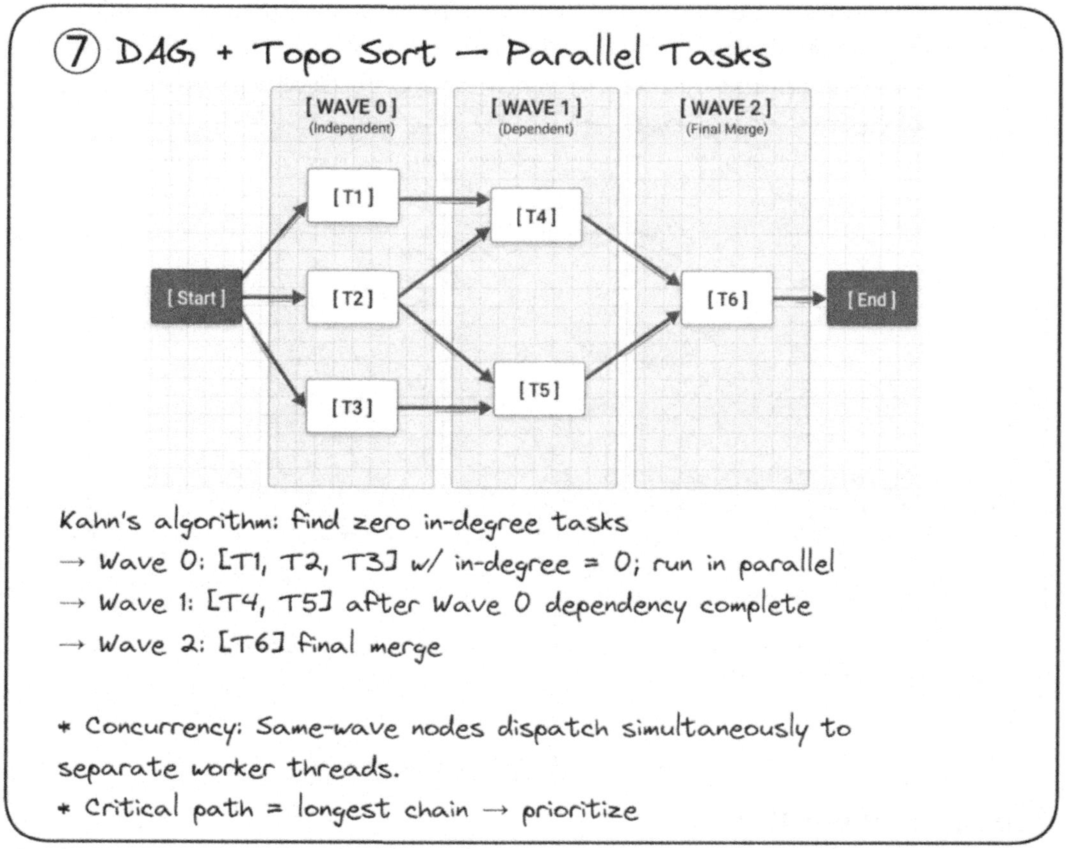

Figure 1.13: DAG topological sort in parallel task scheduling

Code transformation

The foundational step of code understanding involves parsing the existing codebase using an **Abstract Syntax Tree** (**AST**). Unlike superficial text pattern matching, the AST captures the code's true structural syntax. By traversing this tree, the agent accurately pinpoints all synchronous methods, allowing for targeted and precise refactoring. This structural understanding ensures that the target synchronous calls are isolated correctly, regardless of how the code is formatted or commented (*Figure 1.14*).

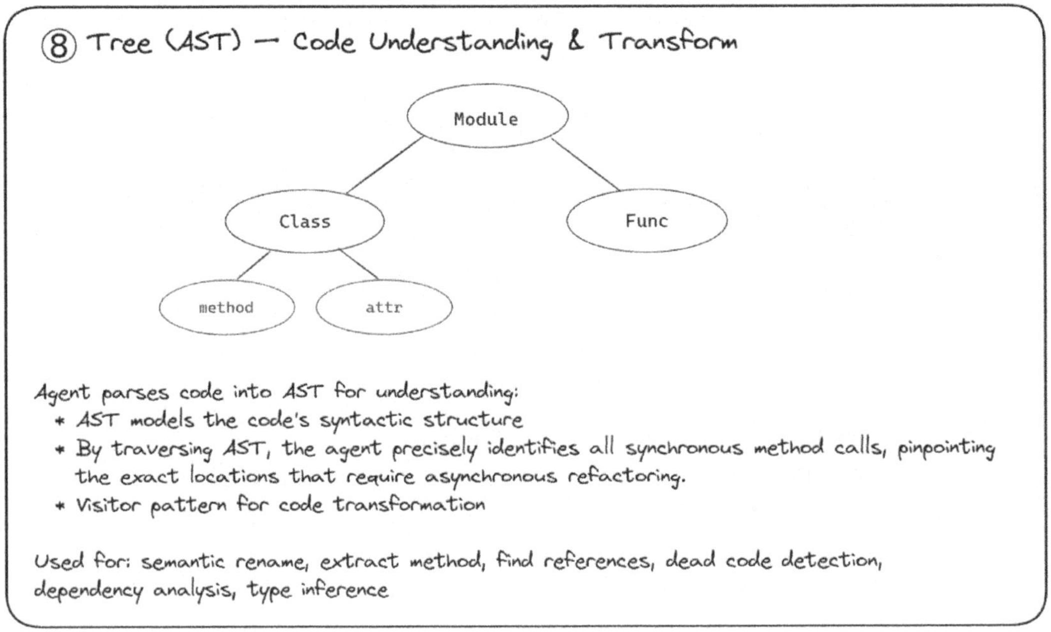

Figure 1.14: AST for code understanding

Routing and verification

Upon successfully optimizing the code, the agent utilizes a DAG traversal, specifically orchestrated via a topologically sorted **Breadth-First Search** (**BFS**), to route the request through its final specialized sequences, transitioning from code generation to infrastructure deployment and ensuring all dependencies are sorted in the correct execution order (*Figure 1.15*).

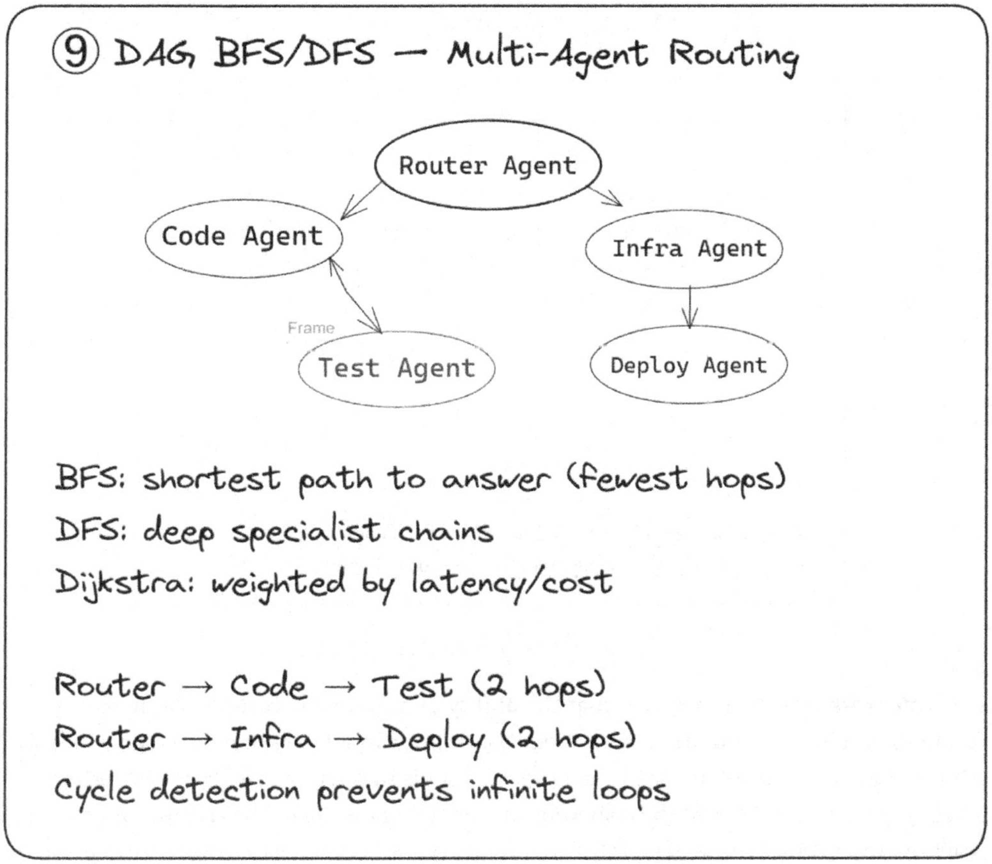

Figure 1.15: DAG traversal for multi-agent routing

The system then passes through the final strict **Deterministic Finite Automaton** (**DFA**) states (Planning -> Executing -> Verifying -> Complete). During the Executing phase, the agent compiles and packages the code. It then transitions to the Verifying state to test the deployment, before entering the final Complete state to deliver the resulting response back to the user (*Figure 1.16*).

Note

DFA is an abstract computational model that translates into software as a unified combination of a data structure and an execution algorithm.

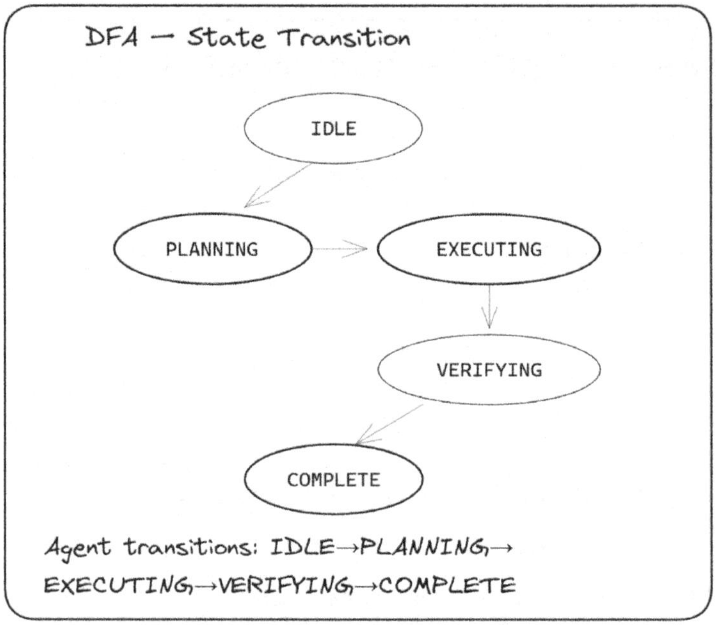

Figure 1.16: DFA state transitions to delivery

The agentic workflow demonstrates that the ability of AI to tackle complex, real-world problems is entirely dependent on a structured computational backbone. DSA provides this backbone, equipping AI agents with the necessary tools to operate efficiently. Whether managing session states through Hash Maps, prioritizing tasks via Min-Heaps, or ensuring logical flow with DAGs, these principles govern every interaction. This journey confirms that mastering these core DSA principles is not merely beneficial for a developer; it is the fundamental, non-negotiable skill required to architect, optimize, and debug the next generation of AI systems.

Moving to abstraction

Having seen these structures in action, we now transition from implementation to design. If DSA teaches us how to build efficient structures, the next logical step is to learn how to define them. We move from the concrete details of code to the abstract principles of system design. To achieve this, we must understand how to define the essential properties and behaviors of a data structure (contract) without being constrained by specific implementations. This is the essence of Abstract Data Types (ADTs).

Abstract data type

An **abstract data type (ADT)** is a contract that defines a set of behaviors or operations that a data structure must have ("what"), without specifying how these behaviors should be implemented ("how"). What does this mean?

An ADT is akin to an architectural blueprint, which includes floor plans, electrical and plumbing layouts, and framing and structural details. In a blueprint, you see the rooms, doors, and walls without knowing the specific construction materials or techniques used (e.g., paint, framing wood, steel, or concrete). Similarly, an ADT specifies the operations, or behaviors, we perform on the data (like insert, delete, search) without defining how these operations are implemented. Different implementations (e.g., arrays or linked lists) can satisfy the ADT requirements, just as various building materials can achieve the same blueprint.

Therefore, an ADT exists as a specification that allows developers to implement a data structure using different algorithms, provided they adhere to the ADT's defined specification. Just like a construction blueprint serves as a high-level guide for building a home, an ADT serves as high-level design specifications for a system. It describes what the system should do rather than how it should do it.

In Java, we can leverage the `interface` keyword to define an ADT as a specification for a data structure. This ADT includes a multitude of defined operations and clear expectations of what each operation should accomplish. For example:

- **The "What"**: An ADT for a queue may define operations such as `enqueue()`, `dequeue()`, `isFull()`, and `isEmpty()`, all following a first-in, first-out (FIFO) access pattern.
- **The "How"**: The implementation details for a queue may vary. A developer can choose any techniques to meet the ADT's specification. For example, we can use an array, linked list, or circular buffer to meet the ADT's requirements. Depending on how these operations are implemented, there may be different levels of efficiency we can achieve on data manipulation. *Figure 1.17* illustrates the core concept of an ADT based on this example.

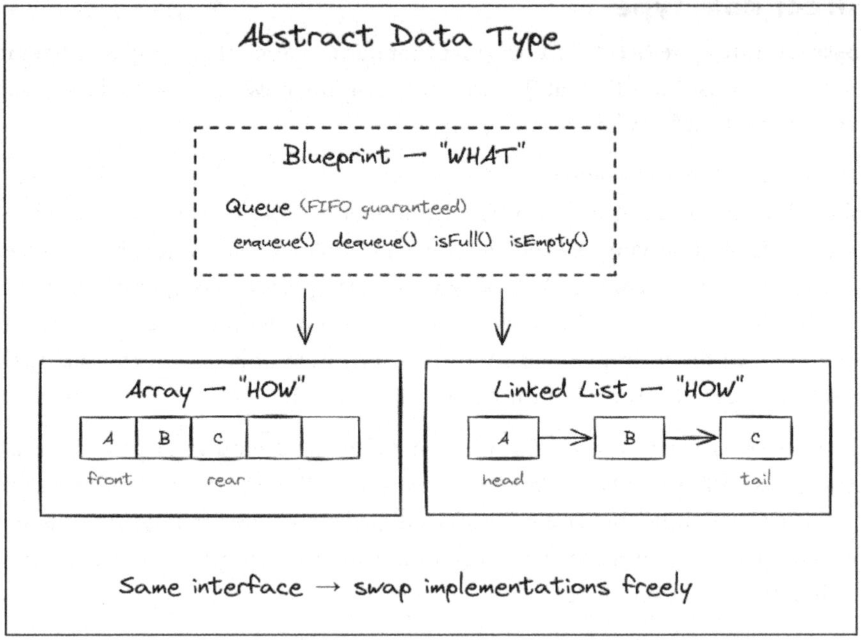

Figure 1.17: What vs how in ADT definition

Here is an example of an ADT using a Java interface. The `Stack<T>` interface class that represents a stack data structure. A stack is a **Last-In-First-Out** (**LIFO**) data structure, meaning that the last element added to the stack will be the first one to be removed:

```
public interface Stack<T> {
    void push(T element);
    T pop();
    T peek();
    boolean isEmpty();
}
```

In the context of the generic `Stack<T>` interface, `T` is a type parameter, which is a placeholder that represents a data type. This allows you to create a flexible stack that can hold any type of data (like Strings, Integers, or custom objects), rather than forcing the stack to be limited to a single type. By using `T`, you defer the choice of the exact data type until the stack is actually created in code. The API for this interface includes:

- `push(T element)`: Adds an element to the top of the stack
- `T pop()`: Removes and returns the top element from the stack

- `T peek()`: Returns the top element from the stack without removing it
- `boolean isEmpty()`: Checks if the stack is empty
- The `Stack<T>` interface does not define any properties; it only provides methods to interact with the stack

After exploring the ADTs that provide a common interface for various data structures, it's time to see how these concepts are implemented in practice. The Java Collections Framework (JCF) offers a powerful set of classes and interfaces that encapsulate and extend the functionality of ADTs. From lists and sets to maps and queues, JCF provides a rich array of data structures that can be used to solve complex problems in Java programming.

In this section, we'll examine how JCF's core components, such as `ArrayList`, `LinkedList`, `HashSet`, and `HashMap`, adhere to the principles of ADTs, including common operations like insertion, deletion, and querying.

Java collections framework

The Java core libraries provide developers with key facilities to efficiently build software requiring functionalities such as I/O, threading, Java Virtual Machine, concurrency, and security, to name a few. These key facilities consist of specific implementations for the ADTs defined. One of these core libraries is the **JCF**, consisting of a hierarchy of interfaces (such as `List`, `Set`, `Map`, `Queue`, etc.) and data structures (such as `ArrayList`, `LinkedList`, `HashSet`, `TreeSet`, `HashMap`, `TreeMap`, `PriorityQueue`, etc.). Several of these data structures are widely used across various industries due to their efficiency, flexibility, and ease of use. For example:

- `ArrayList`: For storing and accessing data in a list format.
- `LinkedList`: For accessing data that requires frequent insertion and deletion, especially at the beginning or end of the list. queues, frequent insertions/removals.
- `PriorityQueue`: For managing a collection of elements with priority, such as tasks or events.
- `HashMap`: For fast lookup and retrieval via key-value pairs.
- `HashSet`: For enabling unique collections without order.
- `TreeMap`: For enabling sorted key-value storage.
- `TreeSet`: For enabling sorted, unique collections.
- `Deque`: For enabling double-ended access for stack/queue uses.

Figure 1.18 shows the hierarchy of classes and interfaces in JCF:

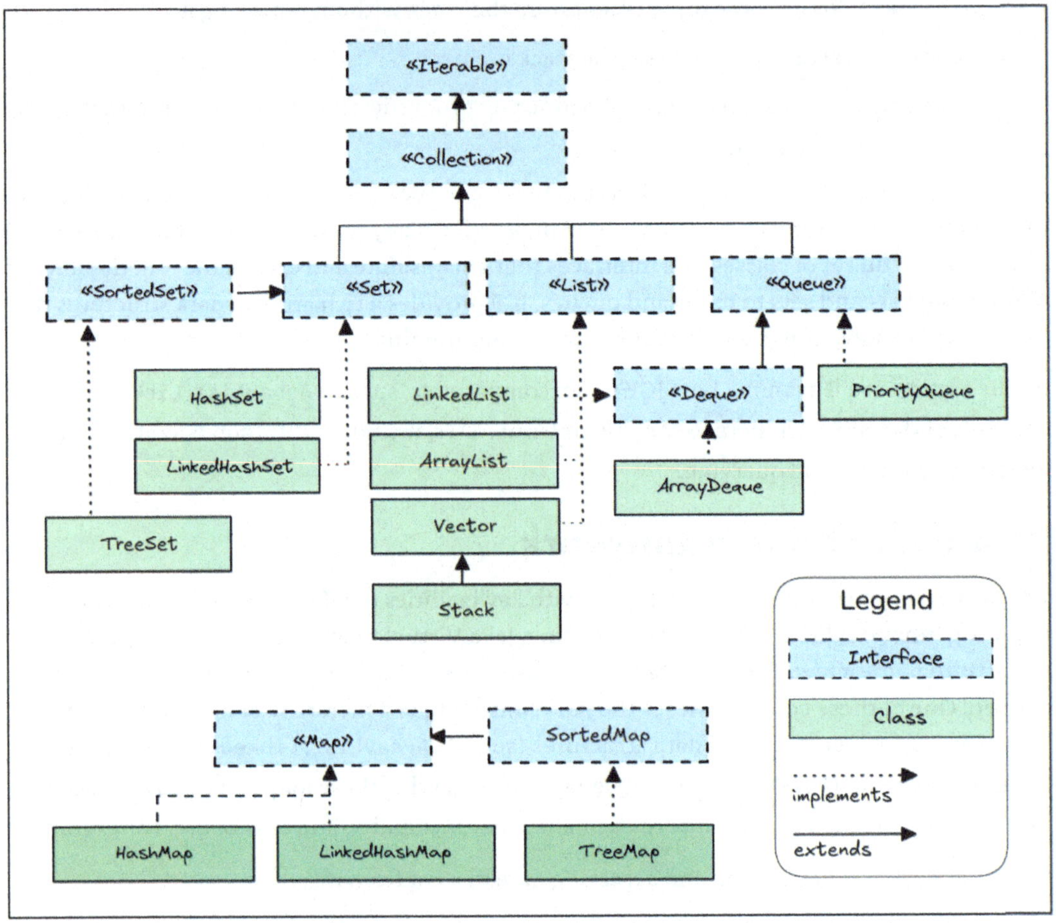

Figure 1.18: JCF Hierarchy of Classes and Interfaces

Throughout this book, we will provide pragmatic examples demonstrating the use of JCF data structures to solve real-world problems. We will explore applying JCF's core components to tackle complex challenges and ensure optimal performance.

While understanding fundamental data structures (such as arrays, linked lists, stacks, and queues) is key for solving complex problems, knowing the right structure is the first step. The real challenge lies in effectively utilizing these structures across various contexts. This realization leads us to algorithms, which serve as the recipe book for solving problems. By mastering their implementation, we can craft efficient and scalable solutions capable of handling demanding data-driven applications.

Algorithms

An algorithm is a set of clear instructions for performing a task or solving a computational problem. In essence, an algorithm can be viewed as a step-by-step guide for achieving a specific objective. Its complexity varies in accordance with the problem's complexities, ranging from straightforward solutions to more intricate and nuanced approaches. Algorithms exist to automate such instructions, making them faster and more efficient.

Imagine you want to build a toy tower with Lego pieces. An algorithm is like a set of easy and correct instructions you follow to build that tower involving:

- Picking up a Lego piece
- Put the piece on the floor
- Pick up another Lego piece
- Put the second block on top of the first one

You keep following these steps until your tower is built. That's how an algorithm works; it tells you exactly what to do, step by step!

Why algorithms?

When developing software, it's often the case that there are multiple approaches to solving a particular computational problem. Each solution may have varying levels of complexity and efficiency, making it essential to carefully evaluate their merits.

A prime example can be seen in machine learning model training for AI applications. Two different models may train faster than one another, yet differ significantly in terms of computing resource utilization. One approach might prioritize speed, while the other focuses on optimization for specific computational resources. This dichotomy highlights the fundamental concept of algorithms: finding the optimal balance between efficiency and performance.

How do we determine the best solution to use in solving a problem? How do we characterize such a solution with respect to its performance when compared to other solutions? In the upcoming sections, we will cover the following:

- Create several algorithms to solve an example problem
- Identify, assess, and measure the complexity of an algorithm
- Learn how to use Big O notation to characterize the complexity of an algorithm

Algorithmic performance

There are two crucial aspects to consider when evaluating algorithmic performance:

- **Time**: the speed at which an algorithm executes, influenced by the number of instructions executed.
- **Space**: the amount of memory (or computing resource) used by the algorithm. This is also predicated on the type and size of data structures employed.

In this discussion, we will focus on time, exploring ways to determine the time required for an algorithm. We will also learn to optimize our approach to reduce the time taken by an algorithm.

> **Note**
>
> Different algorithms call for varying levels of complexity, hence performance. In software development, it is imperative for us to understand how complexity is measured and assessed so we can be more informed about the trade-off of each solution for solving a problem.

Algorithm analysis

In computer science, the study of algorithms is vital as it allows for the evaluation and optimization of various problem-solving methods. When comparing the time efficiency of two algorithms that solve the same problem, a naive approach might involve running them on a particular system to compare their execution times. However, this method can be flawed due to several factors, including:

- **Differences in programming paradigms**: Variations in programming styles and languages can impact performance
- **System resource limitations**: Differences in available memory, CPU power, or other system resources can skew results
- **Hardware configurations**: Variances in hardware architecture, operating system, or driver versions can affect performance
- **Other implementation details**: Factors such as caching, compiler optimizations, or interpreter overhead can also influence execution times

When evaluating algorithms, it's essential to use mathematical techniques that focus on the algorithm itself, rather than specific implementations, computers, or data. To analyze an algorithm, we follow these steps:

- **Count significant operations**: identify and count the key operations in the solution, such as comparisons, additions, or memory accesses
- **Express efficiency using growth functions**: represent the time or space complexity of the algorithm using mathematical expressions, such as Big O notation (e.g., `O(n)`, `O(log n)`), to describe its growth rate relative to input size

Consider an algorithm for searching for a specific person in a phone book. The algorithm works by examining each entry in the phone book one by one. This algorithm is often referred to as a "linear search," where each entry in the phone book is examined sequentially until the desired person is found.

Here's a description of the algorithm:

- Initialize current index to 0 (assuming the first entry is the starting point).
- Iterate through each entry in the phone book.
- For each entry: compare the person's name with the target name. If it matches, return the corresponding phone number.

The running time is primarily determined by the number of entries that need to be scanned, not the actual content of each entry. In algorithm analysis, the running time of an algorithm is often expressed as a function of the input size, denoted as `n`. The time complexity is typically represented by a formula `f(n)`, which describes how the running time changes with respect to the input size.

The key point is that `f(n)` is assumed to be a non-negative value, meaning that the algorithm's running time cannot be negative. By expressing the running time in terms of `n`, we can compare and analyze different algorithms for their efficiency, regardless of the specific input size.

For brevity, we say the "cost" of comparing two phone entries is `c`. This cost can also be the approximate amount of time required to run the algorithm. Since there are `n` entries to compare, the total "cost" of running the log scan algorithm can be represented by a function:

```
f(n) = c * n
```

Here `c` is the constant cost of comparing two phone entries, and `n` is the number of entries in the phone book. This function captures the idea that the total cost grows linearly with the size of the input (number of entries). Formally, the above equation describes the growth rate of the running time of the log scan algorithm.

> **Note**
>
> The growth rate of an algorithm refers to the rate at which the cost (or running time) of the algorithm increases as the size of its input grows. The growth rate can be described using various mathematical terms such as linear, quadratic, exponential, polynomial, etc., depending on the relationship between the input size and the algorithm's running time.

Summarizing what we have learned so far, let's look at a few examples illustrating how algorithm analysis is performed. *Figure 1.19* compares different measures of time complexity with varying growth rates. We will introduce Big O notation in detail in the following section:

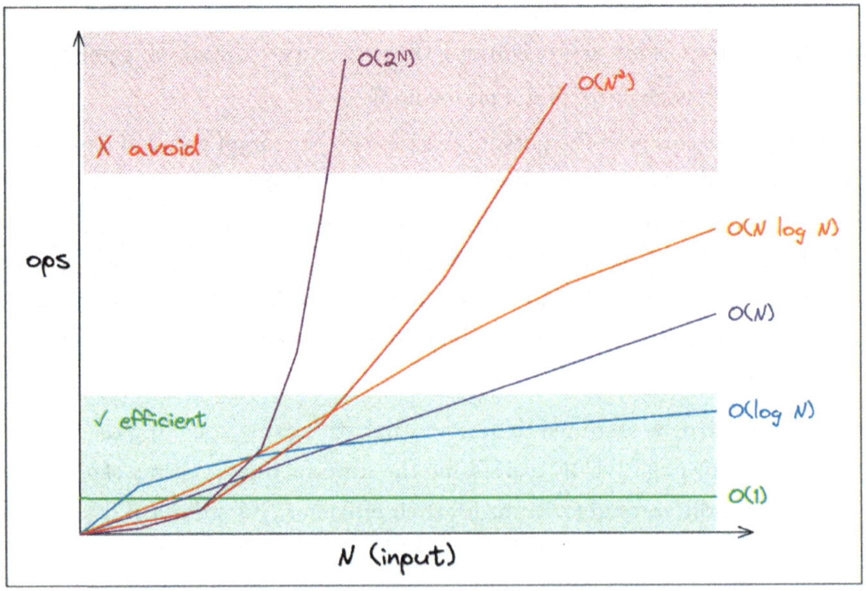

Figure 1.19: Relationship between Time Complexity and Input Size

Let's consider two more algorithms and analyze their execution time.

Algorithm 1

Let's analyze the execution time of a while-loop code snippet:

```
int n = 5;
int i = 0;
```

```
while (i < n) {
    System.out.println(i);
    i += 1;
}
```

The total cost of this algorithm can be broken down into individual costs, which are:

- c_1: declaring and initializing variable n to 5 (constant time)
- c_2: declaring and initializing variable i to 0 (constant time)
- c_3: loop iteration from i=0 to n-1 (cost proportional to n)
- c_4: printing i inside the loop (n times)
- c_5: incrementing i by 1 inside the loop (n times)

The total cost is therefore: $f(n) = c_1 + c_2 + c_3(n+1) + c_4(n) + c_5(n)$

Note the loop condition is checked n+1 times: once for every successful loop iteration, and once at the end when the condition evaluates to false and terminates. Simplifying this expression, we can see that the term $(n+1)*c_3$ dominates the other terms, making the overall time complexity of the algorithm proportional to n. This means that as the input size (n) increases, the running time of the while-loop algorithm will increase linearly.

Algorithm 2

Let's analyze the execution time of the NestedWhileLoops function in Java:

```
public class NestedWhileLoops {
    int n = 5;
    int i = 0;
    int j = 0;
    while (i < n) {
        j = 0;
        while (j < n) {
            j++;
        }
        i++;
    }
}
```

The total cost of this algorithm can be broken down into individual costs, which are:

- c_1: Declaring and initializing n = 5

- c_2: Declaring and initializing `i` = 0
- c_3: Declaring and initializing `j` = 0
- c_4: The outer while loop is checked `n+1` times, running from `i = 0` to `i = n-1` plus the last terminating check
- c_5: Resetting `j = 0` for `n` iterations
- c_6: The inner while loop is entered `n` times by the outer loop, and each time it checks the condition `n+1` times. The total number of iterations is `n*(n+1)`
- c_7: Incrementing `j++` for `n*n` iterations
- c_8: Incrementing `i++` for `n` iterations

Placing the exact execution frequencies into the function yields

$$f(n) = c_1 + c_2 + c_3 + c_4 * (n + 1) + c_5 * (n) + c_6\big(n(n + 1)\big) + c_7(n^2) + c_8(n)$$

If we expand this to consolidate the matching powers of `n`:

$$f(n) = n^2(c_6 + c_7) + n(c_4 + c_5 + c_6 + c_8) + (c_1 + c_2 + c_3 + c_4)$$

Simplifying this expression, we can see that the term, $n^2(c_6 + c_7)$ dominates the others, making the overall time complexity of the algorithm proportional to n^2. This means that as the input size (`n`) increases, the running time of the `NestedWhileLoops` function increases quadratically.

Note

Time complexity or growth rate of an algorithm is invariant to environment-specific factors, whether they are hardware related (e.g., processor speed, disk I/O rate, network connectivity, etc.) or software-related (e.g., operating system, library, and framework dependencies, etc.). The growth rate of running time may be affected by a constant factor under such conditions, but the growth rate remains the same.

Complexity

As we see from analyzing the algorithm's performance, the notion of complexity refers to the amount of computational resources required to solve a problem. It is a measure of how efficiently an algorithm can be executed on a given system. High-complexity algorithms can lead to increased processing time, memory usage, and storage requirements, ultimately affecting the overall performance of the system. As the size of the input data increases, the relationship between the input size and the computational resources required becomes increasingly important. This is where Asymptotic Analysis comes into play, providing a mathematical framework for analyzing and comparing the complexity of different algorithms.

Asymptotic analysis

By considering the input size, n, in the examples to be sufficiently large (i.e., infinity), we can use this value to analyze the asymptotic growth rate of an algorithm's efficiency in time. Such analysis makes use of mathematical notations, such as Big O, Big Ω, and Big Θ, that describe the upper bound, lower bound, and the exact growth rate of an algorithm's running time, respectively:

- An upper bound is an approximation that says "an algorithm will not take more than this much time."
    - Big O notation is used to describe the upper bound of an algorithm's running time. It represents the maximum amount of time an algorithm takes as a function of the input size (n).
    - Example: O(n) notation represents the maximum time complexity of an algorithm as a function of n.
- A lower bound is an approximation that says "an algorithm will take at least this much time"
    - Big Ω notation describes a lower bound of an algorithm's running time, which represents the minimum amount of time an algorithm takes.
    - Example: Ω(n) notation represents the minimum time complexity of an algorithm as a function of n.
- An exact growth rate is between upper and lower bounds that says "an algorithm will take exactly this much time."
    - Big Θ notation describes the exact growth rate of an algorithm's running time, as a function of the input size (n). It represents both the upper and lower bounds of an algorithm's time complexity.
    - Example: Θ(n) notation represents the exact time complexity (upper and lower bounds) of an algorithm as a function of n.

Based on the above definitions, the running times of the aforesaid algorithms are as follows:

- Algorithm 1: f(n) = O(n), meaning the growth rate of f(n) is no faster than the growth rate of n.
- Algorithm 2: f(n) = $O(n^2)$, meaning the growth rate of f(n) is no faster than the growth rate of n^2.

Big O notation

Let's assume that an algorithm for finding entries in our prior phonebook example has a growth function of f(n), which can be more formally expressed as, in Big O notation:

$$f(n) = O(g(n))$$

Here, for a sufficiently large value of n, there exist positive constants c and n_0 such that

$$0 \leq f(n) \leq c \cdot g(n), \; for \; all \; n > n_0$$

In this formulation, n_0 is the positive ($n_0 > 0$) threshold point where the algorithmic growth rate stabilizes and settles into its long-term performance pattern. The above definition of Big O connotes several ideas:

- `g(n)` is a growth function that is asymptotically the upper bound for `f(n)`.
- Our objective in asymptotic analysis is to ascertain the smallest rate of growth `g(n)` that meets the above definition.
- The growth rate of an algorithm becomes significant as `n` passes `n0`, or the threshold of the function. We therefore consider `n` when it approaches infinity or becomes sufficiently large.

We can see that, for any given function `f(n)`, we are trying to find another function `g(n)` which approximates `f(n)` at higher values of `n`. That means `g(n)` approximates `f(n)` at higher values of `n`. For this reason, we call such analysis asymptotic analysis.

Why big O matters

In computer science, Big O notation is more widely used than Big Θ and Big Ω because upper bounds are more relevant than lower bounds in analyzing bottlenecks in code when the worst-case scenario is considered. Upper bounds provide a simple way to estimate the maximum amount of time an algorithm will take, making it easier to understand its performance.

> **Note**
>
> Why is O(n) not the growth rate for 8log (n) + 12?

Common big O examples

Let's take a look at some Big O examples:

- **Example 1**: Find the upper bound for *f(n) = 8n + 8*

Answer: We find $8n + 8 \leq 9n$, where $8 \leq n$ which leads to $8n + 8 = O(n)$, with $c = 9$ and $n_0 = 8$.

- **Example 2**: Find the upper bound for $f(n) = 2n^2 + 1$
  Answer: We find $2n^2 + 1 \leq 3n^2$, where $1 \leq n$ leading to $2n^2 + 1 = O(n^2)$, with $c = 3$ and $n_0 = 1$.
- **Example 3**: Find the upper bound for $f(n) = n^3 - n^2$
  Answer: We find $n^3 - n^2 \leq n^3$ for $1 \leq n$ and $c=1$ which leading to $n^3 - n^2 = O(n^3)$, with $c = 1$ and $n_0 = 1$.
- **Example 4**: Find the upper bound for $f(n) = 8$
  Answer: We find that $8 \leq 8$ for all $n \geq 1$ leading to $8 = O(1)$, with $c = 8$ and $n_0 = 1$. For this problem, you can have infinitely many valid sets of c and n0 in the natural number range.
- **Example 5**: Find the upper bound for $f(n) = 8n$
  Answer: We find $8n \leq 8n$ for all $n \geq 1$ leading to $8n = O(n)$, with $c = 8$ and $n_0 = 1$.
- **Example 6**: Find the upper bound for $f(n) = 3log(n) + n^2 + n + 8$
  Answer: Instead of finding c and n_0, note that we can compare the growth rates of each term as n becomes sufficiently large. Note that the quadratic term, n^2, grows much faster than the other terms, log(n) and n. This means the other terms are "lower-order" and can be ignored when finding the dominant growth rate. Analyzing them separately, we get:

$$3\log(n) + n^2 + n + 8 = O(\log n) + O(n^2) + O(n) + O(1)$$

or, considering the most significant growth factor of all, we arrive at:

$$f(n) = O(n^2)$$

Note

To assess the Big O complexity of any algorithm, we look for a function g(n) such that there exist positive finite constants c and n_0, where $f(n) \leq c\,g(n)$ holds for all $n \geq n_0$. We focus on the asymptotic growth rate of $g(n)$, to ensure that the growth rate of $f(n)$ is properly bounded as n approaches infinity.

Common big O time complexities

In describing the growth rate of an algorithm in Big O, we may come across any of the following:

- `O(1)`: constant time complexity (algorithm runs in constant time regardless of input size)
- `O(log n)`: logarithmic time complexity (algorithm runs in time proportional to the logarithm of the input size)
- `O(n)`: linear time complexity (algorithm runs in time directly proportional to the input size)
- `O(n log n)`: linearithmic time complexity (algorithm runs in time proportional to the product of the input size and its logarithm)
- `O(n2)`: quadratic time complexity (algorithm runs in time proportional to the square of the input size)
- `O(2n)`: exponential time complexity (algorithm runs in time proportional to 2 raised to the power of the input size)

In computer science, `O(1)` is a notation used to describe algorithms with constant time complexity. This means that an algorithm takes the same amount of time to execute, regardless of the size of the input. This is a deterministic behavior such that, for a given input size, `n`, the algorithm always takes the same amount of time to execute.

> **Note**
>
> Some classic examples of algorithms with `O(1)` time complexity include accessing an element in an array by its index, retrieving an element from a hash table, or performing an integer addition or division operation. An overview of common growth rates is presented in *Figure 1.20*, which outlines their varying complexity levels and real-world uses.

Complexity	Name	Example
$O(1)$	Constant	HashMap get, array index access
$O(\log N)$	Logarithmic	Binary search, BST lookup
$O(N)$	Linear	Linear search, iterate array
$O(N \log N)$	Linearithmic	Merge sort, heap sort
$O(N^2)$	Quadratic	Bubble sort, nested loops
$O(2^N)$	Exponential	Recursive Fibonacci, subsets
$O(N!)$	Factorial	Permutations, travelling salesman

Figure 1.20: Common growth rates and their use cases

Algebraic rules for big O analysis

Big O notation provides an upper bound on the running time or space complexity of an algorithm. We can simplify and analyze the Big O of any algorithm by following these practical rules; they serve as practical heuristics for simplifying complexity expressions while maintaining accuracy of the Big O analysis:

Rule 1: Focus on the dominant term

When analyzing a function f(n), ignore all terms of lower order and focus only on the term with the highest degree (the dominant term). If:

$$f(n) = a_i n^i + a_{i-1} n^{i-1} + \cdots + a_0$$

Then:

$$O(f(n)) \approx O(a_i n^i)$$

This means the algorithm's running time scales asymptotically to n^i, which is the most practical way to express complexity.

For example, in $3n^3 + n$, we may drop the lower term, n, from this equation and focus the growth rate on the higher, $3n^3$, term, yielding:

$$O(f(n)) \approx O(3n^3)$$

Rule 2: Ignore multiplicative constants

Multiplicative constant does not affect the asymptotic growth rate. This means the above equation from Rule 1 becomes:

$$O(f(n)) \approx O(a_i n^i) \approx O(n^i)$$

For example, $O(8n^3)$ is equivalent to $O(n^3)$

Rule 3: Ignore constant addition/subtraction

Adding or subtracting a constant to a function will not change its asymptotic order. For a given constant, c, we have:

$$O(f(n) \pm c) \approx O(f(n))$$

For example,

$$O(n^2 - 8) \approx O(n^2)$$

Rule 4: Addition rule

When combining two or more growth-rate functions, we take the maximum of their growth rates.

$$O(f(n)) + O(g(n)) \approx O(\max(f(n), g(n)))$$

Rule 5: Division rule

Dividing a complexity function by a constant factor, c, does not change its asymptotic growth rate.

$$O\left(\frac{f(n)}{c}\right) \approx O(f(n))$$

For example: consider an algorithm with a Big O complexity of O(n/2). By way of the division rule, this complexity is asymptotically equivalent to O(n).

While these heuristics are practical for real-world analysis, the full mathematical derivation for proving the accuracy of the addition and division rules is beyond the scope of this textbook. For a rigorous mathematical breakdown of these asymptotic properties, readers can consult the open-source MIT OpenCourseWare notes on Mathematics for Computer Science or OpenDataStructures.org.

Summary

In this chapter, we established that Data Structures and Algorithms are the essential framework for building efficient and scalable software. By integrating **Data Structures** (linear and non-linear), **Algorithmic Analysis** (complexity), and practical tools like the **Java Collections Framework (JCF)**, we learn that understanding DSA is the prerequisite for writing faster and cleaner code and orchestrating AI to force multiply.

This knowledge is essential for professional development. We now see how these principles are the core of modern technology, especially in AI. AI agents rely on DSA principles, using structures like Hash Maps, Tries, Priority Queues, and DAGs, to manage memory, plan complex actions, and optimize runtime orchestration constraints.

The following chapters will move from foundational concepts to specific data structures and algorithms, tying this knowledge to complex, real-world problems. We will then expand our knowledge into advanced topics like recursion, sorting, dynamic programming, and concurrency, which are essential for building truly efficient, AI-native code.

Part 2

Common Data Structures and Applications

In this part of the book, you will develop a solid foundation in fundamental data structures and algorithms by mastering linear structures and their specialized applications. We will start by exploring **Arrays** and **Linked Lists**, understanding how to efficiently store and manage sequential data. Next, we will examine essential abstract data types like **Stacks** and **Queues**, which govern how data is processed in order. We will then learn how to model relationships between data using **Maps** and **Hash Tables** for fast lookups. Moving to hierarchical structures, we will study **Trees**, learning about their structure, properties, and efficiency. This knowledge culminates in mastering specialized structures like **Priority Queues** and **Heaps**, which optimize selection and ordering. Finally, we will transition to modeling complex systems as **Graphs**, exploring how to represent connectivity, master traversal algorithms like BFS and DFS, and use these tools to solve sophisticated problems involving paths, cycles, and network analysis.

This part of the book includes the following chapters:

- *Chapter 2, Arrays and Linked Lists*
- *Chapter 3, Stacks and Queues*
- *Chapter 4, Maps and Hash Tables*
- *Chapter 5, Trees*
- *Chapter 6, Priority Queues and Heaps*
- *Chapter 7, Graphs*

2

Arrays and Linked Lists

In the world of data structures, linear data structures are characterized by elements being stored in a contiguous sequence of memory locations, where each element can be accessed via a fixed index or pointer. Arrays and linked lists are two fundamental data structures that exemplify this concept, making them ideal starting points for exploring other data structures.

Arrays are fixed-size, linear data structures that store same-type data elements in adjacent memory locations. Each element can be accessed directly via its index, which serves as a unique identifier. This simplicity and efficiency make arrays a popular choice for many applications.

In contrast, linked lists are another fundamental linear data structure that stores elements in a sequential manner by pointers or references. The linear relationship between elements enables efficient traversal and manipulation of the elements, making it suitable for scenarios where elements need to be dynamically added or removed.

As versatile building blocks of programming languages, arrays and linked lists offer a robust foundation for introducing object-oriented programming concepts and understanding how they intersect with data structures. Their fundamental properties and operations provide a solid starting point for exploring more complex data structures and learning about the nuances of programming.

In this chapter, we'll embark on an in-depth exploration of two fundamental data structures: arrays and linked lists. We'll examine the essential characteristics, advantages, and disadvantages of each, as well as their key operations, including insertion, searching, and deletion. Additionally, we'll discuss real-world scenarios where these data structures are commonly employed, highlighting their strengths, weaknesses, and run-time performance.

Arrays

A music streaming service like Spotify offers users a range of features that enable them to create and update their personalized playlists. Specifically, these features include:

- Inserting songs into playlists, which allows users to add new tracks to their existing collections
- Deleting songs from playlists, enabling users to remove unwanted or duplicate tracks
- Searching for specific songs within playlists, allowing users to quickly locate a particular track amidst their collection

We need an efficient data structure that can support frequent insertions, deletions, and searches without any significant performance degradation. In this context, arrays emerge as a suitable solution for modeling this playlist, due to their ability to provide fast access and modification of elements.

An array is a contiguous data structure where a fixed amount of memory is allocated to store all its elements in a linear, sequential order. This organized layout allows for efficient access to any element within the array by referencing its unique position using an index or subscript (*Figure 2.1*). Given that array indexing starts with 0, the index for the last element in an array is equal to the array length minus one:

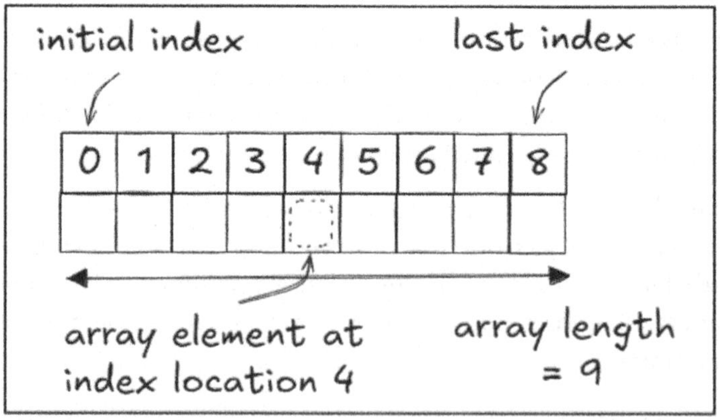

Figure 2.1: An array with 9 elements

An array readily models the aforesaid playlist. For example, a song can be removed from or inserted into an array by using its positional index in memory. This example illustrates two key facts about an array:

- Arrays are stored in contiguous memory locations, which means that each element has a fixed and known address.
- To access an element, you can simply use its index or subscript to calculate its memory location.

In Java, you can create a primitive array and access its elements using their corresponding indices. For example, the following code demonstrates how to allocate an integer array with 8 elements, access the third element, and insert a new value at that index.

```
// Dynamically instantiating an integer array of 8 elements
int[] arr = new int[8];

System.out.println("Accessing the 3rd element: " + arr[2]);

// Inserting 10 into the 3rd element
arr[2] = 10;
```

Accessing an array element using its index takes constant time, typically measured as `O(1)`, regardless of the size of the array or the number of elements it contains. In the following sections, we will discuss a few common array operations and their efficiencies.

Array operations and their efficiency

We will review a few common array operations in this section. The complete code is available in the GitHub repo inside the `ArrayADT.java` file in the `Chapter02` subfolder. To unlock the GitHub repo link, refer to the instructions in the *Download the example code files* section of the *Preface*. We will use the following notations throughout:

- The underlying array is represented by `arr` of capacity `arr.length`
- `n` is the current number of elements in the array
- `i` is an index location in `arr` with a value between 0 and `arr.length-1`
- e is a value to be inserted into `arr`

Assessors are operations that are used to inspect and retrieve information about an array without modifying its content. Let's say we have a wrapper class for an array data structure. This class has assessor methods such as:

- `get(i)`: retrieves the element at index `i` in `arr`. This method returns a data of type T, which is a generic type parameter that acts as a placeholder for an actual data type.
- `length()`: returns the total number of elements in `arr`.

More specifically:

```
T get(int i) {
    if (i < 0 || i >= n) {
       throw new IndexOutOfBoundsException(...);
    }
    return arr[i];
}

int length() {
    return n;
}
```

Their time efficiencies are:

```
get(i): O(1)
length(): O(1)
```

Likewise, mutation operations, as listed below, modify data in the system. These operations change the state of the data structure, either by adding new data of generic type `T`, updating existing data of type `T`, or deleting data.

- `set(int i, T e)`: replaces the element at index `i` with the specified value e.
- `add(int i, T e)`: inserts a new element, e, at position `i`, shifting all subsequent elements to the right.
- `delete(int i)`: removes the element at index i from arr, shifting all subsequent elements to the left.

The `set()` operation has `O(1)` time efficiency:

```
void set(int i, T e) {
     if (i < 0 || i >= n) { throw new IndexOutOfBoundsException(...);}
```

```
    arr[i] = e;
}
```

Whereas the time efficiency for `add(i, e)` is a bit more complex. To understand this better, let's look at its definition:

```
void add(int i, T e) {
1   if (i < 0 || i > n) {throw new IndexOutOfBoundsException(...);}
2   if (n >= arr.length) resize();
3   for (int j=n; j>i; j--) arr[j] = arr[j-1];
4   arr[i] = e;
5   n++;
}
```

Here, `n` is a counter representing the total number of elements in the array at the end. To add an element into the array at index `i`, we need to shift all elements from index `i + 1` to the end one position to the right.

Recall from *Chapter 1* that time efficiency refers to how long an algorithm takes to complete, typically measured in terms of the number of steps or operations it performs. These complexities are often referred to as the "cost" or "time complexity" of an algorithm because they provide a way to estimate how much computational resources (e.g., CPU cycles, memory) will be required to execute it.

The total cost of a single `add(i,e)` operation is therefore the summation of time complexity costs from lines 2, 3, 4, and 5, as follows:

- Line 2: the cost for the resize operation involves allocating a new array of size `x*n` (where `x` is a numeric growth factor greater than 1) and copying all data from the old array into the new one in `O(n)`.
- Line 3: the cost of data shifting is `O(n-i+1)`.
- Line 4: the cost of assigning an element at index `i` is `O(1)`.
- Line 5: the cost for incrementing the total size of the array is `O(1)`.

For trivial data manipulations not exceeding the capacity of an array, the average cost of an `add()` operation, therefore, is `O(n-i+1)`. For a big-sized array, where `n >> i`, the complexity of `add()` converges to `O(n)`. Note that this estimation ignores the occasional array expansion per x number of `add()` operations to trigger a `resize()` operation.

Similarly, as an element is removed from its original position in `delete(i)`, all the following elements must be moved by one position to fill the gap, resulting in a contiguous shift of elements. Namely:

```
T delete(int i) {
1     if (i < 0 || i >= n) {throw new IndexOutOfBoundsException(...);}
2     T e = arr[i];
3     for (int j=i; j<n-1; j++) arr[j] = arr[j+1];
4     arr[i] = e;
5     n--;
6     if(x*n<= arr.length) resize();
7     return e;
}
```

Line 6 indicates that `arr` will resize() down when it is more than half empty. When that happens, we will shrink it, usually by a numeric growth factor greater than 1.

The total cost of one `delete(i)` operation is, therefore, the summation of time complexity costs from lines 2, 3, 4, 5, and 6.

The total cost should be as follows:

- Line 2: the cost for fetching an element and assigning it to a local variable: `O(1)`.
- Line 3: the cost of data shifting is `O(n-i+1)`.
- Line 4: the cost of decrementing a counter is `O(1)`
- Line 5: the cost of assigning an element at index `i` is `O(1)`.
- Line 6: the cost for the resize operation involves allocating a new array of size `n/x` (where `x` is a numeric growth factor greater than 1), and copying all data from the old array into the new one in `O(n)`.

Most of the time, a `delete(i)` operation takes place without triggering `resize()`, costing `O(n-i+1)`. For a big-sized array, where `n>>i`, the complexity of `delete(i)` reduces to `O(n)`. We ignore the effect of occasional array resizing in computing the above cost.

In summary, the time complexity of both `add(i,e)` and `delete(i)` is `O(n-i)`, which converges to `O(n)` when `n>>i`. This is because `arr` has a fixed capacity and shifting neighboring values, either to insert new data or fill the gap left by a deleted value, incurs a cost of `n-i`. *Figure 2.2* summarizes the time complexity for the **create**, **read**, **update**, and **delete** (**CRUD**) operations of a fixed-size array.

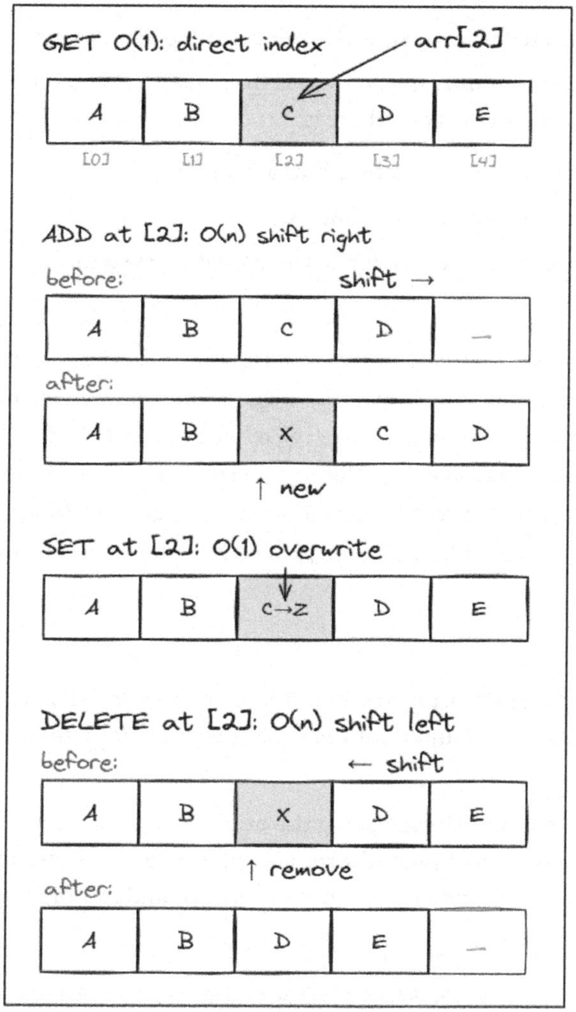

Figure 2.2: Time complexity of CRUD operations in a fixed size array

Resizing arrays: Expansion and contraction

Resizing an array leads to two types of transformations on `resize()`: expansion and compression. When an array expands, its size is increased by adding new elements to the end of the existing data structure. This process involves allocating additional memory to accommodate the growing data set. Expanding an array occurs in response to changes in data volume or frequency, such as:

- New elements are added frequently.

- The existing capacity is insufficient for future growth.
- Memory is allocated from a large block of contiguous memory.

Conversely, when an array compresses, its size is decreased by removing or reusing unused memory. This process can occur when there is:

- Unused space within the array becomes available.
- The data volume decreases or stabilizes.
- Memory needs to be released back to the operating system.

> **Note**
>
> Unused memory must eventually be reclaimed by the runtime environment. In-memory data structure resizing is typically triggered in two ways: explicitly by the user optimizing capacity (e.g., trimming an array), or automatically by the data structure itself using internal threshold metrics like load factors. If the overall system faces critical resource shortages, the Operating System may signal the runtime layer to aggressively run Garbage Collection, though it cannot directly alter individual data structures.

When an array expands, a new array must be created by copying the existing elements into it. This involves allocating new memory for the expanded array and updating the reference to the new location.

The process typically begins with increasing the original array size by a growth factor, followed by allocating a new array of the updated size. The growth factor is often set to 1.5 times the original size, which balances reducing memory overhead and minimizing copying cost.

> **Note**
>
> In OpenJDK, the growth factor is 1.5 times the original size, which is a trade-off between reducing memory overhead and minimizing copying costs.

All elements from the original array are copied into the new array element-wise, ensuring that data remains contiguous.

> **Note**
>
> When choosing an array resizing strategy, we must consider the following factors:
>
> - The amount of data is reasonably small.

- The amount of data can be predicted in advance, and it won't vary in size over time.
- The distribution of data is not sparse. A sparse array may trigger a resizing mechanism.

When dealing with dynamic arrays, it's essential to consider the trade-offs between efficient memory usage and frequent resizing. So far, we have focused on analyzing the maximum amount of work performed by individual operations or small sets of procedures in our mutation methods: `add(i,e)` and `delete(i)`. However, this approach overlooks the continuous effect of performing these operations over time and the triggering of `resize()` operations, which incur additional overhead.

In the following section, we will better understand the trade-off by examining the average cost of a sequence of operations over time.

Amortized analysis: Resizing an array

Amortized analysis is a methodology that extends traditional worst-case analysis by taking into account the long-term effects of repeated calls. It examines the average cost of a sequence of operations over time, rather than just considering individual operations in isolation.

From the prior sections, we know resizing an array is needed when its capacity is either full due to the repeated addition of values or when there is a significant amount of empty space due to the removal of values. Let's understand the cost for doing so.

Evaluating the time complexity, or cost, of one `resize()` operation is trivial. Namely, for each `resize()` on expansion due to `add()`, we need to copy `n` sequence of elements into a new array of size `x*n`, where `x` is the numerical growth factor greater than 1. This calls for `O(n)` time. Conversely, for each `resize()` on compression due to `delete()`, we need to copy `n` sequence of elements into a new array of size `n/x`. This again calls for `O(n)` time. This begs a question: what is the total cost of performing a sequence of `add()` and `delete()` operations on `resize()`?

If we look at the amount of work over time, by repeatedly adding and/or deleting values into an array to eventually trigger a `resize()` operation, we can amortize that work by looking at the number of `add()` or `delete()` operations required.

Assuming we are starting with an empty array with a growth factor of `x` on expansion. Whenever the array capacity grows to `n`, it automatically expands to a new capacity of `x` times `n`, where `x` is a numeric constant greater than 1 on expansion as illustrated in *Figure 2.3*:

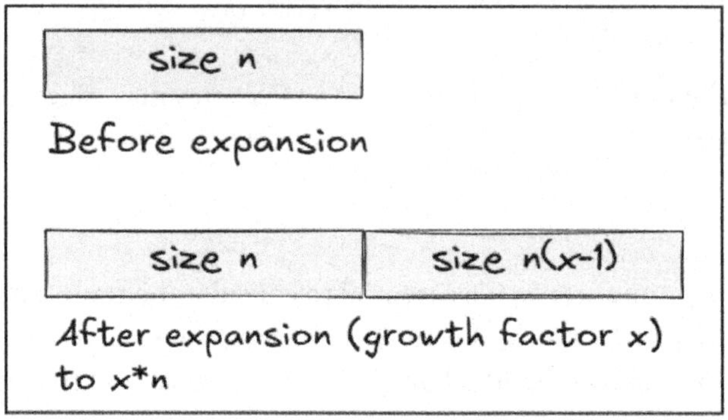

Figure 2.3: Array expansion on a growth factor of x

We say during the ith resizing, a new array of $xn_i = n_{i+1}$ in size is allocated, and n_i elements from the old array are copied into it. During the i+1th resizing, a new array of xn_{i+1} in size is allocated, and the old n_{i+1} elements are copied into it. Therefore, we say the total number of elements copied is:

$$N = n_o + n_1 + n_2 + n_3 + \cdots$$

The above can also be represented as:

$$N = xn_0 + xn_1 + xn_2 + \cdots = x(n_0 + n_1 + n_2 + \cdots)$$

Here, n_o is the initial capacity of the array. During the ith and i+1th resizing, there are at least $n_i(x-1)$ elements added due to a sequence of m_i number of `add()` and/or `delete()` operations. It is not hard to see:

$$n_i(x-1) \leq m_i$$

Over the course of many resizing operations:

$$n_0(x-1) + n_1(x-1) + n_2(x-1) + \cdots \leq m_0 + m_1 + m_2 + \cdots$$

If we say there are M total such `add()` and `delete()` operations over the course of a sufficiently large number of `resize()` operations:

$$(x-1)(n_0 + n_1 + n_2 + \cdots) \leq M$$

The above equations yield:

$$N - n_0 - n_1 - n_2 - \cdots = N - \frac{N}{x} = \frac{N(x-1)}{x} \leq M$$

We can also write the above as:

$$N \leq \frac{x}{x-1}M$$

Since `x` is a numeric constant greater than 1, the total time spent in all `resize()` operations is `O(M)`.

The above result connotes that the total amount of work leading to array resizing, over time, is the number of calls to `add()` and/or `remove()`. In other words, even though a single `resize()` operation costs `O(n)`, if we amortize many `add()` and `delete()` operations to derive a cumulative, average cost of `resize()`, its amortized cost per operation is `O(1)`. Over the course of `M` operations, each of them runs in `O(1)` amortized time. We can derive a similar amortized analysis of array compression to yield a similar result.

Assessing the expansion cost

In the above section, we described how a fixed-size array must grow or shrink when its capacity is reached or exceeded. Now, let's examine the cost of that operation in more detail. For brevity, we'll focus on expansion, noting that the same analysis applies to compression.

To gauge the cost, we need to enumerate every operation that contributes to it. When the array hits its limit, we perform the following steps:

- Allocate a larger buffer: most often twice the previous size
- Copy the contents from the old buffer to the new one
- Release the old buffer

If there is still room, we simply place the next element in the free slot. The total time spent on an expansion is therefore the sum of the copying and the insertion work:

$$Cost_{expansion} = Cost_{copy} + Cost_{insert}$$

Beginning with an array that holds only one element, the structure will grow as more inserts arrive. With a growth factor of two, the process unfolds as follows in *Table 2.1*:

Expansion Step (m)	Insertions	Array Size	Elements copied
1	Insert "a" (n = 1)	$1 \rightarrow 2$	1 element: a
2	Insert "b" (n = 2)	$2 \rightarrow 4$	2 elements: a, b
3	Insert "c", "d" (n = 4)	$4 \rightarrow 8$	4 elements: a, b, c, d

Expansion Step (m)	Insertions	Array Size	Elements copied
4	Insert "e", "f", "g", "h" (n = 8)	8 → 16	8 elements: a, b, c, d, e, f, g, h

Table 2.1: Step-by-step insertion, expansion and copying sequence during array expansion

This is illustrated in *Figure 2.4*:

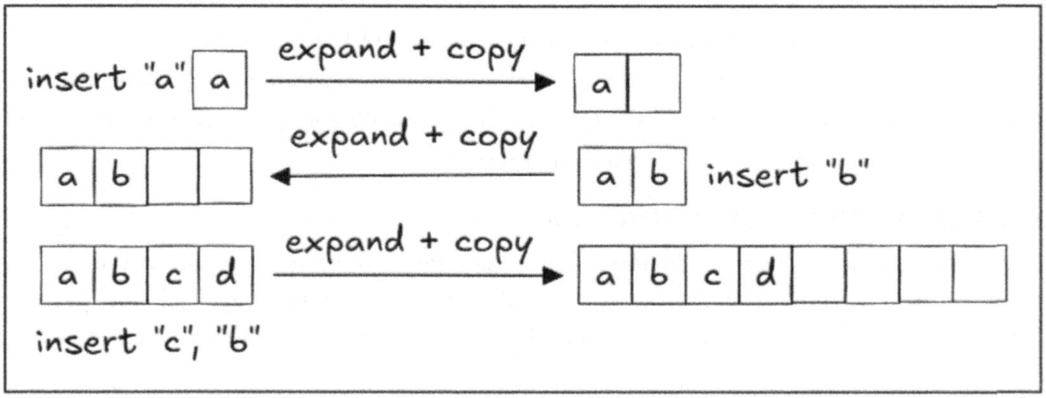

Figure 2.4: Expansion cost as a function of total insertions and copies

When an array starts at size 1 and doubles, it expands at specific milestones:

$$1 \rightarrow 2 \rightarrow 4 \rightarrow 8 \rightarrow 16 \rightarrow \cdots \rightarrow n$$

Mathematically, these milestones are powers of two:

$$2^0 \rightarrow 2^1 \rightarrow 2^2 \rightarrow 2^3 \ldots \rightarrow 2^m$$

where `m` represents the total number of expansions. If the array has reached a size of `n`, it must have doubled *approximately* $\log_2$ n times. We can see this clearly when `n=8`, where the array doubles $\log_2 8$ `= 3 times (1 → 2 → 4 → 8)`. This means the total number of expansions, `m`, is *approximately* $\log_2$ `n`. This is just an approximation. Let's look at a more formal derivation to arrive at the exact inequality for `m` and `n`.

Because an insertion that triggers a resize costs `O(n)`, every one of these `m` expansions must copy all existing elements into the newly expanded array. Summing these sequential copying costs across all expansions up to a capacity of `n` (see *Table 2.1*) yields a geometric series of the powers of two:

$$1 + 2 + 4 + \ldots + 2^{(m-1)}$$

Note

Sum of Powers of 2

Mathematically, the following algebraic formula holds true. The derivation, though straightforward, is beyond the scope of this text:

$$\sum_{i=0}^{m} 2^i = 2^{m+1} - 1$$

Applying the sum of powers of two identity to our array expansions, the total copying cost simplifies to:

$$1 + 2 + 4 + \ldots + 2^{(m-1)} = 2^m - 1$$

Since the array has n elements, and the next expansion occurs at 2^m, we know that n sits somewhere between these two milestones:

$$2^{(m-1)} < n \leq 2^m$$

Multiplying the above member-wise by 2 yields:

$$2^m < 2n \leq 2^{m+1}$$

Summarily, the total copying cost amounts to:

$$1 + 2 + 4 + \cdots + 2^{(m-1)} = 2^m - 1 < 2^m < 2n$$

Since 2n is just a constant multiplied by n, the overall time complexity for all copies is O(n). When divided across n insertions, the average (amortized) cost per insertion is just O(1).

The total cost of expansion is the sum of the copying and the insertion work.

$$(1 + 2 + 4 + \ldots + n) + n = (2n - 1) + n = 3n - 1$$

The amortized cost is calculated by dividing the total operational work by n insertions. This yields an average cost of O(1), as the total runtime simplifies to a constant factor per operation. The amortized effect is visualized by choosing n = 16 in *Figure 2.5*:

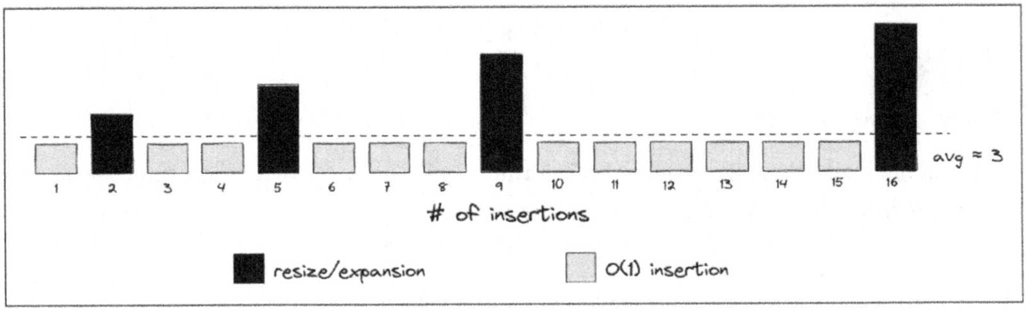

Figure 2.5: Cost of expansion when n = 16

Note

Number of Expansions

The total number of expansions, m, required for an array of n elements (where n > 1) is:

$$m = \lfloor log_2(n-1) \rfloor + 1$$

where ⌊ ⌋ is the floor function.

This reveals a key distinction: while the cost of a single expansion is strictly `O(n)`, this heavy resizing work is distributed across a large number of cheap insertions. This global view yields an `O(1)` amortized cost per insertion, even though an individual operation spikes to `O(n)` during a resize event. In other words, when evaluating the system over a continuous sequence of `add(i, e)` and `delete(i)` operations, the cumulative cost scales as if every individual operation ran in constant `O(1)` time.

While arrays provide a straightforward way to store and manipulate collections of elements, they can become cumbersome when dealing with large datasets or frequent insertions and deletions. In such cases, the time and space complexity of array operations becomes a concern. To address this limitation, a more sophisticated data structure is introduced: the vector. Vectors are the standard, widely used concrete implementation of the dynamic array ADT, built on top of a contiguous raw array buffer. Unlike arrays, which require manual management of size and copying of contents, vectors provide a dynamic and flexible way to store elements. They can grow or shrink in size as needed, making them an attractive choice for applications that involve frequent additions and removals.

Vectors

In a language-agnostic sense, a vector can grow or shrink in size as needed. Elements are stored in an underlying array that dynamically grows or shrinks to accommodate changing capacity requirements.

> **Note**
>
> **Vector in Java**
>
> `Vector` is an obsolete Java 1.0 class whose mandatory internal synchronization creates unnecessary overhead in single-threaded contexts. Modern applications should instead use `ArrayList` or concurrent collections, choosing the implementation that matches their specific threading requirements.

In modern Java, dynamic arrays are created using the new keyword with the List type:

```
java.util.List<Integer> myVector = new java.util.ArrayList<>();
```

The underlying capacity of an `ArrayList` can be pre-adjusted after creation using the `ensureCapacity()` method. Vector indices start at 0. They offer flexibility by not requiring the amount of data to be known in advance. However, this feature comes at the cost of occasional automatic expansion or compression, as described in the previous sections.

In the following section, we'll explore two distinct categories of arrays for how developers manage data inside them: ordered and unordered arrays.

Types of arrays

When managing data within arrays, developers may choose between two algorithmic approaches: ordered (sorted) and unordered (unsorted) arrays. *Table 2.2* shows the difference between the two:

Ordered Arrays	Unordered Arrays
Also known as sequential (or sorted) arrays or lists; they maintain a logical order among their elements.	Also known as unordered lists; they do not maintain any specific order among their elements.
Prioritizes search speed (supports fast binary search).	Prioritizes insertion speed (supports fast `O(1)` appends).

Table 2.2: Comparison of Ordered Arrays and Unordered Arrays

When managing and processing large datasets, choosing between an unordered array and an ordered array significantly impacts system performance. Unordered arrays offer maximum write efficiency, allowing for constant insertions since data is simply appended to the end. However, they require linear scans through the entire dataset.

In contrast, ordered arrays prioritize read efficiency, maintaining data in a strict sequence that enables fast binary search algorithms. The trade-off is significantly slow write times, as inserting or deleting elements requires CPU-intensive shifting to maintain the correct logical order.

Table 2.3 highlights the key differences in performance characteristics between the two data management approaches in arrays:

Operation	Unordered Array	Ordered Array
Write (Insertion)	O(1)	O(n)
Random Index Read	O(1)	O(1)
Search by Value	O(n)	O(log n)

Table 2.3: Operational Efficiencies in Unordered Array vs Ordered Array

Unordered arrays

Unordered arrays are frequently used in software applications where write-insertion speed and maximum throughput are critical. In computer science, an array is classified as "unordered" when elements are simply appended to the next available slot based on their time of arrival, rather than being sorted by their internal values (like alphabetical or numerical order). This allows insertion to run at constant time `O(1)`, as no element shifting or sorting algorithms are required. We illustrate two industry examples.

Example: Drone log buffer

Consider an autonomous drone surveying a region. As it flies, it captures various sensor readings, such as altitude, velocity, and GPS coordinates. To handle this massive stream of data without dropping packets, the flight logger employs an append-only array buffer.

While the entries naturally follow a chronological order in time of arrival, the data structure is an unordered array because the system does not sort the readings by their internal values (e.g., sorting from lowest to highest altitude). It prioritizes capturing data exactly when it arrives:

```
public class LogBuffer {
    private LogEntry[] buffer;
    private int writeIndex = 0;
    private int capacity;

    public LogBuffer(int capacity) {
       this.capacity = capacity;
       this.buffer = new LogEntry[capacity];
    }

    public void addLogEntry(LogEntry entry) {
        // Simple append - O(1) operation
        if (writeIndex < capacity) {
            buffer[writeIndex++] = entry;
        } else {
            flush(); // Log shipping; write to disk and reset
            WriteIndex = 0;
            buffer[writeIndex++] = entry;
        }
    }

    private void flush() { ... }
}
```

Note

Why Logging uses Unordered Arrays

If the drone flies at 500ft, climbs to 600ft, and then drops to 400ft, the array stores [500, 600, 400]. Because 400 comes after 600, the data is unsorted by value. Forcing this into a technically "Ordered Array" would require shifting elements on every tick, destroying the chronological timeline and lagging the drone's processor.

Once the buffer is full, we may log-ship or export the data elsewhere via `flush()` while employing an efficient circular buffer-write pattern, where old logs can be overwritten with new ones.

Example: High-throughput service logger

Consider a streaming platform processing millions of user requests per hour. To monitor system health, it logs events precisely as they occur. Sorting these logs by User ID or Error Severity on the fly would bottleneck the application. Instead, an unordered array structure accepts data based purely on its real-time arrival sequence:

```
// Requests are instantly appended to a buffer in arrival order // The array
remains unordered relative to the
// content of the messages.
logger.info("User ID: " + userId);            // Appended to buffer
logger.error("Streaming connection failed"); // Appended next
logger.debug("Session cache hit for ID: " + uuid); // Appended next
```

The messages vary in severity, length, and user ID. The system does not waste CPU cycles alphabetizing or ranking the logs before saving them; it simply streams them into memory slots sequentially based on their time of arrival. A more extended version of the above can be found inside the `LogBuffer.java` file in the `Chapter02` subfolder on GitHub. To unlock the GitHub repo link, refer to the instructions in the *Download the example code files* section of the *Preface*.

Ordered arrays

These arrays support traversal and are optimized for search speed. They frequently employ a binary search algorithm to locate elements efficiently, in `O(log n)` time. For example, binary search can be used in database query optimization to efficiently locate specific records or values within a vast dataset. Other than searching, ordered arrays are also used in prioritizing data, as the following example illustrates.

Example: Air traffic control priority buffer

Ordered arrays are highly effective when data must be instantly available in priority order, such as in an air traffic control system that must guarantee critical alerts (e.g., collision warnings) are processed ahead of routine data:

```
public class PriorityLogBuffer {
    private LogEntry[] sortedBuffer; // Ordered by severity
    private int size = 0;
```

```
    public void insertLogEntry(LogEntry entry) {
        // Insert maintaining order by priority
        int insertPos = findInsertPosition(entry.severity);
        // Shift and insert - more expensive but
        // prioritizes critical logs
    }
}
```

Prioritizing data in an ordered array can be costly due to the need to consider array expansion and compression because of its fixed capacity, which limits the ability to dynamically adapt to changing data volumes.

If a system requires high-frequency data insertion alongside prioritization, developers typically replace the ordered array with a binary heap (priority queue). A heap provides dynamic insertion and deletion in `O(log n)` time by organizing data as a binary tree, eliminating the need to sequentially shift large blocks of contiguous memory.

Linked lists

Linked lists are another essential data structure used for storing and manipulating collections of data. A linked list is a sequence of elements connected to each other. Each element in a linked list is a separate node that contains the data and a reference (link) to the next node in the sequence, as illustrated in *Figure 2.6*:

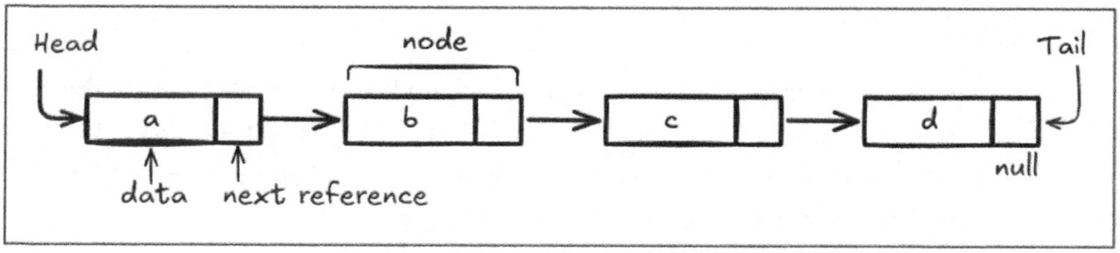

Figure 2.6: The structure of a singly linked list

In the following section, we will review a few key linked list operations and their efficiencies.

Operations and efficiency

A linked list supports similar foundational operations to an array, but with entirely different performance characteristics:

- Insertion
  - `O(1)`: Pointer rewiring at a known node position.
  - `O(1)`: Inserting an element at the beginning of the list, requiring only updating a few head pointers
  - `O(n)`: Traversing the entire list to find the last node and insert at that location. This drops to `O(1)` if the list maintains a direct tail pointer.
- Deletion
  - `O(1)`: Pointer unlinking at a known node position
  - `O(1)`: Deleting an element from the beginning of the list, updating the head pointer to the second node
  - `O(n)`: Deleting a node from the middle or end of the list, requiring traversing it to locate the node and its predecessor to unlink it
- Search
  - `O(n)`: Finding a specific node in the linked list by traversing from the beginning to the target node, as linked lists do not support index-based random access
- Traversal
  - `O(n)` for forward traversal: Traversing each node from the beginning of the list to its end (pointer update). No support for backward traversal: a singly linked list only possesses forward pointers. Traversing backward requires upgrading to a doubly linked list, which operates at `O(n)` time.

The **create-read-update-delete** (**CRUD**) operations are shown in *Figure 2.7*.

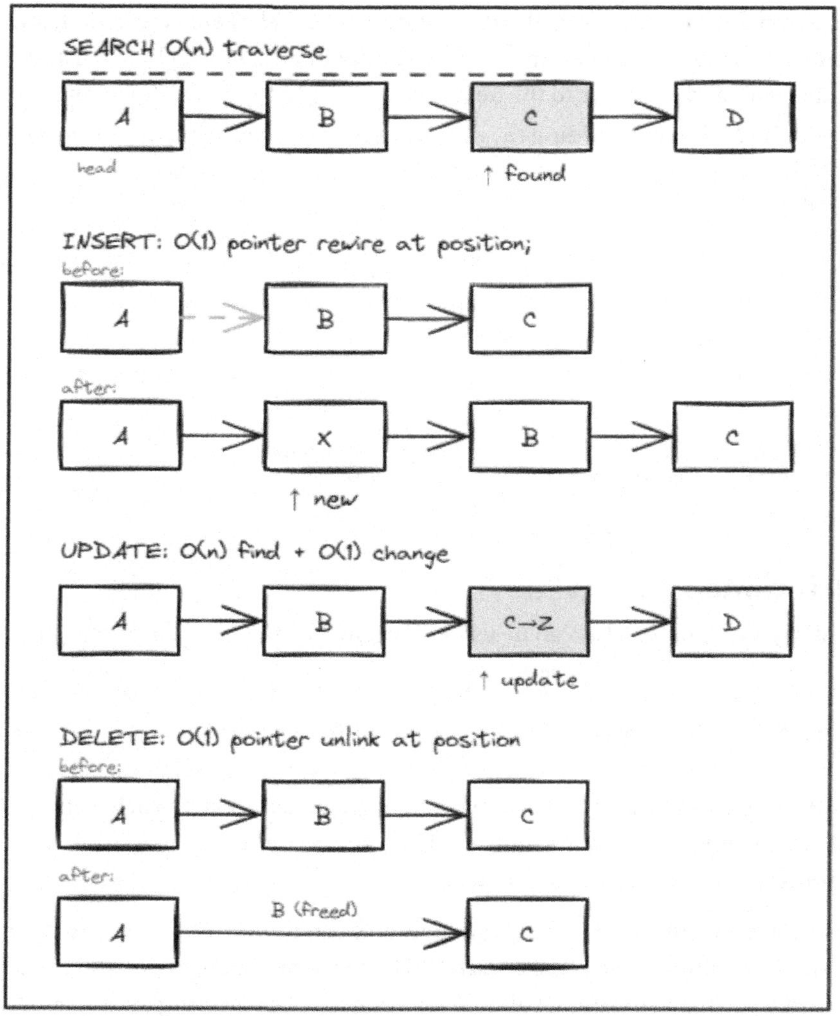

Figure 2.7: CRUD operations in a linked list

Types of linked lists

There are many variations of linked lists; some come equipped as a hybrid by combining other data structures, such as tree-linked lists and hash table-linked lists, to name a few. In Java Collection Framework, we also observe the following Java classes.

ConcurrentLinkedQueue

A **queue** is a **first-in, first-out** (**FIFO**) data structure where elements are added at the rear and removed from the front. Queues can be efficiently implemented using linked lists, where each node contains data and a pointer to the next node, allowing for dynamic sizing and `O(1)` time complexity for both enqueue (adding to rear) and dequeue (removing from front) operations.

```
ConcurrentLinkedQueue<String> queue = new ConcurrentLinkedQueue<>();

  // Enqueue operations (add elements to rear)
queue.offer("First");
queue.offer("Second");
queue.offer("Third");

// Dequeue operations (remove elements from front)
String element1 = queue.poll();  // Returns "First"
String element2 = queue.poll();  // Returns "Second"
```

LinkedHashMap

For ordered key-value pairs. This can be used for cache and buffering, for example:

```
// LRU-style implementations
LinkedHashMap<String, Object> lruCache = new LinkedHashMap<>(16, 0.75f, true);
```

Throughout this chapter, we have discussed singly linked lists, where each element (node) points only to the next node in the sequence. This type is commonly used for basic implementations and for many algorithms.

There's also a doubly linked list, having two pointers per node: one pointing to the previous node and another pointing to the next node. This allows for efficient traversal in both forward and backward directions, making it suitable for applications requiring bidirectional navigation (*Figure 2.8*).

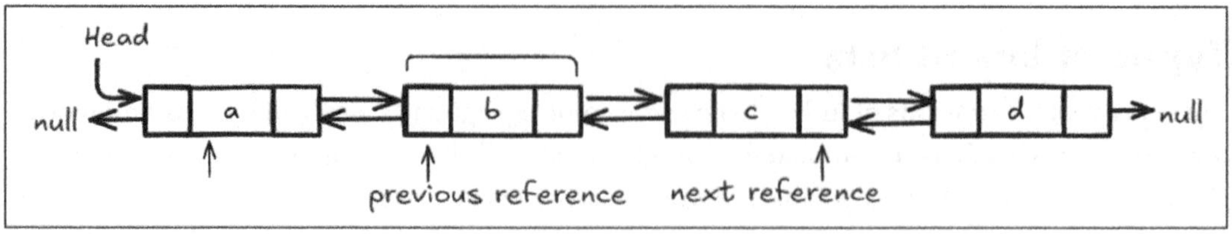

Figure 2.8: The structure of a doubly linked list

Comparing arrays and linked lists

The primary difference between array-based structures (like `ArrayList`) and linked lists lies in how they handle dynamic memory allocation. Arrays require occasional, expensive `O(n)` operations to resize and shift entire memory buffers, leading to unpredictable performance spikes. In contrast, linked lists are inherently dynamic: they allocate or free individual nodes organically, eliminating the need for bulk memory copying.

Flexibility, access, and operations

Linked lists are inherently dynamic, managing memory by allocating individual nodes, which avoids the costly `O(n)` element-shifting penalties associated with array resizing. However, this flexibility introduces a core trade-off: random access. Unlike arrays, linked lists require a sequential `O(n)` walk to reach an arbitrary element.

The efficiency of a linked list is highly dependent on where the operation occurs:

- Boundary Operations `O(1)`: Inserting or deleting at the head or tail is highly efficient.
- Arbitrary Access `O(n)`: While modifying pointers at a known node is `O(1)`, locating that node first requires a linear search, costing `O(n)` time. This limitation contrasts with the `O(1)` random access of arrays.

Real-world application: High-frequency logging

This distinction becomes crucial in high-frequency systems, such as data traceability and observability. While both structures allow fast `O(1)` appending of new log entries (arrays and linked lists), their long-term performance differs significantly.

- **Arrays**: Excel in memory density and random access but suffer from unpredictable `O(n)` latency spikes during mandatory reallocations.
- **Linked Lists**: Offer a smooth, continuous insertion profile, avoiding these spikes. However, the scattered memory locations can reduce CPU cache efficiency compared to the contiguous layout of an array.

Despite the limitation of sequential traversal (`O(n)` access time), linked lists remain exceptionally efficient for scenarios involving continuous data streams, dynamic modifications, or implementing dynamic structures like stacks and queues. This flexibility makes them the optimal choice when memory flexibility outweighs the need for instant random access.

In summary, the choice depends entirely on the workload. Arrays are superior for predictable access; linked lists are superior for dynamic modification and streaming data where bulk reallocation pauses must be avoided.

Summary

As we learn from this chapter, when choosing between arrays and linked lists for storing and manipulating collections of data, it's essential to consider the predictability of the data amount and the frequency of access operations. Arrays are suitable when the data can be accurately predicted and frequent access is necessary, as they provide constant-time access. For instance, in databases, arrays (or specifically, arrays used to represent tables) are often used for storing fixed-size datasets, such as numerical or categorical data, where predictability and regular updates are guaranteed.

However, insertion and deletion operations in arrays can be costly due to shifting existing elements. In contrast, linked lists excel in scenarios where the data amount is uncertain or frequently modified, offering efficient dynamic allocation of memory for insertion and deletion operations. This makes them a better choice when flexibility and adaptability are crucial, such as in applications requiring frequent log additions or updates, found in:

- **Log aggregation systems**: Used to collect and analyze log data from various sources.
- **Real-time analytics platforms**: Utilize linked lists to handle high-frequency updates and dynamic queries.
- **Social media platforms**: Leverage linked lists to efficiently manage user data, such as friends, followers, or post history.

As we move forward, we will delve into two more essential data structures: stacks and queues. Both data structures are ubiquitous in computer science and play vital roles in many applications, including:

- Job scheduling: Stacks are used to manage job execution, where each new task is added on top of the existing ones.
- Network protocols: Queues are used to handle incoming data packets, ensuring that they are processed in a first-come-first-served manner.
- Task management: Both stacks and queues can be used to manage tasks, such as adding new tasks to a queue or executing them from a stack.

The summary diagram of arrays and linked lists is as follows:

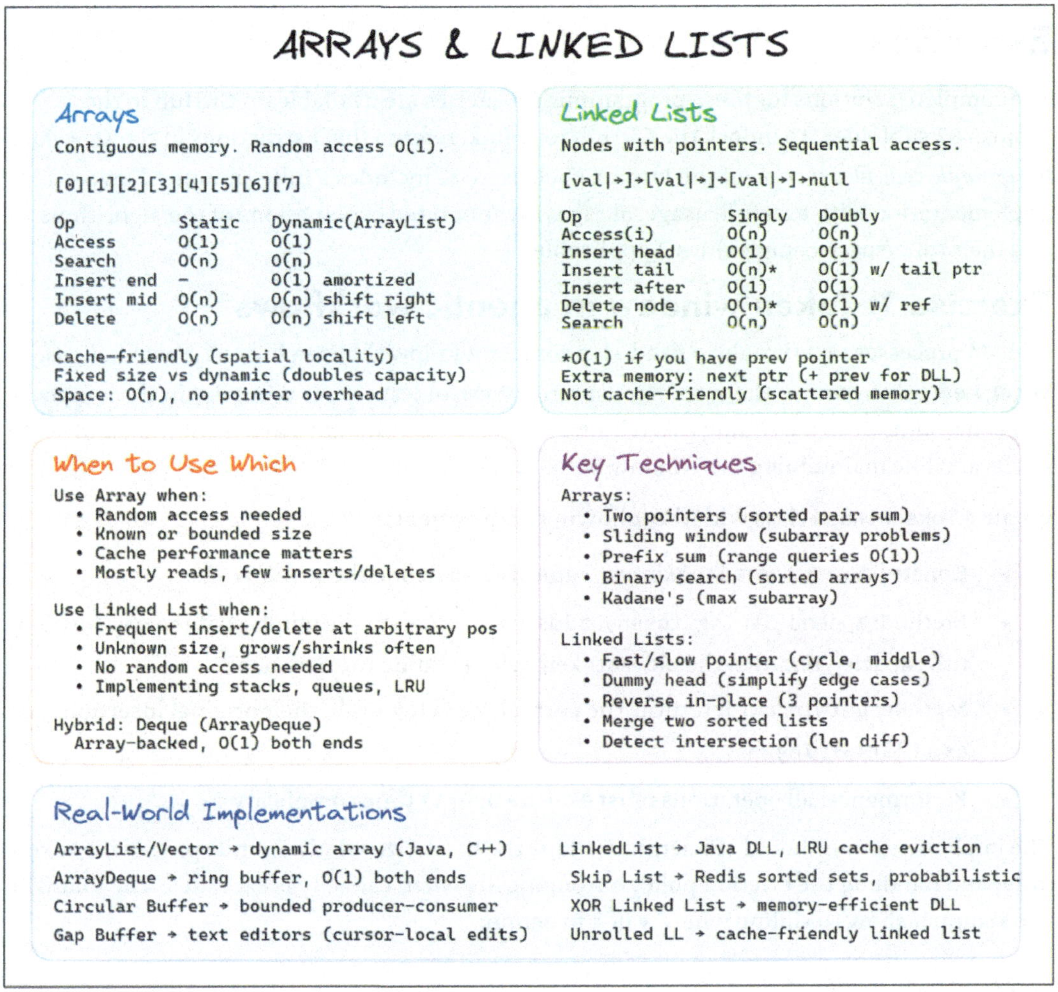

Figure 2.9: Arrays and linked lists summary

In our next chapter, we will delve into the definition of these two data structures using both array and linked list representations. We will explore their fundamental properties, including:

- Stack operations (push, pop, peek)
- Queue operations (enqueue, dequeue, peek)

We will also examine the algorithms used to implement these data structures efficiently and discuss their applications in real-world scenarios.

Exercises

The complete solutions for these programming exercises are available on GitHub in the `Chapter02` subfolder. To unlock the GitHub repo link, refer to the instructions in the *Download the example code files* section of the *Preface*. Each exercise includes a fully annotated Java implementation with example usage, along with annotated explanations of the algorithms and their time/space complexities if applicable.

Exercise 1: Token window in agentic workflows

An LLM processes text through a fixed-size context window that can hold at most `k` tokens. When new tokens arrive, the system must remove the oldest tokens to maintain the window size constraint. Design a sliding token buffer that efficiently handles token addition and retrieval while maintaining the window boundaries.

Create a `TokenWindow` class with the following requirements:

- Constructor: Accepts a maximum capacity `k` to define the window size
- Method: `append(String token)`: adds a new token to the window; if the window is at full capacity, removes the oldest token before adding the new one
- Method: `getWindow()`: returns the current set of tokens in their original insertion order as a `List<String>`
- Performance: all operations must execute in `O(1)` time complexity

The implementation should efficiently manage the fixed-size window while preserving token order and handling the eviction policy automatically when capacity is exceeded. The following code snippet shows a sliding window of 4 in action:

```
// Setting k = 4
TokenWindow window = new TokenWindow(4);
window.append("The");
window.append("agent");
window.append("processes");
window.append("input");
window.getWindow(); // ["The", "agent", "processes", "input"]
window.append("tokens");
window.getWindow(); // ["agent", "processes", "input", "tokens"]
```

Solution

LLMs have finite context windows (like 128K tokens for Claude). When conversations exceed this limit, the system must evict the oldest content automatically. This is fundamentally a fixed-size, first-in-first-out (FIFO) buffer called a queue, where new data pushes out old data following that pattern.

A naive `ArrayList` implementation requires `O(n)` shifts when removing elements from the front, making it inefficient for frequent operations. To meet the `O(1)` requirement, we use a "circular" buffer or linked list as a deque. A linked list provides:

- `O(1)` removal from the head (oldest element)
- `O(1)` append to the tail (newest element)
- Perfect for sliding window operations

This approach ensures that when the window reaches capacity, the oldest token is automatically evicted as new tokens are added, maintaining the fixed-size constraint while keeping all operations efficient. The solution is as follows:

```
public class TokenWindow {
    private final int capacity;
    private final LinkedList<String> buffer;

    public TokenWindow(int capacity) {
        this.capacity = capacity;
        this.buffer = new LinkedList<>();
    }

    public void append(String token) {
        if (buffer.size() == capacity) {
            buffer.removeFirst();          // O(1) eviction
        }
        buffer.addLast(token);             // O(1) append
    }

    public List<String> getWindow() {
        return new ArrayList<>(buffer);  // O(k) snapshot
    }
}
```

The linked list's doubly-linked structure allows `O(1)` operations at both ends. In production, `ArrayDeque` is preferred over `LinkedList` for cache locality (contiguous memory), but the asymptotic behavior is identical.

The linked list implementation is particularly elegant because it naturally supports both ends of the queue without requiring expensive repositioning of elements. The full solution is available in the `TokenWindow.java` file in the `Chapter02` folder on GitHub. To unlock the GitHub repo link, refer to the instructions in the *Download the example code files* section of the *Preface*.

Exercise 2: Remove duplicates from sorted array

Write a `RemoveDuplicates` class with the following `removeDuplicates` method that modifies a sorted integer array (`nums`) in-place to remove duplicate values:

```
public int removeDuplicates(int[] nums)
```

Assumptions and Constraints

- Array is sorted in non-decreasing order
- The array is modified in-place (no extra space for new array)
- Elements are integers
- `0 ≤ nums.length ≤` 10^4
- `-100 ≤ nums[i] ≤ 100`

Hints: Use two pointers approach; one for reading, one for writing

Examples

- **Input**: `[1,1,2]` → **Output**: 2 // `nums = [1,2]`
- **Input**: `[0,0,1,1,1,2,2,3,3,4]` → **Output**: 5 // `nums = [0,1,2,3,4]`

Exercise 3: Merge two sorted lists

Write a `MergeSortedLists` class with the following `mergeTwoLists` method, to merge two sorted linked lists into one sorted list by splicing together the nodes.

```
public ListNode mergeTwoLists(ListNode list1, ListNode list2)
```

The `ListNode` class is defined as follows:

```
    static class ListNode {
        int val;
```

```
        ListNode next;
        // define your own constructor(s)
    }
```

Assumptions and Constraints

- Both input lists are sorted in non-decreasing order
- Each list can be empty
- We need to create a new merged list (not modify existing nodes)
- Number of nodes in both lists is in range `[0, 50]`
- Node values are in range `[-100, 100]`

Hints: Use a dummy node to simplify edge cases and avoid null pointer exceptions.

Examples

- **Input**: `list1 = [1,2,4], list2 = [1,3,4]` → **Output**: `[1,1,2,3,4,4]`
- **Input**: `list1 = [], list2 = []` → **Output**: `[]`

Exercise 4: Rotate array

Write an `ArrayRotation` class with the following rotate method that rotates an integer array (`nums`) to the right by `k` steps, where `k` is non-negative:

```
public void rotate(int[] nums, int k)
```

Assumptions and Constraints

- Array can be modified in-place
- `k` can be larger than array length (use modulo operation)
- Elements are integers
- $1 \leq nums.length \leq 10^5$
- $0 \leq k \leq 10^5$

Hints: Reverse entire array, then reverse first `k` elements, then reverse remaining elements

Examples

- **Input**: `nums = [1,2,3,4,5,6,7], k = 3` → **Output**: `[5,6,7,1,2,3,4]`
- **Input**: `nums = [-1,-100,3,99], k = 2` → **Output**: `[3,99,-1,-100]`

Exercise 5: Remove linked list nodes

Remove all nodes with a specific value from a linked list and return the new head in a class named `RemoveElements` and the method. The same `ListNode` definition from Exercise 3 applies.

```
public ListNode removeElements(ListNode head, int val)
```

Assumptions and Constraints

- List can be empty
- Value to remove exists in the list
- We need to return the new head of the modified list
- Number of nodes in list is in range [0, 10^4]
- Node values are in range [-100, 100]
- Value to remove is in range [-100, 100]

Hints: Use a dummy node to handle cases where the head needs to be removed

Examples

- **Input**: head = [1,2,6,3,4,5,6], val = 6 → **Output**: [1,2,3,4,5]
- **Input**: head = [], val = 1 → **Output**: []

Exercise 6: Find the middle element of a list

Find the middle node of a linked list using the fast and slow pointer technique in a class named `MiddleNodeFinder`, with the method:

```
public ListNode middleNode(ListNode head)
```

The same `ListNode` definition from Exercise 3 applies.

Assumptions and Constraints

- List is not empty
- We can use the fast/slow pointer approach
- If there are two middle nodes, return the second one
- Number of nodes is in range [1, 100]
- Node values are in range [-100, 100]

Hints: Use two pointers; the fast pointer moves 2 steps, and the slow pointer moves 1 step.

Examples

- **Input**: `[1,2,3,4,5]` → **Output**: `[3,4,5]` (middle node with value 3)
- **Input**: `[1,2,3,4,5,6]` → **Output**: `[4,5,6]` (second middle node with value 4)

Exercise 7: Max subarray

Write a class named `MaxSubarray` to find the contiguous subarray with the largest sum (Kadane's algorithm). The method that performs this algorithm is as follows:

```
public int maxSubArray(int[] nums)
```

Assumptions and Constraints

- Array can contain negative numbers
- We need to find the maximum sum of contiguous elements
- At least one element exists
- $1 \leq nums.length \leq 10^5$
- $-10^4 \leq nums[i] \leq 10^4$

Hints: Iterate through the array once. For each loop, decide whether it is better to add the current element to your running subtotal, or to restart the subtotal from the current element. Use a global variable to track the maximum sum seen so far.

Examples

- **Input**: `[-2,1,-3,4,-1,2,1,-5,4]` → **Output**: 6 (subarray `[4,-1,2,1]`)
- **Input**: `[1]` → **Output**: 1

Exercise 8: Intersection of two arrays

Find the intersection of two arrays where each element appears as many times as it appears in both arrays in a class named `ArrayIntersection` and the following method:

```
    public int[] intersect(int[] nums1, int[] nums2)
```

Assumptions and Constraints

- Arrays can contain duplicates
- Order doesn't matter in the result
- We need to preserve the frequency of elements

- `1 ≤ nums1.length, nums2.length ≤ 1000`
- `0 ≤ nums1[i], nums2[i] ≤ 1000`

Hints: Use HashMap to count frequencies of elements in first array, then iterate second array

Examples

- **Input**: `nums1 = [1,2,2,1], nums2 = [2,2]` → **Output**: `[2,2]`
- **Input**: `nums1 = [4,9,5], nums2 = [9,4,9,8,4]` → **Output**: `[4,9]`

3

Stacks and Queues

Stacks and queues are two fundamental data structures that play a crucial role in computer science; they provide efficient ways to store and retrieve elements in a specific order. Both data structures can be implemented using either an array or a linked list. These data structures are widely used in various applications, including parsing algorithms, job scheduling, and network protocols, due to their simplicity and efficiency.

Stacks are a type of linear data structure that stores elements in a Last-In-First-Out (LIFO) sequence, where the most recently added element is always accessed first. Each element can be thought of as a "block" or a unit of information that can be pushed onto the stack and popped off when needed.

In contrast, queues are another fundamental linear data structure that store elements in a First-In-First-Out (FIFO) sequence, where the oldest element is always accessed first. Each element can be thought of as a "block" or a unit of information that can be enqueued and dequeued when needed.

Throughout this chapter, we'll delve into the world of stacks and queues, exploring their properties, operations, and real-world applications. By the end of this journey, you'll have a comprehensive understanding of these fundamental data structures and how they can be applied in a variety of contexts.

What is a stack?

A stack is a linear data structure that follows the Last-In, First-Out (LIFO) principle, where elements are added and removed exclusively from the top end. The top end refers to the position at the end of the stack where the most recently added element resides. Think of it like a stack of plates in a restaurant: you can only add or remove plates from the top of the stack. When you push (add) an element, it goes to the top position. When you pop (remove) an element, it comes from the top position. This topmost element is always the most recently inserted item in the stack.

This LIFO approach lets you store and access data efficiently from a single point. The LIFO convention dictates that the most recently added element is the first one to be taken out, while the earliest added element will be removed only after all newer elements have been popped.

To illustrate this concept, suppose we have a stack with three elements `A`, `B`, and `C` sequentially pushed into it, in that order. The `C` element is now the top element in the stack. Now, if we pop one element from the stack, it will be removed in reverse order of its insertion; `C` is popped off of the stack. The push and pop operations are illustrated in *Figure 3.1* below:

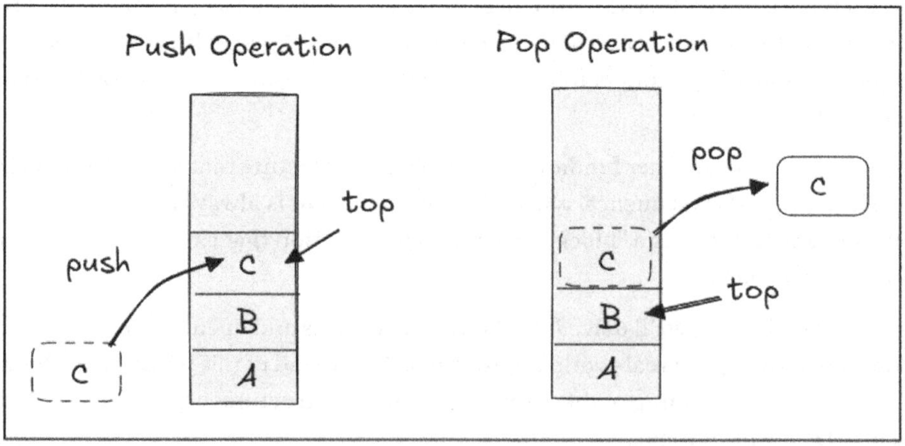

Figure 3.1: Push/Pop operations in a Stack

We can summarize the LIFO access pattern as follows:

- **Adding Elements**: When an element is pushed onto the top of the stack, it becomes the new "top" element. This means that when you add a new element, it always goes on top of the existing elements.
- **Removing Elements**: When an element is popped off of the stack, it is taken away in the reverse order of its insertion. This means that the most recently added element (the one at the top) is always the first one to be removed.

Let's go through some examples of where stacks are most used.

Example 1: Browser back-button navigation

Web browser navigation relies on two Last-In, First-Out (LIFO) stacks. When a browser session begins, both the Back and Forward stacks are completely empty. New page visits populate the Back stack, while clicking the "`Back`" button transfers pages onto the Forward stack.

The first page you visit (let's say page `A`) becomes the current page, but no page is pushed to the back stack yet because there's no previous page to go back to.

```
Back Stack: []
Current Page: Page A
Forward Stack: []
```

When you visit a new web page `B`, the browser pushes the URL of the current page `A` onto the "`Back Stack`". The "`Forward Stack`" remains empty. New page `B` becomes the "`Current Page`":

```
Back Stack: [Page A]
Current Page: Page B
Forward Stack: []
```

When you click the "Back" button on the above-referenced web page `B`, it is pushed onto the "`Forward Stack`". Then, the browser pops the most recent URL from the "`Back Stack`" and loads that page `A` again; this page becomes the "`Current Page`":

```
Back Stack: []
Current Page: Page A
Forward Stack: [Page B]
```

When you click the "Forward" button on the above-referenced web page A, it is pushed onto the "Back Stack". Then, the browser pops the most recent URL from the "Forward Stack" and loads that page B as the new "Current Page":

```
Back Stack: [Page A]
Current Page: Page B
Forward Stack: []
```

The above-described mechanism is depicted in *Figure 3.2* below:

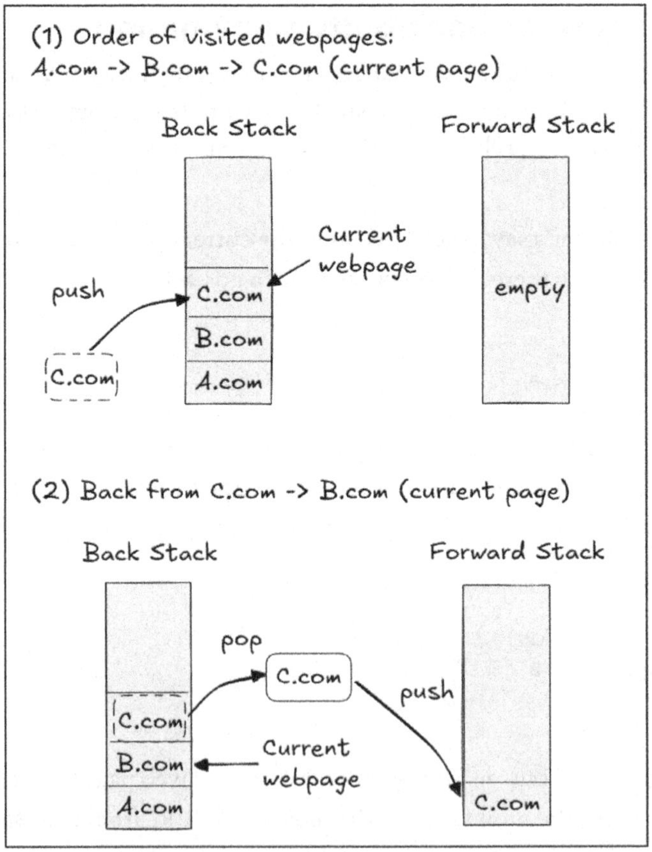

Figure 3.2: Browser Back and Forward mechanisms in two stacks

Because the last page you visited is the first one you retrieve, the stack naturally implements the LIFO principle; the stacks constantly change as the user navigates, pushing and popping pages to maintain the browsing history. This 2-stack mechanism powers the intuitive "time travel" navigation web browsing.

Example 2: Word processor undo/redo mechanism

Code editors like Visual Studio Code let users step through edits with Undo/Redo, powered by a straightforward double stack LIFO, much like a browser's Back/Forward in the prior example.

Whenever a user modifies code within the editor, the current state of the document is captured and pushed onto an Undo stack. This stack maintains a complete record of the document's evolution, with each entry representing a specific state. Namely:

- Undo (`Ctrl + Z`, or `Cmd + Z` on Mac) pops the top state from the Undo stack, restores it, and pushes that state onto the Redo stack
- Redo (`Ctrl + Y`, or `Shift + Cmd + Z` on Mac) pops from the Redo stack, reapplies the change, and pushes the state back onto the Undo stack

By keeping a history of changes in one stack and the undone history in another, this undo/redo functionality is efficient, allowing users to "time-travel" through the document's evolution. This mechanism is all built upon the foundation of a double-stack LIFO system depicted in *Figure 3.3*:

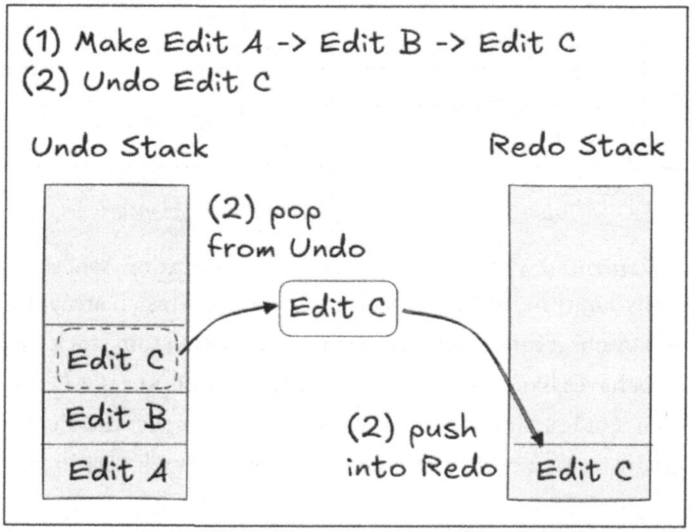

Figure 3.3: Undo/Redo mechanisms in the VSC Editor

To deepen our grasp of stacks, let's examine their abstract data type and defining characteristics.

Abstract data type (ADT): Stack

Stack allows constant time access to the most recently added element. The Stack ADT provides a set of generic methods for manipulating a sequence of elements, allowing for adding, and removing elements in a specific order, with the following operations:

Operation	Purpose	Complexity
`push(x)`	Adds x to the top (end) of the stack	`O(1)` amortized with dynamic array; `O(1)` with a `singly`linked list
`pop()`	Removes and returns the top element	`O(1)` amortized with dynamic array; `O(1)` with a singly linked list
`peek()`	Returns (but does not remove) the top element**	`O(1)`
`isEmpty()`	Checks whether the stack contains any elements	`O(1)`
`size()`	Number of elements currently stored	`O(1)`

Table 3.1: Stack operations and their efficiencies

When a stack is implemented with a dynamic array, each mutation, whether a push or a pop, executes in strict constant time, `O(1)`, unless a mutation requires an array resize, which takes `O(n)` time. Another key observation: although some texts or custom stack classes define a `top()` method that behaves like `peek()`, the official `java.util.Stack` API does not expose such a method. With `java.util.Stack`, you must use `peek()` to inspect the element at the top. The following code demonstrates a basic implementation of the Stack ADT in Java:

```
public interface StackADT<T> {
    // Push an element onto the top of the stack
    void push(T element);

    // Remove the top element from the stack
    T pop();

    // Return a copy of the top element without removing it
    T peek();
```

```
    // Return the number of elements in the stack
    int size();

    // Return whether the stack has any elements in it
    boolean isEmpty();
}
```

The code file of this implementation can be found in the `Chapter03` folder on GitHub. To unlock the GitHub repo link, refer to the instructions in the *Download the example code files* section of the *Preface*.

Concrete implementations

The two primary approaches to implementing stacks are indeed array-based and linked list-based implementations. Each method offers different advantages and disadvantages regarding performance and memory usage. Array-based stacks store elements in an underlying array, while linked stacks use a dynamic memory allocation approach.

Below are two canonical implementations: one backed by a resizable dynamic array (`ArrayDeque`), and one backed by a singly linked list (`LinkedList`). Both satisfy the `StackADT` interface and provide the same public API.

Array-based stack (DynamicArrayStack)

This approach utilizes a dynamic array to store stack elements. Such an array is not a variable-length array where its length is segment allocated at run time without a backing buffer, but a fixed-size segment allocated at run time and resized internally depending on need.

A stack can be efficiently built on a dynamic array: The stack's height is tracked by the number of elements currently stored in the array, with the "top" element always residing at the last occupied index. As long as the underlying array has available capacity, pushing a new element runs in strict `O(1)` constant time. When it's full, the array must be resized, allocating a larger buffer and copying all elements, which incurs a noticeable cost at resizing. Popping remains a constant-time operation.

As discussed in *Chapter 2*, array resizing is locally `O(n)` because it requires copying all elements to a new memory block. However, this cost is amortized to `O(1)` globally when averaged over a long sequence of data insertions. To minimize frequent resizing, dynamic arrays grow by a sizable factor (commonly doubling) so that the newly reserved space can accommodate many future insertions.

A version of the stack implementation that employs a dynamic array buffer can be found on GitHub inside the `DynamicArrayStack.java` file in the `Chapter03` folder. To unlock the GitHub repo link, refer to the instructions in the *Download the example code files* section of the *Preface*. Lastly, in the modern Java Collection Framework, you will see `ArrayDeque` as a lightweight, non-synchronized version of Stack. `ArrayDeque` implements the Deque (double-ended queue) interface and provides the same LIFO behavior as Stack, but with noticeably faster performance and reduced memory consumption.

In the following section, we will look at another implementation option for Stack: a linked list, which is a recursive data structure without a capacity constraint.

List-based stack (LinkedListStack)

When we implement a stack with a singly or doubly linked list, each node contains an element and a pointer to the next node (and, for a doubly-linked list, also a pointer to the previous node). For a standard singly-linked list, the structure can be defined in Java as follows:

```
public class Node<T> {
    public T data;
    public Node<T> next;

    public Node(T data, Node<T> next) {
        this.data = data;
        this.next = next;
    }

    public Node(T data) {
        this(data, null);
    }
}
```

For brevity, we will focus our implementation on using a singly linked list, which can be visualized in *Figure 3.4*:

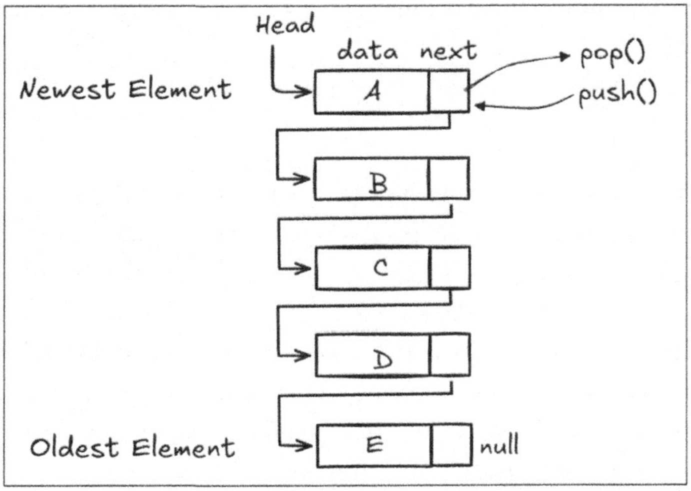

Figure 3.4: Stack implementation using a singly linked list

Note that both push and pop operations occur at the top end of the stack at `O(1)`, along with other `O(1)` operations as shown in *Table 3.1*. For `size()`, we will maintain a counter, making this operation `O(1)`. The trade-off with a linked list implementation is:

- **Higher per-node memory**: Every element in a linked stack requires a wrapper object (the Node). In Java, this means paying for an **Object Header** (12–16 bytes), the **data reference/primitive** (4–8 bytes), and the **next pointer** (4–8 bytes) for *every single item*. A primitive array only stores raw data values without pointers, requiring much less overhead space.
- **Poorer cache performance**: Contiguous arrays store their values in a single, continuous memory block. When you access an array element, the CPU loads that element plus surrounding data into cache lines, creating excellent spatial locality. This results in high cache hit rates during sequential iteration, making array traversal extremely efficient compared to non-contiguous data structures like linked lists.

For many use cases, especially with unbounded growth or frequent mutations (push/pop), a dynamic array implementation is the most efficient compared to a linked list. Unlike arrays that may require expensive resizing operations when growing beyond capacity, linked lists can grow and shrink dynamically without performance penalties. The consistent `O(1)` time complexity for both operations makes linked list stacks particularly advantageous in scenarios with unpredictable usage patterns or when the maximum stack size is unknown. For the implementation, see the `LinkedListStack.java` file inside the `Chapter03` folder on GitHub. To unlock the GitHub repo link, refer to the instructions in the *Download the example code files* section of the *Preface*.

> Note
>
> **Object Arrays in Java**
>
> Unlike primitive arrays, object arrays such as `Integer[]`, `String[]`, or custom class arrays like `Animal[]` store references to objects rather than the objects themselves. These references are stored contiguously in memory, but the actual objects are scattered throughout the heap. While sequential iteration through the array efficiently loads the references, accessing the underlying object data requires dereferencing each pointer to retrieve data from random heap locations. This pointer-chasing overhead can lead to cache misses and increased latency compared to primitive arrays, where data is stored directly and contiguously in memory.

Performance: Linked-based vs. array-based stacks

Before we dive into the detailed performance assessment, let's revisit the broad characteristics of linked-based and array-based structures. A singly linked list delivers `O(1)` insertions and deletions at its head. In contrast, array-based stacks store elements contiguously, enabling amortized `O(1)` push and pop as well. A stack implemented on either structure inherits these `O(1)` push and pop operations. In the following sections, detailed performance analysis will expose the time-space trade-offs inherent to each operation.

Both array-based and linked list stacks run in `O(1)` time, but when you factor in the occasional array resize, the push and pop operations no longer behave identically:

Operation	Array-Based Stack	Linked-Based Stack
`push(x)`	• Amortized `O(1)`, overall complexity by spreading the expansion cost globally. • Otherwise, `O(1)` via array indexing, sequential access. • No iteration is required.	• `O(1)`, pushing an element onto the front of the list through reference reassignment. • No iteration is required.

Operation	Array-Based Stack	Linked-Based Stack
pop()	• Amortized O(1), overall complexity by spreading the compression cost globally. • Otherwise, O(1) via array indexing, sequential access. • No iteration is required.	• O(1), removing an element off of the front of the list through reference reassignment. • No iteration is required.

Table 3.2: Operational efficiency comparison of push() and pop()

In array-based implementation:

```
public void push(T element) {
    if (size == data.length) resize();              // amortized O(1)
    data[size++] = element;                         // O(1)
}
public T pop() {
    if (size  == 0) throw new Exception();          // O(1)
    T element = (T) data[--size];                   // O(1)
    return element;
}
```

In linked-based implementation:

```
public void push(T data) {
    Node<T> n = new Node<T>(data);                          // O(1)
    n.next = top;                                           // O(1)
    top = n;                                                // O(1)
    size++;                                                 // O(1)
}

public T pop() {
    if (isEmpty()) throw new Exception();                   // O(1)
    T item = top.data;                                      // O(1)
    top =  top.next;                                        // O(1)
    size--;                                                 // O(1)
    return item;
}
```

Remember that while resizing an array is a costly operation, `O(n)`, it happens only rarely compared to the many inexpensive pushes and pops that follow it. This sparsity of costly events spreads overhead across all operations, yielding an amortized `O(1)` cost per operation. In practice, when averaging across all mutations, each element is copied a constant number of times (i.e., fewer than 2 times on average in a doubling strategy).

Memory

In a stack backed by an array, removing the top element is a single, direct memory fetch:

```
T item = array[top--];
```

This operation is fast because it accesses the element via an array's sequential index with no pointer indirection. By contrast, a linked list stack requires several memory accesses:

```
T item = top.data;
```

This is followed by:

```
top = top.next;
```

Each step involves dereferencing a node pointer before reaching the data, and then another dereference to advance the head, making the pop operation noticeably slower and less cache-friendly.

When to use what?

We can summarize their trade-offs as follows:

- **Prioritizing speed:** use an array-based stack when the stack size is roughly bounded in advance, performance matters, push/pop operations are frequent, and memory consumption can be predicted. Typical scenarios include expression evaluation or function call stacks in a language interpreter.
- **Prioritizing memory flexibility**: a linked list stack is preferable when the depth is highly variable or unknown, memory conservation is paramount, or occasional deep recursion may occur; common use cases are recursive algorithms with unbounded depth or undo systems where the stack may grow unpredictably.

A stack example

Java's standard collections (namely, `ArrayDeque`, `Stack`, and the like) use a resizable array. This choice gives them excellent cache locality and guarantees constant-time push and pop, aside from the occasional resizing cost.

A natural extension of that approach is a deque (double-ended queue, which we will study in the next section), which stores elements in a contiguous array but exposes operations at both ends. By restricting all deque operations to one end, namely, `addFirst/removeFirst` (or `addLast/removeLast`), we obtain the same LIFO behavior as a stack while retaining the flexibility to treat the other end differently if needed. Thus, a deque can serve as a highly efficient, cache-friendly stack implementation, as illustrated in the example below.

Thread-safe deque

A thread-safe deque guarantees safe concurrent access by multiple threads. In a typical server, several worker threads may simultaneously push and pop data, for example, when parsing multiple streams in parallel. To avoid race conditions on the underlying node pointers and size counter, a deque is protected by either a reentrant lock (as in `LinkedBlockingDeque`) or by a lock-free algorithm (as in `ConcurrentLinkedDeque`). In either case, thread operations are coordinated safely, ensuring that concurrent operations on the same deque remain atomic and free from data corruption. Specifically:

- A **re-entrant lock** (e.g., `ReentrantLock` in Java) guards every operation that reads or mutates the stack (`push`, pop, `peek`). The same thread can acquire the lock multiple times without deadlocking.
- A **lock-free** method leverages atomic operations to deliver the same outcome without blocking, keeping the structure thread-safe while improving scalability under contention.

Below is a re-entrant lock example. Note that it is not completely thread-safe; we will explore these concurrency issues in a later chapter on concurrency.

```
import java.util.concurrent.locks.ReentrantLock;

public final class SynchronizedArrayStack<T> implements StackADT<T> {
    private final Deque<T> backing = new ArrayDeque<>();
    private final ReentrantLock lock = new ReentrantLock();

    @Override public void push(T item) {
        lock.lock();
        try { backing.addLast(item); }
        finally { lock.unlock(); }
    }

    @Override public T pop() {
        lock.lock();
```

```
        try {
            if (backing.isEmpty()) throw new EmptyStackException();
            return backing.removeLast();
        } finally { lock.unlock(); }
    }

    @Override public T peek() {
        if (backing.isEmpty()) throw new EmptyStackException();
        return backing.peekLast();
    }

    @Override public boolean isEmpty() {
        return backing.isEmpty();
    }

    @Override public int size() {
        return backing.size();
    }
}
```

Note

Design Note

Notice that `peek()`, `isEmpty()`, and `size()` lack synchronization locks. While they do not mutate state, accessing a non-thread-safe collection (`ArrayDeque`) concurrently without synchronized read operations introduces dangerous data races and memory visibility bugs.

The following code illustrates a lock-free sketch:

```
class LockFreeStack<T> {
    private static class Node<T> { T value; Node<T> next; }

    private final AtomicReference<Node<T>> top = new AtomicReference<>(null);

    public void push(T value) {
        Node<T> newNode = new Node<>();
        newNode.value = value;
        Node<T> currentTop;
        do {
```

```
            currentTop = top.get();
            newNode.next = currentTop;
        } while (!top.compareAndSet(currentTop, newNode));
    }

    public T pop() {
        Node<T> currentTop, newTop;
        do {
            currentTop = top.get();
            if (currentTop == null) {
                throw new EmptyStackException();
            }
            newTop = currentTop.next;
        } while (!top.compareAndSet(currentTop, newTop));
        return currentTop.value;
    }
}
```

In summary, a thread-safe deque can be implemented by guarding an `ArrayDeque` with a `ReentrantLock` to support concurrency, ensuring that only one thread at a time can modify the internal array, hence preventing race conditions. Alternatively, a lock-free stack can be built with an `AtomicReference` to the top node and a compare-and-set loop, allowing multiple threads to update the stack without blocking. Both designs retain `O(1)` performance profiles while providing safe, concurrent manipulation of the stack.

Queue

After examining the classic Last-In-First-Out (LIFO) stack, we now turn to its natural counterpart: the queue. Whereas a stack draws and pushes elements from a single end of a buffer, a queue interacts with both ends. Namely, elements are enqueued at the rear and dequeued from the front. A queue therefore adheres to a First-In-First-Out (FIFO) discipline. This seemingly modest alteration unlocks a distinct family of application patterns, from breadth-first search and message buffering to resource throttling and data prioritization. In the sections that follow, we will explore the Queue Abstract Data Type (ADT), its core operations, performance characteristics, and a range of real-world industry examples that illustrate its indispensable role.

What is a queue

A queue is a linear collection of elements that supports two fundamental operations: insertion (enqueue) at one end, commonly called the rear or back, and deletion (dequeue) from the opposite end, known as the front. Imagine a line of customers waiting at a ticket counter: the first person to step forward is the first one served, and new customers join the line at the far end. This simple, FIFO discipline ensures that elements are processed in order of arrival. The FIFO pattern is illustrated in *Figure 3.5*:

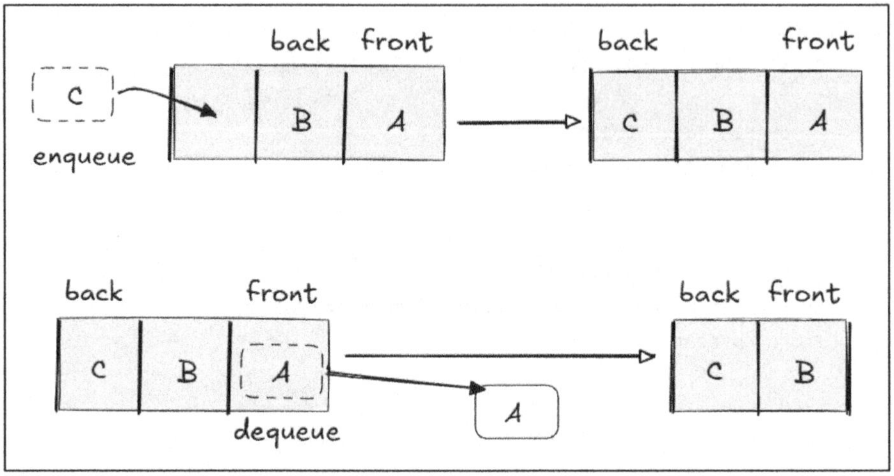

Figure 3.5: Enqueue/Dequeue operations in a Queue

The FIFO enqueue and dequeue operations can be summarized as follows:

- **Adding Elements (Enqueue)**: When a new element is inserted, it is placed at the rear (or back) of the queue. The element simply joins the existing line; it does not displace any earlier items. The element marks the "back" of the queue.
- **Removing Elements (Dequeue)**: When an element is removed, it is taken from the front of the queue. The item that has been waiting for the longest, namely, the one that was inserted earliest, will be the first one to leave regardless of any later insertions. The second element in line marks the "front" of the queue.

Thus, a queue guarantees that elements are processed in the exact order they arrive: first in, first out.

Example 1: Print spooler queue

In a typical office, several users send print jobs to a shared printer. A spooler software receives each job and places it in a FIFO queue. The first job that arrives, say, a brochure from the marketing department, is in front of the queue. Subsequent jobs, such as a report from HR and a legal memo, are appended to the back, in the order of their submittal.

When the printer finishes a job, it dequeues the next one. Thus, the spooler guarantees that jobs are printed in the exact order they were submitted, preventing any single user from monopolizing the printer and ensuring fair resource allocation. This simple queue mechanism serializes access to the limited resource (the printer) and keeps the workflow orderly.

Because of its predictable ordering, the queue structure underpins many everyday and technical systems. For example, whenever a set of items must share a limited resource, a queue can serialize access. Network routers and switches buffer incoming packets in queues before forwarding them, ensuring fair bandwidth allocation and preventing packet loss under congestion.

Example 2: Deferred processing and prioritization

A queue is more than a simple data structure; it provides a flexible abstraction for orderly resource sharing in many computing scenarios. Whenever tasks must wait before execution—such as when a web server receives HTTP requests, a distributed computing platform schedules jobs, or a GUI framework handles user events—a FIFO queue ensures that work proceeds in the order it arrives.

Specialized variants extend this idea, and some come up with a juxtaposition of both LIFO and FIFO properties. As we will see in the latter chapters, a **priority queue** or **heap** reorganizes items so that the most urgent task is processed first. A double-ended queue (deque) allows insertion and removal at both ends, enabling both FIFO and LIFO behaviors as needed.

Abstract data type (ADT): Queue

A queue gives constant-time access to the element that has been waiting the longest. The Queue ADT defines a collection of generic operations that allow elements to be added at one end and removed from the other, preserving the FIFO order. Its primary operations are:

Operation	Purpose	Complexity
`enqueue(x)`	Adds x to the back of the queue	`O(1)` amortized with dynamic array; `O(1)` with a doubly linked list
`dequeue()`	Removes and returns the front element	`O(1)` amortized with dynamic array; `O(1)` with a doubly linked list
`peek()`	Returns (but does not remove) the front element	`O(1)`
`isEmpty()`	Checks whether the queue contains no elements	`O(1)`

Operation	Purpose	Complexity
`size()`	Number of elements currently stored	`O(1)`

Table 3.3: Primary ADT Operations

Just like stack, when a queue is implemented with a fixed-size array, each mutation, whether an enqueue or a dequeue, executes in amortized constant time (`O(1)`) except when the array must be resized. In the `java.util.Queue` interface, there's a `poll()` method which returns and removes the front of the queue, or `null` if this queue is empty.

The code below demonstrates how to implement a Queue ADT in Java:

```
public interface QueueADT<T> {

    // Adds an element to the end of this queue
    void enqueue(T item);

    // Removes and returns the element at the front of this queue
    T dequeue();

    // Returns, but does not remove, the front of this queue
    T peek();

    // Returns the number of elements in this queue
    int size();

    // Returns whether the queue has any elements in it
    boolean isEmpty();
}
```

The code file of this implementation can be found in the `Chapter03` folder on GitHub. To unlock the GitHub repo link, refer to the instructions in the *Download the example code files* section of the *Preface*.

Concrete implementations

The two principal ways to implement a queue are an array-based version and a linked-list-based version. Each has its own trade-offs in terms of speed and memory usage. An array-backed queue keeps its elements in a contiguous block of memory (usually a circular buffer to avoid shifting), while a linked-list queue allocates nodes on the heap as items are added.

Array-based queue (DynamicArrayQueue)

Implementing a queue with a fixed-size array is a bit delicate. In a naïve array-based implementation approach: suppose a queue has `n` elements. If we store them in the first `n` slots of the array and place the `front` at index 0, then a dequeue takes `O(1)` time. However, we must shift all existing `n-1` elements one spot forward to fill that void, costing `O(n)` time (see *Figure 3.6*):

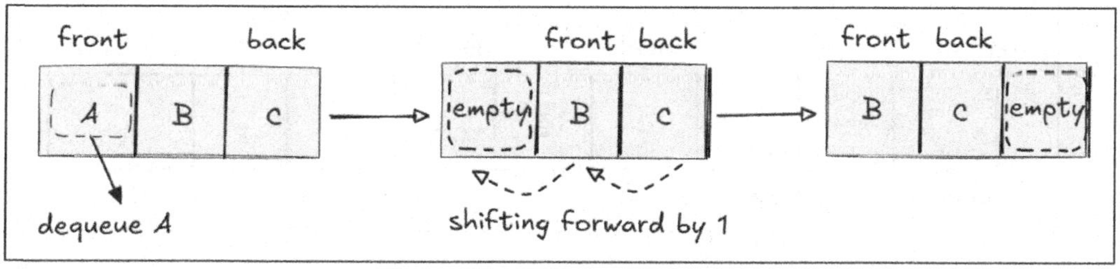

Figure 3.6: Left shifting elements on dequeue operation in O(n) time

Conversely, if we keep the `front` at index `n-1`, a dequeue runs in `O(1)` by decrementing the size tracker. However, an enqueue at index `0` requires shifting all `n-1` elements one spot forward, costing `O(n)` time (see *Figure 3.7*):

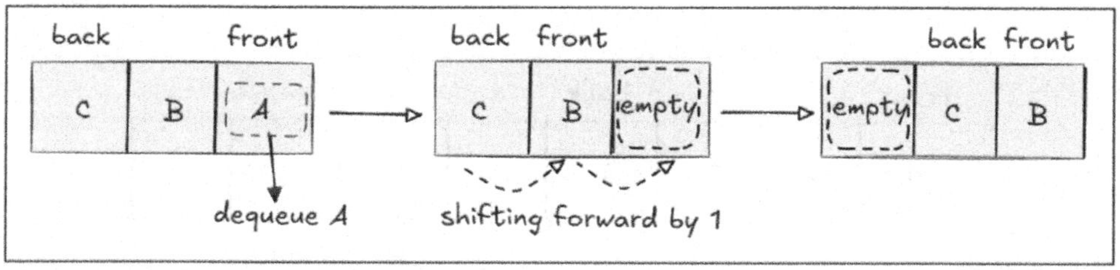

Figure 3.7: Right shifting elements on dequeue operation in O(n) time

Shifting elements is costly. To avoid that overhead while still allowing ordinary enqueue and dequeue operations in a very large (effectively infinite) array, we can treat one end of the array as the queue's `front` and the other as its `back`. The queue elements then occupy a single contiguous segment bounded by these two ends. The entire queue segment shifts to the right if `front < back`, or to the left if `back < front`. Both enqueue and dequeue operate in constant time in this setup. See *Figure 3.8* below:

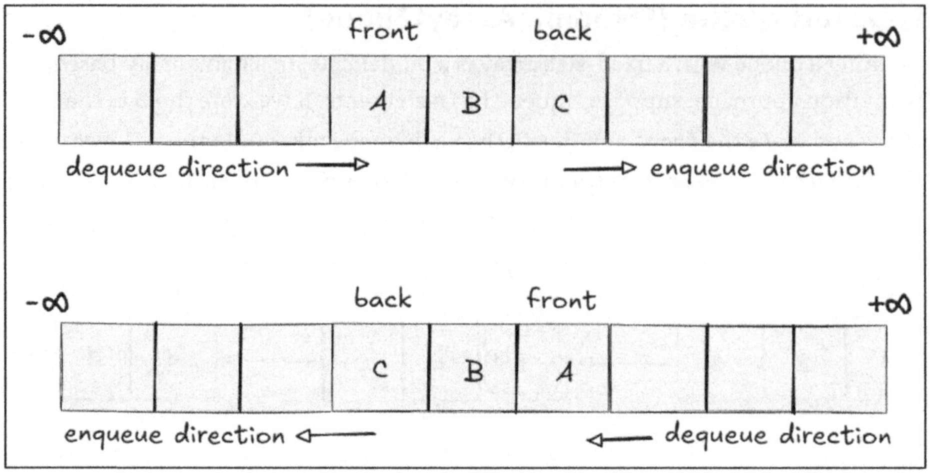

Figure 3.8: Growth direction of a queue based on the locations of both front and back indices in an infinite array

The above example demands an infinite sequence of slots. In a finite world, as elements are enqueued, the logical `back` would eventually run past the physical end of the array, and as elements are dequeued, its logical `front` would move along with the direction of enqueue. After repeated operations, the queue drifts to one end of the array as depicted in *Figure 3.9* below:

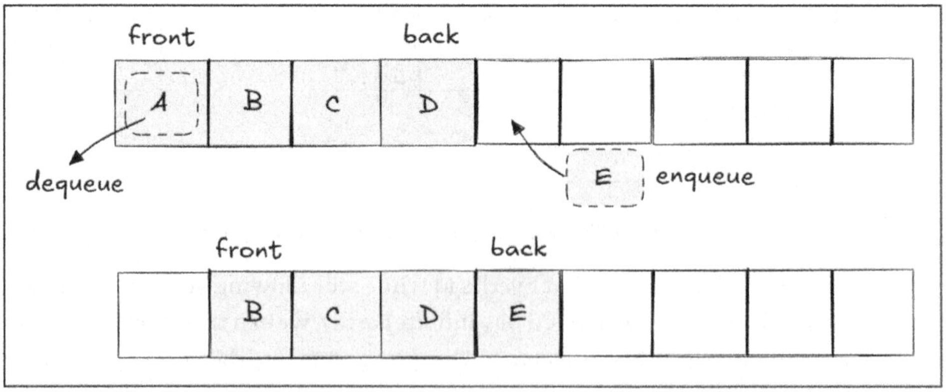

Figure 3.9: In a finite array, element A is dequeued and E is enqueued. As enqueue continues, the back will eventually hit the rightmost end of the array

A natural way to reconcile this mismatch is to treat the array as a circle. That is, letting indices that exceed the array's last slot wrap around to the beginning. This trick is made precisely with modular arithmetic. For example, just as 8 + 5 yields 1 on a 12-hour clock (`8 + 5 = 13 ≡ 1` (mod 12)), we can compute any position by taking the raw index modulo the array length. In Java this is expressed with the % operator (e.g., `index % array.length`), yielding a value in the range `0 … array.length-1`. By storing the queue's elements at `array[j % array.length]`, `array[(j+1) % array.length], …, array[(j+n-1) % array.length]`, we obtain a seamless, wrap-around data structure that behaves as if it were an infinite array, while in fact occupying only a fixed amount of memory. We can visualize this approach by converting the prior linear example in *Figure 3.9* to a circular array in *Figure 3.10*:

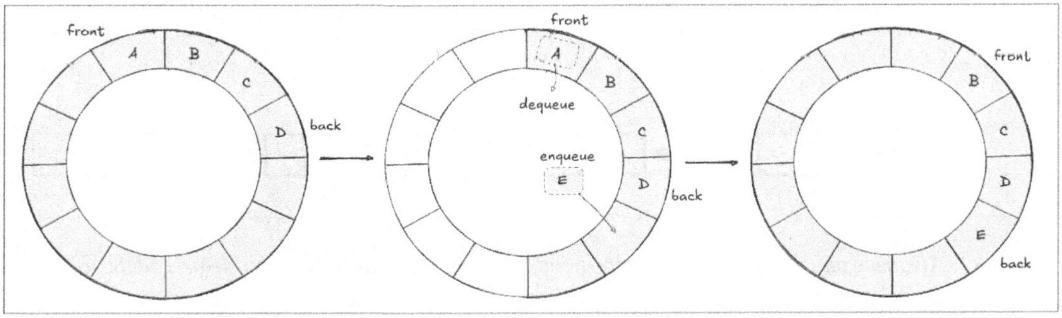

Figure 3.10: In a circular array, element A is dequeued and E is enqueued. As enqueue continues, the back wraps around the circle in a clockwise fashion

See the `DynamicArrayQueue.java` file inside the `Chapter03` folder on GitHub for the implementation of a FIFO queue backed by a resizable circular array buffer. To unlock the GitHub repo link, refer to the instructions in the *Download the example code files* section of the *Preface*. The core fields are an `Object[] data`, a `head` index, a `tail` index, and a `size` counter. `enqueue` writes the new element at tail, increments `tail` modulo the current capacity, and, when `size` equals the array length, calls `resize()` to double the buffer size and copy the elements in FIFO order. `dequeue` removes the element at `head`, advances `head` modulo the length, and decrements `size`. The `peek`, `isEmpty`, and `size` methods run in constant time. Because the array only expands when the queue is full, each insertion or removal runs in `O(1)` amortized time, making the structure efficient for typical FIFO workloads.

Link-based queue (LinkedListQueue)

Compared to the array-based circular queue, the linked-list implementation trades a modest per-element memory overhead for true `O(1)` enqueue and dequeue without any costly `resize` operations. The linked-list queue never has to shift or reallocate data. The `head` represents the element to be removed next as the front of the queue, whereas the `tail` represents the most recently added element as the back of the queue. Thus, both `enqueue` and `dequeue` are strict

`O(1)` regardless of queue length, which grows indefinitely. *Figure 3.11* illustrates both enqueue and dequeue operations performed in constant time.

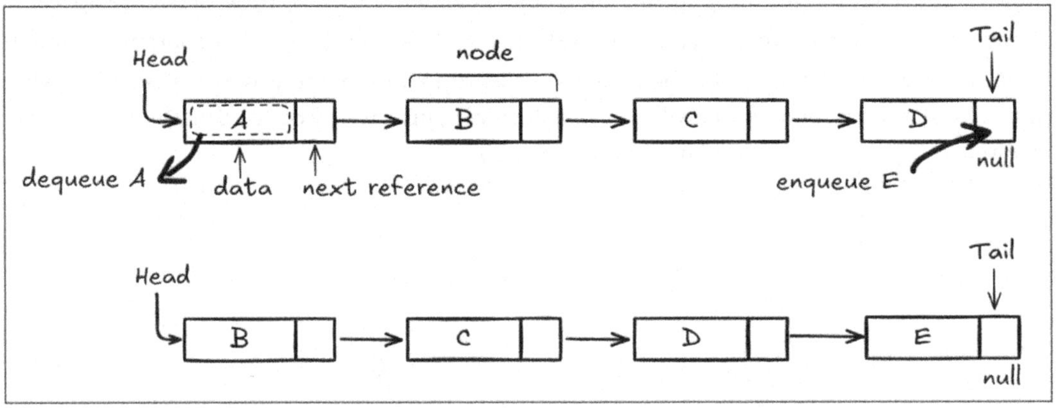

Figure 3.11: Dequeue removes the element at the head, whereas enqueue adds a new element at the tail in O(1) time

The linked list implementation of the above-referenced queue is available in the `LinkedListQueue.java` file inside the `Chapter03` folder on GitHub. To unlock the GitHub repo link, refer to the instructions in the *Download the example code files* section of the *Preface*.

Summary

Stacks and queues model LIFO and FIFO behaviors, respectively. Their performance depends on the chosen internal buffer, i.e., an array gives `O(1)` amortized access with good cache locality, while a linked list offers `O(1)` operations without resizing but incurs per-node overhead. Typical stack uses include expression evaluation, back-tracking, and undo/redo applications; queue uses include producer-consumer pipelines, time-shifting buffers, and request throttling. *Figure 3.12* is a summary diagram of stacks and queues for a quick overview.

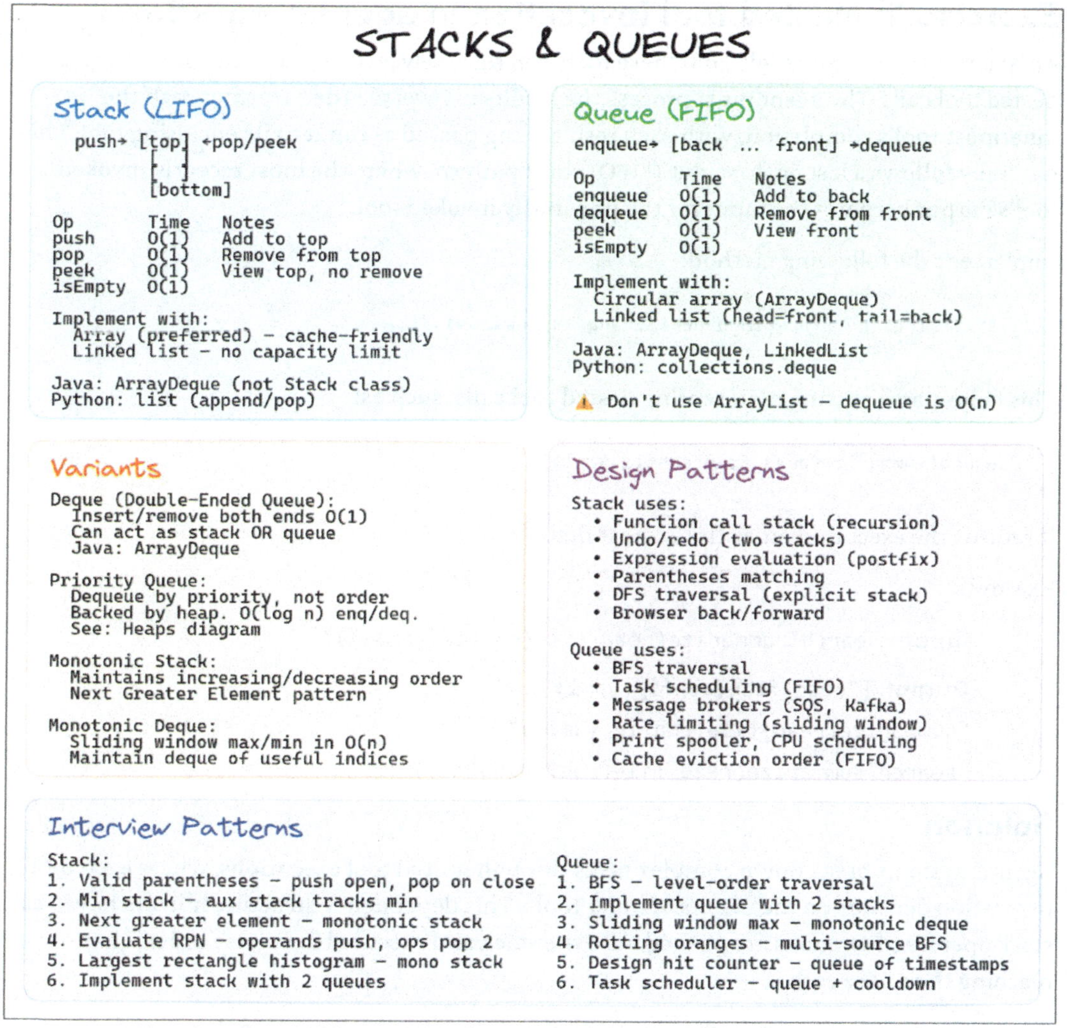

Figure 3.12: Summary of stacks and queues

In the next chapter, we will discuss Maps and Hash Tables.

Exercises

The complete solutions for these programming exercises are available in the `Chapter03` folder on GitHub. To unlock the GitHub repo link, refer to the instructions in the *Download the example code files* section of the *Preface*. Each exercise includes a fully annotated Java implementation with example usage, along with annotated explanations of the algorithms and their time/space complexities if applicable.

Exercise 1: Nested tool invocation in agentic workflows

An AI agent can execute tools, and these tools can themselves invoke additional tools, creating nested tool calls. The agent must process the results in reverse order: starting with the innermost tool's completion, with each result being passed as input to its enclosing tool. This naturally follows a last-in, first-out (LIFO) stack pattern, where the most recently invoked tool's output becomes the input for the previously invoked tool.

Implement the following method:

```
List<String> getExecutionOrder(String expression)
```

This helps parse a string representing nested tool calls, such as:

```
"search(summarize(read_file(config.yaml)))"
```

It returns the execution order (innermost first).

Example

- **Input**: `"search(summarize(read_file(config.yaml)))"`
- **Output**: `["read_file(config.yaml)", "summarize(read_file(config.yaml))", "search(summarize(read_file(config.yaml)))"]`

Solution

Agentic systems break down complex tasks through nested tool executions, where each tool invocation depends on the results of inner tools. This dependency structure mirrors how a call stack operates. Functions are pushed onto the stack and executed in reverse order when reaching their base case.

We will implement a stack-based algorithm that processes the input from left to right, in the following patterns:

- Push each character onto the stack
- When encountering a closing parenthesis `")"`, begin popping elements until you find the matching opening parenthesis `"("`
- This popped sequence represents a complete tool invocation that should be recorded in execution order

The key insight is that this process naturally captures the dependency hierarchy, executing innermost tools first before their outer wrappers. The key mechanism is captured in the following code:

```
public List<String> getExecutionOrder(String expression) {
    List<String> order = new ArrayList<>();
    Deque<Integer> openParens = new ArrayDeque<>();

    for (int i = 0; i < expression.length(); i++) {
        if (expression.charAt(i) == '(') {
            openParens.push(i);
        } else if (expression.charAt(i) == ')') {
            int start = openParens.pop();
            // Find the function name: scan backward
            // from '(' to find start of identifier
            int nameStart = start;
            while (nameStart > 0 &&
               Character.isLetterOrDigit(expression.charAt(nameStart - 1))
                 || (nameStart > 0 &&
                    expression.charAt(nameStart - 1) == '_')) {
                nameStart--;
            }
            String toolCall = expression.substring(nameStart, i + 1);
            order.add(toolCall);
        }
    }
    return order; // innermost first
}
```

The stack naturally tracks nesting depth. The first ")" matched corresponds to the deepest nested call, which is the first to execute. This mirrors how programming language interpreters evaluate nested expressions.

Exercise 2: MinStack

Design a stack (`MinStack` class) that supports `push`, `pop`, `top`, and `getMin`. All operations run in `O(1)` time. Note that a regular stack gives you `O(1)push/pop/top` but `O(n)getMin`. The trick is to track the minimum alongside each element so you never need to scan.

Hints

- Use a second stack that only stores values when they are ≤ the current minimum
- On pop, also pop from the min stack if the popped value equals the current min

Exercise 3: Queue using two stacks

Design a queue data structure using two stacks to achieve `O(1)` amortized operations for all operations: `enqueue`, `dequeue`, `peek`, `isEmpty`.

Note, since a stack reverses the order of elements, using two stacks allows us to maintain the first-in, first-out (FIFO) property of a queue. The "lazy transfer" optimization ensures that elements are only moved between stacks when necessary.

Hints

- Stack 1 (inbox) accepts all pushes
- Stack 2 (outbox) serves all pops/peeks
- Transfer inbox ⟶ outbox only when outbox is empty

Exercise 4: Daily temperatures: Next warmer day

Given an array of daily temperatures, determine how many days you must wait after each day to encounter a warmer temperature. For each day, return the number of days until the next higher temperature occurs. If no warmer temperature exists in the future, return 0 for that day. That is:

Given an array `temperatures`, return an array `answer` where `answer[i]` is the number of days until a warmer temperature. If no warmer day exists, `answer[i] = 0`.

```
public class DailyTemperatures {
    public int[] dailyTemperatures(int[] temps) {
        // YOUR CODE HERE
    }
}
```

Example

- **Input**: `[73, 74, 75, 71, 69, 72, 76, 73]`
- **Output**: `[1, 1, 4, 2, 1, 1, 0, 0]`

Exercise 5: Sliding window maximum

Given array nums and window size k, return the maximum in each sliding window of size k:

```
public class SlidingWindowMaximum {
    public int[] maxSlidingWindow(int[] nums, int k) {
        // YOUR CODE HERE
    }
}
```

Assumptions and Constraints

- $1 \leq n \leq 10^5$ temperatures
- $30 \leq T \leq 100°F$
- O(n) time and space complexity
- Valid input array
- Sequential day processing
- Each day has one integer answer (0 or positive)
- O(1) stack operations

Hints

Brute force is O(nk). A monotonic deque (double-ended queue) maintains a decreasing window of candidates in O(n) total. Elements that can never be the max are discarded eagerly. You may consider:

- Deque stores indices; front is always the max of the current window
- Remove from back any index whose value ≤ current (it can never win)
- Remove from the front any index that has slid out of the window

Exercise 6: Reverse polish notation

Evaluate an expression given in Reverse Polish Notation (postfix). Tokens are either integers or operators +, -, *, / (integer division truncating toward zero).

Note: RPN eliminates the need for parentheses by placing operators after their operands. A stack processes it naturally: push numbers, apply operators to the top two:

```
public class EvalRPN {
    public int evalRPN(String[] tokens) {
        // YOUR CODE HERE
```

```
    }
}
```

Assumptions and Constraints

- 1 ≤ tokens.length ≤ 10^4
- Tokens are integers or operators (+, -, *, /)
- Integer division truncates toward zero
- Valid RPN expression guaranteed
- Valid RPN expression with proper operator-operand relationships
- All tokens are either valid integers or valid operators
- Division by zero will not occur
- Stack operations are `O(1)` amortized

Hints

- On a number token, push it
- On an operator, pop two operands, apply, push the result
- Watch operand order for `-` and `/`: pop `b` then pop `a`, compute `a op b`

Exercise 7: Task scheduler

Given a list of CPU tasks (letters A–Z) and a cooldown `n`, find the minimum number of intervals to finish all tasks. Identical tasks must be at least `n` intervals apart; idle slots count.

Note, the most frequent task creates "gaps" that must be filled. Use a max-heap (priority queue) for available tasks and a cooldown queue to re-release tasks after their cooldown expires.

```
public class TaskScheduler {
    public int leastInterval(char[] tasks, int n) {
        // YOUR CODE HERE
    }
}
```

Assumptions and Constraints

- 1 ≤ `tasks.length` ≤ 10^4
- Tasks: A-Z letters
- 0 ≤ `n` ≤ 100

- Valid task list with A–Z letters
- Non-negative cooldown period
- Tasks scheduled within constraints

Hints:

- Max-heap orders tasks by remaining count (most frequent first)
- A queue holds (`count`, `readyTime`) pairs for tasks in cooldown
- Each cycle: take from heap if available; else idle

Exercise 8: LRU cache

Design a data structure that follows the Least Recently Used (LRU) cache policy with capacity `cap`. `get(key)` returns the value or -1; `put(key, value)` inserts or updates, evicting the LRU entry when over capacity. Both operations must be `O(1)`.

A `LinkedHashMap` in Java maintains insertion/access order and has a clean override for eviction. The doubly-linked-list + hashmap approach gives you the same `O(1)` from scratch.

Assumptions and Constraints

- `1 ≤ cap ≤ 3000`
- `get()` and `put()` operations `O(1)`
- Valid integer keys/values
- Valid capacity > 0
- Integer keys/hashable types
- `LinkedHashMapaccessOrder=true`
- Eviction based on access order (recent at tail)

Hints

- `LinkedHashMap` with `accessOrder=true` moves accessed entries to the tail
- Override `removeEldestEntry` to auto-evict when over capacity
- The eldest (head) is the LRU entry

4

Maps and Hash Tables

A map is the intuitive way to model any scenario in which a distinct identifier (the key) must be linked to some arbitrary data (the value). Thus, a Map as an abstract data type (ADT) associates unique keys with corresponding values, enabling software to retrieve, insert, or delete a value by looking up its key. Each key must be unique; duplicate keys are not permitted. The most common concrete implementations of the Map ADT are hash-based tables, where the key's hash code is used to compute an index into an underlying array. The power of maps lies in their ability to locate an entry in virtually no time, regardless of how large the collection grows.

Hash-based maps, also known as hash tables, achieve this by hashing a key to compute an index into an underlying array. In the ideal case, insertion, lookup, and deletion all run in `O(1)` time. Thus, hash tables deliver extremely fast insertions and lookups. In practice, this translates to a few nanoseconds per operation, enabling applications such as spell checkers, caching layers, and any scenario that must probe tens of thousands of entries in a fraction of a second. For example, a spelling checker that must look up every word in a large dictionary may complete the spelling check in a fraction of a second.

Throughout this chapter, we will explore map and hash table properties, operations, and real-world applications. We will look at textbook applications of maps, including address books and inventory systems, where a unique identifier is linked to rich metadata. These examples illustrate the everyday relevance of maps and hash tables across software engineering, from low-level systems to high-level application logic.

What is a map?

A map, also referred to as an associative array or dictionary, is a collection of key-value pairs. Each key serves as a unique identifier that allows you to locate a particular value that holds the data; this data can be a simple scalar, such as a number, or a more complex object like a record containing many fields. A doubly linked-list based map is illustrated in *Figure 4.1*:

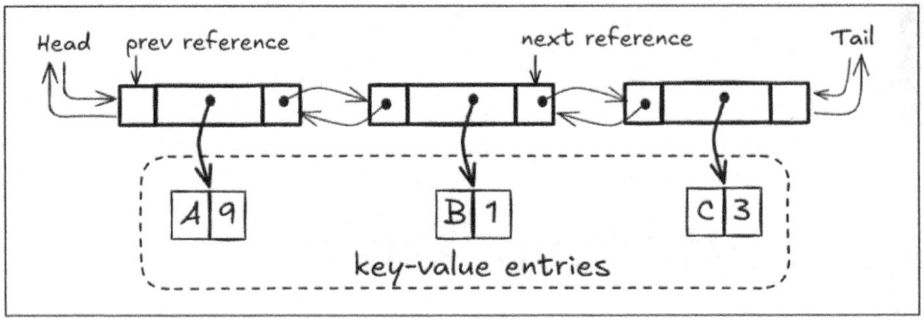

Figure 4.1: A map implemented with a doubly-linked list, with each node containing a key-value entry

The defining property of a map is its uniqueness: no two entries may share the same key. This restriction turns the map into a perfect lookup table. That is, if you know the key, you can find the corresponding value in linear time `O(n)` using a list, or constant time `O(1)` using a hash table. There are five key features of a map (dictionary) data structure:

1. Key-value pairing: each entry is a unique key linked to a value.
2. Fast access: lookup, insertion, and deletion run in `O(1)` (hash table) or `O(log n)` (balanced tree).
3. Key uniqueness: duplicate keys are disallowed; every key identifies a single value.
4. No ordering guarantee: keys are not necessarily stored in any particular order.
5. Dynamic size: the container resizes automatically as keys are added or removed, and values are updated.

Maps excel at performing key-value searches, implementing caches, managing configuration data, and modeling relationships between objects. Classic computer science problems frequently employ maps, and this section will spotlight two common examples. Later in the chapter, we'll dive into more sophisticated hash-based map implementations.

Example 1: Address books

In a conventional address book, the primary search for locating any particular entry ("key") is normally done by a name lookup. In a digital system, the name is often the natural key because it is human readable. On the other hand, the "value" that is associated with each unique key packs all the ancillary information that a user might need when looking up a contact in the address book. An example of a value is the record containing a person's phone number, email address, mailing address, company, job title, birthday, etc. With a map, a query like "What is John Doe's phone number?" becomes a single dictionary lookup, rather than scanning a long list of entries. This example illustrates that even with organization (alphabetical or grouped entries), the search process remains fundamentally different from digital lookup; it's still a manual search through the list of entries, whereas digital systems provide direct dictionary-style access. *Figure 4.2* shows the key search difference between the linear scan in a paper address book versus the `O(1)` lookup in a digital address book.

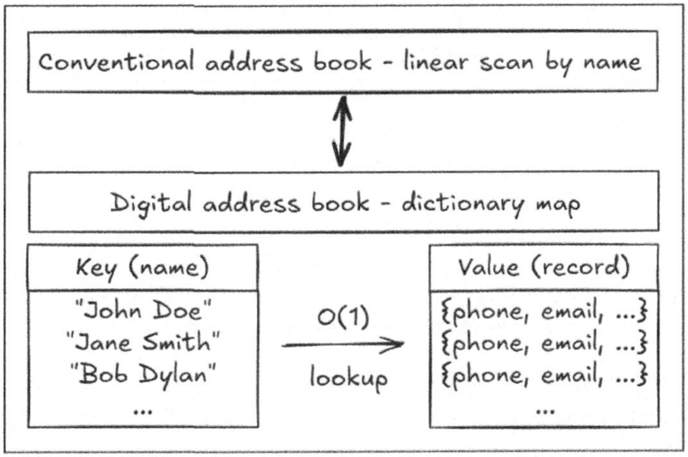

Figure 4.2: In a paper-bound address book, you must scan every entry to find a name, whereas a digital system keeps the same information in a hash table (or balanced tree), giving constant-time (O(1)) lookups instead of a linear scan through all rows

Example 2: Parking garage ticketing system

In a parking garage ticketing system, each vehicle that enters is issued a unique ticket number, which serves as the key in a map (dictionary) that stores a rich value record containing the car's license plate, owner, entry time, assigned spot, etc. At the exit, the attendant scans the ticket, and the ticketing system performs a fast hash lookup to retrieve the vehicle record in `O(1)` time, allowing the fee to be computed, payment accepted, and the spot released. This ticketing system uses a map data structure, where its underlying key-value mechanism replaces a linear search of all parked cars with a single constant-time dictionary lookup. *Figure 4.3* shows this ticketing system in action.

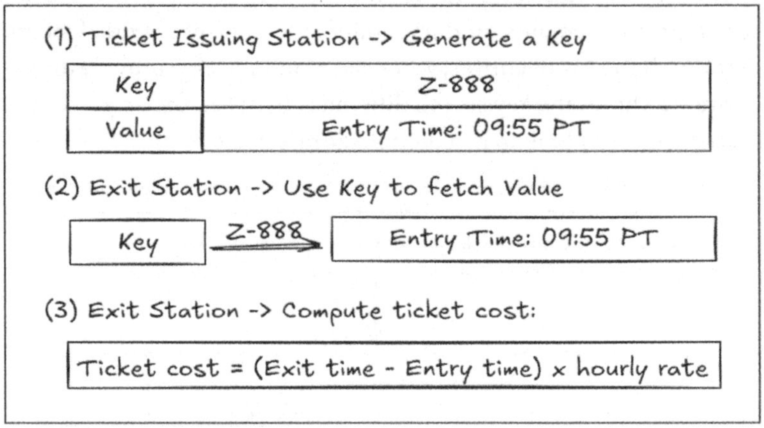

Figure 4.3: The ticketing station tags each car with a unique key (e.g., Z-888) and logs the entry time; on exit, it looks up that key to compute the fee

A parking garage ticketing system functions as a real-time map: the ticket number (a unique, human-readable key) points to a detailed record of that stay. Using a map, the system can insert or fetch these records in constant time, ensuring accurate timing and fast ticket computation.

Abstract data type (ADT): Map

The defining property of a map is a unique key: no two entries may share the same key. This restriction turns the map into a perfect lookup table. Namely, if you know the key, you can find the corresponding value instantly. Specifically, we define a generic `Map<K,V>` where we choose exactly the key type (`K`) and the value type (`V`) at compile-time. Every entry inside the map is a unique key-value pair. Keys are compared for equality. No duplicates are permitted. The core operations that a map must support are:

Operation	Purpose	Complexity
`put(k, v)`	Insert a new key-value pair or overwrite the value for an existing key.	`O(1)`
`get(k)`	Retrieve the value associated with key `k`.	`O(1)`
`remove(k)`	Delete the entry identified by key `k`.	`O(1)`
`isEmpty()`	Check whether the map contains any elements	`O(1)`

Operation	Purpose	Complexity
`size()`	Get the number of elements stored	`O(1)`

Table 4.1: Map operations and their efficiencies

The following code demonstrates a basic implementation of the Map ADT in Java:

```
public interface Map<K,V> {

    // Insert a new key-value pair or overwrite w/ an existing key
    V put(K key, V value);

    // Retrieve the value associated with key k
    V get(K key);

    // Delete the entry identified by key k
    V remove(K key);

    // Checks whether the map contains any elements
    boolean isEmpty();

    // Number of elements currently stored
    int size();

}
```

The code file for this demonstration can be found in the `Chapter04` folder in the GitHub repo. To unlock the GitHub repo link, refer to the instructions in the *Download the example code files* section of the *Preface*.

Depending on the language implementation, a map may expose several helper methods that let you query the number of keys and values and test whether a specific key is present. The common examples are:

- `boolean containsKey(K key)`
- `Set<K> keySet()`
- `Collection<V> values()`

`containsKey(K key)` is a lookup method checking whether a particular key is present in the map, returning `true` if the key exists and `false` otherwise. `containsKey` runs constant-time `O(1)` for hash maps. We will introduce hashing in the next section of this chapter.

> **Note**
>
> Developers frequently mistake `TreeMap` for hash-based collections like `HashMap`, which provide `O(1)` average-case lookup performance. `TreeMap`, however, focuses on maintaining sorted order and delivering guaranteed `O(log n)` performance instead of constant-time lookups. This type of lookup requires traversing a tree structure, which will be introduced in *Chapter 5*.

Both `keySet()` and `values()` methods in Map are essentially "view" factories, returning a constant view consisting of all keys and values currently stored in the map, respectively. Both run in constant time `O(1)`; the only non-constant work is when you iterate over the returned collection, which costs linear time in the number of `n` entries, plus the array capacity, `N`, totaling `O(n + N)` in iteration.

All operations are performed on the underlying data structure, so their asymptotic behavior matches that of the structure's lookup and traversal costs.

Concrete implementations

The concrete implementation of Map using `ArrayList` is in the `Map.java` file inside the `Chapter04` folder on GitHub. To unlock the GitHub repo link, refer to the instructions in the *Download the example code files* section of the *Preface*.

In this chapter, we have introduced the Map ADT, explained its essential operations, and shown a minimal yet concrete implementation using a plain `ArrayList`. While this example suffices to illustrate the concept of key-value associations, it is far from efficient for real-world workloads: lookups, insertions, and deletions degrade to linear time as the collection grows. In industry-grade systems, developers routinely replace such naïve structures with hash tables or tree-based implementations that guarantee sublinear performance. With this foundation in mind, we now turn our attention to hashing, an efficient technique for enabling high-performance map structures.

Fundamentals of hashing

The map Abstract Data Type (ADT) formalizes a collection of key-value pairs, exposing operations such as insertion, lookup, and deletion that run in constant or near-constant time.

Hashing provides a practical mechanism for realizing these operations by mapping arbitrary keys to a fixed-size array of "buckets" or "chains" via a deterministic hash function. This type of hashing is illustrated in *Figure 4.4*:

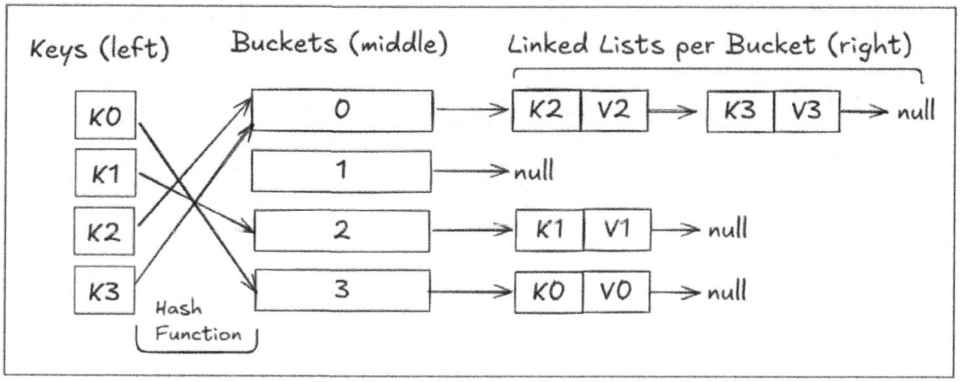

Figure 4.4: This illustration depicts a classic hash map that uses separate chaining to resolve hash collisions. On the left, we have a set of keys on the map, mapping into the buckets in the middle. Because multiple keys can map to the same bucket (a collision), each bucket contains a linked list of all key-value pairs that hash to that index. This linked list is shown on the right

When a key is inserted, its hash value determines the target bucket, and the value is stored there. Subsequent lookups recompute the same hash to retrieve the entry directly. Thus, hashing turns the conceptual map ADT into a highly efficient data structure by distributing entries uniformly across memory and reducing search time from linear to average case `O(1)`, while collision resolution strategies (e.g., chaining, probing, cuckoo hashing) preserve correctness in the face of hash collisions.

What is a hash and hash function?

A hash, short for hash value or hash code, is a fixed-size numerical representation that is deterministically produced from an arbitrary-size input, such as a string, file, or data structure, by applying a hash function. The hash captures the essence of the input in a compact form: identical inputs always produce the same hash, while even tiny differences in the input are intended to produce drastically different hashes. Hashes are used for fast key-value lookups; they are useful for detecting data corruption, digital signatures, and many other purposes in computing.

A hash function is a mathematical function that maps input data of arbitrary size to fixed-size values (hash codes), used to determine where to store or find elements in a hash table.

Key properties of good hashing

A hash is considered good when it exhibits the following desirable traits:

- **Uniformly distributed**: this example routine disperses distinct strings evenly across the table, minimizing collisions:

```
public int balancedHash(String key) {
    int h = 0;
    for (int i = 0; i < key.length(); i++) {
        h = 31 * h + key.charAt(i);
    }
    return h % tableSize;
}
```

  The multiplier, 31, is popular because it is a small, odd prime that lets the JVM use a fast shift-and-subtract multiplication, effectively blending high-order bits into the low-order part for good dispersion. When combined with per-character accumulation and a final modulo by the table size, this yields a quick, deterministic hash that spreads keys evenly and exhibits the avalanche effect. A hash with an avalanche effect turns tiny changes in the input into large changes in the output, preventing many similar keys from falling into the same bucket. This keeps the hash table's lookup, insert, and delete operations near `O(1)` by minimizing collisions, making the hash behave like random mapping and ensuring efficient performance.

- **Deterministic**: This code snippet illustrates that identical strings consistently produce the same hash value, ensuring each key maps to a unique, repeatable hash code:

```
String key = "apple";
int h1 = key.hashCode();    // 93029210
int h2 = key.hashCode();    // always 93029210
```

- **Fast computation**: The example routine relies on a simple modulo operation, yielding a hash in constant time:

```
public int fastHash(int key) {
    return key % tableSize;    // O(1)
}}
```

A well-designed hash function should compute in time linear in the key size, `O(k)`. We will look at why that is the case next.

Why hashing amortizes to O(1)?

The statement "hashing amortized to `O(1)`" encapsulates two key observations:

- Each individual insert, delete, or lookup takes expected constant time, provided the hash function distributes keys uniformly across the table (the classic "uniform hash" assumption).
- When the table is resized, grown when it becomes too dense or shrunk when it is sparsely populated, the expensive rehashing is spread over many subsequent cheap operations. Thus, the average cost over a long sequence of operations remains `O(1)`; this is the amortized guarantee.

To understand why this holds, namely that every map operation amortizes constant time `O(1)`, let's examine the situation from a mathematical perspective. Suppose we insert n keys into a hash table with m buckets, using separate chaining (see the section on *Separate Chaining* later), and the hash function distributes the keys uniformly so that every bucket is equally likely to receive a key. Taking $E[L_i]$ as the expected length, `L`, of bucket `i`, where `1 ≤ i ≤ m`, we can express

$$E[L_i] = E\left[\sum_{j=1}^{n} \mathrm{N_j}\right]$$

Where $\mathrm{N_j}$ is either 1 if element `j` hashes to bucket `i`, or `0` otherwise, because the hash is uniform:

$$E[N_j] = \frac{1}{m}$$

Summing over all n keys, $E[L_i] = \sum_{j=1}^{n} \frac{1}{m} = \frac{n}{m} = \alpha$

Here, α is the load factor. Thus, on average, each chain contains α elements, and every operation touches only a constant-size chain, yielding expected `O(1)` time even when resizing occasionally occurs. *Figure 4.5* shows the load factor as a function of occupied over the total slots in a hash table.

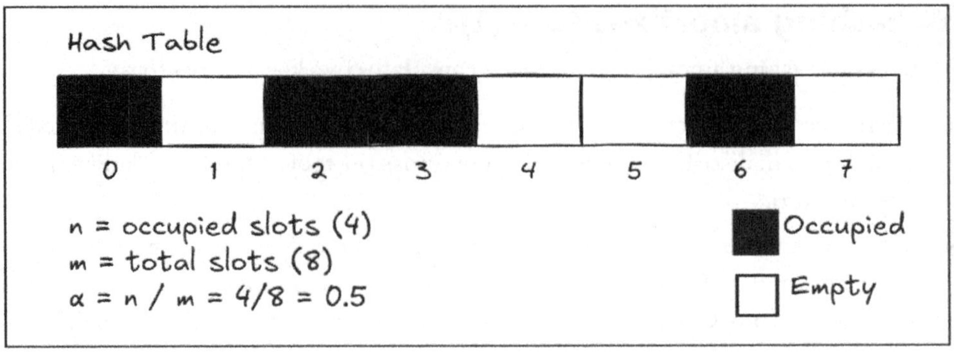

Figure 4.5: Load factor

To look up or delete a key, we first compute its hash in constant time to jump to the appropriate bucket, then scan that bucket until we either hit the key or reach its end. Consequently:

- Unsuccessful search: we compare against every element in the bucket, yielding an expected $O(1 + \alpha)$ comparisons
- Successful search: on average, we only inspect half the bucket, giving the following

$$O(1 + \frac{E[L_i]}{2}) = O(1 + \frac{\alpha}{2})$$

If we keep the load factor αbounded by a modest constant c, such that $\alpha \leq c$, the costs collapse to constant time:

- Unsuccessful search:$1 + \alpha \leq 1 + c = O(1)$
- Successful search:$1 + \frac{\alpha}{2} \leq 1 + \frac{c}{2} = O(1)$

Even if the hash function is biased and some buckets grow disproportionately large, maintaining a constant load factor α cannot protect localized performance, which can degrade within those clusters.$O(1)$. However, the mechanism that keeps those operations efficient under such uneven distributions is the choice of collision resolution strategy, which preserves a near constant or sub-linear average cost.

In what follows, we explore the two canonical families: separate chaining and open addressing. We will examine how each one handles the inevitable clashes that arise when distinct keys hash to the same slot.

Collision resolution techniques

In a hash table, a hash function `h(k)` maps a key `k` to an index. When two distinct keys, k_1 and k_2, produce the same index, a collision occurs. How the structure resolves that collision decides the table's performance, memory overhead, and concurrent behavior.

Open addressing

In an open-addressing hash table, the storage is a compact, contiguous array of `Entry<K,V>` objects. Every key/value pair is stored directly in this single array. When a computed slot is already in use, the algorithm searches by "probing" the array until it finds an empty position. There are multiple probing strategies. We'll focus on two: linear probing and quadratic probing.

Linear probing

You can illustrate the method with Java's native `hashCode()` function and a table of size `m`. The probe sequence is calculated as

$$index(i) = (h(k) + i) \ mod \ m$$

Here `h(k)` is the initial hash index, and `i` is the step counter. For example, to compute the hash for a key:

```
// h(key)
int h = Math.abs(key.hashCode() % m);
```

If the slot at `h(k)` is already taken, linear probing simply looks at the next slot `h(k)+1`, then the next `h(k)+2`, and so on, wrapping around the array when it reaches the end. In other words, it "walks one step at a time" through the table until it finds an empty slot. The lookup time depends entirely on the number of steps required to find either the matching key or an empty slot; the latter indicating that a key is absent. In a largely empty hash table with few clusters, keys can typically be found within 1-2 steps on average: `O(1)`. A well-designed table with uniform hashing minimizes long search sequences through proper resizing and rehashing before the table fills up. This keeps the average number of steps small and the clusters of occupied slots in the table sparse, resulting in an expected, average-case `O(1)` lookup time.

Quadratic probing

This technique is like linear probing with a slight twist: quadratic probing skips progressively farther gaps instead of taking one step at a time, using the following formula:

$$index(i) = (h(k) + i^2)\ mod\ m$$

Here, `h(k)` is the initial hash index and `i` is the step counter starting at 0.

For example, with the same `h(key)` treatment on collision, this technique probes the table for the next available, empty slot in this fashion: first `h(k)+1`, then `h(k)+4` (`i=2`; 2^2`=4`), then `h(k)+9`, etc. Each step grows quadratically farther away from the origin.

Open addressing techniques are straightforward to implement. In practice, many modern Java hash maps (e.g., `HashMap`) use linear probing for its speed and simplicity, while `ConcurrentHashMap` and other high concurrency variants adopt more complex open addressing techniques such as double hashing, to preserve the uniformity of probe sequences under lock-free updates. Quadratic probing remains a useful "middle ground" when you want better dispersion than linear but still need a very fast, low overhead implementation.

Closed addressing

When designing a hash table, collisions are unavoidable since multiple distinct keys may map to the same array index. Open addressing resolves this by having colliding elements search for alternative empty slots within the main array, while closed addressing uses a contrasting approach. In closed addressing, elements are confined to their designated hash index and cannot occupy other slots. Each array bucket functions as a portal to an external container capable of storing multiple items. The most common and intuitive implementation of this strategy is separate chaining as we will see next.

Separate chaining

Separate chaining is a straightforward collision resolution technique. Each bucket of the hash table is an independent chain of, say, a linked list, but it can also be of any dynamic container. When a key hashes to bucket `i`, the entry is appended to that chain. The key idea is that the table's physical array holds only pointers to these lists, so the actual data can grow independently of the number of buckets.

When a client asks for a value, the hash function tells us which bucket to investigate:

$$bucket_{index} = h(k)\ mod\ m$$

We can append a new key-value pair as a node to the end of the specific bucket:

$$bucket[bucket_{index}].append(k, v)$$

We then walk through the short list for that bucket, comparing keys until we find a match or exhaust the list. Deletion is identical to a lookup, except that we splice out the matched node once we locate it.

With separate chaining, the chance that every key collides into one bucket is tiny if the hash function is decent. We keep the load factor $\alpha = n/m$ below a constant (≈0.75) so the average chain stays short, and each operation is constant time. *Figure 4.6* displays the closed addressing technique via separate chaining.

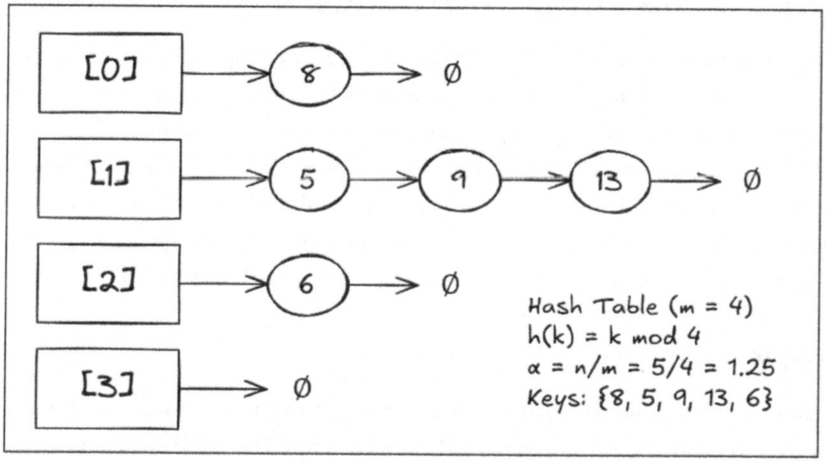

Figure 4.6: Closed addressing via separate chaining

From a concurrency perspective, separate chaining is advantageous because threads can lock only the specific bucket they're working on instead of the whole table, boosting scalability in multi-threaded contexts. In essence, separate chaining delivers a straightforward, reliable method for maintaining fast hash-table operations even when the hash function isn't ideal, which is why it's widely adopted in language runtimes and standard data-structure libraries.

Hashing and the core map operations

The analysis of hashing complexity applies equally to the two most common collision resolution techniques: separate chaining and open addressing. Below, we show how the three fundamental map operations (`put`, `get`, and `remove`) behave under the core strategies:

- In the worst case, if we have all `n` keys mapping to the same bucket, the cost of any operation becomes `O(n)` for collision resolution techniques. For chaining, all keys pile into a single linked list, while for open addressing they all occupy a single probe chain.
- In the expected case, when a hash function is reasonably uniform and the load factor α is small, i.e.

$$\alpha = \frac{n}{m} \ll 1$$

A successful search (`get`) on average is `O(1)` as described before. This constant search behavior applies to open addressing as well, where the number of probes before finding a free slot or a target key is proportional to $\frac{1}{1-\alpha}$ giving the same `O(1)` expectation.

Examples of hashing in practice

There are many hashing algorithms in the industry. For example, Robin-hood hashing is an open-addressing scheme that keeps probe distances of all entries as equal as possible: when inserting a key, it compares the "age" (number of steps from its ideal home bucket) of the new key with that of the occupant; if the new key is older (has traveled farther), it swaps places with the occupant, and the displaced key continues probing. This "kicking out" strategy evens out the distribution of probe lengths, yielding very low and predictable lookup times even at high load factors (`α≈90%`), while keeping insertion cost amortized to `O(1)`.

Summary

In this chapter, we examined the fundamentals of maps and hash tables, i.e., how they store key-value pairs, the core operations (`put`, `get`, `remove`), and the collision resolution strategies that keep performance constant on average. We then grounded the theory in practical examples, from address books and inventory systems to other real-world use cases, highlighting how hash-based maps underpin software across the stack, from low-level system components to high-level application logic. The method of resolving collisions, whether by separate chaining, where each bucket holds a small list, or by open addressing, where the array itself is probed for free slots, determines the real cost in the unlikely worst case, the memory layout, and the concurrency model. *Figure 4.7* is the summary diagram of hash maps for overview.

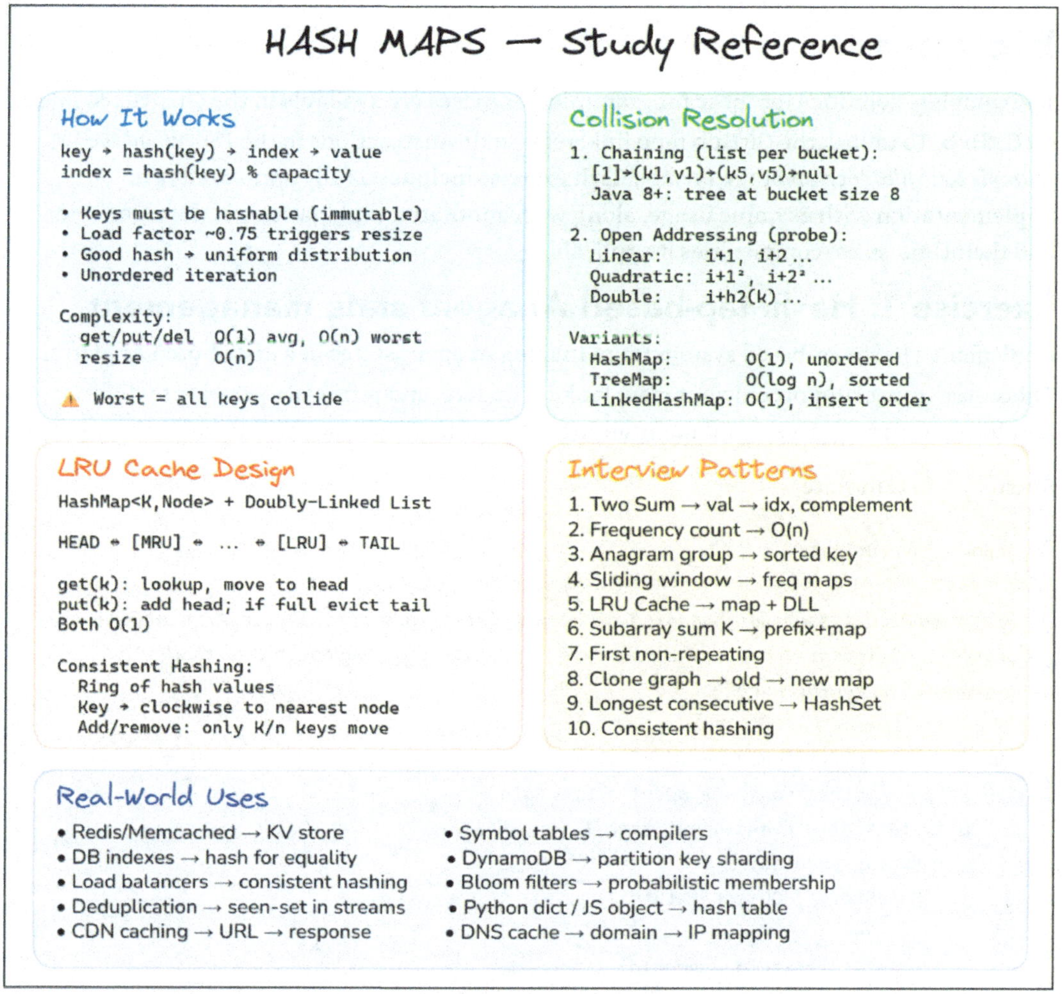

Figure 4.7: Summary of hash maps

Having unpacked how hash tables turn a collection of key-value pairs into an almost constant-time lookup, we now shift our attention to a different family of data structures that are hierarchical in nature: trees. They preserve order while guaranteeing logarithmic worst-case bounds. The next chapter will introduce binary search trees and their balanced variants, showing how they can support ordered queries, range searches, and dynamic updates with provable $O(\log n)$ performance.

Exercises

The complete solutions for these programming exercises are available in the `Chapter04` folder on GitHub. To unlock the GitHub repo link, refer to the instructions in the *Download the example code files* section of the *Preface*. Each exercise includes a fully annotated Java implementation with example usage, along with annotated explanations of the algorithms and their time/space complexities if applicable.

Exercise 1: HashMap-based AI agent state management

Implement a `HashMap`-based system for managing AI agent states in a distributed AI platform. The system must support efficient state lookup, update, and retrieval operations while handling concurrent access and maintaining `O(1)` average-case performance for all operations.

Starter code template

```
import java.util.*;
/**
HashMap-based system for managing AI agent states in a distributed AI platform
Supports efficient state lookup, update, and retrieval operations with O(1)
average-case performance
*/
public class AIStateHashMap {
    // Inner class to store agent state data
    private static class AgentState {
        String agentId;
        Map<String, Object> state;

        AgentState(String agentId) {
            this.agentId = agentId;
            this.state = new HashMap<>();
        }
    }

    // HashMap to store agent states
    private Map<String, AgentState> agentStates;

    /**
    * Constructor to initialize the AI state HashMap
    */
    public AIStateHashMap() {
```

```
        this.agentStates = new HashMap<>();
    }

    /**
     * Put a key-value pair in agent's state
     * @param agentId Unique identifier for the agent
     * @param key State key to set
     * @param value State value to set
     * @throws IllegalArgumentException if agentId is null
     */
    public void put(String agentId, String key, Object value) {
        if (agentId == null) {
            throw new IllegalArgumentException("Agent ID cannot be null");
        }
        // TODO: Implement put operation with O(1) lookup
    }

    /**
     * Get a value from agent's state
     * @param agentId Unique identifier for the agent
     * @param key State key to retrieve
     * @return State value or null if not found
     * @throws IllegalArgumentException if agentId is null
     */
    public Object get(String agentId, String key) {
        if (agentId == null) {
            throw new IllegalArgumentException("Agent ID cannot be null");
        }
        // TODO: Implement get operation with O(1) lookup
        return null;
    }

    /**
     * Get all state for an agent
     * @param agentId Unique identifier for the agent
     * @return Complete state map or null if agent not found
     * @throws IllegalArgumentException if agentId is null
     */
    public Map<String, Object> getAgentState(String agentId) {
        if (agentId == null) {
            throw new IllegalArgumentException("Agent ID cannot be null");
```

```
        }
        // TODO: Implement agent state retrieval with O(1) lookup
        return null;
    }

    /**
     * Remove an agent's state
     * @param agentId Unique identifier for the agent
     * @return Removed state or null if agent not found
     * @throws IllegalArgumentException if agentId is null
     */
    public Map<String, Object> remove(String agentId) {
        if (agentId == null) {
            throw new IllegalArgumentException("Agent ID cannot be null");
        }
        // TODO: Implement remove operation with O(1) lookup
        return null;
    }

    /**
     * Get the number of agents in the system
     * @return Number of agents
     */
    public int size() {
        return agentStates.size();
    }

    /**
     * Check if the system is empty
     * @return true if no agents, false otherwise
     */
    public boolean isEmpty() {
        return agentStates.isEmpty();
    }

    /**
     * Check if an agent exists in the system
     * @param agentId Unique identifier for the agent
     * @return true if agent exists, false otherwise
     * @throws IllegalArgumentException if agentId is null
     */
```

```
    public boolean containsAgent(String agentId) {
        if (agentId == null) {
            throw new IllegalArgumentException("Agent ID cannot be null");
        }
        return agentStates.containsKey(agentId);
    }

    /**
     * Clear all agent states from the system
     */
    public void clear() {
        agentStates.clear();
    }

}
```

Assumptions and Constraints

- Agent IDs are unique strings
- Agent states are key-value pairs stored as `Map<String, Object>`
- All operations must maintain `O(1)` average-case lookup performance
- `getAgentState` and `remove` return copies to prevent external modification
- No concurrency access support; `HashMap` is used without synchronization
- Java's built-in `String.hashCode()` is used via `HashMap` to hash agent IDs

Test case 1

- **Input**: `put("agent-001", "status", "active"), get("agent-001", "status")`
- **Expected Output**: "active"

Test case 2

- **Input**: `put("agent-002", "cpu_usage", 85.5), put("agent-002", "memory_usage", 42.3), get("agent-002", "cpu_usage")`
- **Expected Output**: 85.5

Solution

`AIStateHashMap` manages AI agent states using a two-layer `HashMap` structure where each agent ID maps to its own key-value state map.

It supports four core operations: `put` writes a value to an agent's state, creating the agent entry if it doesn't exist yet; `get` retrieves a single value by agent and key; `getAgentState` returns a full copy of an agent's state; and `remove` deletes an entire agent and returns its last state. Both `getAgentState` and `remove` return defensive copies to prevent external mutation.

Utility methods `size`, `isEmpty`, `containsAgent`, and `clear` delegate directly to the outer map. All operations throw `IllegalArgumentException` on null agent IDs.

Two-layer HashMap structure

The core design uses Java's `HashMaps`. The outer map keys agent IDs to `AgentState` objects, and each `AgentState` holds its own inner map of key-value pairs. This gives `O(1)` average-case lookup at both levels: first resolving the agent, then resolving the state key:

```
private Map<String, AgentState> agentStates; // outer map: agentId → AgentState
// inside AgentState:
Map<String, Object> state = new HashMap<>();  // inner map: key → value
```

Put operation: lazy agent creation

On `put`, the outer map is checked first. If the agent doesn't exist yet, a new `AgentState` is created and inserted into the outer map before writing to the inner one. This avoids a separate "register agent" step as agents are created on first write:

```
AgentState agentState = agentStates.get(agentId);
if (agentState == null) {
    agentState = new AgentState(agentId);
    agentStates.put(agentId, agentState);
}
agentState.state.put(key, value);
```

Get operation: two-step lookup

Retrieval traverses both maps in sequence. If the outer map returns null (agent not found), the method short-circuits immediately rather than risking a `NullPointerException` on the inner map lookup:

```
AgentState agentState = agentStates.get(agentId);
if (agentState == null) return null;
return agentState.state.get(key);
```

Copying on read and remove

Both `getAgentState` and `remove` return `new HashMap<>(agentState.state)` rather than the internal map directly. This prevents callers from mutating agent state from outside the class, preserving encapsulation.

Exercise 2: Uniform hash function

Implement a hash function for strings that distributes keys uniformly across a hash table of given size. The hash function should use the polynomial rolling hash technique with a prime base.

Starter Code Template

```
public class HashFunction {
    public static int hash(String key, int tableSize) {
        // TODO: Implement polynomial rolling hash function
        return 0;
    }
}
```

Assumptions and Constraints

- String keys can be `null` or empty
- Table size is always a positive integer
- Use base 31 for polynomial rolling hash
- Handle negative hash values properly

Test Case 1

- **Input**: `key = "hello", tableSize = 1000`
- **Expected Output**: 995

Test Case 2

- **Input**: `key = "abc", tableSize = 100`
- **Expected Output**: 29

Exercise 3: Linear probing hash map

Implement a `HashMap` using linear probing for collision resolution. The implementation should support put, get, and remove operations with proper handling of deleted entries.

Starter Code Template

```
public class LinearProbingHashMap<K, V> {
    private static final int INITIAL_CAPACITY = 16;
```

```
    private static final double LOAD_FACTOR_THRESHOLD = 0.75;

    private Object[] keys;
    private Object[] values;
    private boolean[] occupied;
    private int size;
    private int capacity;

    public LinearProbingHashMap() {
        this.capacity = INITIAL_CAPACITY;
        this.keys = new Object[capacity];
        this.values = new Object[capacity];
        this.occupied = new boolean[capacity];
        this.size = 0;
    }

    public void put(K key, V value) {
        // TODO: Implement put with linear probing
    }

    @SuppressWarnings("unchecked")
    public V get(K key) {
        // TODO: Implement get with linear probing
        return null;
    }

    @SuppressWarnings("unchecked")
    public V remove(K key) {
        // TODO: Implement remove with linear probing
        return null;
    }
}
```

Assumptions and Constraints

- `HashMap` uses linear probing with tombstone markers for deleted entries
- Load factor is maintained at 0.75
- Rehash when load factor exceeds threshold
- Handle `null` keys and values appropriately

Test Case 1

- **Operations:** `put("a", 1), put("b", 2), get("a")`
- **Expected Output:** 1

Test Case 2

- **Operations:** `put("x", 10), put("y", 20), remove("x"), get("y")`
- **Expected Output:** 20

Exercise 4: Quadratic probing hash map

Implement a `HashMap` using quadratic probing for collision resolution. The implementation should support all standard operations with a quadratic probing sequence.

Starter Code Template

```
public class QuadraticProbingHashMap<K, V> {
    private static final int INITIAL_CAPACITY = 16;
    private static final double LOAD_FACTOR_THRESHOLD = 0.75;

    private Object[] keys;
    private Object[] values;
    private boolean[] occupied;
    private int size;
    private int capacity;

    public QuadraticProbingHashMap() {
        this.capacity = INITIAL_CAPACITY;
        this.keys = new Object[capacity];
        this.values = new Object[capacity];
        this.occupied = new boolean[capacity];
        this.size = 0;
    }

    public void put(K key, V value) {
        // TODO: Implement put with quadratic probing
    }

    @SuppressWarnings("unchecked")
    public V get(K key) {
        // TODO: Implement get with quadratic probing
        return null;
```

```
    }

    @SuppressWarnings("unchecked")
    public V remove(K key) {
        // TODO: Implement remove with quadratic probing
        return null;
    }
}
```

Assumptions and Constraints

- Quadratic probing sequence: `h + i²` where `i` = 0, 1, 2, ...
- Handle load factor management
- Support null keys and values
- Maintain `O(1)` average case performance

Test Case 1

- **Operations**: `put("key1", 100), put("key2", 200), get("key1")`
- **Expected Output**: 100

Test Case 2

- **Operations**: `put("a", 1), put("b", 2), put("c", 3), remove("b"), get("c")`
- **Expected Output**: 3

Exercise 5: Chaining hash map

Implement a `HashMap` using separate chaining for collision resolution. Each bucket should be a linked list of key-value pairs.

Starter Code Template

```
public class ChainingHashMap<K, V> {
    private static final int INITIAL_CAPACITY = 16;
    private static final double LOAD_FACTOR_THRESHOLD = 0.75;

    private class Node {
        K key;
        V value;
        Node next;

        Node(K key, V value) {
```

```
            this.key = key;
            this.value = value;
            this.next = null;
        }
    }

    private Node[] buckets;
    private int size;
    private int capacity;

    public ChainingHashMap() {
        this.capacity = INITIAL_CAPACITY;
        this.buckets = new Node[capacity];
        this.size = 0;
    }

    public void put(K key, V value) {
        // TODO: Implement put with chaining
    }

    @SuppressWarnings("unchecked")
    public V get(K key) {
        // TODO: Implement get with chaining
        return null;
    }

    @SuppressWarnings("unchecked")
    public V remove(K key) {
        // TODO: Implement remove with chaining
        return null;
    }
}
```

Assumptions and Constraints

- Use linked list for chaining
- Handle load factor management
- Support `null` keys and values
- Maintain `O(1)` average case performance

Test Case 1

- **Operations**: `put("apple", 5), put("banana", 3), get("apple")`
- **Expected Output**: 5

Test Case 2

- **Operations**: `put("x", 10), put("y", 20), remove("x"), get("y")`
- **Expected Output**: 20

Exercise 6: Hash table with open addressing

Implement a hash table that supports multiple open addressing strategies (linear, quadratic, double hashing). The implementation should be flexible enough to switch between strategies.

Starter Code Template

```
public class OpenAddressingHashMap<K, V> {
    private static final int INITIAL_CAPACITY = 16;
    private static final double LOAD_FACTOR_THRESHOLD = 0.75;

    public enum Strategy {
        LINEAR, QUADRATIC, DOUBLE_HASHING
    }

    private Object[] keys;
    private Object[] values;
    private boolean[] occupied;
    private int size;
    private int capacity;
    private Strategy strategy;

    public OpenAddressingHashMap(Strategy strategy) {
        this.strategy = strategy;
        this.capacity = INITIAL_CAPACITY;
        this.keys = new Object[capacity];
        this.values = new Object[capacity];
        this.occupied = new boolean[capacity];
        this.size = 0;
    }

    public void put(K key, V value) {
        // TODO: Implement put with selected strategy
```

```
    }

    @SuppressWarnings("unchecked")
    public V get(K key) {
        // TODO: Implement get with selected strategy
        return null;
    }

    @SuppressWarnings("unchecked")
    public V remove(K key) {
        // TODO: Implement remove with selected strategy
        return null;
    }
}
```

Assumptions and Constraints

- Support three open addressing strategies: linear, quadratic, double hashing
- Use double hashing for collision resolution
- Handle load factor management
- Support `null` keys and values

Test Case 1

- **Operations**: `put("test", 100), put("example", 200), get("test")`
- **Expected Output**: 100

Test Case 2

- **Operations**: `put("a", 1), put("b", 2), put("c", 3), remove("b"), get("c")`
- **Expected Output**: 3

Exercise 7: HashMap with load factor monitoring

Implement a `HashMap` that tracks load factor and automatically rehashes when it exceeds a threshold. Include monitoring capabilities to observe performance characteristics.

Starter Code Template

```
public class LoadFactorHashMap<K, V> {
    private static final int INITIAL_CAPACITY = 16;
    private static final double LOAD_FACTOR_THRESHOLD = 0.75;

    private Object[] keys;
```

```
    private Object[] values;
    private boolean[] occupied;
    private int size;
    private int capacity;
    private int rehashCount;

    public LoadFactorHashMap() {
        this.capacity = INITIAL_CAPACITY;
        this.keys = new Object[capacity];
        this.values = new Object[capacity];
        this.occupied = new boolean[capacity];
        this.size = 0;
        this.rehashCount = 0;
    }

    public void put(K key, V value) {
        // TODO: Implement put with load factor monitoring
    }

    @SuppressWarnings("unchecked")
    public V get(K key) {
        // TODO: Implement get
        return null;
    }

    @SuppressWarnings("unchecked")
    public V remove(K key) {
        // TODO: Implement remove
        return null;
    }

    public double getLoadFactor() {
        // TODO: Implement load factor calculation
        return 0.0;
    }

    public int getRehashCount() {
        // TODO: Implement rehash count getter
        return 0;
    }
}
```

Assumptions and Constraints

- Monitor load factor during operations
- Rehash when load factor exceeds threshold
- Provide methods to get current load factor
- Support standard `HashMap` operations

Test Case 1

- **Operations**: `put("a", 1), put("b", 2), get("a"), getLoadFactor()`
- **Expected Output**: 1, 0.25 (for load factor)

Test Case 2

- **Operations**: `put("x", 10), put("y", 20), remove("x"), getLoadFactor()`
- **Expected Output**: 0.5 (for load factor)

Exercise 8: HashMap with collision statistics

Implement a `HashMap` that tracks and reports collision statistics during operations. The implementation should provide insights into how often collisions occur and how they're resolved.

Starter Code Template

```
public class CollisionTrackingHashMap<K, V> {
    private static final int INITIAL_CAPACITY = 16;

    private Object[] keys;
    private Object[] values;
    private boolean[] occupied;
    private int size;
    private int capacity;
    private int collisionCount;
    private int totalProbes;

    public CollisionTrackingHashMap() {
        this.capacity = INITIAL_CAPACITY;
        this.keys = new Object[capacity];
        this.values = new Object[capacity];
        this.occupied = new boolean[capacity];
        this.size = 0;
        this.collisionCount = 0;
```

```
        this.totalProbes = 0;
    }

    public void put(K key, V value) {
        // TODO: Implement put with collision tracking
    }

    @SuppressWarnings("unchecked")
    public V get(K key) {
        // TODO: Implement get with probe tracking
        return null;
    }

    @SuppressWarnings("unchecked")
    public V remove(K key) {
        // TODO: Implement remove with probe tracking
        return null;
    }

    public int getCollisionCount() {
        // TODO: Implement collision count getter
        return 0;
    }

    public int getTotalProbes() {
        // TODO: Implement total probes getter
        return 0;
    }

    public double getAverageProbes() {
        // TODO: Implement average probes calculation
        return 0.0;
    }
}
```

Assumptions and Constraints

- Track the number of collisions during put operations
- Provide methods to get collision statistics

- Support standard `HashMap` operations
- Maintain performance characteristics

Test Case 1

- **Operations**: `put("a", 1), put("b", 2), getCollisionCount()`
- **Expected Output**: 0 (no collisions)

Test Case 2

- **Operations**: `put("x", 10), put("y", 20), put("z", 30), getCollisionCount()`
- **Expected Output:** 0 (assuming no collisions in a small table)

5

Trees

A tree is a nonlinear, hierarchical data structure that literally conceptually mirrors an upside-down tree in nature. Picture a branching diagram in which every element (a node) is attached to a single parent, except for the root, which stands alone at the top. Each node may spawn zero or more children, and because the links are purely parent-child, no horizontal connections or cycles ever occur.

Unlike linear structures such as stacks, queues, or linked lists, where elements line up one after another, a tree fans out in multiple directions. Visual examples help cement this idea:

- Family tree: The root is the earliest ancestor; each generation sprouts from its parent.
- File-system directory: The root folder branches into subfolders, which in turn branch into their own subfolders and files.

There are no horizontal links or loops, only a clear top-to-bottom hierarchical order that mirrors many real-world systems. This structure not only makes the data intuitive to model but also gives us powerful algorithmic guarantees when we search, insert, or delete nodes.

In this chapter, we will dissect the properties that differentiate tree variants: height, balance, node capacity, and more. We'll examine how these characteristics govern the efficiency of common operations, explore concrete use cases, and dive into the algorithms that let us build, traverse, and maintain these structures with optimal performance.

What is a tree?

A tree is defined by the way its nodes are linked: each node may have zero or more children, and all edges point from a parent to a child. The two most common variations we'll explore differ mainly in the maximum number of children a node can have: a binary tree, where each node may have at most two children, and a general n-ary tree, where a node can have an arbitrary number of children. *Figure 5.1* illustrates the branching difference between binary and n-ary trees, where binary nodes have at most two children, and n-ary nodes can have up to n children.

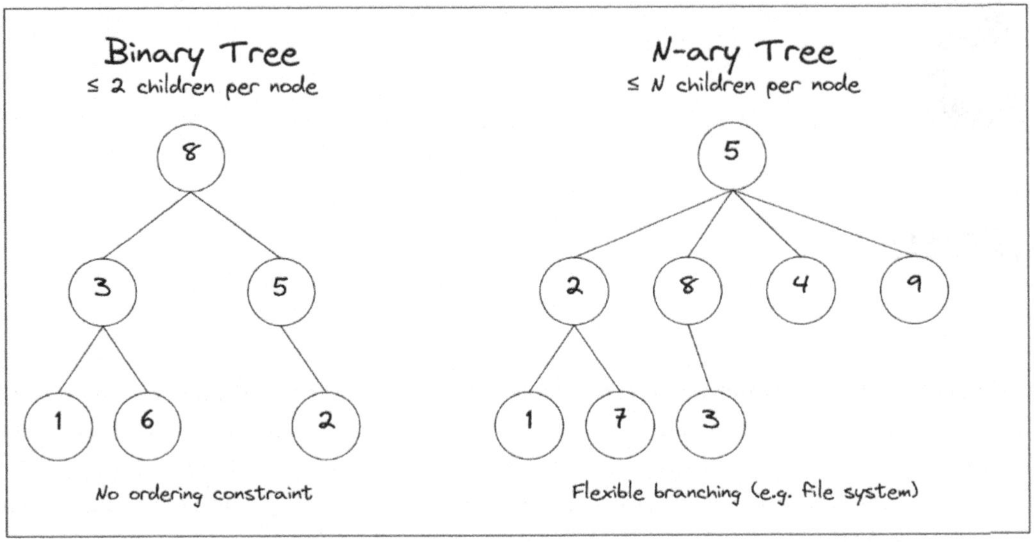

Figure 5.1: Binary tree vs n-ary tree

Binary trees and properties

A binary tree consists of a finite set of nodes. Every node in this tree may have at most two children, conventionally called the left and right child; any node that has children acts as a parent node. *Figure 5.2* shows a simple binary tree relation.

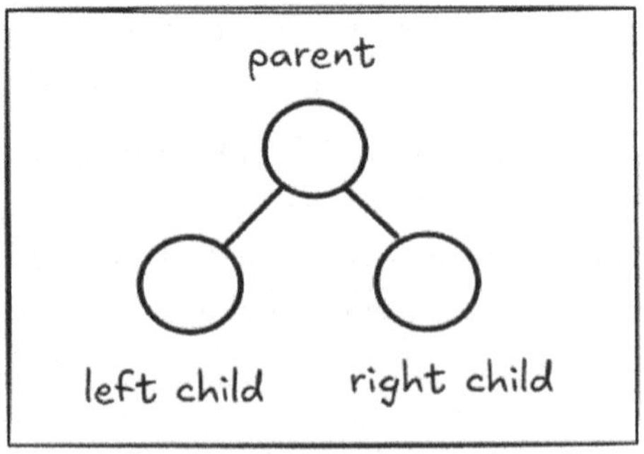

Figure 5.2: The binary tree relation

The topmost node in this set of finite nodes is called the root. The children of any given node, if they exist, recursively branch into distinct left and right subtrees. No nodes are in common; hence disjoint, in both subtrees. *Figure 5.3* depicts a simple binary tree structure:

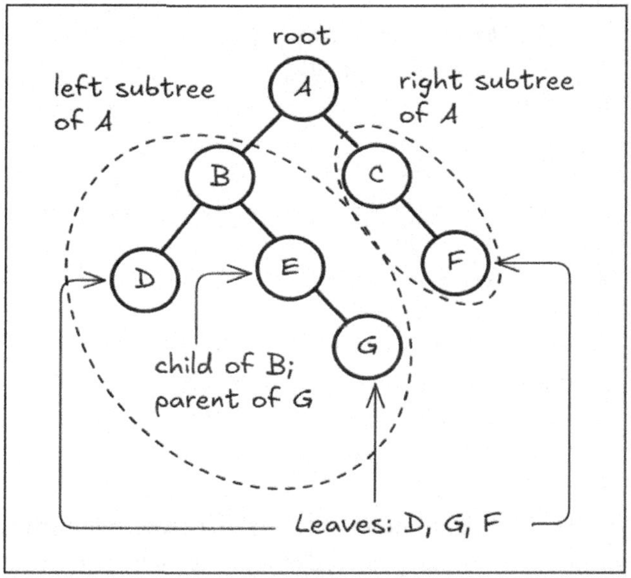

Figure 5.3: A simple binary tree structure

There is an edge from a node to each of its children. By extension, node D in *Figure 5.3* is the left single-node subtree of B, whereas nodes E-G are the right subtree of B. Any node that does not have any child is called a leaf, or a terminal node. Nodes D, G, and F are leaves. Additional terminology will be defined when we discuss tree traversals.

Java representation

A binary tree may be represented in a linked structure. Each node keeps references to its descendants instead of a single "next" link. In a singly linked list, a node carries one field that points to the following element. In a binary tree, a node carries two fields, one for the left child and one for the right child. These two references allow us to walk down the left or right subtrees, just as the single reference lets us walk down a list. Below is a minimal, but complete, Java representation of a binary tree node:

```
public class BinaryTreeNode<T> {
    private T value;
    private BinaryTreeNode<T> left;
    private BinaryTreeNode<T> right;

    public BinaryTreeNode(T value) {
        this(value, null, null);
    }
```

```
    public BinaryTreeNode(T value,
                          BinaryTreeNode<T> left,
                          BinaryTreeNode<T> right) {
        this.value = value;
        this.left  = left;
        this.right = right;
    }
    public T getValue()         { return value; }
    public void setValue(T v)  { value = v; }
    public BinaryTreeNode<T> getLeft()    { return left; }
    public void setLeft(BinaryTreeNode<T> l) { left = l; }
    public BinaryTreeNode<T> getRight()   { return right; }
    public void setRight(BinaryTreeNode<T> r) { right = r; }
}
```

As we will see later, the left and right references in a binary tree enable the classic recursive traversals, namely in-order, pre-order, post-order, and the many algorithms that rely on branching such as search, balancing, etc. Common variations include binary search trees (BSTs), AVL trees, and Red-Black trees. The next section introduces the binary search tree and its key properties.

Binary search trees (BST) and properties

A binary search tree, or BST, is a binary tree in which every node satisfies the invariant that all keys in its left subtree are strictly less than the node's key, and all keys in its right subtree are strictly greater than the node's key:

```
Max(leftsubtree) < node.key < Min(rightsubtree)
```

This simple ordering allows logarithmic time to search, insert, and delete on average, while keeping the data in sorted order for in-order traversal (see the In-Order Traversal section). In the worst case where a BST degenerates into a linked list, the cost of these operations becomes `O(n)`. *Figure 5.4* shows a balanced BST and its degenerate (skewed) case:

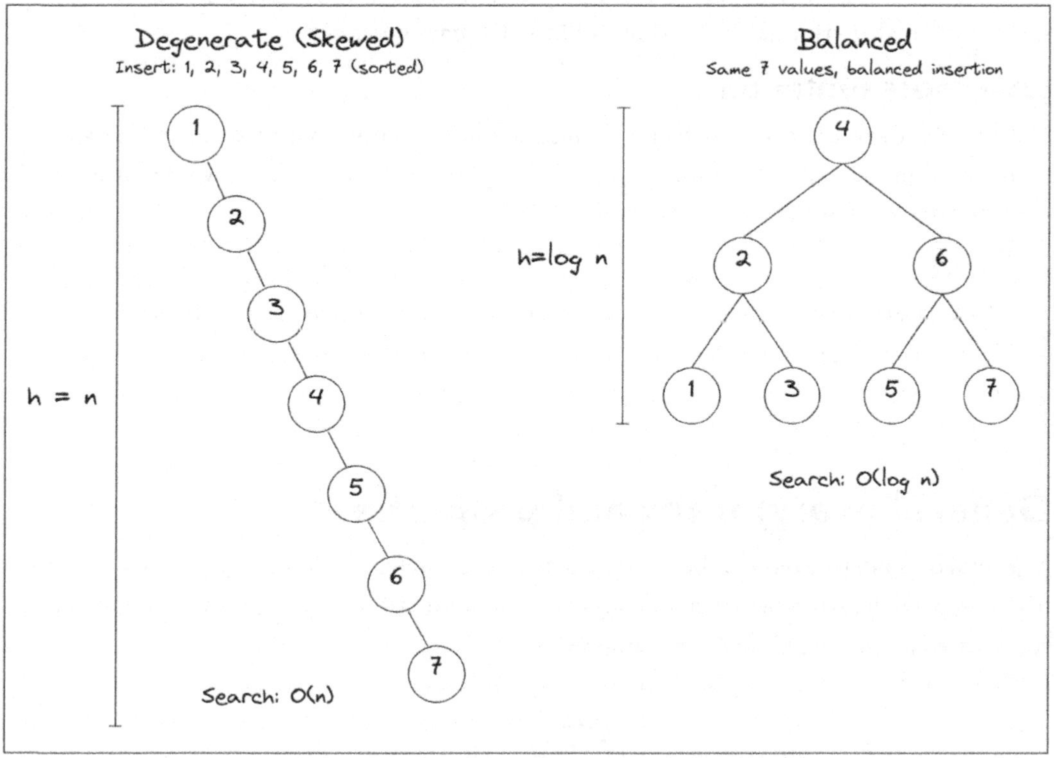

Figure 5.4: A balanced binary search tree vs. the degenerate (skewed) case

A binary search tree maintains order by guaranteeing that every left descendant holds a key smaller than the parent while every right descendant holds a key larger. As explained later, an in-order traversal (a mechanism visiting the left subtree, the current node, and then the right subtree) produces the node values in strictly increasing order, making BSTs naturally suited for sorted access.

However, if the inserted nodes happen to be in already sorted order (or all go to one side), the tree becomes a degenerate linked list whose height equals the number of nodes, `h=n`. In that degenerate case, each search, insertion, or deletion must walk along this chain, yielding a linear time complexity of `O(n)` rather than the desired logarithmic `O(log n)`. This is structurally equivalent to scanning a linked list in `O(n)`.

Binary search trees are widely used because they combine a sorted representation of data with fast, dynamic modifications. This makes them an obvious choice whenever a system must keep a constantly changing set of keys in order. For instance, in database engines and file systems, sorted map variants keep records organized for range queries. On disk-resident systems, well-known B-Trees and B+Trees extend the binary search concept into multi-way branching to serve as the high-performance backbone of SQL database indexing.

Java representation

A BST uses the same `BinaryTreeNode<T>` class definition as the binary tree. In Java, `<T>` represents a generic type, allowing a single class definition to operate on any reference or custom data type (e.g., `Integer`, `String`, etc.).

> **Note**
>
> For a type to be compatible with a BST, it must implement the `Comparable` interface so that its keys can be programmatically compared during search and insertion operations.

General (n-ary) trees and properties

A general or `n`-ary tree relaxes the binary constraint; namely, a node can have zero or `n` number of children, where n can be any integer or even unbounded. *Figure 5.5* shows a general `n`-ary tree with nodes having more than 2 children.

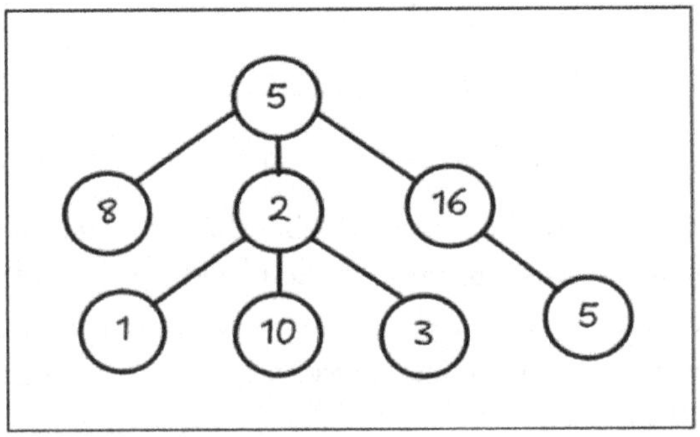

Figure 5.5: An n-nary tree

There is no inherent ordering of children, unless an order is explicitly imposed. The max number of children per node is up to a specified n, where n ≥ `0`.

General trees are the natural representation of many real-world hierarchies where a parent node may spawn an arbitrary number of sub-entities. Common examples of such applications include filesystem directories, XML/JSON parser trees, business organizational charts, and abstract syntax trees (ASTs) in programming language compilers.

Note

Do not confuse the variable n in an n-ary tree with the variable n in Big-O time complexity analysis.

- Tree Structure (n or k): Represents the branching factor, or the maximum number of children any single node has.
- Time Complexity (n): Represents the total number of nodes in the entire tree structure.

Java representation

The n-ary node keeps a list of children, allowing a node to have zero, one, or an arbitrary number of immediate children. This single collection field replaces the left and right references found in binary nodes, turning the node into a flexible container that can model any arbitrary branching factor. Below is a robust Java representation of an n-ary tree node:

```
public class NAryTreeNode<T> {
    private T value;
    private List<NAryTreeNode<T>> children = new ArrayList<>();
    public NAryTreeNode(T value) {
        this.value = value;
    }
    public NAryTreeNode(T value, List< NAryTreeNode<T>> children) {
        this.value = value;
        if (children != null) {
            this.children.addAll(children);
        }
    }
    public T getValue()
    {
        return value;
    }
    public void setValue(T v)
    {
        value = v;
    }
    public List< NAryTreeNode<T>> getChildren()
    {
```

```
        return Collections.unmodifiableList(children);
    }

    public void addChild(NAryTreeNode<T> child) {
        if (child != null) {
            children.add(child);
        }
    }
    public void addChildren(List< NAryTreeNode<T>> newChildren) {
        if (newChildren != null) {
            children.addAll(newChildren);
        }
    }
    public boolean removeChild(NAryTreeNode<T> child) {
        return children.remove(child);
    }
}
```

Abstract data type (ADT)

Before coding a complex algorithm, we must define the **Abstract Data Type (ADT)**. The ADT serves as a blueprint, separating conceptual behavior (what the structure does) from physical memory management (how the data is stored using arrays, pointers, or objects). This separation is key for writing flexible, reusable, and maintainable code. We begin with the n-Ary Tree ADT, a generalization to model nodes capable of having an arbitrary, unbounded number of children. We then specialize this concept into the Binary Tree ADT, which imposes the strict, yet mathematically powerful, constraint that limits every node to a maximum of two children (left and right). These interfaces define essential operations: accessing data, managing parent/child references, and checking structural properties.

N-ary tree ADT

The general, n-ary tree ADT is a hierarchical data structure where each node can have an arbitrary number of children. It consists of three primary components: the data stored within the node, a reference to its parent node (`null` for the root), and a list of its children.

Key operations include adding and removing children while maintaining bidirectional parent-child relationships, as well as checking if a node is a root (having no parent) or a leaf (bearing no children). The dynamic nature of this structure allows the children's list to expand dynamically as needed. The following code models the abstraction of an n-ary tree node:

```
public interface TreeNode<T> {
    T getData();
    void setData(T data);
    TreeNode<T> getParent();
    List<TreeNode<T>> getChildren();
    void addChild(TreeNode<T> child);
    void removeChild(TreeNode<T> child);
    boolean isRoot();
    boolean isLeaf();
}
```

Binary tree ADT

The binary tree ADT is a specialized tree structure in which every node may have at most two children: a left child and a right child. Each node holds a value along with two references that indicate when a child is absent.

The `BinaryTreeNode<T>` interface exposes the minimal set of operations needed to build and manipulate such a tree. `getData()` and `setData(T)` provide access to the node's value. `getLeft()/setLeft()` and `getRight()/setRight()` allow clients to attach or detach the two child subtrees. `getParent()` provides upward navigation, while the boolean predicates `isRoot()` and `isLeaf()` give constant-time checks for a node's position in the hierarchy. Together, these operations define the core interface for any binary tree implementation, enabling traversal, insertion, deletion, and other structural queries without exposing the underlying representation.

```
public interface BinaryTreeNode<T> {
    T getData();
    void setData(T data);
    BinaryTreeNode<T> getParent();
    BinaryTreeNode<T> getLeft();
    BinaryTreeNode<T> getRight();
    void setLeft(BinaryTreeNode<T> left);
    void setRight(BinaryTreeNode<T> right);
    boolean isRoot();
    boolean isLeaf();
}
```

Having defined ADT and its essential operations, we can now consider how to visit the nodes in a systematic way. Traversal is the mechanism that allows us to walk through the entire structure, whether for printing, searching, or performing computations that depend on the ordering of nodes. The next section will explore the classic traversal strategies (pre-order, in-order, post-order, and level order), explain how each relates to the tree's inherent hierarchy, and show how they can be implemented efficiently using the tree's minimal interface.

What is a traversal?

A traversal is an algorithmic approach for visiting every node in a tree exactly once, following a well-defined order. Depth-first search (DFS) and breadth-first search (BFS) traversals are two complementary ways to visit the nodes of any tree, binary or n-ary, with each imposing a different hierarchy on the exploration process. *Figure 5.6* illustrates the general traversal orders involving BFS vs. DFS in a tree.

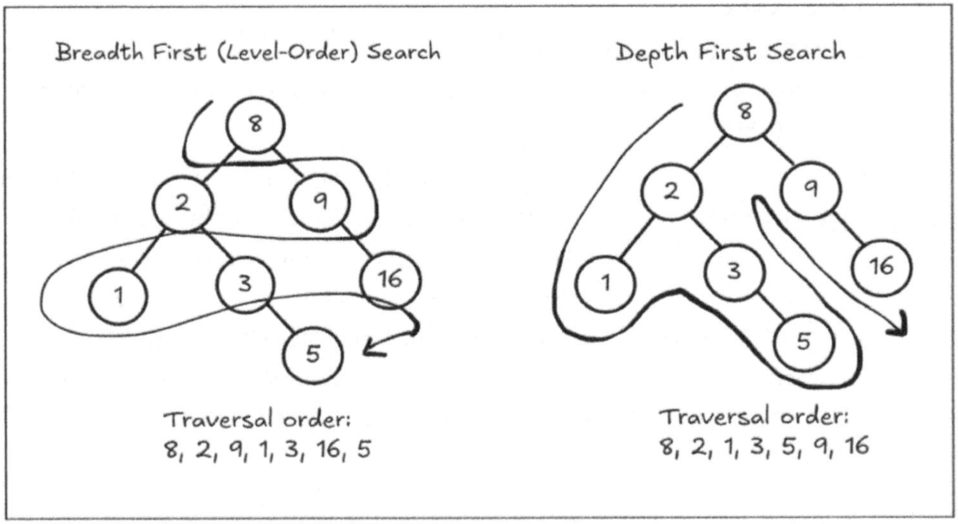

Figure 5.6: BFS vs DFS traversal orders

These traversal techniques underpin a wide range of tree-based algorithms. Common real-world examples include:

- Exploring file system via DFS to navigate directory trees to calculate folder size, list subdirectories, and recursively delete nested files.

- Manipulating web content in the Document Object Model (DOM) tree to render CSS, or locate specific HTML elements to dynamically modify application state.
- Serializing hierarchical tree structures into linear arrays or strings for efficient HTTP transmission and database storage.

Next, we will examine the DFS and BFS traversal mechanisms.

Depth-first traversal

DFS traversals can be implemented either recursively or iteratively. We will examine both approaches next, using binary trees as the underlying structure to demonstrate these traversal patterns.

Recursive methods: DFS

There are three classic **depth-first** strategies using recursion: pre-order, in-order, and post-order. Their visitation pattern can be summarized as follows:

- **Pre-order** (node, left, right): visit(node) → traverse(node.left) → traverse(node.right)
- **In-order** (left, node, right): traverse(node.left) → visit(node) → traverse(node.right)
- **Post-order** (left, right, node): traverse(node.left) → traverse(node.right) → visit(node)

Recursion follows the natural tree hierarchy: to traverse a subtree, call the same routine on that subtree. In the above, "left" signifies the left subtree of the node in question, whereas "right" signifies its right subtree. The base case is an empty (null) node.

Pre-order traversal (node, left, right)

This method calls for visitation (node) before exploration (children, or both the left and right subtrees, in that order).

```
public void preorder(Node root) {
    if (root == null) return;
    visit(root);            // Visit the node
    preorder(root.left);  // recurse left
    preorder(root.right); // recurse right
}
```

This approach is depth-first; stack depth equals tree height.

In-order traversal (left, node, right)

This method explores the left subtree first, then visits the current node, followed by exploring the right subtree.

```
public void inorder(Node root) {
    if (root == null) return;
    inorder(root.left);         // recurse left
    visit(root);                // visit root
    inorder(root.right);        // recurse right
}
```

This approach naturally produces values in ascending sorted order when applied to a binary search tree (BST). *Figure 5.7* shows the application of in-order traversal on a BST:

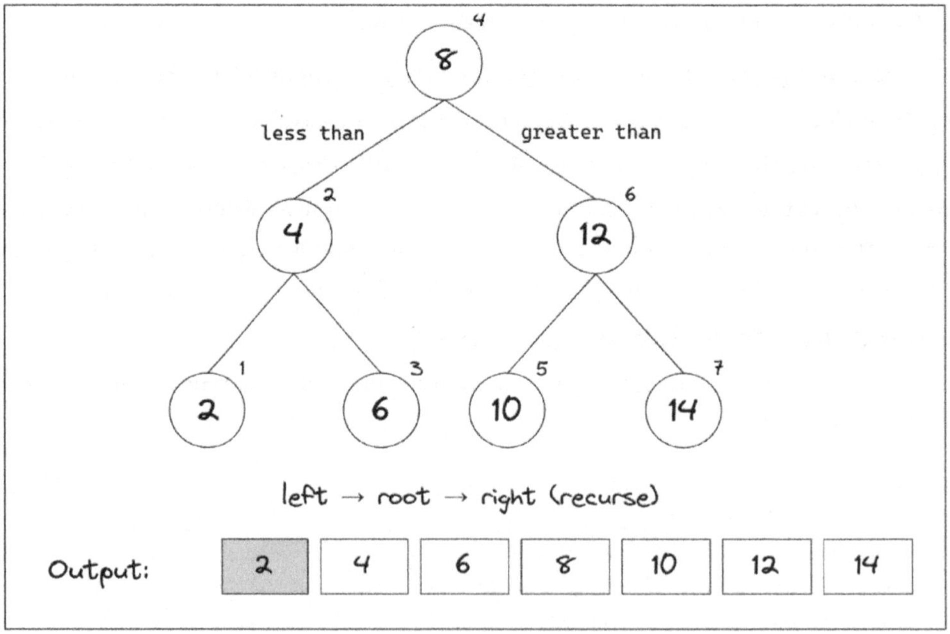

Figure 5.7: In-order traversal of a BST

In-order traversal is ideal for printing sorted lists and generating human-readable reports because it exploits the core BST property: all values in the left subtree are smaller than the node, and all values in the right subtree are larger than the node.

Post-order traversal (left, right, node)

This method calls for exploration (both left and right subtrees, in that order) before visitation. In other words, all children are processed before their parents.

```
public void postorder(Node root) {
    if (root == null) return;
    postorder(root.left);      // recurse left
    postorder(root.right);     // recurse right
    visit(root);               // visit root
}
```

This bottom-up approach is effective for operations that require deleting a tree, where we must safely free the children before freeing their parents, or computing the total size of a file directory, to name a few.

In summary, all three traversals maintain a time complexity of `O(n)` (linear time) and use `O(h)` space for the recursive call stack, where `h` is the height of the tree. However, the moment you process the data is critical: use pre-order for copying or writing; use in-order for reading sorted data; and use post-order for cleanup or deletion. *Figure 5.8* compares all three traversal approaches:

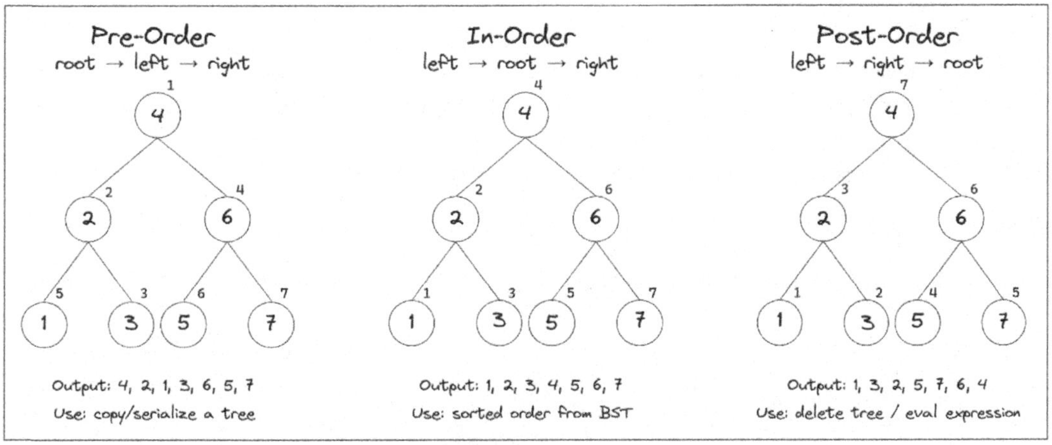

Figure 5.8: Comparison of pre-order, in-order, and post-order traversals

Iterative methods: DFS

Recursive DFS relies on the system's call stack. To avoid overflowing in a computing environment with limited recursion, we replace it with an explicit stack data structure. The following pseudocode demonstrates how this stack is used to perform a pre-order traversal.

Each node's right child is pushed first, followed by the left child, so that the left child is popped and processed before the right one.

```
procedure preorderIter(root):
    if root is null:
        return
    stack ← new empty stack
    stack.push(root)
    while stack is not empty:
        node ← stack.pop()
        visit(node)
        if node.right ≠ null:
            stack.push(node.right)
        if node.left ≠ null:
            stack.push(node.left)
```

In Java, the pre-order traversal is implemented as follows:

```
public <T> void preorderIter (Node<T> root) {
    if (root == null) return;
    Deque<Node<T>> stack = new ArrayDeque<>();
    stack.push(root);
    while (!stack.isEmpty()) {
        Node<T> cur = stack.pop();
        visit(cur);
        if (cur.getRight() != null) {
            stack.push(cur.getRight());
        }
        if (cur.getLeft() != null) {
            stack.push(cur.getLeft());
        }
    }
}
```

Figure 5.9 shows the step-by-step illustration of this pre-order iteration:

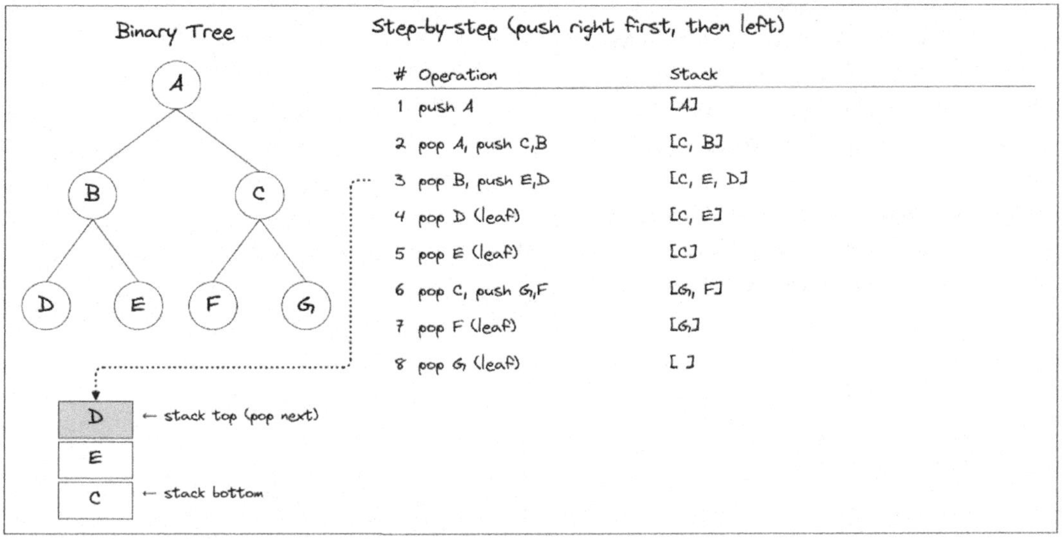

Figure 5.9: Iterative preorder mechanism using stack

The classic in-order algorithm uses a stack to mimic recursion, pushing all left ancestors along the current navigation path before processing the node and moving to its right child:

```
public <T> void inorderIter(Node<T> root) {
    Deque<Node<T>> stack = new ArrayDeque<>();
    Node<T> cur = root;
    while (cur != null || !stack.isEmpty()) {
        while (cur != null) {
            stack.push(cur);
            cur = cur.getLeft();
        }
        cur = stack.pop();
        visit(cur);
        cur = cur.getRight();
    }
}
```

Post-order is slightly more involved because we must process children *before* the node. We use one stack with last-visited tracking as follows:

```
public <T> void postorderIter(Node<T> root) {
    Deque<Node<T>> stack = new ArrayDeque<>();
    Node<T> lastVisited = null;
```

```
    Node<T> cur = root;
    while (cur != null || !stack.isEmpty()) {
        while (cur != null) {
            stack.push(cur);
            cur = cur.getLeft();
        }
        Node<T> peek = stack.peek();
        if (peek.getRight() != null && lastVisited != peek.getRight()) {
            cur = peek.getRight();
        } else {
            visit(peek);
            lastVisited = stack.pop();
        }
    }
}
```

DFS traversal complexity: recursion vs. iteration

When we traverse a tree recursively, the *time* cost is always linear in the number of nodes, `O(n)` because every node must be visited exactly once. The real difference lies in space consumption.

Recursive traversal uses the call stack; each call adds a frame of a few references, so the stack depth equals the tree height, yielding an `O(h)` space cost where:

- In a perfectly balanced tree, $h = O(\log n)$, which is quite memory efficient
- In the worst case, when the tree collapses into a linked list shape, its height $h = O(n)$, which can quickly deplete the call stack and trigger a stack overflow on large input

Iterative traversal uses an explicit stack whose depth is bounded by the tree's height, yielding $O(h)$ space.

Breadth-first traversal

BFS, also known as level-order traversal, visits the nodes level by level, starting at the root and moving downwards. Unlike depth-first search (DFS), which maps natively to the system call stack via recursion, true recursion cannot perform a level-order traversal because the call stack is inherently a **Last-In, First-Out (LIFO)** structure. Instead, BFS relies on a **First-In, First-Out (FIFO)** ordering mechanism, which can be implemented using iteration coupled with an explicit queue data structure. We will illustrate this using a binary tree as the underlying structure.

Iterative methods: BFS

Unlike recursive mechanisms, iterative BFS naturally employs a `Queue` (typically an `ArrayDeque`) because it follows a First-In, First-Out discipline that cascades traversal from the root level to the bottom of a tree in a level-order fashion. The canonical BFS for an `n`-ary tree follows the structure below:

```
public void bfs(Node root) {
    if (root == null) return;
    Queue<Node> q = new ArrayDeque<>();
    q.add(root);
    while (!q.isEmpty()) {
        Node cur = q.poll(); // FIFO: front
        visit(cur);
        for (Node child : cur.children)
            q.add(child);
    }
}
```

Node represents an `n`-ary node (or a binary node with `left` and `right` children) with a `List<Node> children`. Each iteration removes the next node from the front of the queue, visits its value, and enqueues its immediate children.

Since every node at level d is inserted into the queue before any node at level d+1 is removed, the traversal follows the tree's structural breadth. Consequently, BFS efficiently explores all nodes near the starting point (the root) without venturing deeply into the structure. This property makes it ideal for applications such as searching for degrees of separation between contacts, ranking mutual users in social networks, or generating localized news feeds that prioritize proximity content. *Figure 5.10* illustrates how a queue is used to process a binary tree in the BFS order:

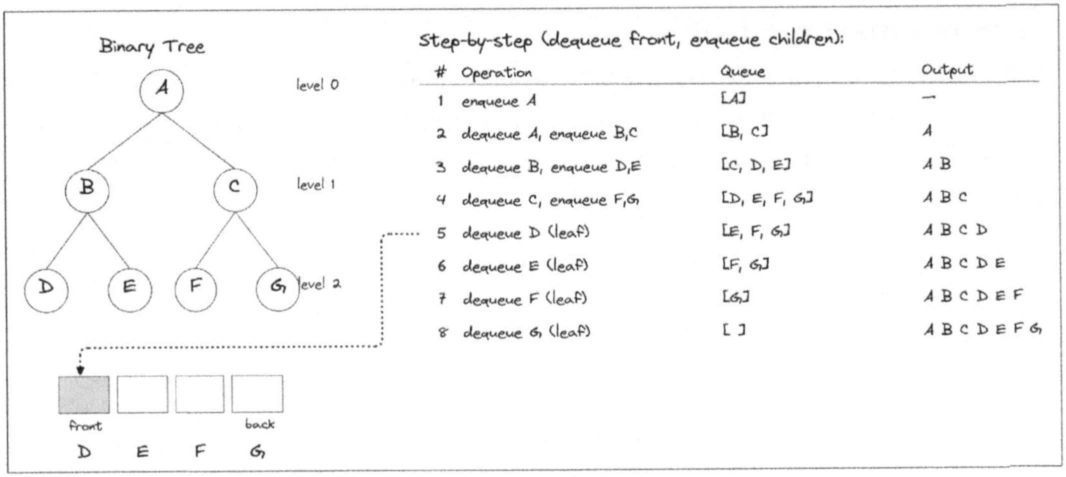

Figure 5.10: BST using queue

BFS traversal complexity: recursion vs. iteration

When deciding between a recursive or an iterative (queue-based) implementation of breadth-first search, we will consider three practical dimensions: time, space, and overhead.

The time cost is essentially identical for both strategies. Each node is visited once, and the algorithm performs a constant amount of work per node (insertion, deletion, and iterating over children). Thus, the asymptotic running time is linear: `O(n)`.

Space is more nuanced based on the traversal strategy employed:

- An **iterative** BFS keeps a single queue that, at its peak, holds all nodes residing at the widest horizontal layer of the tree. The maximum size of this queue equals the tree's maximum width `w` at any level/height: `O(w)`. For balanced binary trees, each level contains exactly twice as many nodes as the level above it. Because of this exponential growth, the bottom-most level (leaf) contains approximately half (`n/2`) of all the nodes in the entire tree. Therefore, the peak level-width simplifies asymptotically to `w = O(n)`. Conversely, in highly unbalanced (degenerate) trees, width collapses to `w = 1`. Thus, BFS can consume more memory than DFS for wide trees.
- A **recursive** BFS constructs a list for the current level and another for the next level, which together also occupy at most `w` nodes. The key distinction lies in the recursion stack: each level adds a call frame. For a tree of height `h`, the recursive version requires `O(h)` additional stack space beyond the frontier lists. For balanced trees, `h=O(log n)`,

so the extra space is negligible; but in highly unbalanced (degenerate) trees, `h=O(n)`, which may lead to stack overflow.

Stack frame overhead is a practical penalty that does not appear in the iterative form. Every recursive call consumes a stack frame that includes return addresses, local variables, and parameter slots. The iterative approach, by contrast, relies on a single loop and a queue object, resulting in a leaner memory profile and fewer JVM operations per node.

In short, both algorithms achieve the same theoretical efficiency, but the iterative queue implementation avoids the extra `O(h)` stack usage and associated overhead, making it the safer, more scalable choice in Java, especially for trees that may be wide, deep, or both.

BFS vs. DFS

Both BFS and DFS are systematic algorithms to visit every node in a tree or graph. Both traversal techniques achieve their goals by exploring nodes in fundamentally different patterns (*Figure 5.11*). The choice between the two is not about which one is "better," but which one is structurally appropriate for the problem at hand.

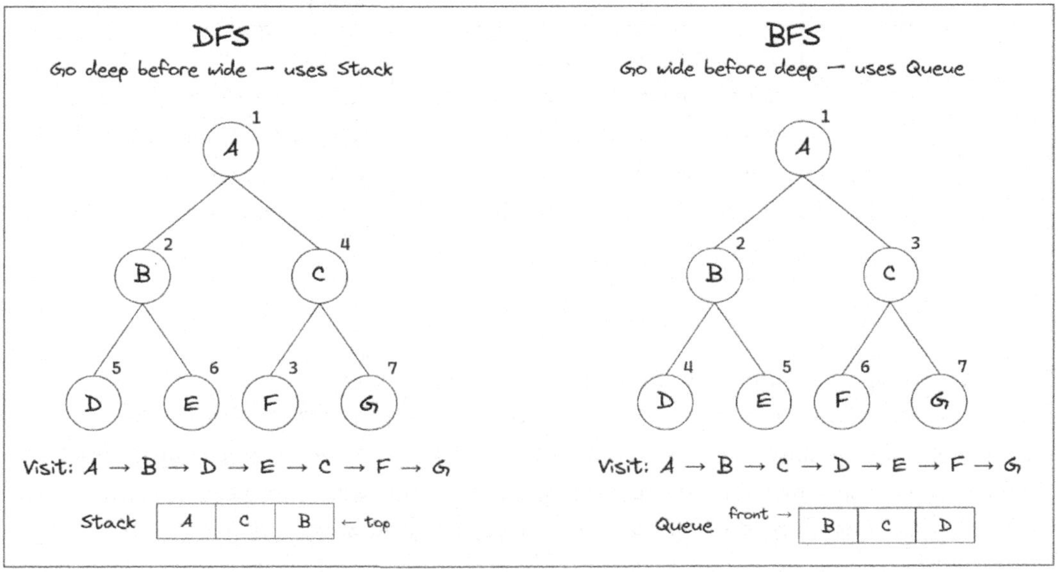

Figure 5.11: DFS vs BFS traversal mechanisms

The following table lists the difference between Breadth-first and Depth-first search side by side:

Feature	Breadth-First Search (BFS)	Depth-First Search (DFS)
Search Pattern	Level-Order (Wide)	Zig-Zag-Order (Deep)
Mechanism	Uses a queue (FIFO).	Uses a stack (LIFO) or recursion.
Traversal Order	Visits all neighbors at the current depth before moving to the next level.	Goes as far down a single path as possible before backtracking to explore siblings.
Space complexity	`O(w)` (Width): Requires space proportional to the maximum number of nodes at any one level.	`O(h)` (Height): Requires space proportional to the deepest path from the root to a leaf (the call stack).
Time Complexity	`O(n)` (Nodes): Visits every node exactly once.	`O(n)` (Nodes): Visits every node exactly once.
Best For	Shortest Path: Finding the minimum number of edges to reach a target. Connectivity-graph component checking, nearest neighbor search, level-order traversal.	Exhaustive Search: Backtracking algorithms, finding all paths, cycle detection, topological sorting, and tree serialization.

Table 5.1: Difference between Breadth-first and Depth-first searches

In terms of the space requirement, DFS explores deep down one path at a time; its memory footprint (namely, the recursion stack) is dictated by the depth of the tree `O(h)`. This is advantageous for shallow, wide trees, as the memory usage remains low. In contrast, BFS must track all nodes at the current level simultaneously; its memory usage is dictated by the width of the tree `O(w)`, benefiting tall, narrow trees where each level width remains small.

Trees in java collection framework

The **Java Collection Framework** (**JCF**) lacks a generic, hierarchical tree node structure for general-purpose use. Instead, it employs self-balancing binary search trees internally to deliver specific, sorted collection functionalities (*Figure 5.12*). There are several tree-based data structures that implement the `NavigableMap` and `NavigableSet` interfaces. These structures offer logarithmic `O(log n)` time complexity for basic operations and provide powerful navigation capabilities. The most used tree-based collections are `TreeMap` and `TreeSet`, which are implemented using red-black trees (a type of self-balancing binary search tree). Let's look at some canonical examples.

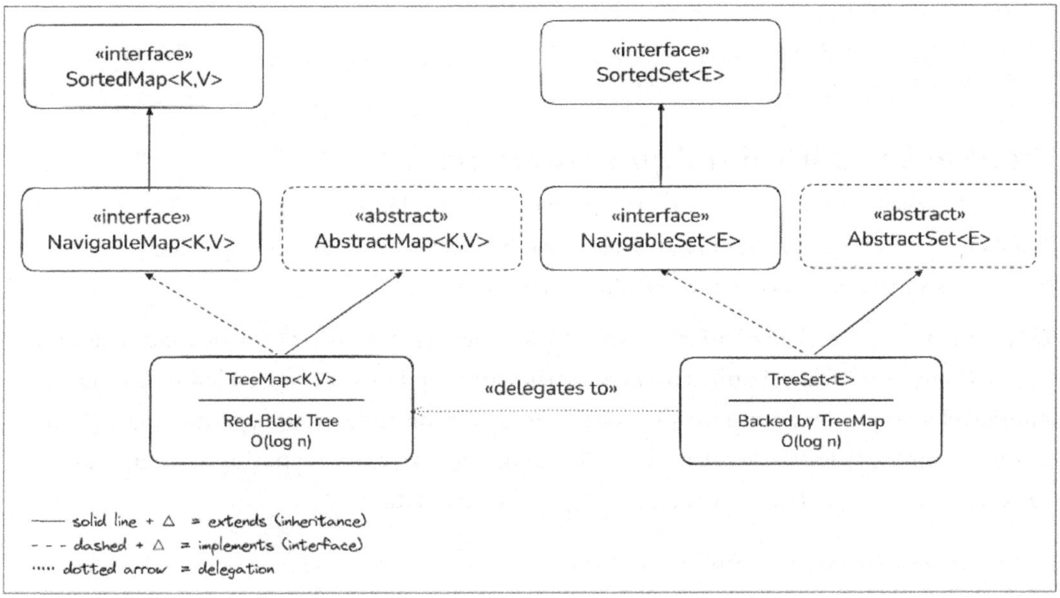

Figure 5.12: Tree-related components in JCF

TreeMap for sorted Key-Value storage

In Java, `TreeMap` is part of the `java.util` package and implements the `NavigableMap` interface. `TreeMap` maintains key-value pairs in sorted order by keys. It's useful when you need to iterate through elements in sorted order or perform range-queries on keys. Unlike `HashMap` which has no ordering guarantee, `TreeMap` maintains this sort dynamically, guaranteeing `O(log n)` time complexity for individual insertion, deletion, and lookup operations, and allowing full linear `O(n)` iteration of the sorted entries. Compared to `LinkedHashMap` which maintains insertion order, `TreeMap` sorts by keys, making it ideal for applications like grade books, dictionaries, or any scenario requiring sorted data access.

```
Map<String, Integer> grades = new TreeMap<>();
grades.put("Charlie", 78);
grades.put("Alice", 85);
grades.put("Bob", 92);
```

```
// The entries are automatically sorted
// by their keys in ascending order
// Outputs: {Alice=85, Bob=92, Charlie=78}
System.out.println(grades);

// Returns the lowest key in the map
// Outputs: Alice
System.out.println(grades.firstKey());
```

TreeSet for sorted unique elements

In Java, `TreeSet` is part of the `java.util` package and implements the `NavigableSet` interface. `TreeSet` stores unique elements in sorted order. It's useful for maintaining collections of distinct items that need to be accessed in sorted order.

Compared to `HashSet` which offers no structural ordering, a `TreeSet` provides sorted access. Unlike `ArrayList` which requires manual sorting after updates, a `TreeSet` maintains its internal element order automatically upon every insertion and deletion, guaranteeing `O(log n)` time complexity for these operations. This makes it perfect for scenarios like maintaining sorted lists of unique IDs, or extracting ranges of sorted data.

```
Set<Integer> numbers = new TreeSet<>();
numbers.add(5);
numbers.add(2);
numbers.add(8);
numbers.add(2); // Duplicate ignored

// [2, 5, 8]
System.out.println(numbers);
// 5 (greatest element < 6)
System.out.println(numbers.lower(6));
```

NavigableMap interface operations

`NavigableMap` as a Java interface provides ceiling and floor operations for finding elements relative to a given key, enabling efficient range-queries and navigation. While `HashMap` offers `O(1)` average access, it lacks navigation capabilities. `NavigableMap` provides `O(log n)` ceiling/floor operations that are essential for applications like time-series data analysis, range-based queries, or any scenario where you need to find elements within a specific range rather than exact matches.

```
NavigableMap<Integer, String> map = new TreeMap<>();
map.put(10, "Ten");
map.put(20, "Twenty");
map.put(30, "Thirty");

// Ceiling and floor operations
// 20=Twenty (least entry >= 15)
System.out.println(map.ceilingEntry(15));
// 20=Twenty (greatest entry <= 25)
System.out.println(map.floorEntry(25));
```

NavigableSet interface range operations

`NavigableSet` as a Java interface enables efficient `O(log n)` subset operations in its balanced tree, allowing you to work with ranges of elements within the sorted collection. Compared to `HashSet` or `ArrayList`, `NavigableSet` provides fast range operations without requiring manual sorting. This is invaluable for applications like database query results, time-based filtering, or any scenario where you need to process elements within a specific range rather than all elements.

```
NavigableSet<String> fruits = new TreeSet<>();
fruits.add("apple");
fruits.add("banana");
fruits.add("cherry");
fruits.add("date");

// Subsets based on range
// Up to and including cherry
NavigableSet<String> subset =fruits.headSet("cherry", true);
// Output: [apple, banana, cherry]
System.out.println(subset);
```

Custom tree sorting with comparator

`TreeSet` with custom comparator allows sorting by custom criteria rather than natural ordering, providing flexible sorting options. While `ArrayList` can be sorted with `Collections.sort()`, it requires expensive re-sorting after each modification. In contrast, a `TreeSet` maintains its sorted order automatically based on the custom criteria during every insertion and deletion, making it useful for applications like sorting by multiple fields (i.e., ordering student records by courses and grades received), or any scenario requiring automatic sorting based on a non-natural ordering pattern.

```
// [elephant, cat, dog] (by length)
System.out.println(words);
TreeSet<String> words =
new TreeSet<>(Comparator
.comparingInt(String::length)
.reversed()
.thenComparing(Comparator.naturalOrder()));
words.add("cat");
words.add("elephant");
words.add("dog");
System.out.println(words); // [elephant, cat, dog]
```

Tree-based collections (`TreeMap`, `TreeSet`) are ideal when you need data maintained in sorted order and efficient (`O(log n)`) range queries or navigation operations (`floor`, `ceiling`, `subMap`, etc.). These capabilities are not available on hash-based collections. If you don't need ordering, hash-based collections are typically faster for basic lookup/insert (`O(1)` average).

Summary

Trees are fundamental, non-linear data structures used to model hierarchical relationships, ranging from file systems to organizational charts. The general N-Ary Tree allows nodes to branch arbitrarily, while the Binary Tree imposes the restriction of having at most two children (left and right), giving rise to specialized variants like the Binary Search Tree (BST). Defining these structures via an Abstract Data Type (ADT) allows us to separate the conceptual rules (parent/child relationships, constraints) from the physical memory implementation, ensuring code is flexible and robust.

To interact with these structures, we use systematic traversal algorithms. These are grouped into two complementary strategies: Breadth-First Search (BFS), which explores all nodes at a given level before moving to the next (ideal for shortest path problems), and Depth-First Search (DFS), which drills deep into one path before backtracking (ideal for exhaustive searching). DFS further utilizes specific patterns: pre-order (process parent first, useful for copying), in-order (process elements in sorted sequence, ideal for BSTs), and post-order (process children first, crucial for cleanup or deletion). Ultimately, choosing the correct tree type and the appropriate traversal pattern determines whether the solution can efficiently and correctly solve a problem in `O(n)` time.

Now that we have explored how trees organize data hierarchically, how to construct and traverse them, and how to manage their memory and performance characteristics, we can turn our attention to priority queues and heaps. This specialized, tree-based data structure is designed to instantly surface the highest or lowest priority item. *Figure 5.13* is a summary diagram of trees for a quick overview.

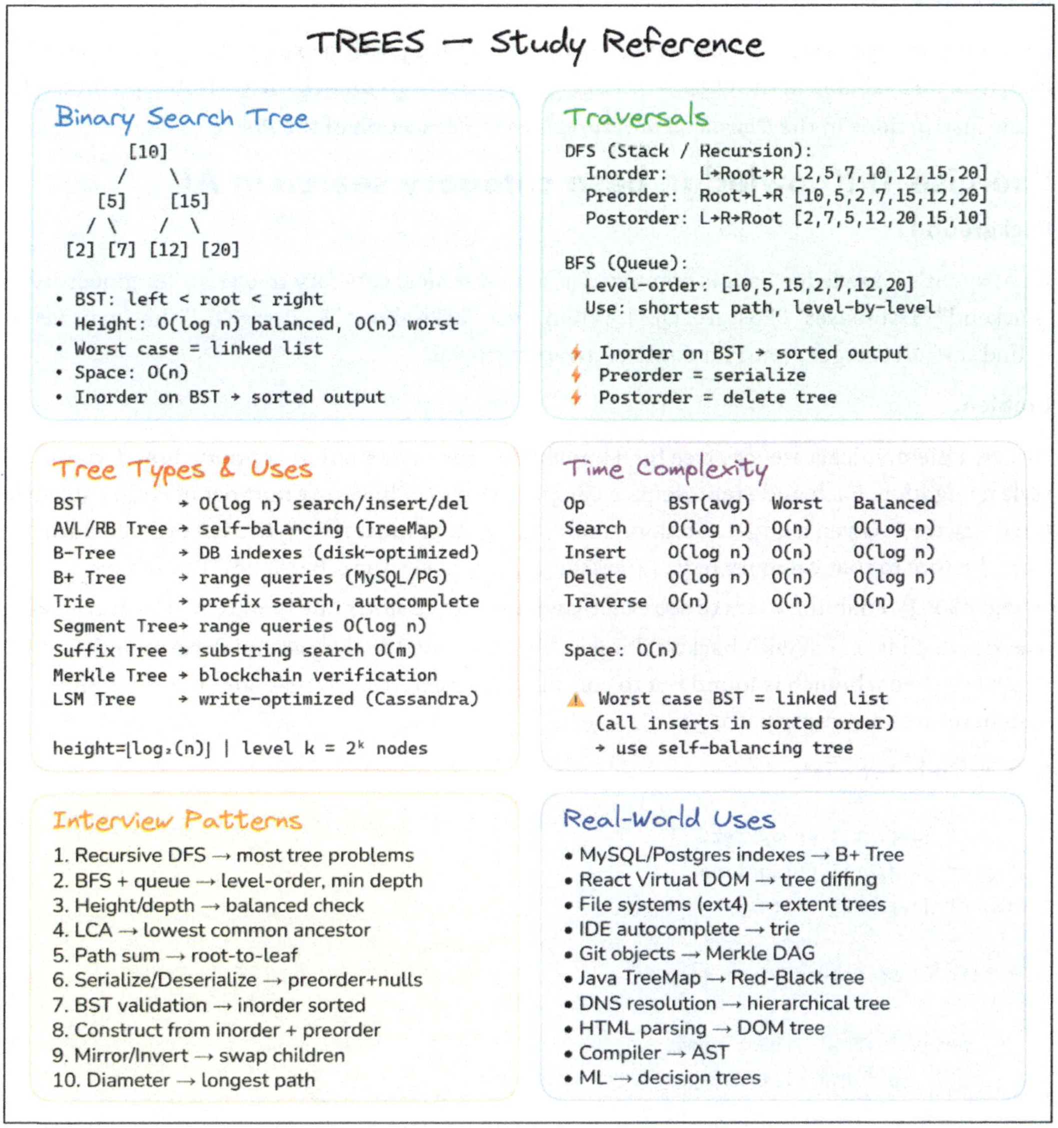

Figure 5.13: Summary diagram of trees

In the next chapter, we will introduce the fundamentals of priority queues and heaps, discuss how they organize elements directly via index mathematics, and examine the core operations that operate on them: from insertion and extraction to efficient element restructuring, building upon our foundational data structure concepts.

Exercises

Fully annotated Java solutions, practical examples, and algorithm explanations for these exercises are available in the `Chapter05` folder on GitHub. To unlock the GitHub repo link, refer to the instructions in the *Download the example code files* section of the *Preface*.

Exercise 1: Knowledge base category search in AI

Background

An AI agent's knowledge base is organized as a hierarchical category tree (e.g., "Engineering" "Backend" "Databases" "PostgreSQL"). When a user asks about "PostgreSQL," the agent needs to find the full category path for context-aware retrieval.

Problem

Design a hierarchical category tree for a knowledge base system that supports breadcrumb-style navigation. Each node represents a category and may have any number of child categories (an n-ary tree). Given a target category name, the system must return the full ordered path from the root to that category (e.g., `[Knowledge, Engineering, Backend, Databases, PostgreSQL]`), enabling users to see exactly where a topic sits in the hierarchy. The traversal uses depth-first search with backtracking: nodes are added to the path on descent and removed when a branch is found not to contain the target. If the target does not exist, the system returns an empty path.

Starter Code Template

```
import java.util.ArrayList;
import java.util.Collections;
import java.util.List;

public class CategoryTree {

    private final String name;
    private final List<CategoryTree> children;

    public CategoryTree(String name) {
        this.name = name;
```

```
        this.children = new ArrayList<>();
    }

    // Add a child category and return it (for fluent tree construction)
    public CategoryTree addChild(String childName) {
        // TODO: create child node, add to children list, return it
    }

    public List<String> findPath(String target) {
        // TODO: initialize path, call dfs, return path or empty list
    }

    private boolean dfs(CategoryTree node, String target, List<String> path) {
        // TODO:
        // 1. Add current node name to path
        // 2. Base case: if node matches target → return true
        // 3. Recurse into each child → return true if found
        // 4. Backtrack: remove current node, return false
    }

    public static void main(String[] args) {
        // Build tree
        CategoryTree root = new CategoryTree("Knowledge");
        // TODO: add categories, e.g. Engineering → Backend → Databases →
PostgreSQL

        // Test 1: existing target → full path
        // Test 2: missing target → empty list
    }
}
```

Assumptions and Constraints

1. Tree is built once, queried many times (read heavy)
2. Single-threaded; no concurrent modification during traversal
3. Category names are non-null caller-provided strings
4. Tree fits in memory; recursion depth won't overflow the stack
5. Exactly one path from root to any node (tree, not graph)
6. Time: `O(n)` worst case, each node visited once

7. Space: `O(h)`, bounded by tree height
8. Duplicate names allowed; returns first match in DFS order
9. Target not found returns an empty immutable list, never null
10. No parent pointers; every lookup traverses from root
11. Append only; no deletion or restructuring after construction
12. No input validation; caller ensures non-null names and no cycles

Test Case 1: Target exists deep in the tree

- **Input**:
  - See *Figure 5.14* for the knowledge tree structure
  - **Target:** `"PostgreSQL"`
- **Expected Output**: `["Knowledge", "Engineering", "Backend", "Databases", "PostgreSQL"]`
- **Verification:** Path contains all ancestors in order from root to target

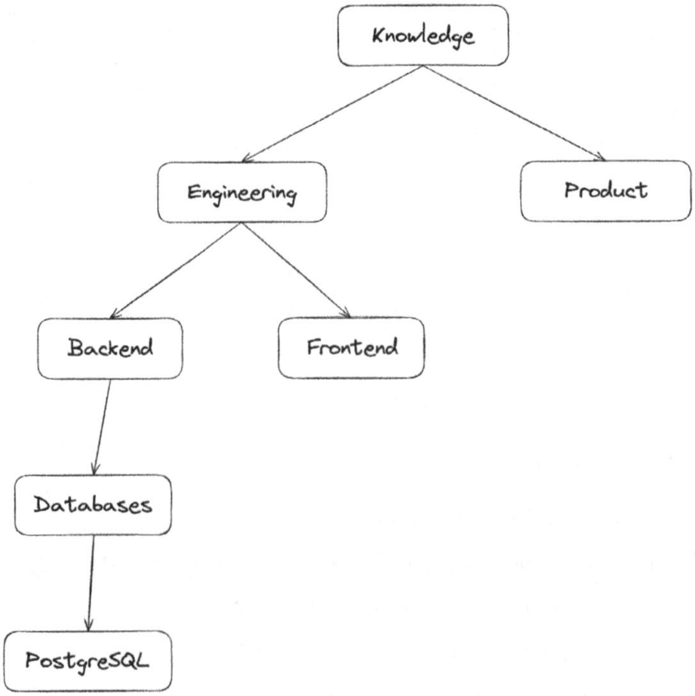

Figure 5.14: Knowledge tree

Test Case 2: Target does not exist

- **Input**:
  - Same tree structure as shown in *Figure 5.14*
  - **Target:** "Redis"
- **Expected Output**: [] (empty list)
- **Verification**:
  - Returns `Collections.emptyList()`, not `null`
  - All nodes were visited and backtracked (no residual state in path)

Solution

The algorithm answers a simple question: "*What is the route from the root category down to a target category?*" It does this with DFS, exploring one branch as deeply as possible before trying another, while maintaining a running path that acts as a breadcrumb trail.

Everything begins in the public entry point, which sets up an empty path and kicks off the recursive search from the root node (`this`):

```
public List<String> findPath(String target) {
    List<String> path = new ArrayList<>();
    if (dfs(this, target, path)) {
        return path;
    }
    return Collections.emptyList();
}
```

If the `dfs` traversal succeeds, the `path` list has been populated with the full route and we return it. If it fails, the target doesn't exist anywhere in the tree, so we return an empty list rather than `null`. Callers never have to null-check.

Inside `dfs`, the first thing we do at every node is optimistically assume it might be part of the route, so we add its name to the path:

```
path.add(node.name);
```

Path is an ArrayList running in LIFO order (acting as a Stack) to enable this traversal. This is the "push": dropping a breadcrumb. Immediately after, we check whether we've actually arrived at our destination:

```
if (node.name.equals(target)) {
    return true;
}
```

If this node is the target, we're done. Returning true here is significant: it means the path, exactly as it stands right now, spells out the complete root-to-target route, and that true will ripple all the way back up the call chain without disturbing the path.

If this node isn't the target, we don't give up. We descend into each of its children and recurse, hoping one of their subtrees contains what we're looking for:

```
for (CategoryTree child : node.children) {
    if (dfs(child, target, path)) {
        return true;
    }
}
```

The moment any child reports success, we short-circuit and propagate true upward without bothering to check the remaining siblings. This is why, in a tree where the target sits deep on the left, branches to the right are never even visited.

But if we exhaust every child and none of them leads to the target, then this node is a dead end. It is not on the route, so we must undo the breadcrumb we dropped on the way in and report failure to our parent:

```
path.remove(path.size() - 1);
return false;
```

This removal is the backtracking step, and it's what keeps the path honest; any node still in the list is guaranteed to be a true ancestor of the target. The path list grows and shrinks in perfect lockstep with the recursion, i.e., pushing a name on every descent and popping it on every dead-end return, so by the time the target is found, the list contains precisely the nodes along the successful route and nothing else. Putting everything together, we arrive at the following:

```
public class CategoryTree {
    String name;
    List<CategoryTree> children;
```

```
    public CategoryTree(String name) {
        this.name = name;
        this.children = new ArrayList<>();
    }

    public List<String> findPath(String target) {
        List<String> path = new ArrayList<>();
        if (dfs(this, target, path)) {
            return path;
        }
        return Collections.emptyList();
    }

    private boolean dfs(CategoryTree node, String target, List<String> path) {
        if (node == null) return false;
        path.add(node.name);
        if (node.name.equals(target)) return true;
        for (CategoryTree child : node.children) {
            if (dfs(child, target, path)) return true;
        }
        path.remove(path.size() - 1);
        return false;
    }
}
```

Running this through *Test Case 1*, the code builds the tree as follows:

```
CategoryTree root = new CategoryTree("Knowledge");

CategoryTree engineering = root.addChild("Engineering");
root.addChild("Product");

CategoryTree backend = engineering.addChild("Backend");
engineering.addChild("Frontend");

CategoryTree databases = backend.addChild("Databases");
databases.addChild("PostgreSQL");

root.findPath("PostgreSQL");
// → [Knowledge, Engineering, Backend, Databases, PostgreSQL]
```

The runtime trace (DFS with backtracking) is as follows:

- **Knowledge** path `[Knowledge]` not target, recurse into children
- **Engineering** path `[Knowledge, Engineering]` not target, recurse into children
- **Backend** path `[Knowledge, Engineering, Backend]` not target, recurse into children
- **Databases** path `[Knowledge, Engineering, Backend, Databases]` not target, recurse into children
- **PostgreSQL** path `[Knowledge, Engineering, Backend, Databases, PostgreSQL]` match, return `true`
- Path unwinds with no backtracking (target found on first descent); `Frontend` and `Product` never visited due to short-circuit on `return true`

Complexity

- **Time: O(n)**
  The time complexity is `O(n)`, where n is the number of nodes. Each node is visited at most once with constant work per node (an `equals` check, an `add`, and possibly a `remove`). The worst case occurs when the target is missing or last-visited, requiring a full traversal; finding the target early short-circuits via `return true`. Notably, `path.remove(path.size() - 1)` removes from the end of an `ArrayList` in `O(1)`, which prevents the total from degrading to $O(n^2)$.
- **Space: O(h)**
  The space complexity is `O(h)`, where h is the tree height. Both the recursion call stack and the `path` list hold at most one entry per level, growing and shrinking together as the search descends and backtracks. This means `O(log n)` for a balanced tree and `O(n)` for a degenerate, linear one. In short, the `O(n)` time is unavoidable since confirming absence requires checking every node, but the `O(h)` space is far more economical than `O(n)` for balanced trees.

Exercise 2: Validate binary search tree

Complete the following function definition to test if a binary tree is a BST or not:

```
public boolean isBST(TreeNode node, int min, int max) {
// YOUR CODE HERE
}
```

Assumptions and Constraints

- The tree is a binary tree of integer-valued nodes accessed via `getValue()`, `getLeft()`, `getRight()`
- A node is a valid BST node following the BST ordering property
- An empty tree (`node == null`) is trivially a BST, returning `true`
- The root call uses the widest range: `isBST(root, Integer.MIN_VALUE, Integer.MAX_VALUE)`
- Duplicates are disallowed in the strict definition (`min < v < max`); if allowed, the chosen side (left or right) must be applied consistently
- Each node is visited once; traversal is conducted in `O(n)` or `O(|v|)` time and `O(height)` space

Test Case 1

- Root `5`, left subtree `3` (children `1, 4`), right subtree `8` (children `7, 9`). Every node respects its inherited bounds. `isBST(root, MIN, MAX)` returns `true`.

Test Case 2

- Root `5`, left child `3`, right child `8`, where `8`'s **left child is 4**. Although `4 < 8` satisfies the immediate parent, `4` sits in `5`'s right subtree where the inherited bound requires values `> 5`. `isBST(root, MIN, MAX)` returns `false`.

Exercise 3: Pre-order from in-order implementation

Given the **in-order** and **post-order** traversal sequences of a binary tree (values are **distinct**), reconstruct the tree and output its **pre-order** traversal.

```
import java.util.*;
public class PreOrderFromInPost {
    public static String preOrder(int[] inorder, int[] postorder) {
        // TODO: Last of postorder is the root; split inorder around it; recurse.
        return "";
    }
}
```

Assumptions and Constraints

- All node values are distinct (required to locate the root unambiguously in in-order)
- `Inorder` and `postorder` have the same length and represent the same tree

- Empty inputs (`length == 0`) represent an empty tree, leading to empty pre-order output
- Values are integers; output is comma-separated, no trailing comma
- Each value is processed once with a hash-map index: `O(n)` time, `O(n)` space
- Inputs are assumed valid (no need to detect malformed/mismatched sequences for the base problem)

Test Case 1

- **Input (in-order):** `[9,3,15,20,7]`
- **Input (post-order):** `[9,15,7,20,3]`
- **Output:** `3,9,20,15,7`

The worked example above verifies the split/recursion and right-before-left post-order consumption

Test Case 2

- **Input (in-order):** `[1]`
- **Input (post-order):** `[1]`
- **Output:** `1`

Smallest non-empty tree; checks base case and no-trailing-comma formatting

Hints

- The **last** element of post-order is the **root**.
- Find that root in in-order: everything to its **left** is the left subtree, everything to its **right** is the right subtree. The split index gives the sizes of each subtree.
- Recurse to rebuild the tree, then do a normal pre-order walk over it.
- Consume post-order from the right (root, then right subtree, then left subtree), so build the right child before the left when walking post-order backward. This keeps the moving post-order pointer aligned with the values you pop.

Exercise 4: Iterative post-order traversal with a single stack

Given the root of a binary tree, implement an iterative post-order traversal that uses a single stack and prints the node values separated by commas (no trailing comma).

Note that recursion is not allowed; the point is to simulate the recursive call stack explicitly.

Starter Code Template

```
import java.util.*;
class TreeNode {
    int val;
    TreeNode left, right;
    TreeNode(int val) { this.val = val; }
}
public class PostOrder {
    public static String postOrder(TreeNode root) {
        // TODO: single-stack iterative post-order.
        return "";
    }
}
```

With the following test harness:

```
    public static void main(String[] args) {
        int passed = 0, total = 0;

        //          1
        //         / \
        //        2   3
        //       / \
        //      4   5
        TreeNode root = new TreeNode(1);
        root.left = new TreeNode(2);
        root.right = new TreeNode(3);
        root.left.left = new TreeNode(4);
        root.left.right = new TreeNode(5);
        total++; passed += check("full tree", postOrder(root), "4,5,2,3,1");
        TreeNode single = new TreeNode(1);
        total++; passed += check("single node", postOrder(single), "1");
        System.out.printf("%n%d/%d checks passed.%n", passed, total);
    }
    private static int check(String name, String actual, String expected) {
        boolean ok = actual.equals(expected);
        System.out.printf("[%s] %-12s expected=\"%s\" actual=\"%s\"%n",
                ok ? "PASS" : "FAIL", name, expected, actual);
        return ok ? 1 : 0;
    }
```

Assumptions and Constraints

- Input is the root of a binary tree; `root == null` is valid (prints an empty string)
- Node values are integers, printed via `toString`; values may repeat
- The tree may be skewed (degenerate to a linked list); iteration must not assume balance
- Output is a single line: values separated by `commas` with no trailing comma or spaces
- Each node is visited once `O(n)` time, `O(n)` space for the stack

Test Case 1

- Full small tree `4,5,2,3,1`.
- Root `1`, left `2` (children `4`, `5`), right `3`. Post-order processes the leaves first, then their parents, then the root.

Test Case 2

- Single node `1`.
- Root `1` with no children. Output is just `1` with no commas (verifies the no-trailing-comma joining logic and the smallest non-null case).

Hints

- Use a **single stack** to simulate the recursive post-order traversal.
- Push the root, then pop-and-record each node while pushing its children **left before right**. This produces the reverse of post-order (`node right left`); **reverse the result** at the end.
- Equivalently: build the sequence `root, right, left` and reverse it to get `left, right, root`.

Exercise 5: Level-order traversal without a queue

Given the root of a **binary tree**, perform a **level-order traversal** (top to bottom, left to right within each level) **without using a queue**. Group the output by level.

Output format: values within a level joined by "," levels separated by ";", no trailing separators.

Example: 1;2,3;4,5

```
      1
     / \
    2   3
   / \
```

```
    4   5


Level order:  level 0 = [1], level 1 = [2,3], level 2 = [4,5]
Output:       1;2,3;4,5
```

Starter Code Template

```
import java.util.*;
class TreeNode {
    int val;
    TreeNode left, right;
    TreeNode(int val) { this.val = val; }
}

public class LevelOrder {
    public static String levelOrder(TreeNode root) {
        // TODO: no queue - use level-indexed DFS (or two stacks).
        return "";
    }
}
```

Assumptions and Constraints

- Input is the root of a binary tree; `root == null` is valid (prints an empty string)
- Node values are integers; values may repeat
- "No queue" means no FIFO structure. Use the recursion stack (level-indexed DFS) or stacks
- The tree may be skewed; the algorithm must not assume balance
- Within each level, values must appear left to right
- Output: levels separated by semicolons, and values of each level by commas. No trailing ...
- Each node visited once `O(n)` time, `O(n)` space (buckets + recursion/stack depth)

Test Case 1

- Full tree `1;2,3;4,5`.
- Root `1`, left `2` (children `4`, `5`), right `3`. Verifies correct level grouping and left-to-right order.

Test Case 2

- Single node `1`.
- Root `1`, no children. One level, no separators; checks the smallest non-null case and the no-trailing-separator logic.

Hints

The natural tool is a queue (BFS) but you can avoid it in two ways:

- **Track level counts/level index:** DFS while passing the current depth; append each value into the bucket for its level. The recursion call stack replaces the queue.
- **Two stacks:** maintain a "current level" stack and a "next level" stack; pop the current, push children to next, then swap when the current empties (this is also the basis of *zigzag*).

Exercise 6: Memory-efficient traversal

Explain how you can reduce the stack space used by iterative DFS in a highly unbalanced tree.

A standard iterative DFS pushes *both* children of every node:

```
stack.push(node);
// ... pop, then:
if (node.right != null) stack.push(node.right);
if (node.left  != null) stack.push(node.left);
```

On a tree skewed to one side, you keep pushing the "other" child at every level, so peak stack size grows to `O(n)`, the height of the tree.

Detailed explanations of memory-efficient traversal alternatives are available in the `MemoryEfficientTraversal.text` file inside the `Chapter05` folder on GitHub. To unlock the GitHub repo link, refer to the instructions in the *Download the example code files* section of the *Preface*.

Exercise 7: Maximum depth of binary tree

Given the root of a binary tree, return its maximum depth. The maximum depth is the number of nodes along the longest path from the root node down to the farthest leaf node.

Starter Code Template

```
public class MaxDepthBinaryTree {
    public int maxDepth(TreeNode root) {
        // Your code here
```

```
        return 0;
    }
}
```

Assumptions and Constraints

- Binary tree node structure: `TreeNode` with `val`, `left`, and `right` fields
- Node values can be any integer (positive, negative, or zero)
- Tree can be empty (root is `null`)
- Number of nodes can be up to 10^4
- Must use a recursive or iterative approach
- Time complexity should be `O(n)`, where `n` is the number of nodes

Test Case 1

- **Input**: `[3,9,20,null,null,15,7]`
- **Output**: `3`

Test case 2

- **Input**: `[1,null,2]`
- **Output**: `2`

Exercise 8: Binary tree side view

Given the root of a binary tree, imagine yourself standing on the right side of it. Return the values of the nodes you can see, ordered from top to bottom.

Starter Code Template

```
import java.util.*;
public class RightSideView {
    public List<Integer> rightSideView(TreeNode root) {
        // Your code here
        return new ArrayList<>();
    }
}
```

Assumptions and Constraints

- Binary tree node structure: `TreeNode` with `val`, `left`, and `right` fields
- Node values can be any integer

- Tree can be empty (root is `null`)
- Number of nodes can be up to 10^4
- Must return the rightmost node value at each level
- Time complexity should be `O(n)`, where n is the number of nodes

Test case 1

- **Input**: `[1,2,3,null,5,null,4]`
- **Output**: `[1,3,4]`

Test case 2

- **Input**: `[1,null,3]`
- **Output**: `[1,3]`

Exercise 9: Lowest common ancestor of a binary tree

Given a binary tree, find the **lowest common ancestor** (**LCA**) of two given nodes in the tree. The LCA is defined as the lowest node that has both `p` and `q` as descendants (where we allow a node to be a descendant of itself).

Starter Code Template

```
public class LowestCommonAncestor {
    public TreeNode lowestCommonAncestor(TreeNode root, TreeNode p, TreeNode q) {
        // Your code here
        return null;
    }
}
```

Assumptions and Constraints

- Binary tree node structure: `TreeNode` with `val`, `left`, and `right` fields
- All node values are unique
- Both nodes `p` and `q` exist in the tree
- Node values can be any integer
- Tree can be empty (root is `null`)
- Number of nodes can be up to 10^4
- Must find the actual node reference, not just the value
- Time complexity should be `O(n)`, where n is the number of nodes

Test case 1

- **Input:** `[3,5,1,6,2,0,8,null,null,7,4], p = 5, q = 1`
- **Output**: 3

Test case 2

- **Input:** `[3,5,1,6,2,0,8,null,null,7,4], p = 5, q = 4`
- **Output**: 5

6

Priority Queues and Heaps

In many real-world systems, we must process items not in the order they arrive, but according to their relative importance or urgency. Think of an emergency room where patients are treated by the severity of their condition, or of an operating-system scheduler that grants CPU time to processes based on a priority level. In both cases, a naïve strategy, like scanning the entire set of waiting elements to pick the next one, would take `O(n)` time per decision and quickly become a performance bottleneck.

In this chapter, we will explore the priority queue data structure in depth, examining its structural properties, implementation strategies, and the algorithms that maintain its invariants such as heaps. We will see how binary heaps serve as the most common building block for realizing these "process-by-priority" workloads, to drive relative ordering over absolute position dynamically.

What is a priority queue?

A priority queue is an abstract data type that holds a set of elements, each paired with a numeric or comparable priority value. The data structure guarantees that the most important element can be identified in constant time, unlike a conventional FIFO queue. *Figure 6.1* shows a simple array-based representation of this structure, where the priorities are explicitly stored alongside the data.

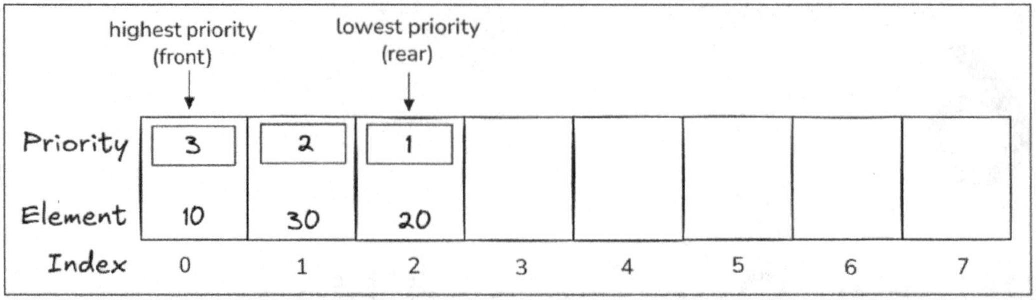

Figure 6.1: Priority queue implementation in an array

The above figure also hints at the drawbacks of a naïve, unsorted array implementation. While adding to the very end of a pre-allocated array is `O(1)`, finding the highest-priority element requires an exhaustive linear scan through all items, resulting in `O(n)` time complexity for removal. Conversely, while linking a new node in a sorted linked list is `O(1)`, we must first locate its proper sorted position by traversing the list from the beginning (linear scan), making the overall enqueue operation `O(n)`. This is shown in *Figure 6.2*.

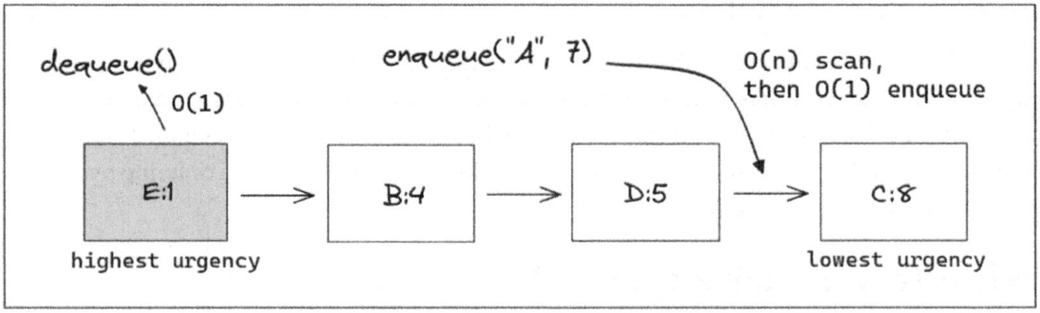

Figure 6.2: Priority queue implementation in a sorted linked list

Regardless of using array or linked list as the implementation details, either the insertion or the removal operation must scan the entire collection and incur an `O(n)` cost, which quickly becomes a bottleneck in high-throughput environments such as emergency room triage or operating-system schedulers.

The heap data structure addresses this inefficiency by enforcing a partial-ordering invariant that allows both insertion and extraction of the extreme-priority element to run in `O(log n)` time while still enabling `O(1)` access to the top element. We will detail this implementation later in the chapter, using the terms insertion/enqueue and deletion/dequeue interchangeably.

In short, the priority queue defines the interface of the operations required, whereas the heap provides an efficient implementation of those operations. We will study heap in detail in a later section. For now, let's look at two common applications of priority queues next.

Example 1: Seat assignment on a flight

Flight seat assignments often use a priority-queue system. Each passenger receives a priority tag that reflects ticket class, frequent-flyer tier, or special needs. When cabin managers begin boarding, they consult the queue to decide who sits first: a business-class traveler, an elite frequent-flyer, or a family traveling with a newborn will all outrank a standard economy guest. The crew removes the passenger with the highest priority from the queue and assigns the best available seat, typically first-class or premium economy, before moving on to the next highest-priority individual. If a new reservation is made during this process, the system inserts it into the queue and re-evaluates the ordering, which can reposition a freshly booked first-class ticket ahead of an economy passenger who is still waiting to board. This dynamic ordering guarantees that higher-status passengers receive preferential seating early, while still allowing all remaining passengers to be accommodated efficiently and transparently.

Example 2: Top K elements

In a massively multiplayer online racing game, millions of players finish races every minute, each generating a new score update that must be ingested with sub-second latency. The challenge is to maintain a globally accurate "top-10" leaderboard in real time, despite the high throughput (tens of thousands of updates per second) and the distributed nature of the game servers. Every score change potentially alters a player's position in the ranking, so the system must support fast insertions, deletions, and priority updates while consuming only modest memory and allowing concurrent updates from multiple regions. The goal is to deliver the current top-10 list to users instantly, with no stale data, and to recover quickly from any node failure without losing recent results. *Figure 6.3* shows an example of a top-10 leaderboard aggregated based on the use of a priority queue, where each node in the tree represents a unique player ID:

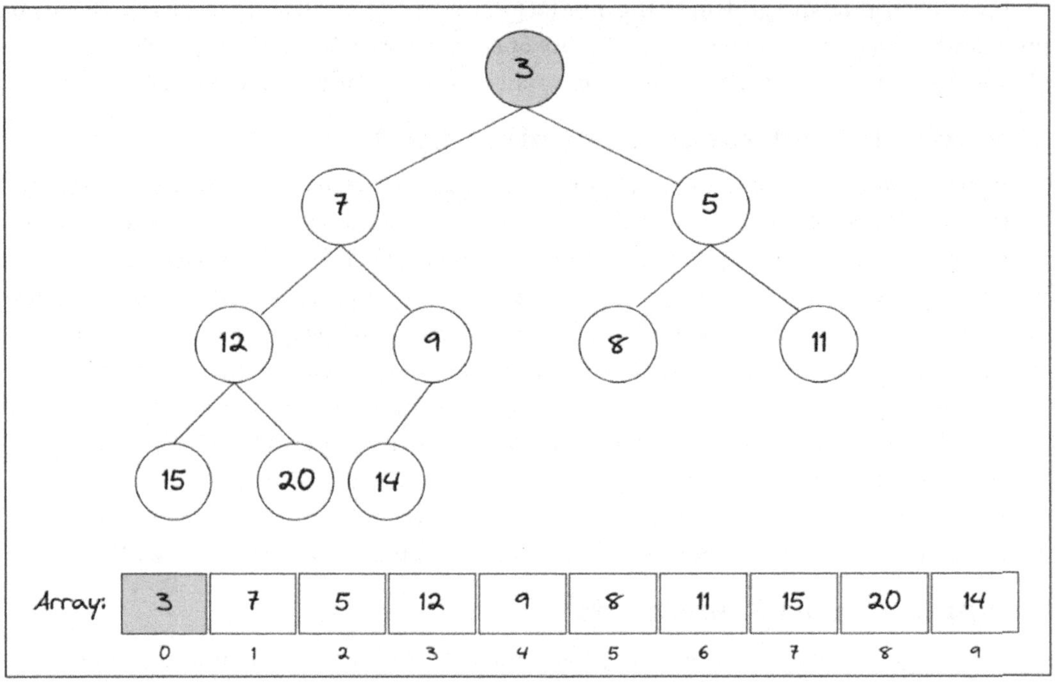

Figure 6.3: Top-10 leaderboard representation

Typical real-world use cases involve keeping an up-to-date list of the most popular items, such as the top 10 best-selling products on an e-commerce site or the 100 stocks that experienced the biggest daily price swings in a trading platform. In general, the task is to maintain a top-N ranking for things like leaderboards, trending topics, top performers, or the most active users. At its core, the problem reduces to identifying the K largest or smallest elements within a continuous data stream or a massive dataset. The complete implementation is available in the GitHub repo in the file named `Top10Leaderboard.java`. To unlock the GitHub repo link, refer to the instructions in the *Download the example code files* section of the *Preface*.

Having described how a priority queue can be built to answer **"top N"** queries in near-constant time, the structure offers more than just a convenient heap wrapper. In real-world workloads we require not only that the most important elements be retrieved swiftly, but also that the storage overhead remains bounded by `O(n)` even when the data set contains billions of entries. This trade-off, namely, fast access to the largest element paired with minimal cost to preserve global order, makes priority queues ideal for high-throughput systems such as live leaderboards, event schedulers, and dynamic ranking engines.

The following section introduces the **Priority Queue ADT** itself, outlining its core operations, invariants, and the abstract interface that underpins these efficient data-management patterns.

Abstract data type (ADT): priority queue

A priority queue is an abstract data structure that stores elements tagged with a numeric or comparable key. This key represents the element's priority level. It guarantees that the element with the extreme priority (maximum or minimum) can be accessed in constant time, while removing that element costs `O(log n)`. Unlike a FIFO queue, a priority queue does not honor insertion order; instead, ordering is solely dictated by the priority key. There are three core operations:

- Insert: Add element with priority
- Find Min/Max: Peek at the highest priority element
- Delete Min/Max: Remove and return the highest-priority element

All operations must maintain the invariant that the root (or top) always holds the current extreme priority.

Order, priority, and efficiency

At its heart, a priority queue arranges items around a user-defined key, doing so without re-sorting the entire collection after each update. The structure ensures immediate access to the highest or lowest priority element, while the remaining items are stored locally to enable efficient subsequent operations. Because of this local ordering, advanced heap implementations enable insertion, deletion, and peeking to execute in logarithmic or constant time, depending on the underlying implementation.

Performance can be measured in three dimensions: time complexity, space usage, and scalability. Different designs, namely arrays, reference-based trees, or hybrid layouts, trade off these axes in various ways.

The next sections will examine several common implementations to illustrate how the choice of underlying structure shapes these trade-offs.

Implementing priority queues using arrays

A priority queue can be implemented using a simple unsorted or sorted array, though this approach involves significant trade-offs compared to heap-based implementations. This section explores two fundamental, non-heap implementations of the Priority Queue ADT using simple, fixed-size arrays. The complete implementation is available in the GitHub repo in the file named `PriorityQueueDemo.java`. To unlock the GitHub repo link, refer to the instructions in the *Download the example code files* section of the *Preface*.

Unsorted array

In an unsorted array implementation, insertion is efficient by appending the new element to the end in `O(1)` time, but extracting the highest-priority element requires scanning the entire array to find the Min/Max, resulting in `O(n)` time complexity:

- **Insert/Enqueue**: `O(1)`; append to the end of the array
- **Find Min/Max**: `O(n)`; scan the entire array for max/min in `O(n)`, e.g., for locating min:

```
int minIndex = 0;
for (int i = 1; i < currentSize; i++) {
    if (storage[i] < storage[minIndex]) {
        minIndex = i;
    }
}
```

- **Delete/Dequeue Min/Max**: `O(1)`; the precondition for this is that the min/max element has already been located. The key insight is that we can swap the element to be deleted with the last element in the array, then decrement the size counter. This avoids the expensive `O(n)` shifting operation. Thus, deletion becomes a combination of a single assignment operation followed by a single decrement operation; both are `O(1)` operations regardless of the array size:

```
:storage[minIndex] = storage[--currentSize];
```

An unsorted array is a viable choice for a priority queue when the workload is write-heavy but read-light, because:

- Insertions happen frequently (`O(1)` each)
- Find/Remove operations are rare (`O(n)` each, but acceptable)
- Memory efficiency is important
- High write throughput is needed with minimal contention

This use case is ideal for high-throughput environments, such as a telemetry system ingesting millions of events per second while deferring the computation of the top-N items until the end of the reporting cycle.

Because the underlying array stays compact and avoids any reordering overhead, it can handle a high write throughput with minimal contention. This makes it highly suitable for scenarios where priority extractions are infrequent and can tolerate a one-time `O(n)` cost.

Sorted array

A sorted array implementation maintains elements in priority order, making extraction trivial at `O(1)` by removing the element at the end of the array. However, insertion is expensive at `O(n)` because we must find the correct position and shift elements to maintain sorted order:

- **Insert/Enqueue**: `O(n)`; find the correct position and shift elements.
- **Find Min/Max**: `O(1)`; locate the min or max element at the end of the array.
- **Delete/Dequeue Min/Max**: `O(1)`; remove the element at the end of the array without shifting by simply decrementing the size variable (`currentSize--`). Note that deleting the element at the beginning of the array would require an O(n) shift operation.

A sorted array is a perfectly adequate implementation of a priority queue when the workload is write-light and read-heavy, such as in a static leaderboard that is only refreshed at the end of a gaming session or in a reporting system that pre-computes rankings once per day. In this scenario, insertions cost `O(n)` because elements must be shifted to maintain order. However, if those modifications occur rarely, the overhead is negligible compared to the `O(1)` time required to peek or delete the top element, or the `O(log n)` time to binary-search for a specific key. Consequently, the array's simplicity and cache-friendly layout make it an attractive choice when the priority queue state changes infrequently while reads dominate the operation mix.

Complexity of unsorted array vs. sorted array

Space complexity for any array-based approach is `O(n)` for storing `n` elements. However, when working with arrays, one must account for their fixed-capacity nature and structural limitations:

- **Insertion**: As the data scale grows, the overhead of scanning or shifting elements becomes prohibitive at `O(n)` time complexity.
- **Expansion**: Like all fixed-size arrays, resizing is expensive because it requires allocating a larger block of memory and copying existing elements to the new array in `O(n)` time. While this cost amortizes to `O(1)` per insertion if a geometric resizing strategy (like doubling the capacity) is used, individual expansion events still cause noticeable performance spikes.

While array-based implementations are simple and suitable for small datasets or specialized workloads (such as read-heavy or write-heavy scenarios), they become impractical for large-scale applications where both insertions and extractions occur frequently.

In the next section, we explore a more powerful alternative, heaps, whose hierarchical structure yields better performance for high-frequency mixed workloads. We will examine heap properties and operations in depth.

The heap abstraction

A heap is a binary or multi-way tree that implements the priority queue abstract data type (ADT) in a space-efficient and cache-friendly way. A heap's popularity stems from the fact that it achieves an `O(n)` space footprint while offering constant-time `O(1)` access to the optimum element (min or max) and logarithmic `O(log n)` time for insertions and deletions.

When implemented as an array-based structure, the heap stores its elements in a contiguous block of memory, delivering great cache locality (where data may be loaded into an ultra-fast CPU cache). This makes the heap an ideal choice for high-throughput applications such as event schedulers, Dijkstra's shortest-path algorithm, and real-time applications.

The shape property

A binary heap is structured as a **complete binary tree**. That means every level of the tree is fully populated except possibly the bottom level, which is populated sequentially from left to right. *Figure 6.4* illustrates the shape of a complete binary tree.

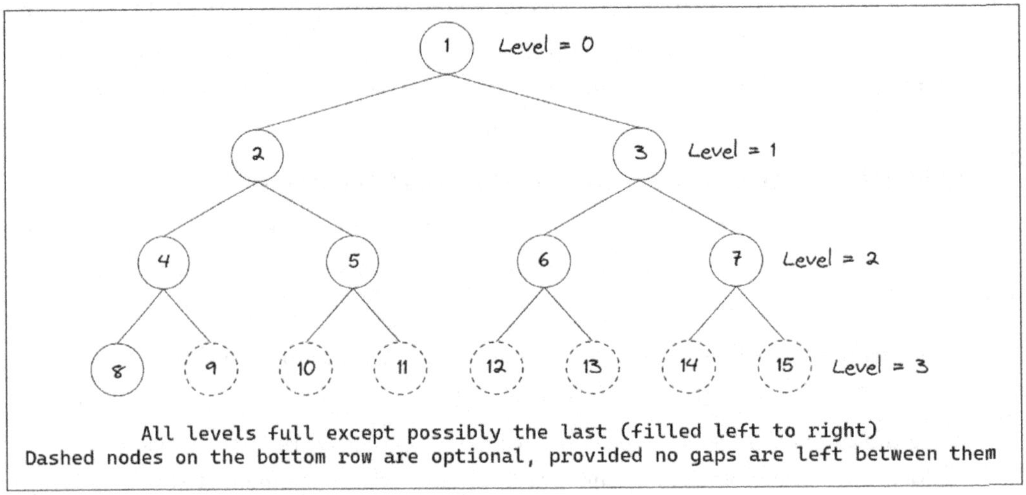

Figure 6.4: Complete binary tree

This regular layout guarantees that the tree's depth grows only logarithmically with the number of nodes, while enabling a contiguous array representation where each child's index is derived from its parent's index. The result is a compact, cache-friendly data layout that eliminates pointer overhead and supports the efficient heapify-up and heapify-down operations that give heaps their logarithmic performance guarantees.

Implementations: Array- and Tree-based heap

A heap can be codified either as a one-dimensional array or as a reference-based tree of node objects. *Figure 6.5* depicts both representations of the heap and their interoperability:

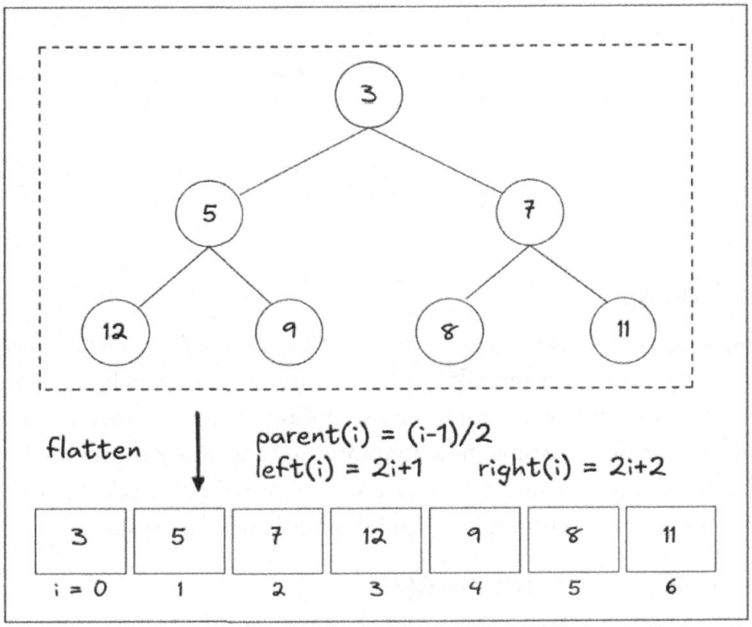

Figure 6.5: Heap representation in array vs tree

Array-based heap

Because a binary heap is a complete tree, its structure can be flattened into a single contiguous array. This mapping eliminates explicit node objects and pointer chasing, resulting in excellent cache locality, no per-node pointer overhead, and minimal memory fragmentation. The root always contains the global minimum or maximum, allowing constant-time `O(1)` access. In its zero-based array form, the complete-tree property allows a node's relationships to be calculated using simple index arithmetic:

Node	Index Formula
Current Node	`i`
Parent	`⌊(i-1)/2⌋`
Left Child	`2i + 1`
Right Child	`2i + 2`

Table 6.1: Nodes and their corresponding index formula

The total space complexity remains `O(n)`, as the array capacity scales proportionally with the number of stored elements.

Tree-based heap

Tree-based heaps explicitly store child references for each node to enable more flexible node structures, e.g., storing auxiliary, metadata, enabling multi-way branching, facilitating lazy deletions, or integrating with other graph representations. However, tree-heaps incur per-node pointer overhead, consume more memory, and can suffer from poorer cache performance due to pointer chasing, which is a performance bottleneck that occurs when a program must resolve a long sequence of dependent memory addresses to access data.

Minimum and maximum heaps

Both min and max heaps are the two fundamental forms of the heap structure. In both cases, the root always holds the extreme value (minimum for a min-heap, maximum for a max-heap). Specifically:

- In a min heap, the tree is complete and no parent element is larger than its children, so the globally smallest element sits at the root
- In a max heap, the tree is complete and no parent element is smaller than its children, placing the largest element at the root

Both variations enable constant-time `O(1)` access to the extreme element, alongside logarithmic `O(log n)` insertion and deletion. This performance makes them ideal for workloads requiring repeated access to extreme values such as heap sort, Dijkstra's shortest path, and tracing top-K elements in large datasets.

Heap operations

All mutations or structural modifications run in logarithmic time by performing localized "heapify-up" or "heapify-down" adjustments that restore the heap property along a single tree path. Searching for an arbitrary element requires a linear scan as the data structure is not fully sorted. *Figure 6.6* illustrates the heapify-up mechanism (enqueue) in a tree:

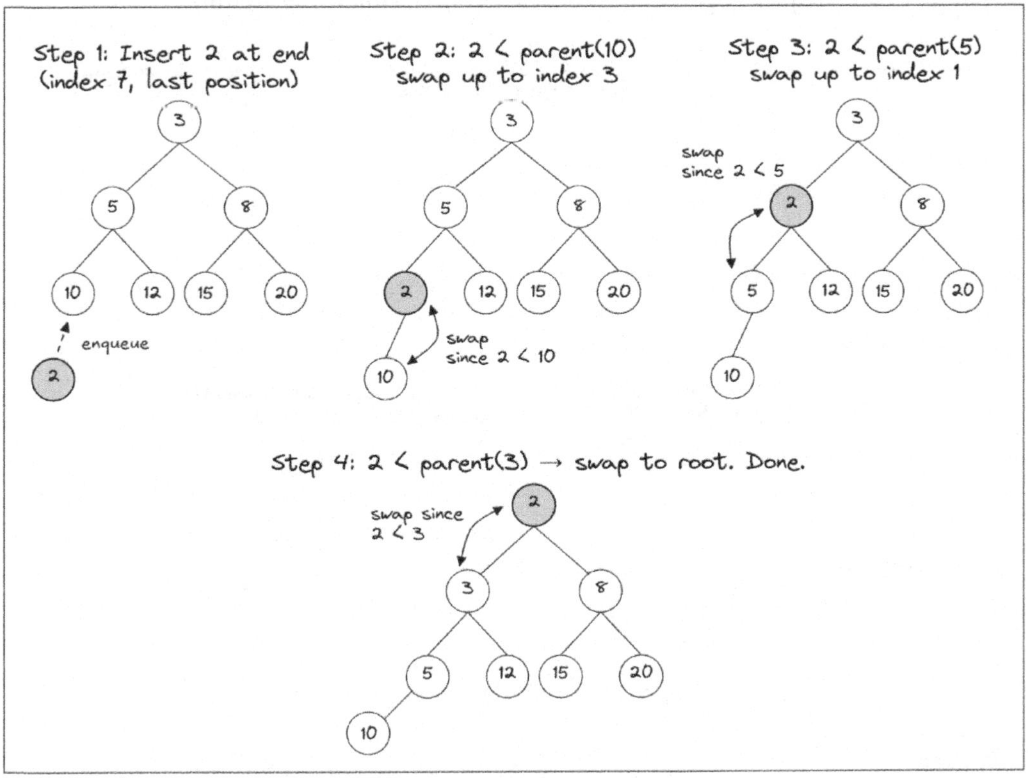

Figure 6.6: Heapify-up mechanism for enqueuing

As we can see in *Figure 6.6*, enqueuing an element, 2, in a heap structure requires inserting it into the next open slot to keep the tree binary-complete, then bubbling it up to the root. In Step 1, we place 2 in the next available slot, which is the left child of 10. In the next three steps, we compare 2 with its new parent up to the root via a series of parent swaps. In the last swap, 2 reaches the root and stops as there's no parent beyond the root to swap with.

Figure 6.7 shows the heapify-down mechanism (dequeue) in a tree. The process starts with the outcome of enqueuing 2 in *Figure 6.6*. We proceed to dequeue the root element, 2, leaving the root spot empty. As the next step, we replace the root with the very last element in the complete binary tree, which is 10. In Step 3, we down swap (heapify-down) by comparing 10 with its two children, 3 and 8. The smaller child or `min(3, 8)` is 3. Since 10 is greater than 3, we swap 10 and 3. In Step 4.

10 is now at index 2 in the tree. We compare it with its new children, 5 and 12. The smaller child or `min(5, 12)` is 5. Since 10 is greater than 5, we swap 10 and 5. In Step 5, 10 is now at index 4 which is a leaf; it has no children left in the tree, so the operation is complete. We will look at both enqueue and dequeue operations more closely in the following section.

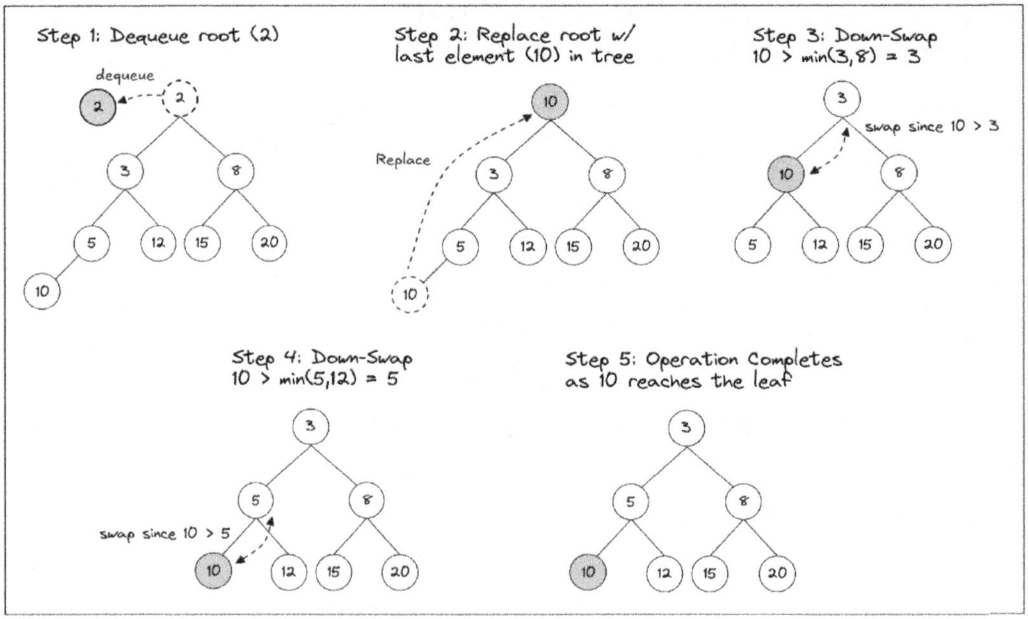

Figure 6.7: Heapify-down mechanism for dequeuing an element

> **Note**
>
> Deletions (heapify-down operations) do not leave a heap tree incomplete. In a standard binary heap implementation, the algorithm is explicitly designed to ensure the tree always remains complete at every single stage of a deletion. However, in a **binary search tree (BST)**, if you delete an internal element, you must lift entire subtrees or relink structural pointers, which can cause the tree to warp, become unbalanced, or lose its complete shape.

In practice, heaps are almost always implemented as arrays because they offer superior performance through better cache locality, use much less memory by eliminating reference overhead, provide simpler code that's easier to maintain, and represent the industry standard adopted by all major libraries including Java's `PriorityQueue`, C++'s `std::priority_queue`, and Python's `heapq` module. For example, a native integer requires only 4 bytes in an array, whereas the same integer stored in a tree node with parent and child references requires 20–28 bytes, plus additional overhead from object instantiation.

In the next section, we will illustrate both insert (heapify up) and remove (heapify down) operations using an array as the underlying data structure.

Heapify-up

When a new element is inserted into a heap, the new element is placed at the next available leaf position, keeping the tree complete. It is then compared with its parent element. If the parent element is larger (in a min-heap) or smaller (in a max-heap), the two nodes are swapped. This comparison-swap cycle continues upward, moving the new element toward the root, until the comparison condition terminates or the root is reached. The following pseudocode illustrates inserting an element into a min-heap:

Pseudocode: insert(value)

```
   1. if heap is full, resize array (double capacity)
   2. heap[size] = value    // Add to the left-most open
                             // leaf at the bottom level
   3. size = size + 1             // Increase size
   4. heapifyUp(size - 1):        // Restore heap property
          i = size - 1                // Start at last element
          while i > 0:                // While not at root
              parent = (i - 1) / 2    // Calculate parent index

              // If element >= parent, done (heap property satisfied)
              if heap[i] >= heap[parent]:
                  break

              // Swap element with parent
              swap(heap[i], heap[parent])
              i = parent                  // Move up to parent position

   5. done when the new
element satisfies the heap property relative to its parent, or when the root is
reached.
```

The following code snippet illustrates the min-heap construction using a 0-indexed array. The complete implementation is available in the GitHub repo in the file named `MinHeapDemo.java`. To unlock the GitHub repo link, refer to the instructions in the *Download the example code files* section of the *Preface*.

```
public void insert(int value) {
        // Step 1: Resize if full
        if (size == capacity) resize();
        // Step 2 & 3: Add to left-most open leaf and increase size
        heap[size] = value;
        size++;
        // Step 4 & 5: Restore heap property by moving up
        heapifyUp(size - 1);
}
// Step 4 implementation: Heapify Up
private void heapifyUp(int index) {
        int i = index; // Start at the last element
        while (i> 0) { // While not at root
            // Calculate parent index
            int parent = (i - 1) / 2;
            //Ifelement>= parent, done; heap property satisfied
            if (heap[i]>= heap[parent]) break;
            // Swap element with parent
            swap(i, parent);
            // Move up to parent position
            i = parent;
        }
}
// Step 1 helper: Double the array capacity
private void resize() {
        capacity = capacity * 2;
        heap = Arrays.copyOf(heap, capacity);
}
// Swap helper method
private void swap(int index1, int index2) {
        int temp = heap[index1];
        heap[index1] = heap[index2];
        heap[index2] = temp;
}
```

Heapify-down

When the highest-priority element is removed from a heap, the last leaf node in the tree is moved to the vacant root position to preserve completeness. From that root, the displaced key is compared with its children. In a min-heap, if the element is larger than one of its children, it is swapped with the smallest child; in a max-heap, it is swapped with the largest child. This compare-and-swap sequence propagates the element downward, ensuring the heap property is restored, until the element is no longer greater than (min-heap) or smaller than (max-heap) its children, or it reaches a leaf. The following pseudocode illustrates removing an element from a min-heap. The complete implementation is available in the GitHub repo in the file named `MinHeapDemo.java`. To unlock the GitHub repo link, refer to the instructions in the *Download the example code files* section of the *Preface*.

Pseudocode: removeMin()

```
1. if heap is empty, return error
2. minValue = heap[0]              // Save root (minimum)
3. heap[0] = heap[size - 1]        // Move last element to root
4. size = size - 1                 // Decrease size
5. heapifyDown(0):                 // Restore heap property
   i = 0
   while i has at least one child:
       leftChild = 2*i + 1
       rightChild = 2*i + 2

       // Find smaller child
       smallerChild = leftChild
       if rightChild exists and heap[rightChild] < heap[leftChild]:
           smallerChild = rightChild

       // If parent <= smaller child, done
       if heap[i] <= heap[smallerChild]:
           break

       // Swap parent with smaller child
       swap(heap[i], heap[smallerChild])
       i = smallerChild

6. return minValue
```

Complexity analysis

The performance of heap-based algorithms is fundamentally governed by the logarithmic height of the underlying complete binary tree. By tracing how structural constraints translate into operational work, we can establish tight asymptotic bounds for all core heap operations. This analysis examines how the tree's height directly dictates the maximum number of comparisons and swaps required for both insertion and deletion, revealing why these operations consistently achieve logarithmic time.

O(insert)

Because a heap is a complete binary tree, adding a new element never changes the tree's height. The new element merely fills the next open leaf. The work associated with insertion is the heapify-up mechanism, where the newly inserted element is repeatedly compared with its parent and swapped if the heap property is violated. In a complete tree with n elements (nodes), its height `h` satisfies:

$$2^h \leq n < 2^{h+1}$$

Alternatively, height is bounded by the logarithmic function: $h = \lfloor log_2 n \rfloor$

Since at each level in a tree, the new element is compared and possibly swapped in constant time, the total amount of work needed to percolate this element up to its destination in a heap is proportional to `O(h)` or `O(log n)` in logarithmic time.

O(delete)

A comparable argument holds for the inverse operation when an item is deleted from the heap. The heap-down process likewise costs `O(log n)` in time.

Finally, what is the running time for creating a heap from an array of *n* unsorted items? A naive approach is to start with an empty array and perform insertion n times. Because each insertion takes `O(log n)` time, the approach takes a total of `O(n log n)` time. More efficient approaches exist that can construct the heap in `O(n)` time instead.

The heap mechanics detailed in this chapter establish a robust framework for dynamic priority management. Structured as complete binary trees, heaps guarantee `O(log n)` time complexity for both element insertion and extraction, thereby maintaining predictable performance under scaling workloads. Coupled with an `O(n)` linear-time construction process that drastically outperforms naive sequential insertion, these mathematical bounds elevate this data structure from a theoretical tree model to a practical priority-queue foundation. We now shift our focus to real-world applications.

Applications and use cases

The heap's ability to expose the maximum or minimum element in constant time while maintaining logarithmic insertion and deletion costs makes it a natural choice for efficient, deterministic priority handling. There are many applications in the industry, to name a few:

- **Task Scheduling & Job Queues**: Priority queues form the core of numerous schedulers, such as Kubernetes' job queue and Jenkins' build queue, by assigning each task a priority key and always extracting the highest-priority job. This guarantees that critical work runs first while insertion and deletion operations remain fast. A min heap is commonly used for deadline-based scheduling, where the task with the closest deadline is located at the root, enabling `O(1)` peek operations. The heap property ensures that the minimum element is always at the root, maintaining efficient priority-based task order (*Figure 6.8*).

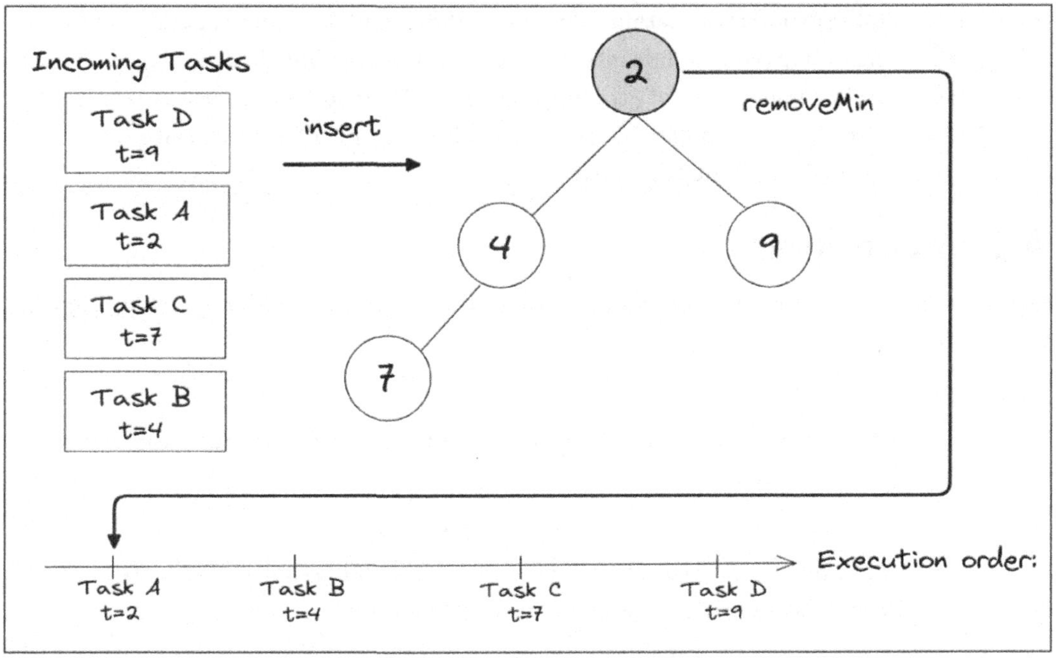

Figure 6.8: Task scheduler using a min heap

> **Note**
>
> Unlike Binary Search Trees (BST) that enforce strict horizontal ordering (Left < Parent < Right), binary heaps only maintain partial vertical ordering where each parent is smaller (min-heap) than its children. This relaxed ordering allows heaps to achieve `O(1)` access to the root element, whereas balanced BSTs require `O(log n)` time to find their absolute minimum or maximum elements.

- **Simulation and Event-Driven Systems**: Event-driven simulators, such as network or discrete-event physics engines, employ a min-heap of timestamps to fetch the next event chronologically, ensuring that each event dispatch occurs in `O(log n)` time and that the total simulation runtime remains nearly linear relative to the number of events
- **Real-Time Systems and Latency-Sensitive Workload**: Real-time operating systems use priority heaps to schedule interrupts and tasks, providing deterministic worst-case latency, while high-frequency trading engines and embedded controllers also employ heaps to reorder incoming messages or work items by deadline or priority, guaranteeing low-latency processing

Advanced heaps

Advanced heap structures offer specialized trade-offs beyond standard binary heaps. Here are key examples:

- Binomial Heaps
  - Efficient `O(log n)` merging through the union operation that combines two heaps
  - Each tree maintains the binomial tree property
  - Ideal for distributed systems; the merging capability makes it suitable for scenarios requiring frequent queue consolidation
  - Logarithmic time operations for insert and extract-min operations with `O(log n)` complexity
- Fibonacci Heaps
  - Achieve amortized `O(1)` insert and decrease-key through lazy evaluation
  - Theoretically optimal for graph algorithms like Dijkstra's shortest path
  - Despite practical overhead, provide superior asymptotic performance

- D-ary Heaps
  - Generalized version of binary heaps
  - Allow `d` children per node, reducing tree height to $\log_d(n)$
  - Optimize insert-heavy workloads and cache performance in external memory algorithms
- Pairing Heaps
  - Balance simplicity with performance through straightforward sibling-pointer structures
  - Often outperform Fibonacci heaps in practice due to lower constant factors and better cache locality
  - Preferred for computational geometry and network flow algorithms

Having surveyed the rich landscape of advanced heap structures, we now shift focus to the most readily available heap implementation in everyday Java development.

Heaps in java collections framework

The **Java Collections Framework** (**JCF**) provides a single structural class for traditional heap implementation in a non-concurrent setting: `PriorityQueue`. Its thread-safe counterpart, also backed by a dynamic array, is available in the concurrency package as `PriorityBlockingQueue`.

There is no standalone `Heap` class in Java; instead, heap functionality is fully encapsulated within the concrete `PriorityQueue` class, which implements the standard `Queue` interface (*Figure 6.9*). Internally, this class uses a binary heap backed by a contiguous array to represent a complete binary tree. You can find the official Java 21 documentation with details in `https://docs.oracle.com/en/java/javase/21/docs/api/`. Besides using arrays as the underlying buffer to implement heap, we can also use `TreeSet` and `ArrayDeque` to emulate heap functionalities.

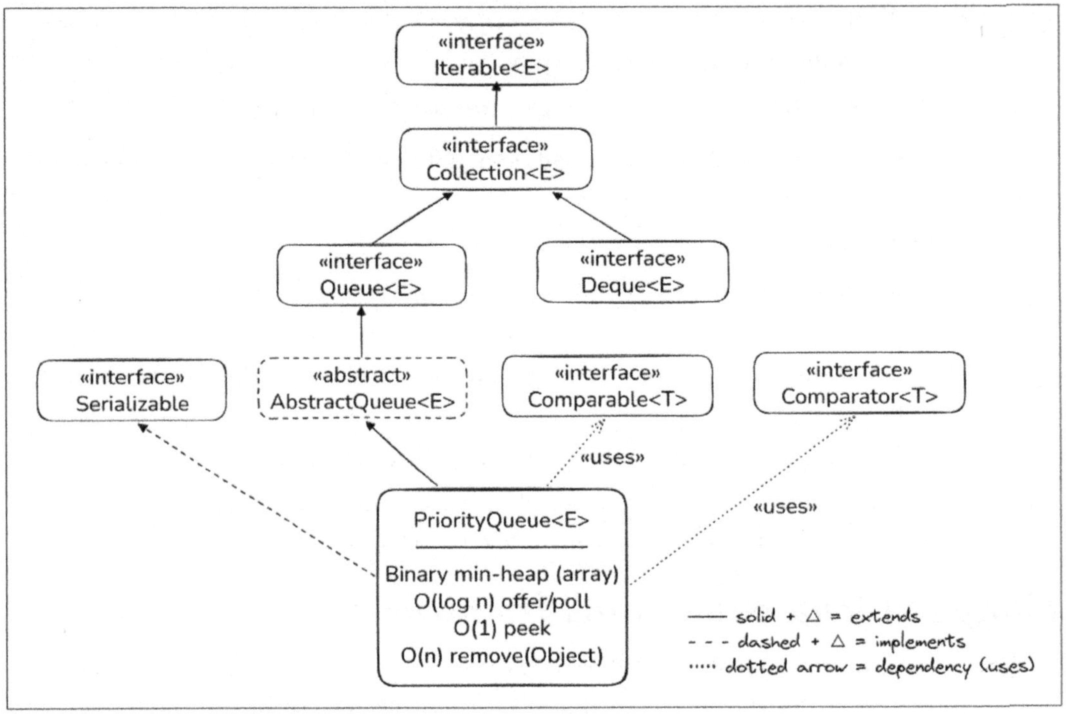

Figure 6.9: PriorityQueue and related components in JCF

Note

While alternative collections can simulate priority queue behavior, they introduce performance penalties.

- `TreeSet` (Red-Black Tree): Maintains sorted order but degrades from `O(1)` to `O(log n)` and automatically removes duplicate priorities
- `ArrayDeque` (Double-Ended Queue): Allows duplicates but requires manual sorting on each insertion, reducing performance from `O(log n)` to `O(n)` time complexity

We recommend using `PriorityQueue` for native heap operations to maintain optimal `O(1)peek()` and `O(log n)` insertion and deletion performance.

PriorityQueue as heap

By default, a `PriorityQueue` instance is a min-heap. You can reverse this behavior by using either a lambda expression or `Comparator.reverseOrder()`:

```
// Default: Min-heap
Queue<Integer> pq = new PriorityQueue<>();

// Max-heap with reverse order: Option 1 & Option 2
// Option 1: Safe lambda with no overflow risk
PriorityQueue<Integer> maxHeap =
new PriorityQueue<>((a, b) ->
Integer.compare(b, a));

// Option 2: Built-in
PriorityQueue<Integer> maxHeap =
new PriorityQueue<>(Collections.reverseOrder());
```

ArrayDeque with custom heap logic

For academic study, an `ArrayDeque` can be repurposed to serve as a max-heap or min-heap through custom logic, as demonstrated in `ArrayDequeHeap.java` in the `Chapter06` folder on GitHub. However, because `ArrayDeque` lacks random-access indexing (`O(1) get(i)` and `set(i, v)`), the actual execution efficiency degrades to an expensive `O(n log n)`. A binary heap relies on mathematical array arithmetic (`2i + 1` and `⌊(i-1)/2⌋`) to navigate between parents and children, which requires a sequential memory buffer capable of instant, arbitrary reads and writes. For production-ready engineering, this queue-cycling approach is a performance anti-pattern. Real-world systems demand true `O(log n)` heap efficiency. This is natively achieved using Java's built-in `PriorityQueue`, which is internally backed by a dynamically resizing, contiguous array structure. This layout ensures optimal CPU cache localization and native tree-navigation mechanics, making it much more efficient than custom, non-random-access alternatives.

`ArrayDeque` is a double-ended queue implementation:

```
Deque<Integer> deque = new ArrayDeque<>();
// Add to front in O(1)
deque.offerFirst(10);
// Add to back in O(1)
deque.offerLast(20);
```

```
// Remove from front in O(1)
int front = deque.pollFirst();
// Remove from back in O(1)
int back = deque.pollLast();
```

TreeSet with heap-like functionality

While not a heap per se, `TreeSet` provides heap-like functionality with `O(log n)` insertion and retrieval. The example implementation of `TreeSet` is available in the GitHub repo in the file named `TreeSetMaxHeap.java`. To unlock the GitHub repo link, refer to the instructions in the *Download the example code files* section of the *Preface*.

```
import java.util.TreeSet;
import java.util.Collections;
// Max-heap using TreeSet with reverse order
TreeSet<Integer> maxHeap = new TreeSet<>(Collections.reverseOrder());
maxHeap.add(10);
maxHeap.add(30);
maxHeap.add(20);
// First element is the maximum
Integer max = maxHeap.first(); // Returns 30
```

We choose `TreeSet`-based heap over `PriorityQueue` when we need to remove specific elements from the collection efficiently; `TreeSet` provides `O(log n)` removal time for any specific element, while `PriorityQueue` requires `O(n)` time to find and `O(log n)` time to remove an element (and re-heapify the tree). This makes the `remove(Object)` operation bounded by search, with the overall operation `O(n)`. Note that removing an arbitrary element is different than dequeuing an element from a binary tree. Additionally, `TreeSet` inherently maintains elements in sorted order, making it ideal when you need to iterate them in sorted order or perform range queries using methods like `headSet()`, `tailSet()`, and `subSet()`.

As seen from the above, the alternatives are mainly useful when you need specific behaviors or are working in constrained environments where you can't use standard collections. For most heap use cases, `PriorityQueue` is still the best choice due to its optimization, built-in support for both min-heap and max-heap, and ease of use.

Summary

At its core, the Priority Queue is an abstract concept, and the heap is the highly efficient algorithmic implementation that solves the critical problem of dynamic ordering. We established that naive collection structures, namely unsorted arrays or linked lists, are impractical in high-throughput environments, forcing expensive linear-time `O(n)` scans just to find the next most important item. The heap structure bypasses this bottleneck entirely by leveraging the physical constraints of a complete binary tree. This structural guarantee is the mathematical engine behind its power: it allows us to achieve `O(1)` constant-time access to the highest (or lowest) priority element while maintaining the invariant through highly efficient, localized `O(log n)` adjustments during both insertion (heapify-up) and extraction (heapify-down). The heap serves as a dependable tool for managing critical systems, ranging from operating system task scheduling to tracking real-time rankings. *Figure 6.10* is a summary diagram of heaps for quick overview.

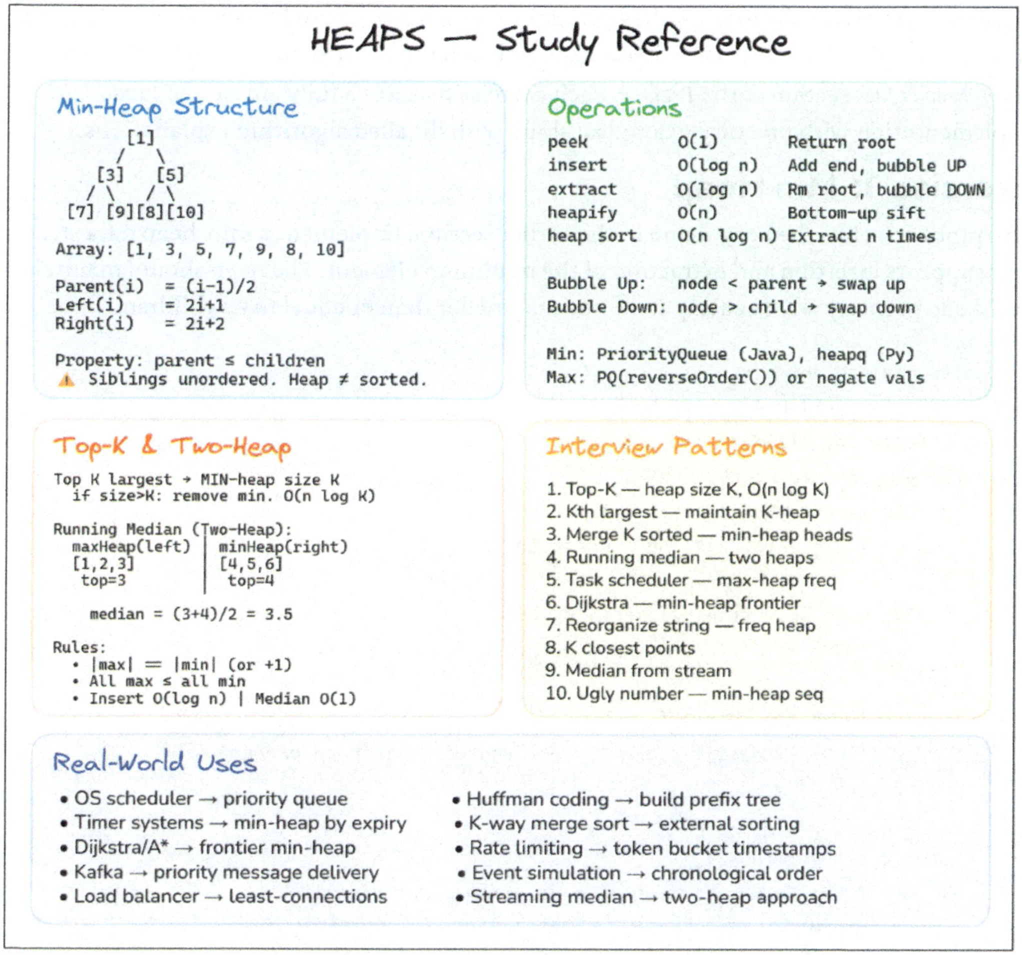

Figure 6.10: Summary diagram of heaps

In the next chapter, we will transition from managing ordered sequences to modeling interconnected relationships in graph theory. We will explore how discrete entities, called nodes (or vertices), are linked by edges, and how this simple structure can power the most complex computational systems in social networks, mapping applications, to name a few.

Exercises

These exercises are designed to move you beyond rote implementation and develop algorithmic thinking. They do not merely test your ability to use heaps; they help you identify when and how heaps provide the optimal solution for real-world problems with specific constraints.

The comprehensive solutions for these programming exercises can be found on GitHub, in the `Chapter06` folder. To unlock the GitHub repo link, refer to the instructions in the *Download the example code files* section of the *Preface*. Each exercise features a fully annotated Java implementation with practical examples, along with detailed algorithm explanations.

Exercise 1: Min-Heap

This problem is like the heap demo in the earlier section. Implement a min-heap data structure that supports insertion and extraction of the minimum element. The heap should maintain the min-heap property where each parent node is smaller than or equal to its children.

```
public class MinHeap {
    private int[] heap;
    private int size;
    private int capacity;
    public MinHeap(int capacity) {
        // TODO: Initialize heap array and set capacity
    }
    public void insert(int element) {
        // TODO: Insert element and maintain heap property
    }
    public int extractMin() {
        // TODO: Extract minimum element and maintain heap property
        return 0;
    }
    public int getMin() {
        // TODO: Return minimum element without removing it
        return 0;
    }
    public boolean isEmpty() {
```

```
        // TODO: Check if heap is empty
        return false;
    }

}
```

Assumptions and Constraints

- Heap capacity is fixed at initialization
- All elements are integers
- Heap supports duplicate values
- Indexing starts from 1 (not 0) for heap operations
- `extractMin()` throws a `RuntimeException` when the heap is empty
- `getMin()` throws a `RuntimeException` when the heap is empty

Test Case 1

- **Input**: `insert(5)`, `insert(3)`, `insert(8)`, `insert(1)`, `extractMin()`
- **Expected Output**: 1

Test Case 2

- **Input**: `insert(10)`, `insert(5)`, `insert(15)`, `insert(2)`, `insert(7)`, `extractMin()`, `extractMin()`
- **Expected Output**: 2, 5

Solution

At the onset, we construct our heap buffer with a 1-based array layout strategy:

```
this.heap = new int[capacity + 1];
```

Array is sized `capacity + 1` because index 0 is deliberately skipped. Using 1-based indexing lets the parent/child math work out to clean integer division `(index / 2)`, instead of needing `(index - 1) / 2` everywhere.

For insertion (enqueue), the new element is dropped at the very next open slot of the array buffer, namely at its end. This is the "bottom" of the heap, not necessarily the correct final position.

```
size++; heap[size] = element;
```

Because the newly added element is simply appended at the end, it may break the min-heap property relative to its parent. The `heapifyUp` function resolves this by repeatedly swapping the element upward until it reaches its correct level:

```
heapifyUp(size);
```

The mechanism for restoring the heap property when an element is appended at the end is as follows:

```
while (index > 1) {
    int parentIndex = index / 2;
    if (heap[parentIndex] <= heap[index]) {
        break;
    }
    swap(parentIndex, index);
    index = parentIndex;
}
```

The `heapifyUp` process relies on a `while` loop that continuously moves a newly inserted element up the binary heap array until it reaches its valid position. During each iteration, the algorithm calculates the parent's position by dividing the current index by two, leveraging integer division to find the exact upper node instantly.

```
int parentIndex = index / 2;
```

It then compares the values; if the parent node is already smaller than or equal to the current element, the min-heap invariant is satisfied and the loop terminates early.

```
swap(parentIndex, index); index = parentIndex;
```

Otherwise swap up one level, and continue checking from the new position until the element either finds its rightful spot or reaches the root of the tree at index one.

For deletion (dequeue), which removes the root element (the minimum), we must employ the `heapifyDown` operation to restore the min-heap invariant after the root element is removed. This algorithm migrates the replacement root downward through the tree structure until all parent-child constraints are satisfied.

The algorithm identifies the left and right children of the current node at:

```
int leftChild = 2 * index;
int rightChild = 2 * index + 1;
```

using boundary checks (≤ `size`) to ensure it does not look past the valid logical array size. The approach compares the parent node against both children to isolate the absolute smallest value among the three, which prevents structural violations on either branch:

```
int smallest = index;
if (leftChild <= size && heap[leftChild] < heap[smallest]) {
    smallest = leftChild;
}
if (rightChild <= size && heap[rightChild] < heap[smallest]) {
    smallest = rightChild;
}
```

If the parent node is already the smallest, the min-heap property holds true, and the loop terminates early via a `break` statement:

```
if (smallest == index) { break; }
```

If the parent itself is already the smallest of the three, the heap property is restored. We then stop here.

```
swap(index, smallest); index = smallest;
```

That is how a `MinHeap` works line by line. A `MaxHeap` works the exact same way, except you swap the "less than" and "greater than" rules.

Exercise 2: Max-Heap

Implement a max-heap data structure that supports insertion and extraction of the maximum element. The heap should maintain the max-heap property where each parent node is greater than or equal to its children.

Starter Code Template

```
public class MaxHeap {
    private int[] heap;
    private int size;
    private int capacity;
```

```
    public MaxHeap(int capacity) {
        // TODO: Initialize heap array and set capacity
    }
    public void insert(int element) {
        // TODO: Insert element and maintain heap property
    }
    public int extractMax() {
        // TODO: Extract maximum element and maintain heap property
        return 0;
    }
    public int getMax() {
        // TODO: Return maximum element without removing it
        return 0;
    }
    public boolean isEmpty() {
        // TODO: Check if heap is empty
        return false;
    }
}
```

Assumptions and Constraints

- Heap capacity is fixed at initialization
- All elements are integers
- Heap supports duplicate values
- Indexing starts from 1 (not 0) for heap operations
- `extractMax()` throws a `RuntimeException` when the heap is empty
- `getMax()` throws a `RuntimeException` when the heap is empty

Test Case 1

- **Input**: `insert(5), insert(3), insert(8), insert(1), extractMax()`
- **Expected Output**: 8

Test Case 2

- **Input**: `insert(10), insert(5), insert(15), insert(2), insert(7), extractMax(), extractMax()`
- **Expected Output**: 15, 10

Exercise 3: Find the kth largest element

Given an array of integers and an integer k, find the kth largest element in the array. You must solve this using a min-heap of size k.

Starter Code Template

```
import java.util.*;

public class KthLargestElement {
    public int findKthLargest(int[] nums, int k) {
        // Your code here
        return -1;
    }
}
```

Assumptions and Constraints

- Input array contains integers (can be negative)
- 1 ≤ k ≤ array length
- Array length can be up to 10^5
- Must use a min-heap of size k for optimal solution
- Time complexity should be `O(n log k)`

Test Case 1

- **Input**: `int[] nums = {3, 2, 1, 5, 6, 4}; int k = 2`
- **Output**: 5

Test Case 2

- **Input**: `int[] nums = {3, 2, 3, 1, 2, 4, 5, 5, 6}; int k = 4`
- **Output**: 4

Exercise 4: K closest points to the origin

Given an array of points on the X-Y plane and an integer k, return the k closest points to the origin (0, 0). Use Euclidean distance for comparison.

Starter Code Template

```
import java.util.*;
public class KClosestPoints {
    public int[][] kClosest(int[][] points, int k) {
```

```
        // Your code here
        return new int[0][0];
    }
}
```

Assumptions and Constraints

- Points array contains valid 2D coordinates
- Each point has exactly 2 coordinates [x, y]
- 1 ≤ k ≤ number of points
- All points are distinct
- Distance is calculated using Euclidean distance (without the square root for optimization)
- Time complexity should be `O(n log n)`

Test Case 1

- **Input**: `int[][] points = {{1, 3}, {-2, 2}}; int k = 1`
- **Output**: `[[-2, 2]]`

Test Case 2

- **Input**: `int[][] points = {{3, 3}, {5, -1}, {-2, 4}}; int k =2`
- **Output**: `[[3, 3], [-2, 4]]`

Exercise 5: Top K frequent elements

Given an array of integers, return the k most frequent elements. You may return the answer in any order.

Starter Code Template

```
import java.util.*;
public class TopKFrequent {
    public int[] topKFrequent(int[] nums, int k) {
        // Your code here
        return new int[0];
    }
}
```

Assumptions and Constraints

- Input array contains integers (can be negative)

- 1 ≤ k ≤ number of unique elements
- Array length can be up to 10^4
- All elements are within the range [-1000, 1000]
- Must use heap-based approach for efficient solution
- Time complexity should be `O(n log k)`

Test Case 1

- **Input**: `int[] nums1 = {1, 1, 1, 2, 2, 3}; int k = 2`
- **Output**: `[1, 2]`

Test Case 2

- **Input**: `int[] nums2 = {1}; int k = 1`
- **Output**: `[1]`

Exercise 6: Merge K sorted arrays

Given k sorted arrays, merge them into one sorted array using a min-heap approach.

Starter Code Template

```
import java.util.*;
public class MergeKSortedArrays {
    public int[] mergeKArrays(int[][] arrays) {
        // Your code here
        return new int[0];
    }
}
```

Assumptions and Constraints

- All input arrays are sorted in ascending order
- Input arrays can have different lengths
- Number of arrays k can be up to 10^4
- Each array can contain up to 10^4 elements
- Total number of elements across all arrays can be up to 10^6
- Must use heap-based approach for optimal solution
- Time complexity should be `O(N log k)`, where N is the total number of elements

Test Case 1

- **Input**: `int[][] arrays = {{1, 4, 5}, {1, 3, 4}, {2, 6}}`
- **Output**: `[1, 1, 2, 3, 4, 4, 5, 6]`

Test Case 2

- **Input**: `int[][] arrays = {{1, 2, 3}, {4, 5, 6}, {7, 8, 9}}`
- **Output**: `[1, 2, 3, 4, 5, 6, 7, 8, 9]`

Exercise 7: Task scheduler

Given an array of tasks and a cooling period n, determine the minimum number of intervals required to complete all tasks. Each task takes one interval to complete, and there must be at least n intervals between two tasks of the same type.

Starter Code Template

```
import java.util.*;
public class TaskScheduler {
    public int leastInterval(char[] tasks, int n) {
        // Your code here
        return -1;
    }
}
```

Assumptions and Constraints

- Tasks are represented by uppercase letters A-Z
- Cooling period n is a non-negative integer
- Number of tasks can be up to 10^4
- Each task takes exactly one interval to complete
- Must use max-heap approach for optimal solution
- Time complexity should be `O(n)`, where n is the number of tasks

Test Case 1

- **Input**: `char[] tasks1 = {'A','A','A','B','B','B'}; int n = 2`
- **Output**: 8

Test Case 2

- **Input**: `char[] tasks = {'A','A','A','B','B','B'}; int n = 2`
- **Output**: 6

Exercise 8: Last stone weight

You are given an array of integers representing stone weights. In each round, you pick the two heaviest stones and smash them together. If their weights are equal, both are destroyed. If not, the smaller is destroyed and the larger is reduced by the weight of the smaller. Return the weight of the last remaining stone, or 0 if none remains.

Starter Code Template

```
import java.util.*;
public class LastStoneWeight {
    public int lastStoneWeight(int[] stones) {
        // Your code here
        return -1;
    }
}
```

Assumptions and Constraints

- Input array contains positive integers (stone weights)
- Array length can be up to 30
- Stone weights can be up to 1000
- Must use max-heap approach for optimal solution
- Time complexity should be `O(n log n)`

Test Case 1

- **Input**: `int[] stones = {2, 7, 4, 1, 8, 1}`
- **Output**: 1

Test Case 2

- **Input**: `int[] stones = {1}`
- **Output**: 1

7

Graphs

Graphs are the abstract mathematical structure that represent relationships among distinct entities. A graph can be directed or undirected, weighted or unweighted, and may even permit multiple edges or self-loops. Since most practical problems involve connections, such as roads, social ties, web links, or software dependencies, graphs provide the natural framework for modeling connectivity, distances, and flows.

This chapter introduces the formal graph **abstract data type** (**ADT**), outlines the key properties and definitions that distinguish different kinds of graphs, and surveys the two classic storage formats: adjacency matrices for dense graphs and adjacency lists for sparse graphs. We'll cover the core traversal algorithms, namely, depth-first and breadth-first search, and highlight how they can be implemented both recursively and iteratively. We will analyze their time-space tradeoffs for each storage choice. By the end, you'll know how to choose the right graph representation for a problem, implement it efficiently in Java, and apply the foundational graph algorithms that underpin many modern applications.

What is a graph?

A graph is a data structure composed of vertices, nodes, and edges, or connections that link pairs of vertices. We define `G` as the graph itself, with `V` being the vertex set and `E` as the edge set comprising this graph. Each edge connects two vertices and represents a relationship between them. We denote the equation for a graph as:

$$G = (V, E)$$

Where `V` is a finite, nonempty set of vertices and E is a finite set of *distinct* pairs of vertices. We may think of `V` as the list of people in a social network, and `E` as the list of friendships among these people. *Figure 7.1* shows a graph data structure:

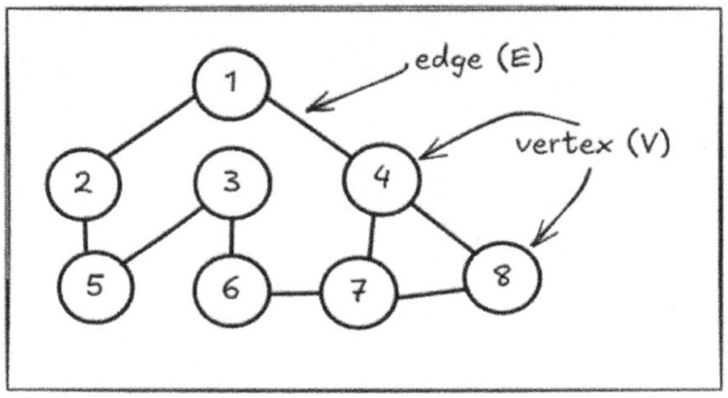

Figure 7.1: Graph data structure showing connected edges and vertices

Let's explore key terminology:

- Two vertices are **adjacent** if an edge links them; the set of all vertices adjacent to a given vertex is its set of neighbors.
- A **path** is a sequence of edges that starts at one vertex and ends at another, passing through intermediate vertices. For example, in *Figure 7.1*, the path `6-7-8` connects vertex `6` to vertex `8` by traversing the edges `6-7` and `7-8`, while the alternative path `6-7-4-8` accomplishes the same connection via a different route.
- The structure of a graph is fundamentally defined by its **vertices**, the **edges** that connect them, the **adjacency** relation between vertices, and the possible **paths** that can be formed by chaining edges together.
- The **degree** of a vertex `v`, written `deg(v)`, is the number of edges that touch `v`. Thus, `deg(v)` measures the local connectivity of a vertex: a high degree means `v` is highly connected, while a degree of zero means `v` is isolated.
- In a directed graph where each edge has a direction, we use in-degree and out-degree to define the connectivity of vertices. In directed graphs, in-degree represents the number of edges pointing toward a vertex (incoming connections), while out-degree represents the number of edges pointing away from a vertex (outgoing connections). *Figure 7.2* depicts this connectivity relationship.

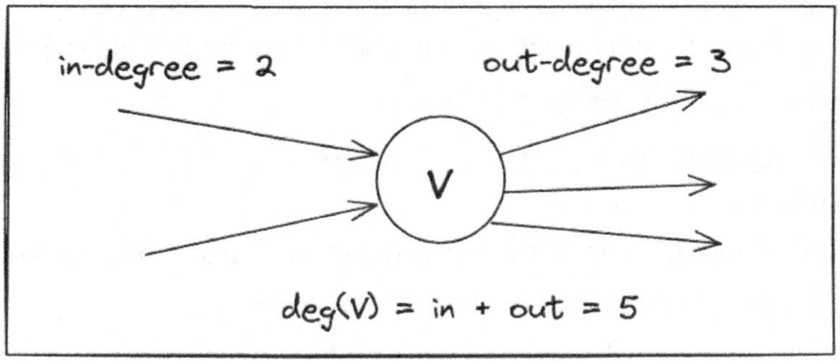

Figure 7.2: Degree (in/out)

Types of graphs

There are different types of graphs in practice. We will look at the most common ones.

Undirected and directed graphs

In a directed graph, each edge carries a direction. Namely, think of a "follows" link on X (Twitter) where the relationship points from one user to another. Conversely, in an undirected graph, the edges are bidirectional, representing a mutual connection like a LinkedIn connection or a Facebook friendship. Here, the edge set consists of unordered pairs of distinct vertices. Mathematically, the differences lie in how edges are structured:

- *Directed* graphs: the edge set is a finite collection of *ordered* pairs. An edge from A to B does not imply an edge from B to A.
- *Undirected* graphs: the edge set is a finite collection of *unordered* pairs of distinct vertices. If a connection exists between A and B, it automatically works both ways. *Figure 7.3* shows the structural difference between an undirected and a directed graph.

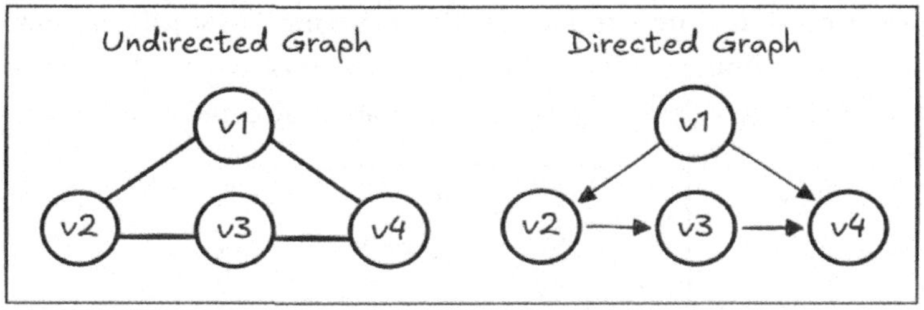

Figure 7.3: Undirected vs Directed Graph

In Java, both directed and undirected graphs can be declared similarly using an adjacency list, often represented as `Map<V, List<Edge<V>>>` in `G`, as we will study in the latter section. The structural difference lies in the `addEdge` method:

- **Undirected Graph**: The `addEdge(u, v)` method adds `v` to `u`'s list and `u` to `v`'s list to ensure bidirectional traversal.
- **Directed Graph**: The `addEdge(u, v)` method adds `v` to `u`'s list only, representing a one-way edge from a source vertex to a destination vertex.

Graphs can contain cycles, which are closed loops of connected vertices and edges that start and end at the same vertex without repeating any intermediate steps. A **Directed Acyclic Graph (DAG)** is a directed graph completely devoid of directed cycles, ensuring that no sequence of directed edges can form a path that returns to its starting vertex.

Weighted graphs

A weighted graph is just a graph in which every edge carries a numeric value that tells you something about that connection, like how far apart two cities are (distance), how expensive it is to travel along a road (cost), or how strong a friendship is (similarity). For example:

- **Distance or cost**: In a street network, the weight might be the length of a street segment or the time it takes to traverse it.
- **Capacity or strength**: In a network of HVAC pipes, the weight could be the maximum flow each pipe can handle.
- **Similarity or preference**: In a recommendation system, the weight could represent how closely two items are related in categories.

Because the weight is often numeric, you can perform calculations that involve adding weights, comparing them, or finding the path that minimizes the total weight. Weighted edges are essential for several foundational algorithms. For instance, Dijkstra's relies on weights to find the shortest path, while Prim's and Kruskal's use them to determine minimum spanning trees. Additionally, the Bellman-Ford algorithm uses weights to identify negative cycles and calculate paths with negative costs. *Figure 7.4* shows an undirected weighted graph:

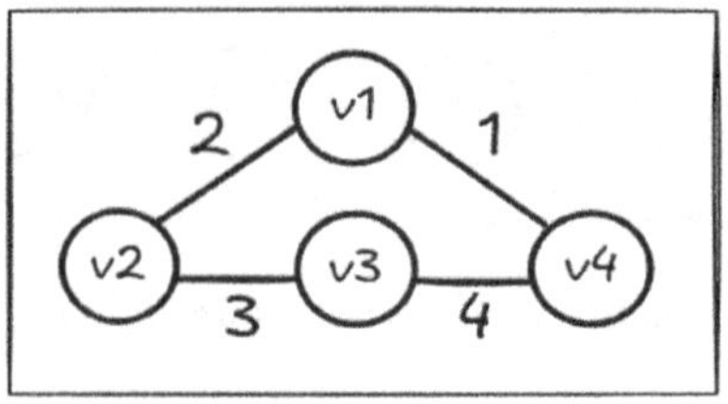

Figure 7.4: An undirected weighted graph

In the same notation we use for a common graph, `G = (V, E)`, we define a weight function, `W`, that assigns a numeric value to each edge in `G`.

$$G = (V, E, W)$$

In a data-structure, a weighted edge is typically stored as a triple `(u, v, w)`, where `w` is the weight associated with the edge from `u → v`:

```
void addEdge(V u, V v, W w);
```

To implement a weighted graph, we can create an adjacency list that maps each vertex to its outgoing neighbors and their associated weights. This structure can be represented as:

```
// Maps a vertex to its outgoing neighbors and their weights
// u → {v → w}
private final Map<V, Map<V, W>> adj = new HashMap<>();
private final boolean isDirected;
```

To mimic the weight function for edge-weight assignment, for example:

```
public void addVertex(V v) {
    adj.computeIfAbsent(v, k -> new HashMap<>());
}

public void addEdge(V u, V v, W w) {
    // Ensure both vertices exist in the graph
    addVertex(v);
    addVertex(u);

    // Add the forward edge (u -> v) with weight w
    adj.get(u).put(v, w);

    // If the graph is undirected, add the reverse
    // edge (v -> u)  with the same weight
    if (!isDirected)
        adj.get(v).put(u, w);
}
```

The above snippet demonstrates a flexible approach for handling both *directed* and *undirected* weighted graphs through a toggle switch (`isDirected`). Alternatively, we may also represent a weighted graph using separate classes for Vertex, Edge, and the Graph itself. This object-oriented approach provides encapsulation and scalability for complex graph operations:

```
public class Edge<V, W extends Number> {
    private final Vertex<V, W> destination;
    private final W weight;

    public Edge(Vertex<V, W> destination, W weight){
        this.destination = destination;
        this.weight = weight;
    }
    public Vertex<V, W> getDestination() { return destination; }
    public W getWeight() { return weight; }
}

public class Vertex<V, W extends Number> {
    private final V value;
    private final List<Edge<V, W>> edges = new ArrayList<>();

    public Vertex(V value) { this.value = value; }

    public void addEdge(Vertex<V, W> destination, W weight) {
        edges.add(new Edge<>(destination, weight));
    }

    public V getValue() { return value; }
    public List<Edge<V, W>> getEdges() { return edges; }
}
```

Graph implementation remains flexible. The graph structure we choose should align with the specific constraints of the problem we are solving. For example, while this approach is customizable, the previous Map-based adjacency list is often faster for direct edge lookups.

To conclude our introduction, understanding these graph variations is essential to solve complex problems. The visual comparison in *Figure 7.5* illustrates six fundamental configurations (undirected, directed, weighted, unweighted, cyclic, and acyclic) that form the foundation for advanced graph theory applications.

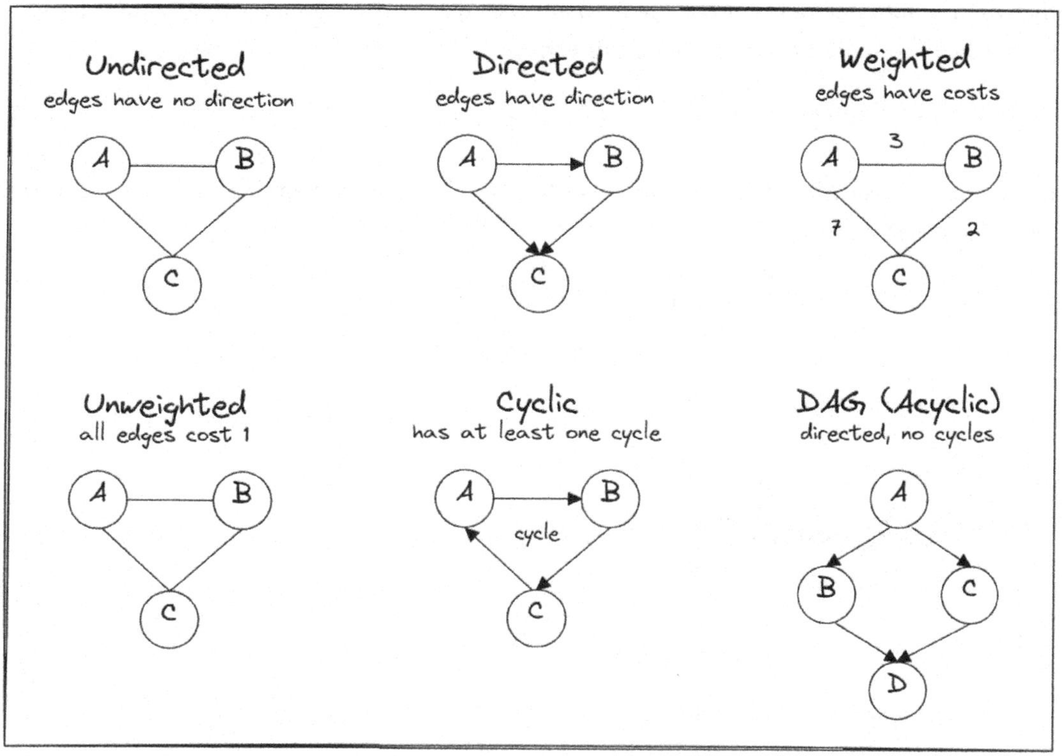

Figure 7.5: Graph data structure representation

Graph components

A graph is fundamentally a collection of two kinds of entities: vertices and edges that connect them. In Java, the most idiomatic way to model these building blocks is to treat a vertex as an arbitrary object, and an edge as either a lightweight pair of vertex references or as a richer object that can carry metadata such as a weight or label. Collections such as `HashMap`, `HashSet`, or primitive arrays are then used to map each vertex to its adjacency information. This representation lays out the basic concept of graph components that we will explore next.

Vertex

Each vertex in a graph represents an entity in it. Here is a compact, idiomatic Java example for a graph vertex using generics and **immutability**. If you're using Java 16+, records are ideal for this, as they automatically generate boilerplate code like constructors, accessors, and `equals`, `hashCode` for immutable data carriers, namely:

```
public record Vertex<T>(T value) { }
```

If you prefer classic **Plain Old Java Objects** (**POJOs**), the same idea applies by replacing `record` with a class as follows:

```
public final class Vertex<T> {
    private final T value;

    public Vertex(T value) {
        this.value = value;
    }

    public T getValue() {
        return value;
    }

    @Override
    public boolean equals(Object o) {
        if (this == o) return true;
        if (!(o instanceof Vertex<?> other)) return false;
        return Objects.equals(value, other.value);
    }

    @Override
    public int hashCode() {
        return Objects.hashCode(value);
    }

    @Override
    public String toString() {
        return "Vertex[value=" + value + "]";
    }
}
```

Since the vertex set V is simply a list of all vertices in the graph, we can codify V using a HashSet, as each vertex is distinct from the others:

```
public class Graph<T> {
    private final Set<Vertex<T>> vertices = new HashSet<>();
}
```

Hashset relies on equals or hashCode to determine object uniqueness. If Vertex is a record or a POJO with value-based equality, identical values are treated as duplicates, leaving only one instance in the set, even when separate nodes were intended. For identity-based vertex distinction, either implement identity-based equality or employ IdentityHashMap-backed structures rather than plain HashSet.

Edge

Each edge captures the pairwise relationship between a source and destination vertex. In Java, an edge may be modeled as an immutable final object that bundles together the two endpoint vertices. A common pattern is to make the edge a simple POJO with final fields for the source and destination, namely:

```
public final class Edge<V> {
    // Source and destination vertices
    private final Vertex<V> src;
    private final Vertex<V> dst;

    public Edge(Vertex<V> src, Vertex<V> dst) {
        if (src == null || dst == null) {
            throw new IllegalArgumentException(…);
        }
        this.src = src;
        this.dst = dst;
    }
    …
}
```

In lieu of the above POJO implementation, we may opt for the record syntax (Java 16+):

```
public record Edge<V>(Vertex<V> src, Vertex<V> dst) {
    public Edge {
        if (src == null || dst == null) {
            throw new IllegalArgumentException(...);
```

```
        }
    }
}
```

There is no explicit "`this.src = src; this.dst = dst;`" needed. The compiler does this automatically after the compact `Edge` constructor body runs. By keeping the edge immutable, we guarantee thread safety and avoid accidental mutation that could corrupt the overall graph or cause memory leak issues.

Vertex-to-Edge

Instead of keeping track of both vertices and edges separately, it is also effective to model the 1: N vertex-to-edge relationship in a composition design, where each vertex contains a list of outgoing edges:

```
public class Vertex<T> {
    // List of outgoing edges
    private final List<Edge<T>> edges = new ArrayList<>();

    public void addEdge(Vertex<T> destination) {
        edges.add(new Edge<>(destination));
    }
    ...
}
```

In this composition design, `Vertex` is mutable, as its `edges` list reference is `final`, but the list content can be henceforth updated via the `addEdge` operation. We define an immutable `Edge` class employing the generic Vertex class as follows:

```
public class Edge<V> {
    private final Vertex<V> destination;
    public Edge(Vertex<V> destination) {
        this.destination = destination;
    }
    public Vertex<V> getDestination() {
        return destination;
    }
}
```

The `Edge` class is immutable because its destination is `final` and set once in the constructor with no public setter; once an `Edge` is instantiated, it cannot be changed.

> **Note**
>
> In this design approach, we make `Vertex` mutable while keeping `Edge` immutable, departing from a fully immutable approach. This is a reasonable decision since we require mutability to enable the adjacency list structure to grow incrementally.

By nesting edges within the vertex that originates from them, the model aligns the data structure with the natural flow of graph traversal, specifically in a directed graph, as we will see later (*Figure 7.6*). Adding a new edge can be done via `vertexSource.addEdge(vertexDestination)`, which appends the new edge to the source vertex's local neighbor list. Instead of searching through a global list of all edges in the graph, we only need to modify the internal list of the specific source vertex, which is quick when a graph is sparse:

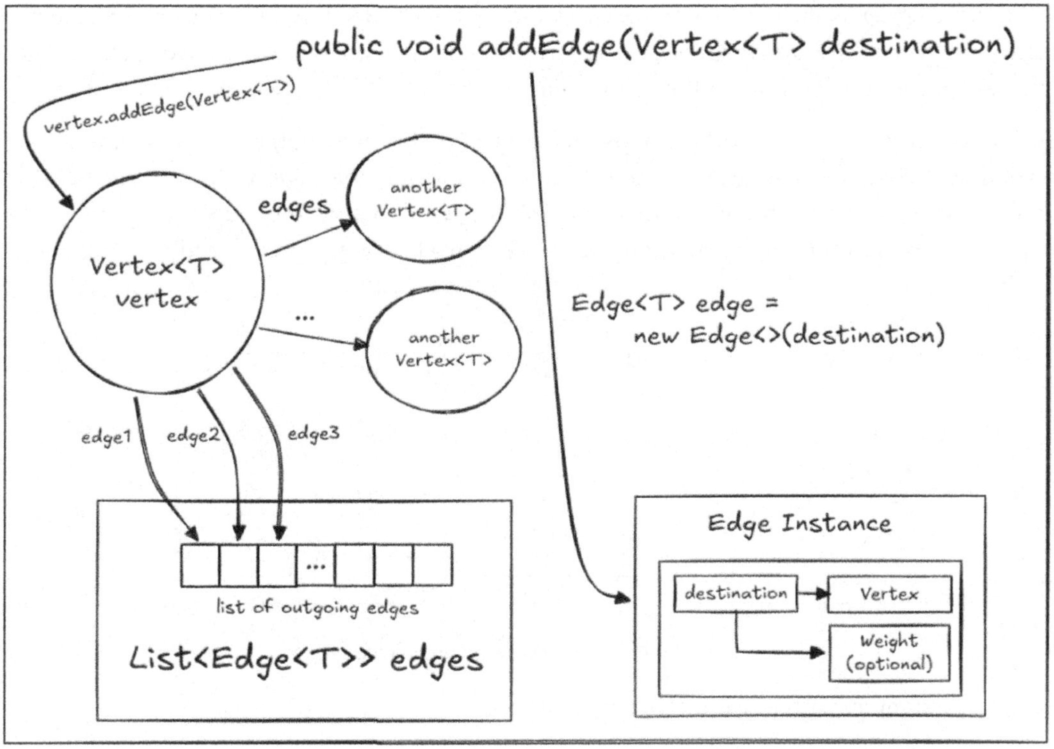

Figure 7.6: Vertex-Edge Relationship Diagram

With the vertex and edge components now defined, the following sections dive into how graphs are implemented, their performance characteristics, and the scenarios in which one or the other should be chosen.

Graph representation

A graph is a set of vertices and a set of edges that connect them. There are two canonical formats for encoding a graph:

- Adjacency list
- Adjacency matrix

We will look at their trade-offs in terms of memory usage versus query speed, and ease of manipulation versus sparsity awareness in the following sections.

Adjacency list

The adjacency list is the most common way to store that connection information in memory, especially when the graph is sparse, i.e., having few edges compared to the maximum number of edges possible, resulting in a low graph density.

At its core, an adjacency-list graph maps each vertex to a list of its outgoing edges, optionally including metadata like weights or other values, storing only the edges that exist. *Figure 7.7* depicts an adjacency list for an undirected graph (i.e., v1, v2, v3, v4 with edges without direction). In this representation, each node is a key in a list that points to its direct neighbors:

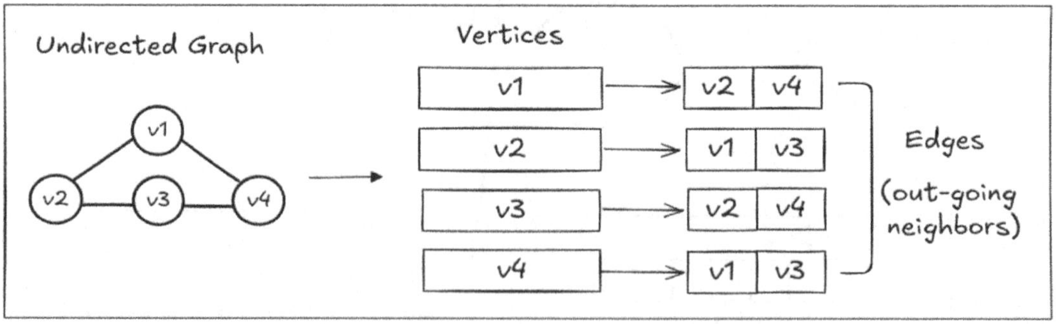

Figure 7.7: Adjacency list for an undirected graph

The most common pattern for this list is as follows:

```
Map<V, List<Edge<V>>>
```

This is done with each vertex mapping to a collection of its outgoing edges:

```
private final Map<V, List<Edge<V>>> adjList = new HashMap<>();
```

Edges are stored in an `ArrayList`, which implements the `List` interface, preserving insertion order and providing cache-friendly traversal. Because `List` is backed by a dynamic array, appending elements is amortized `O(1)`.

To achieve membership checks in `O(1)`, we may replace the list with a `HashSet` to avoid linear iteration. A `HashSet` implements `Set` and is backed by a `HashMap`, so we could go with `Map<Vertex, Set<Edge>>`. Since a set's iteration order is essentially random, this approach is suitable when the order of edges is irrelevant and you need constant-time lookups.

Following is a minimal, type-safe implementation adhering to this contract:

```
public interface Graph<V> {
    void addVertex(V v);
    void addEdge(V src, V dst);
    List<Edge<V>> neighbors(V v);
    Collection<Vertex<V>> getVertices();
}
```

We can likewise implement this adjacency list graph as follows:

```
import java.util.*;

public class AdjacencyListGraph<V> implements Graph<V> {
    private final Map<Vertex<V>, List<Edge<V>>> adjacencyMap = new HashMap<>();
    private final Map<V, Vertex<V>> vertexLookup = new HashMap<>();

    @Override
    public void addVertex(V v) {
        vertexLookup.computeIfAbsent(v, val -> {
            Vertex<V> vertex = new Vertex<>(val);
            adjacencyMap.putIfAbsent(vertex, new ArrayList<>());
            return vertex;
        });
    }

    @Override
    public void addEdge(V src, V dst) {
```

```
        addVertex(src);
        addVertex(dst);
        Vertex<V> srcVertex = vertexLookup.get(src);
        Vertex<V> dstVertex = vertexLookup.get(dst);
        adjacencyMap.get(srcVertex).add(new Edge<>(dstVertex));
        adjacencyMap.get(dstVertex).add(new Edge<>(srcVertex));
    }

    @Override
    public List<Edge<V>> neighbors(V v) {
        Vertex<V> vertex = vertexLookup.get(v);
        if (vertex == null) return Collections.emptyList();
        return adjacencyMap.getOrDefault(vertex, Collections.emptyList());
    }

    @Override
    public Collection<Vertex<V>> getVertices() {
        return adjacencyMap.keySet();
    }
}
```

The cardinality |V| is of `getVertices().size()`, and |E| is obtained by iterating through all the adjacency lists and cumulatively summing their sizes:

```
adjacencyMap.values().stream().mapToInt(List::size).sum() / 2;
```

Because the above implementation is an undirected graph, every edge is stored twice (once in the source vertex's list and another in the destination vertex's list). Therefore, the above stream computation yields exactly 2 times |E|. To get the actual number of unique undirected edges in the graph, we divide the resulting sum by 2.

Most graph algorithms, such as search, shortest-path, and connectivity, work with this basic (V, E) structure. In the next section, we'll look at the adjacency matrix alternative, contrasting its performance and memory usage with the adjacency list we just explored.

Adjacency matrix

The adjacency matrix is another classic alternative to implementing a graph. This matrix allows for efficient edge lookups in constant time when the graph is dense. In a matrix, we allocate a two-dimensional grid of entries, one per possible vertex pair and set a flag (or store a weight) to indicate the presence of an edge. For an undirected graph, the matrix is symmetrical (see *Figure 7.8*):

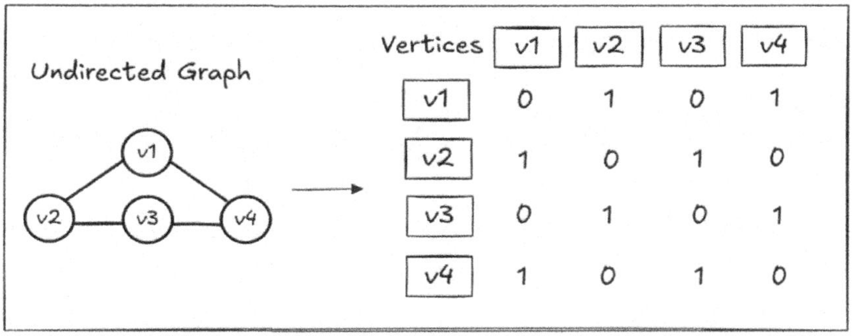

Figure 7.8: Adjacency matrix for an undirected graph

We can represent this relationship in an adjacency matrix, `M`, as `M[i][j] = M[j][i]`, where M[i][j] = 1 if and only if there is an edge between vertex `i` and vertex `j`. That is, each row-column pair corresponds to a vertex; a "1" denotes an undirected edge between the two vertices, whereas a "0" represents no edge. Structurally, `M` is a `|V| x |V|` table of vertices costing $O(|V|^2)$ in storage regardless of sparsity, where `|V|` is the cardinality of vertices.

The Adjacency matrix is highly efficient for dense graphs and allows for constant-time lookup to check if an edge exists between two nodes. However, because it requires quadratic space, it can be memory-intensive for large, sparse graphs. For weighted graphs, the implementation is easily adapted by storing the specific weight of the edge in the corresponding matrix cell instead of a binary value.

A simplified, primitive index-based Java example for an unweighted, undirected graph is as follows:

```
public class Graph {
    private int[][] adjMatrix;
    private int numVertices;

    public Graph(int numVertices) {
        this.numVertices = numVertices;
        this.adjMatrix = new int[numVertices][numVertices];
    }

    // For undirected graph, set both [i][j] and [j][i])
    public void addEdge(int i, int j) {
        if (i >= 0&&i< numVertices &&j>= 0&&j< numVertices){
            adjMatrix[i][j] = 1;
            adjMatrix[j][i] = 1;
```

```
        }
    }

    public void removeEdge(int i, int j) {
        if (i >= 0&&i< numVertices &&j>= 0&&j< numVertices){
            adjMatrix[i][j] = 0;
            adjMatrix[j][i] = 0;
        }
    }

    public boolean hasEdge(int i, int j) {
        if (i >= 0&&i< numVertices &&j>= 0&&j< numVertices){
            return adjMatrix[i][j] == 1;
        }
        return false;
        }
}
```

Performance characteristics

When choosing a graph representation, the tradeoffs between space and time are decisive. Below, we lay out the key characteristics of the two canonical data structures, with a side-by-side comparison:

Operation	Adjacency List	Adjacency Matrix
Space Complexity	O(V + E); store only existing edges	O(V²); fixed-size matrix
Add Vertex	Amortized O(1); hash map insertion	O(V²); requires array resizing and copying
Add Edge	Amortized O(1); append to adjacency list	O(1); matrix cell update
Delete Edge	O(deg(v)); linearly scan neighbor list	O(1); reset cell to 0
Edge Existence	O(deg(u)); linearly scan outgoing list	O(1); direct access

Operation	Adjacency List	Adjacency Matrix
Retrieve Neighbors	`O(deg(v))`; iterate list	`O(V)`; scan row/column
Typical Use-Case	Sparse graphs (e.g., social networks)	Dense or near-complete graphs

Table 7.1: Characteristics of an adjacency list and an adjacency matrix

Choosing a graph representation

When deciding between an adjacency list and an adjacency matrix, the choice hinges entirely on graph density and the specific operations your algorithms perform.

For sparse graphs, where $E \approx V$ but much less than V^2, choose an Adjacency List to save memory; adjacency lists eliminate wasted space by storing actual connections. For dense graphs, where `E` approaches V^2, choose the Adjacency Matrix where the fast edge lookup (`O(1)`) justifies the memory cost.

When to use adjacency list

When our graph is sparse, namely the number of edges `E` is much smaller than the maximum V^2, an adjacency list is almost always the better choice as it eliminates wasted space by storing actual connections. Since the neighbors are stored contiguously in a list, we can traverse it in `O(deg(v))` time. The list stores only the edges that exist; the overall memory footprint is linear in the size of the graph `O(V + E)`. This can lead to dramatic savings compared to a dense representation, making adjacency lists ideal for scenarios where memory is at a premium, and we frequently need to explore the local structure of the graph.

When to use adjacency matrix

When the graph is densely connected, namely when `E` is close to the maximum V^2, an adjacency matrix becomes the ideal representation. The cost of storing every possible connection is amortized, and we can test the presence of an edge in constant time (`O(1)`) by simply indexing the matrix. Moreover, many graph algorithms, such as all-pairs shortest paths or reachability queries, are expressed most naturally as operations on the adjacency matrix (e.g., boolean matrix multiplication or repeated squaring for pathfinding). The ability to apply bulk linear algebraic operations directly to the matrix thus yields significant performance gains, especially when combined with hardware acceleration or parallel processing.

In the next section, we will look at how to model a graph as an Abstract Data Type (ADT), describe its public interface, and see a few minimal concrete implementations in Java. This decoupling ensures that any graph algorithm we write can operate across both memory-efficient adjacency lists and performance-optimized adjacency matrices without modifying a single line of downstream code.

Abstract data type (ADT) – graph

We examine a graph's specification and its operations with a generic interface consisting of the following components of a graph:

- Vertices: A set of unique objects
- Edges: A set of directed or undirected pairs of vertices, optionally with weight

The key operations include:

- `addVertex`: inserts a new vertex into the graph.
- `addEdge(v, u, w?)`: establishes a connection from vertex `v` to vertex `u`. An optional weight `w` may be attached to encode cost, capacity, or any other attribute. If either vertex does not already exist in the graph, it is automatically created and added first.
- `vertices()`: return a collection of all vertices.
- `getVertexCount`: get the number of vertices, `|V|`.
- `getEdgeCount`: get the number of edges, `|E|`.
- `getNeighbors(v)`: get the set of vertices emanating from `v` (out-neighbors in a directed graph).

Following is a minimal but fully generic Java interface that captures the essential graph ADT:

```
public interface Graph<V, W> {

    // Insert a vertex; no effect if the vertex already exists.
    void addVertex(V v);

    // Insert a directed edge v → u with weight.
    void addEdge(V v, V u, W weight);

    // Return an unmodifiable view of the vertex set.
    Set<V> vertices();

    // Return an unmodifiable list of neighbors.
    // Note: out-neighbors for directed.
    List<V> getNeighbors(V v);
```

```
    // Return the weight of edge v → u, or null if no such edge.
    W getWeight(V v, V u);

    // Get the number of vertices |V|.
    int getVertexCount();

    // Get number of edges |E|.
    // Note: for directed graph, each edge is counted once.
    int getEdgeCount();

    // Is the graph directed or not
    boolean isDirected();
}
```

As we studied earlier, we may employ either an adjacency list or a matrix to implement a graph. In some instances, we may employ an edge list that is a simple collection of tuples (u, v, w). This representation is ideal for algorithms that process all edges globally, such as finding a minimum spanning tree (a subset of edges that connects all vertices with the minimum total weight). This structure, however, is less efficient for per-vertex neighbor queries.

In summary, choosing the right representation hinges on the graph's density, the frequency of neighbor lookups versus edge checks, and the nature of the algorithms that will operate on it. With the underlying structure selected, the next fundamental step is learning how to navigate the graph. This process, known as graph traversal, serves as the backbone for nearly all advanced graph algorithms.

What is a traversal?

Much like tree traversal, a graph traversal is an algorithmic strategy for systematically visiting every vertex and edge in a graph exactly once, following a well-defined order. There are two classic traversal methods in a graph:

- Depth-First Search (DFS)
- Breadth-First Search (BFS)

Each of the methods imposes a distinct exploration hierarchy on the search process. In DFS, the algorithm dives deep along a path before backtracking, while BFS explores all vertices at a given distance from the source before moving to the next level. *Figure 7.9* illustrates these contrasting traversal orders in a simple graph:

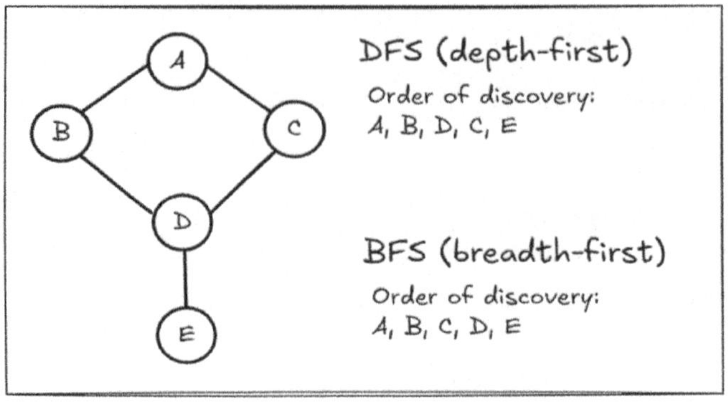

Figure 7.9: DFS vs. BFS in a graph

These traversal techniques underpin a wide range of practical applications:

- **Social-network analysis**: DFS can identify all reachable users from a profile, map connected communities, or clean up orphan sub-networks
- **Route-planning**: BFS can find the fewest edges between two locations, while DFS can enumerate all possible alternative routes
- **Recommendation engines**: graph traversal is used to walk through a product-user interaction graph, discovering connected items and calculating influence scores for personalized suggestions
- **Data serialization**: traversal allows an arbitrary graph (e.g., a module dependency network), to be flattened into a linear sequence for JSON storage, database persistence, or network transmission

In each case, the choice of DFS or BFS, and the underlying graph representation (adjacency list, matrix, or edge list), shapes the efficiency and feasibility of the task.

In the sections that follow, we will delve deeper into the mechanics of DFS and BFS, exploring their time complexities, implementation nuances, and the problem domains for which they shine.

Depth-first traversal

DFS prioritizes vertical exploration, traversing as far down a branch as possible before retreating to explore alternative paths. In a graph, it systematically explores one branch as far as possible before retreating to the previous vertex and trying an alternative route. DFS backs many algorithms, including topological sorting, cycle detection, and connected-component enumeration.

We can generalize this algorithm with the following pseudocode:

- Pick a start vertex, V_{start}
- Push V_{start} onto a stack
- While the stack is not empty:
    - Pop a vertex v
    - If v has not been visited, mark it as visited
    - Push all unvisited neighbors of v onto the stack

The order in which vertices are marked visited defines the DFS traversal order. Below is an implementation utilizing our `Graph` interface and the Java Collections Framework's `Deque` as the stack mechanism:

```
import java.util.*;

public class DFS<V> {
    private final Graph<V> graph;
    public DFS(Graph<V> graph) {
       this.graph = graph;
    }

    public List<V> traverse(V start) {
        Set<V> visited = new HashSet<>();
        List<V> order = new ArrayList<>();
        Deque<V> stack = new ArrayDeque<>();
        stack.push(start);

        while (!stack.isEmpty()) {
            V v = stack.pop();
            if (visited.contains(v)) continue;
            visited.add(v);
            order.add(v);

            List<V> neighbors = graph.getNeighbors(v);

            for (int i = neighbors.size() - 1; i >= 0; --i) {
                V nb = neighbors.get(i);
                if (!visited.contains(nb)) stack.push(nb);
            }
        }
```

```
        return order;
    }
}
```

Note

Instead of managing a separate `HashSet` for `O(1)` fast lookups and an `ArrayList` to preserve tracking sequence, we can consolidate both into a single `LinkedHashSet` to reduce our data tracking down to a single collection. This hybrid Java collection combines a hash table with a doubly linked list, natively guaranteeing constant-time uniqueness checks while maintaining the exact insertion order of traversal as elements are popped and visited.

The DFS mechanism is captured in *Figure 7.10*:

Undirected Graph:

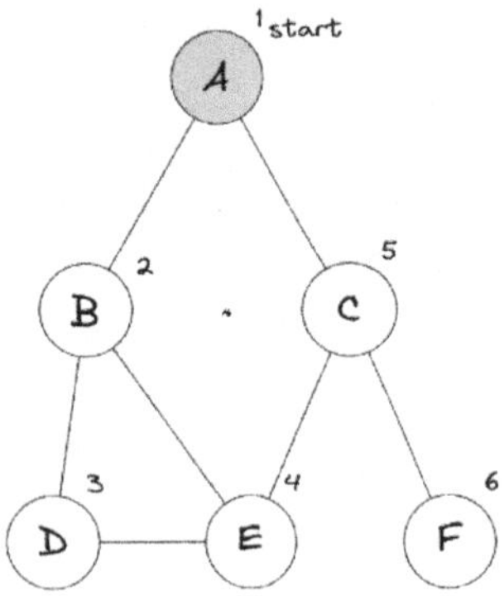

Steps (start from A, iterative):

#	Action	Stack	Visited	Output
1	push A	[A]	{}	—
2	pop A, mark, push C,B	[C, B]	{A}	A
3	pop B, mark, push E,D	[C, E, D]	{A,B}	A B
4	pop D, mark, push E(dup)	[C, E, E]	{A,B,D}	A B D
5	pop E, mark, push C(dup)	[C, E, C]	{A,B,D,E}	A B D E
6	pop C, mark, push F	[E, C, F]	{A,B,C,D,E}	A B D E C
7	pop F, mark	[E, C]	{A,B,C,D,E,F}	A B D E C F
8	pop C,E (visited,skip)	[ ]	all	A B D E C F

Figure 7.10: DFS with stack

For DFS, we have several key observations:

- `visited` **Set**: this is used to mark visited vertices to avoid infinite loops in cyclic graphs.
- **Ordering**: the choice of pushing neighbors in natural or reverse order affects the exact traversal sequence, but it does not alter the final set of reachable vertices.
- **Iterations vs recursions**: we employ an explicit stack to drive the iterable approach, which remains memory-safe even for large graphs. While DFS can be written recursively, doing so risks stack overflow errors if the graph's depth exceeds the runtime's call stack capacity.

Breadth-first traversal

Unlike Depth-First Search (DFS), which easily adapts to recursion, Breadth-First Search (BFS) is inherently iterative and relies on a queue data structure to manage its execution. BFS is the "wavelike" strategy: it explores all vertices at a given distance from the start before moving to the next level. In an unweighted graph, this approach guarantees finding the shortest path (measured by the fewest edges) from a source to every reachable vertex. It also serves as the backbone for many network analysis tasks, such as computing levels in a hierarchy, performing flood fills, and executing level-order tree traversals.

We present the iterative pseudocode:

- Pick a start vertex V_{start}
- Enqueue V_{start} into a queue
- While the queue is not empty:
    - Dequeue a vertex v
    - If v has not been visited, mark it as visited
    - Enqueue all unvisited neighbors of v

The order in which vertices are dequeued defines the BFS traversal order. By employing the same `Graph` interface used for DFS as before, we arrive at the following canonical example for running BFS on a graph:

```
import java.util.*;

public class BFS<V> {
    private final {Graph<V, ?> graph;

    public BFS(Graph<V, ?> graph) {
        this.graph = graph;
    }
    public List<V> traverse(V start) {
        Set<V> visited = new HashSet<>();
        List<V> order = new ArrayList<>();
        Deque<V> queue = new ArrayDeque<>();

        queue.add(start);

        while (!queue.isEmpty()) {
            V v = queue.poll();
```

```
            if (visited.contains(v)) continue;
            visited.add(v);
            order.add(v);

            for (V nb : graph.getNeighbors(v)) {
                if (!visited.contains(nb)) queue.add(nb);
            }
        }
        return order;
    }
}
```

The BFS mechanism is captured in *Figure 7.11*.

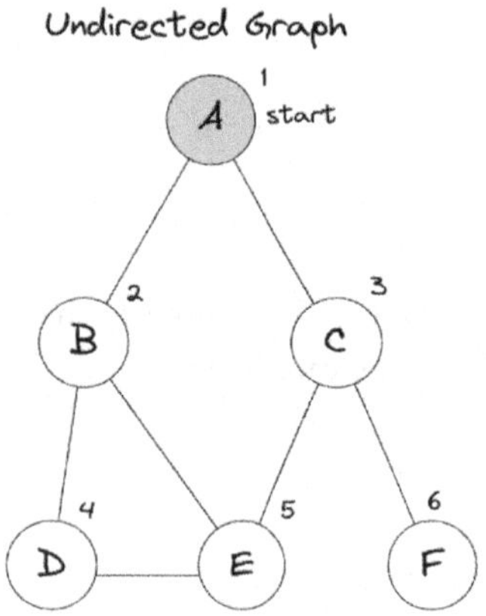

Steps (start from A):

#	Action	Queue	Visited	Output
1	enqueue A, mark visited	[A]	{}	A
2	dequeue A, enqueue B,C	[B, C]	{A}	A
3	dequeue B, enqueue D,E	[C, D, E]	{A,B}	A B
4	dequeue C, enqueue F	[D, E, F]	{A,B,C}	A B C
5	dequeue D (E visited)	[E, F]	{A,B,C,D}	A B C D
6	dequeue E (all visited)	[F]	{A,B,C,D,E}	A B C D E
7	dequeue F	[ ]	{A,B,C,D,E,F}	A B C D E F

Figure 7.11: BFS with queue

For BFS, we have several key observations:

- `visited` **Set**: similar to its role in DFS, this tracking mechanism marks visited vertices to avoid infinite loops in cyclic graphs.
- **Iterations vs recursions**: the algorithm is naturally iterative. Using an explicit Queue keeps the memory usage stable and predictable. Recursion (e.g., by passing the current frontier as a parameter), on the other hand, may lead to stack overflows on large graphs.
- **Level (Height) tracking**: since BFS traversal calls for level-by-level visitation of the graph, we can track the level-distance from the source by maintaining a `Map<V, Integer>` that stores the level as we enqueue vertices.

> **Note**
>
> The term "frontier" in graph search refers to the set of all vertices that have been discovered but have not yet been fully explored or processed. For example, during a BFS, the frontier consists of the vertices currently waiting in the queue, which can span across two adjacent levels at the same time. On the other hand, the DFS frontier is strictly limited to nodes on the active path, and the immediate alternative branches are bypassed during descent.

BFS serves as the driving engine behind many graph utilizations in the industry, such as connected component enumeration, bipartite graph checking, and proximity-based processing in social network analysis.

Trade-off analysis: DFS vs. BFS

The same tradeoffs that apply to tree traversals carry over to graphs. DFS and BFS are complementary; the right one depends on the graph structure (deep versus wide), the algorithmic goal (shortest path versus component or connectivity checks), and practical limits such as memory usage and recursion depth.

For instance, DFS's stack-based approach is ideal for detecting cycles and for generating topological orders, whereas BFS's queue guarantees the shortest edge count path in an unweighted graph and lends itself to level order labeling. DFS explores one branch as far as possible before backtracking, which keeps the frontier small but can lead to deep recursion; BFS visits all vertices at a given distance before expanding, yielding a larger, unpredictable frontier depending on the graph's width.

In deep graphs, DFS is often more memory-efficient because its stack size is limited by the graph depth, while in wide or dense graphs, BFS's queue can grow very large because it must store all nodes at the current level.

> **Note**
>
> "Wide or dense" means a high branching factor at specific levels. An overall sparse graph can still cause a BFS queue spike if a single level is very wide. Conversely, a dense graph can remain memory-efficient if its edges are concentrated depth-wise.

These nuances, namely cycle detection, path optimality, frontier size, and stack versus queue behavior, guide the choice between DFS and BFS in many graph-based problems.

Graphs in java collections framework

Java lacks a native graph class, relying instead on its collections framework to construct custom graph structures from `Map`, `Set`, and `Collection` interfaces (*Figure 7.12*). For a robust, production-ready alternative, readers may refer to the Google Guava libraries, which provide comprehensive graph implementations. For a complete guide, visit the Google Guava Graphs Explained Wiki in `https://github.com/google/guava/wiki/GraphsExplained`.

In Java, key classes for implementing and optimizing graph algorithms include `HashMap`, `HashSet`, `PriorityQueue`, `Deque`, `Stack`, `TreeMap`, `ConcurrentHashMap`, and `LinkedHashSet`, to name a few. Each collection type offers unique advantages for different graph problems. Moving past these foundational structures, the next section details practical use cases for these tools.

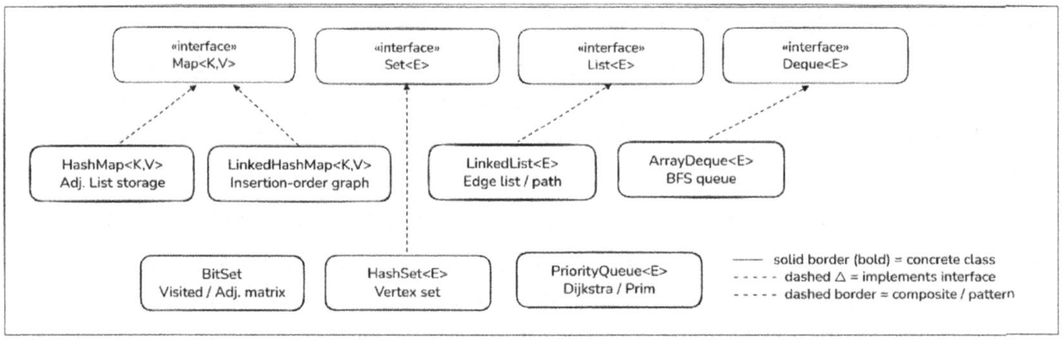

Figure 7.12: Graph-related components in JCF

HashSet for unweighted graphs

This approach utilizes HashSet to store vertices or edges, enabling fast membership testing and preventing duplicate entries in graph operations. What problem is solved here? This implementation solves the problem of fast membership testing and avoids duplicate edges during graph traversal and connectivity checks.

```
Set<Integer> visited = new HashSet<>();
Set<String> edges = new HashSet<>();
int u1 = 1, v1 = 2;
edges.add(Math.min(u1, v1) + "-" + Math.max(u1, v1));

int u2 = 2, v2 = 1;
edges.add(Math.min(u2, v2) + "-" + Math.max(u2, v2));
```

Priority queue: Dijkstra's algorithm

This approach uses `PriorityQueue` to maintain vertices in order of their distances, enabling efficient selection of the next vertex with minimum distance in shortest path algorithms. This implementation solves the problem of efficiently selecting the next vertex with minimum distance in Dijkstra's algorithm, which is essential for finding shortest paths in weighted graphs.

```
PriorityQueue<int[]> pq = new PriorityQueue<>((a, b) -> Integer.compare(a[1] -
b[1]));
pq.offer(new int[]{vertex, 0});
while (!pq.isEmpty()) {
    int[] current = pq.poll();
    int vertex = current[0];
    int distance = current[1];

    if (distance > distArray[vertex]) { continue; }

    // Process neighbors and edges here}
}
```

Deque: BFS implementation

This approach uses `ArrayDeque` as a queue for breadth-first search traversal, providing efficient FIFO operations for level-by-level graph exploration. This implementation solves the problem of efficient level-by-level graph traversal in breadth-first search algorithms, which is essential for finding the shortest paths in unweighted graphs and exploring graph neighborhoods systematically.

```
Deque<Integer> queue = new ArrayDeque<>();
queue.offer(startVertex);
while (!queue.isEmpty()) {
    int vertex = queue.poll();
    // Process neighbors
    for (int neighbor : adjList.get(vertex)) {
        if (!visited.contains(neighbor)) {
            queue.offer(neighbor);
        }
    }
}
```

Stack: DFS implementation

This approach uses an explicit stack to drive a depth-first search traversal, enabling recursive behavior without relying on the system call stack. This implementation minimizes the risk of stack overflow in deep graphs.

```
Deque<Integer> stack = new ArrayDeque<>();
stack.push(startVertex);
while (!stack.isEmpty()) {
    int vertex = stack.pop();

    if (visited.contains(vertex)) { continue; }

    // Mark visited and process the vertex here
    visited.add(vertex);

    // Push unvisited neighbors onto the stack
    for (int neighbor : adjList.get(vertex)) {
        if (!visited.contains(neighbor)) {
            stack.push(neighbor);
        }
    }
}
```

TreeMap: Ordered map operations

This approach uses a `TreeMap` to construct an adjacency list where vertices are in their natural sorted order.. This implementation solves the problem of non-deterministic outputs in applications requiring predictable vertex processing, such as guaranteeing a repeatable, stable sequence during topological sorting and dependency resolution.

```
Map<Integer, List<Integer>> orderedAdjList = new TreeMap<>();
orderedAdjList.put(1, new ArrayList<>());
orderedAdjList.put(2, new ArrayList<>());

// Vertices processed in sorted order
for (Map.Entry<Integer, List<Integer>> entry :
    orderedAdjList.entrySet()) {
    int vertex = entry.getKey();
    List<Integer> neighbors = entry.getValue();
```

```
    // Process vertices and their adjacency lists }
}
```

ConcurrentHashMap: Parallel graph processing

This approach uses `ConcurrentHashMap` to enable thread-safe graph operations, allowing multiple threads to modify the graph structure simultaneously without synchronization overhead. This implementation solves the problem of thread-safe graph modifications and parallel processing of graph algorithms, which is essential for multi-threaded applications and concurrent graph algorithms.

```
Map<Integer, List<Integer>>parallelAdjList = new ConcurrentHashMap<>();

parallelAdjList.computeIfAbsent(1,k-> Collections.synchronizedList( new
ArrayList<>())).add(2);

// Alternate choice for read-heavy graphs:
CopyOnWriteArrayList parallelAdjList.computeIfAbsent(3, k -> new
CopyOnWriteArrayList<>()).add(4);
```

LinkedHashSet: Maintaining insertion order

This approach uses `LinkedHashSet` to maintain the insertion order of vertices while ensuring uniqueness, combining the benefits of ordered traversal with duplicate prevention. This implementation solves the problem of preserving vertex insertion order while avoiding duplicates, which is essential for applications like topological sorting and dependency resolution where both order and uniqueness matter.

```
Set<Integer> vertexOrder = new LinkedHashSet<>();
vertexOrder.add(1);
vertexOrder.add(2);
vertexOrder.add(3);
// Maintains insertion order for vertex processing
for (Integer vertex : vertexOrder) {
    // Process vertices in insertion order
}
```

Summary

Graphs represent abstract mathematical structures capturing relationships among entities, serving as the foundation for applications like social networks, route planning, and dependency resolution. A graph `G = (V, E)` consists of vertices (`V`) and edges (`E`), classified as either directed or undirected, and weighted or unweighted. The two primary storage formats are:

- Adjacency lists for sparse graphs (`O(|V| + |E|)` space)
- Adjacency matrices for dense graphs ($O(|V|^2)$ space)

The Java Collection Framework provides essential data structures for graph implementation: `HashMap` for adjacency lists, `HashSet` for membership testing, `PriorityQueue` for Dijkstra's algorithm, `Deque` for BFS traversal, `Stack` for DFS traversal, `ConcurrentHashMap` for thread-safe operations, and `TreeMap` for ordered processing. These collections enable efficient implementation of core graph operations, including vertex/edge management, neighbor retrieval, and connectivity analysis. *Figure 7.13* is a summary diagram of graphs for overview.

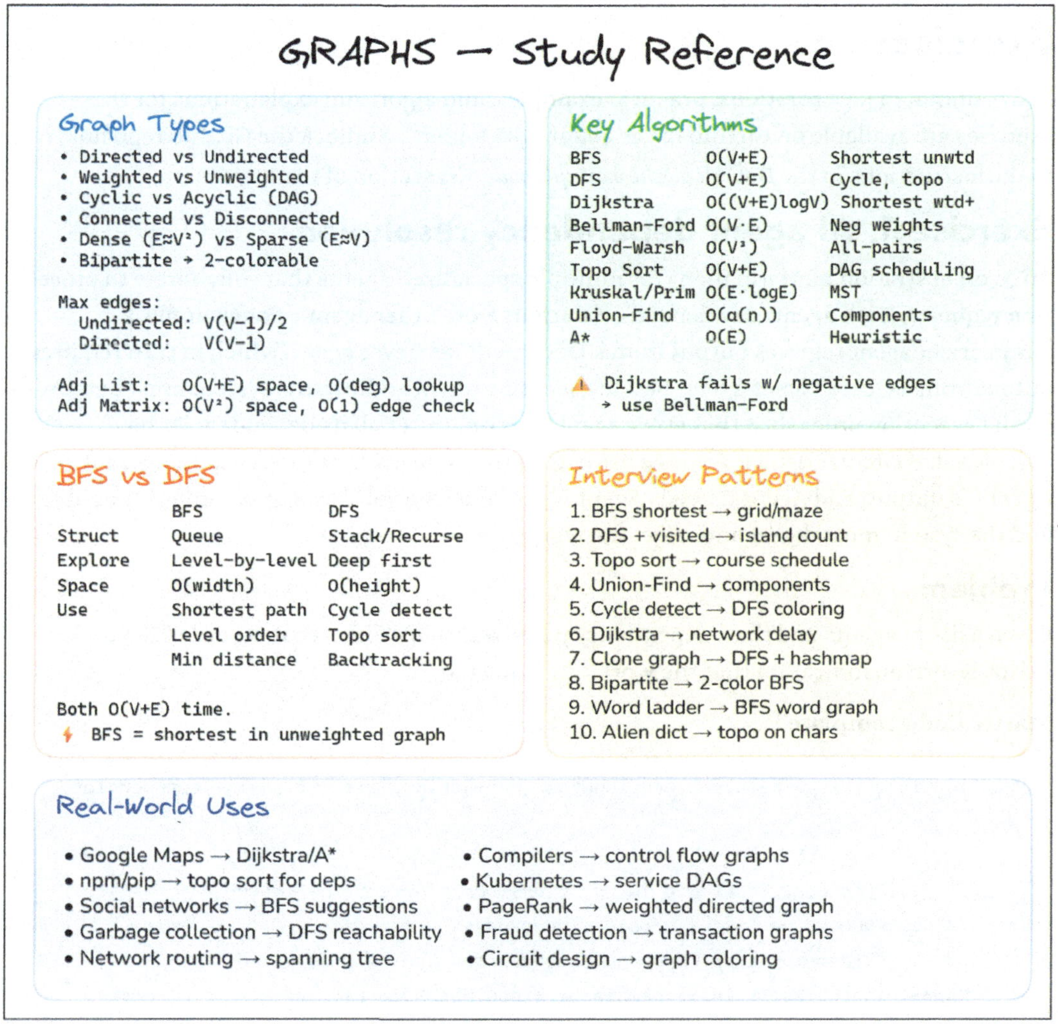

Figure 7.13: Summary of Graphs

In the next chapter, we will explore how to combine the graph abstractions we build (adjacency lists, matrices, and traversal utilities) with dynamic-programming paradigms involving memoization. We'll see how a DAG can be topologically sorted to compute shortest paths in linear time, how Bellman-Ford relaxes edges repeatedly to handle negative weights, and how graph-based DP underlies algorithms such as the **traveling-salesman problem (TSP)**, longest path in a DAG, and many combinatorial counting problems.

Exercises

Fully annotated Java solutions, practical examples, and algorithm explanations for these exercises are available on GitHub in the `Chapter07` folder. To unlock the GitHub repo link, refer to the instructions in the *Download the example code files* section of the *Preface*.

Exercise 1: AI agent dependency resolution

An AI orchestration platform manages multiple specialized agents that collaborate to process user requests. Each agent may depend on outputs from other agents. For example, a Summarizer agent requires output from a Document Retriever agent, which in turn requires output from a Query Parser agent. Before executing any workflow, the system must determine a valid execution order such that every agent runs only after all its dependencies have completed. If circular dependencies exist (e.g., Agent A needs Agent B's output, Agent B needs Agent C's output, and Agent C needs Agent A's output), no valid execution order is possible, and the system must detect and reject the workflow.

Problem

Given a list of agents and their dependency pairs, return a valid execution order. If a cycle exists, return an indication that the workflow is invalid.

Starter Code Template

```
public List<String> resolveExecutionOrder(Map<String, List<String>> dependencies)
{

    // [1] Deep copy input map so mutations don't affect the caller
    //      Each value list is copied independently (new ArrayList) to allow
    //      safe removal of resolved dependencies during processing
    Map<String, List<String>> remaining = new HashMap<>();
    for (Map.Entry<String, List<String>> entry : dependencies.entrySet()) {
        remaining.put(entry.getKey(), new ArrayList<>(entry.getValue()));
    }

    // [2] Accumulates the final execution order
    //      Agents are appended layer by layer as they become ready
    List<String> order = new ArrayList<>();

    // [3] Main loop: each iteration processes one "layer" of ready agents
    //      Terminates when: all agents placed (success) or cycle detected
(exception)
```

```
    while (!remaining.isEmpty()) {

        // [4] Scan all remaining agents to find those with empty dependency lists
        //     Empty list = all dependencies already resolved = safe to execute
now
        //     This is the O(n) scan that makes the overall algorithm O(n²)
        List<String> ready = new ArrayList<>();
        for (Map.Entry<String, List<String>> entry : remaining.entrySet()) {
            if (entry.getValue().isEmpty()) {
                ready.add(entry.getKey());
            }
        }

        // [5] Cycle detection: if no agent has zero dependencies, they're all
        //     waiting on something that's also waiting - circular deadlock
        //     Example: A→B, B→C, C→A - none will ever have an empty list
        if (ready.isEmpty()) {
            throw new IllegalStateException("Circular dependency detected");
        }

        // [6] Commit this layer to the execution order
        //     All agents in 'ready' can execute in parallel (no
interdependencies)
        order.addAll(ready);

        // [7] Remove resolved agents from the remaining pool
        //     They've been placed in the order - no longer need tracking
        for (String agent : ready) {
            remaining.remove(agent);
        }

        // [8] Remove resolved agents from everyone else's dependency lists
        //     This "unblocks" dependents - their list shrinks toward empty
        //     When a dependent's list becomes empty, it will be picked up next
round
        for (List<String> deps : remaining.values()) {
            deps.removeAll(ready);
        }
    }

    // [9] All agents successfully placed - return valid execution order
```

```
    return order;
}
```

Assumptions and Constraints

- Each agent has a unique string identifier
- An agent with no dependencies executes immediately
- Graph is given as directed edges (dependency → dependent)
- Single-threaded ordering; parallelism is handled separately
- `n` = number of agents (nodes in the graph), e.g., Summarizer, Document Retriever, Query Parser would contribute to `n`
- `m` = number of dependency pairs/relationships (edges), e.g., "Summarizer depends on Document Retriever" is one edge
- Cycle must be detected and rejected; no partial execution
- Self-dependencies count as cycles
- An $O(n^2)$ time complexity solution is acceptable

Test Case 1: Valid workflow to produce execution order

- **Input**:
    - **Agents** (n = 5): `["QueryParser", "DocumentRetriever", "Summarizer", "Ranker", "ResponseGenerator"]`
    - **Dependencies**:
        - `QueryParser → DocumentRetriever`
        - `QueryParser → Ranker`
        - `DocumentRetriever → Summarizer`
        - `Ranker → Summarizer`
        - `Summarizer → ResponseGenerator`
- **Output**: A valid topological order, e.g., `["QueryParser", "DocumentRetriever", "Ranker", "Summarizer", "ResponseGenerator"]` or `["QueryParser", "Ranker", "DocumentRetriever", "Summarizer", "ResponseGenerator"]`
- **Verification**:
    - Every agent appears exactly once

- For every dependency A ⟶ B, A appears before B in the output
- `QueryParser` is always first (no dependencies; in-degree = 0), `ResponseGenerator` is always last (nothing depends on it)

This use case calls for a directed acyclic graph (DAG) as illustrated in *Figure 7.14*:

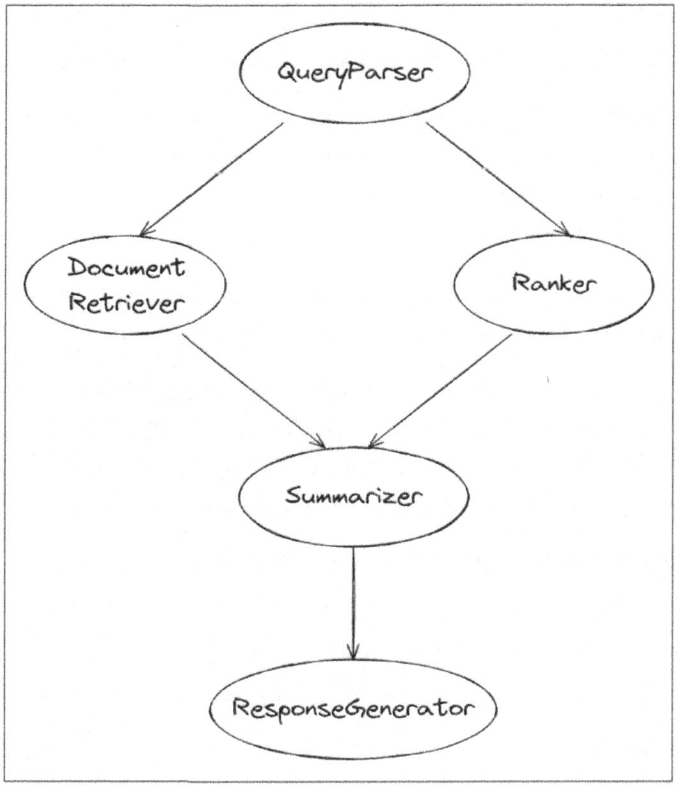

Figure 7.14: DAG consisting of 5 agents and their dependencies

Test Case 2: Invalid workflow involving circular dependency

- **Input**:
  - **Agents** (n = 4): `["Planner", "Executor", "Validator", "Reporter"]`
  - **Dependencies**:
    - `Planner → Executor`
    - `Executor → Validator`

    - `Validator` → `Planner` ← cycle exists here
    - `Validator` → `Reporter`

- **Output**: Cycle detected; workflow rejected (e.g., return empty list, or throw exception, or return error indicator)
- **Verification**:
    - System identifies the cycle: `Planner` → `Executor` → `Validator` → `Planner`.
    - `Reporter` depends on `Validator`. `Validator` can never complete because it's waiting on `Planner`, which is waiting on `Executor`, which is waiting on `Validator`, leading to deadlock.

Solution

To handle this at scale, production systems use topological sorting. Implementing this via Kahn's algorithm (BFS) or DFS post-order reversal yields a fast `O(n + m)` algorithm.

For educational purposes, we will derive an $O(n^2)$ solution with iterations, without the use of a queue, in-degree mapping, or graph traversal. This is also otherwise known as the topological sort algorithm. The iterative solution is fine when we have, say, under 1,000 agent nodes in a graph. Our algorithm can be summarized in the following steps:

- Find all agents with no dependencies → they go first
- Remove them from everyone else's dependency lists
- Repeat until all placed (success) or nothing is ready (cycle)

This algorithm consists of nine sequential implementation steps:

Step 1: Deep copy

This is the first step in the algorithm for creating an isolated, independent duplicate of the input dependency list. We want to preserve the original input by making a deep copy of it for subsequent processing.

```
Map<String, List<String>> remaining =
new HashMap<>();
for (Map.Entry<String, List<String>> entry : dependencies.entrySet()){
    remaining.put(entry.getKey(),
    new ArrayList<>(entry.getValue()));
}
```

Step 2: Results list

We set up an empty list called `order` to store the final sequences of tasks.

```
List<String> order = new ArrayList<>();
```

Step 3: Outer loop

The loop acts as an engine that processes independent tasks one by one, until there are no more tasks left to schedule in the remaining list.

```
while (!remaining.isEmpty()) { ... }
```

Step 4: Find ready

This step scans all remaining tasks to find those ready to run. By checking each item's prerequisite list, it identifies any tasks that have zero dependencies left, meaning they are completely safe to execute immediately. These unblocked tasks are gathered into a temporary "ready" list. However, because the code must look at every single leftover task during every single round, this repetitive scanning creates a bottleneck that slows down the system as the workload grows.

```
List<String> ready = new ArrayList<>();
for (Map.Entry<String, List<String>> entry : remaining.entrySet()) {
    if (entry.getValue().isEmpty()) {
        ready.add(entry.getKey());
    }
}
```

Step 5: Cycle detection

This step acts as a deadlock detector that guards against endless loops. If the previous scan fails to find even a single task that is ready to run, it means every remaining task is stuck waiting on something else that is also waiting. This creates a circular deadlock, where nothing can ever move forward. Recognizing that progress has completely stalled, the system immediately triggers the alarm and stops the program by throwing an error.

```
if (ready.isEmpty()) {
    throw new IllegalStateException("Circular dependency detected");
}
```

Step 6: Commit layer

This step locks in the current wave of safe tasks by adding them all to the final schedule. Because every task in this "ready" list has zero remaining prerequisites, none of them depend on each other. This means they can all be executed at the exact same time in parallel, maximizing efficiency. The code simply transfers this entire batch out of the waiting area and appends them straight into the master execution order.

```
order.addAll(ready);
```

Step 7: Remove from pool

This step cleans up the backlog by permanently deleting the newly scheduled tasks from the tracking pool. Since these tasks have already been successfully committed to the final execution order, the system no longer needs to monitor them. The code loops through each item in the "ready" list and pulls it out of the remaining pool, ensuring the system doesn't waste time checking them again during the next round of processing.

```
for (String agent : ready) {
    remaining.remove(agent);
}
```

Step 8: Unblock dependents

This final step triggers a domino effect that unblocks the remaining tasks in the backlog. The code loops through every single leftover task and scrubs the newly completed "ready" tasks from their prerequisite lists. As these individual lists shrink toward zero, the roadblocks disappear. Any task whose checklist becomes completely empty from this cleanup is now fully unlocked, setting it up to be picked up as "ready" in the very next round of processing.

```
for (List<String> deps : remaining.values()) {
    deps.removeAll(ready);
}
```

Step 9: Return after order completion

All agents successfully placed; return a valid execution order.

```
return order;
```

Complexity: O(n^2)

The overall time complexity of this solution is `O(n²)`, which can be seen by observing the following:

- **The Inefficient Scan** (Step 4): In the worst-case scenario (like a straight line of tasks where A -> B -> C), only one agent becomes ready per round. The loop runs `n` times. In each round, the algorithm checks every remaining item. This repetitive scanning creates a heavy `O(n²)` workload.
- **The Bulk Cleanup** (Step 8): Using .removeAll() requires the system to scan through the dependency lists of every remaining agent to wipe out the ready ones. Doing a full list scan inside an already repeating loop compounds the time complexity, pushing it to `O(n²)`.
- **The Efficient Exception** (Step 7): Removing scheduled agents from the master pool is highly efficient. Because each agent is only processed and removed exactly once over the entire lifecycle of the program, its cumulative cost stays linear at `O(n)`.

We may intuitively observe the worst case from this linear-chain input:

```
A → B → C → D → E
```

This calls for:

- Round 1: scan 5, find A, remove A from 4 lists
- Round 2: scan 4, find B, remove B from 3 lists
- Round 3: scan 3, find C, remove C from 2 lists

The total number of scans is therefore 3.

In summary, this solution does not scale to hundreds of thousands of agents. We pay `O(n²)` because each round asks, "who's ready?" from scratch instead of remembering the answer from the last round.

The fully annotated solutions for both the iterative layer-removal approach (`AgentExecutionOrder.java`) and Kahn's algorithm (`AgentDependencyResolver.java`) are provided in the `Chapter07` folder in the GitHub repository. To unlock the GitHub repo link, refer to the instructions in the *Download the example code files* section of the *Preface*

Exercise 2: Undirected weighted graph

Implement an **undirected, weighted graph** using an **adjacency-list** representation (`Map<Integer, List<Edge<Integer>>>`). Provide methods to:

- `addVertex(v)`: add a vertex
- `addEdge(u, v, weight)`: add a weighted undirected edge between u and v
- `totalWeight()`: return the sum of the weights of all edges in the graph

Starter Code Template

```
import java.util.*;
class Edge {
    final T to; final int weight;
    Edge(T to, int weight) {
        this.to = to;
        this.weight = weight;
    }
}
public class Graph {
    private final Map<Integer, List<Edge<Integer>>>
    adjacency = new HashMap<>();

    /** Add a vertex with no edges. No-op if it already exists. */
    public void addVertex(int v) {
        // TODO
    }

    /** Add an undirected weighted edge between u and v. */
    public void addEdge(int u, int v, int weight) {
        // TODO
    }

    /** Return sum of all edge weights (each undirected edge counted once). */
    public long totalWeight() {
        // TODO
        return 0L;
    }
}
```

Assumptions and Constraints

- The graph is undirected: an edge (u, v, w) is stored from both u's and v's sides
- The graph is **weighted**; weights are integers (maybe negative for this exercise)
- Adding an edge between vertices that don't exist yet should **auto-create** them (or document the chosen behavior)
- **No parallel edges** and **no self-loops** for the base problem (discuss handling if raised)
- `totalWeight()` counts each undirected edge **once**, even though it is stored twice in the adjacency list
- Vertex IDs are unique integers; the graph fits in memory
- Methods are not required to be thread-safe

Test Case 1

- **Input**: `addEdge(1,2,5); addEdge(2,3,7); addEdge(1,3,2)`
- **Output**: `totalWeight()` yields 14

Test Case 2

- **Input**: `addVertex(1); addVertex(2)` (no edges)
- **Output**: `totalWeight()` yields 0

Exercise 3: Cycle detection in DAG

Given a directed graph (DG) as an adjacency list (`Map<Integer, List<Integer>>`), write a DFS routine that returns a boolean indicating whether the graph contains a cycle. *Figure 7.15* shows two directed graphs: one cyclic and another, acyclic (DAG).

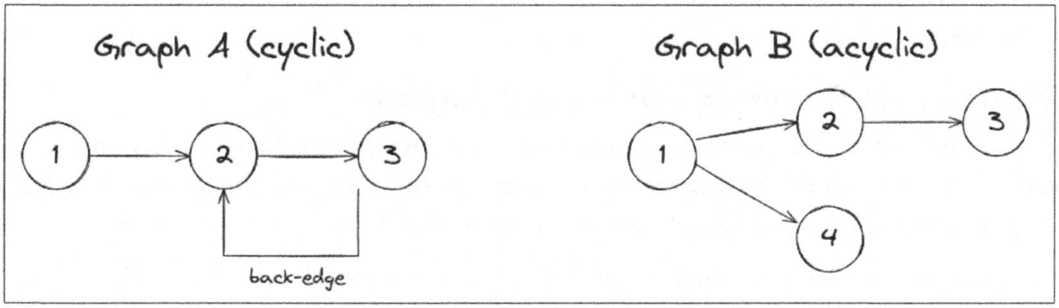

Figure 7.15: Cyclic (A) vs. acyclic (B) directed graphs

Starter Code Template

```
import java.util.*;
public class CycleDetection {
    public static boolean hasCycle(Map<Integer, List<Integer>> graph) {
        // TODO: DFS from every unvisited vertex
        // using visited + recursion-stack sets.
        return false;
    }
}
```

Assumptions and Constraints

- The graph is **directed**; an edge `u -> v` does not imply `v -> u`
- The graph may be **disconnected**; it must start DFS from every unvisited vertex
- A **self-loop** (`u -> u`) counts as a cycle
- Vertex IDs are unique integers; the graph fits in memory
- A vertex with no outgoing edges may be absent from the map or map to an empty list
- Return as soon as the first cycle is found (no need to count or enumerate cycles)

Test Case 1

- **Input**: `{1:[2], 2:[3], 3:[1]}` // 3-cycle
- **Output**: `true`

Test Case 2

- **Input** `{1:[2,3], 2:[3], 3:[]}` // DAG, no cycle
- **Output**: `false`

Exercise 4: Counting connected regions

Count the number of disconnected sensor groups in an `R` rows by `C` columns grid. Each cell is either active (`1`) or inactive (`0`). Active sensors belong to the same group if they share an edge horizontally or vertically. Diagonal connections are excluded.

This problem is modeled as an implicit undirected graph where cells are vertices and connections are edges.

Starter Code Template

```
import java.util.*;
public class SensorClusterCounter {
```

```
    // Input: 2D grid of '1' (activated) and '0' (inactive) sensors
    // Output: count of distinct connected sensor clusters
    public int countClusters(char[][] grid) {
        // Step 1: Handle null/empty grid edge case
        // Step 2: Initialize visited tracking structure (rows x cols)
        // Step 3: Scan every cell in the grid
        // Step 4: On finding an unvisited activated sensor, increment cluster
count
        // Step 5: Flood-fill (BFS) from that sensor to mark the entire cluster
visited
        // Step 6: Return total cluster count
    }
    private void bfs(char[][] grid, boolean[][] visited,
                     int startRow, int startCol, int rows, int cols) {
        // Step 1: Initialize queue with starting cell, mark visited
        // Step 2: While queue is not empty, dequeue a cell
        // Step 3: Check all 4 cardinal neighbors (up, down, left, right)
        // Step 4: If neighbor is valid, activated, and unvisited -
> mark visited, enqueue
    }

    private boolean isValid(int row, int col, int rows, int cols) {
        // Step 1: Check row and col are within grid bounds
    }

    public static void main(String[] args) {
        // Test Case 1: Multiple distinct clusters
        // Test Case 2: No activated sensors
    }
}
```

Assumptions and Constraints

- Grid Representation: 2D char array with `1` (activated) or `0` (inactive) sensors
- Connectivity: Only horizontal/vertical adjacency counts (diagonal doesn't connect)
- Edge Cases:
  - Empty grid: 0 clusters
  - No activated sensors: 0 clusters
  - Isolated sensors: 1 cluster each

- Processing: Grid unchanged; separate visited tracking structure
- Boundary: No wraparound—clusters don't cross grid edges

Test Case 1

- **Input**:

```
[
  ['1','1','0','0','0'],
  ['1','1','0','0','0'],
  ['0','0','1','0','0'],
  ['0','0','0','1','1']
]
```

- **Output**: 3

Test Case 2: No activated sensors

- **Input**:

```
[
  ['0','0','0'],
  ['0','0','0'],
  ['0','0','0']
]
```

- **Expected Output**: 0

Exercise 5: Can all courses be finished?

You have `numCourses` courses numbered from 0 to `numCourses`-1. Each prerequisite relationship `prerequisites[i] = [a, b]` indicates that course `b` must be completed before course a can be taken. Determine whether it's possible to complete all courses, returning true if feasible and false if not.

Example

- `numCourses = 2`, `prerequisites = [[1,0]]` → true (take course 0 first, then course 1)
- `numCourses = 2`, `prerequisites = [[1,0],[0,1]]` → false (circular dependency between courses 0 and 1)

This problem is equivalent to detecting cycles in a directed graph. A complete schedule exists if and only if the dependency graph forms a directed acyclic graph (DAG).

Assumptions and Constraints

- Build a directed edge `b -> a` (take `b` before `a`)
- The graph may be disconnected; must consider every course
- Duplicate prerequisite pairs are possible; self-prerequisite (`[a,a]`) is an immediate cycle
- `numCourses ≥ 0`; an empty prerequisite list is always finishable

Test Case 1

`numCourses=4, prerequisites=[[1,0],[2,1],[3,2]]` (linear chain) → true

Test Case 2

`numCourses=3, prerequisites=[[0,1],[1,2],[2,0]]` (3-cycle) → false

Exercise 6: Shortest path with BFS

You're given an undirected, unweighted graph, and two vertices, start and target. Write a function that returns the length of the shortest path (number of edges) from start to target. Return -1 if no path exists. The graph is provided as an adjacency list: a map from a vertex to the list of its neighbors. *Figure 7.16* shows such a graph.

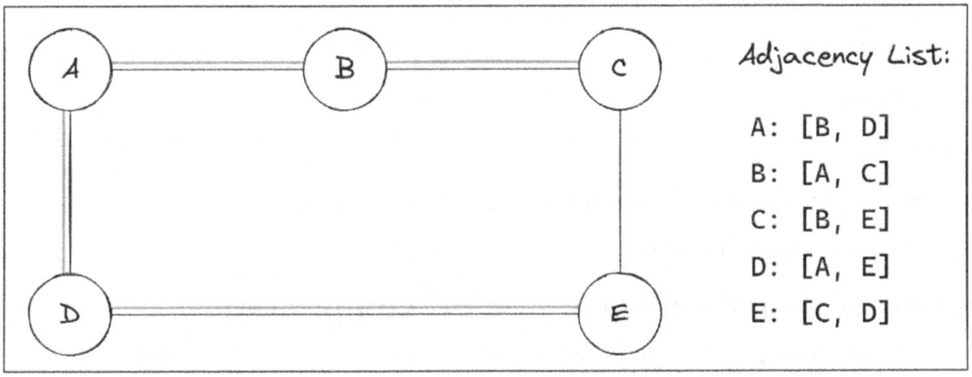

Figure 7.16: Shortest path in an undirected graph Starter Code Template

```
import java.util.*;
public class ShortestPath {
    public static int shortestDistance(Map<String,
                          List<String>> adjacency,
                          String start,
                          String target) {
        // TODO: implement using BFS.
```

```
        return -1;
    }
}
```

Assumptions and Constraints

- The graph is **undirected** and **unweighted**; every edge counts as distance 1.
- Vertices are labeled with unique identifiers (e.g. strings); no duplicate vertex IDs.
- The adjacency list is consistent for an undirected graph (if `B` is in `A`'s list, `A` is in `B`'s).
- Distance is the **number of edges**, not the number of vertices (`start == target` → `0`).
- Return -1 when no path exists, including when `start` or `target` are absent from the graph.
- The graph may contain **cycles**; the traversal must not loop forever.
- The graph may be **disconnected**; `target` is not guaranteed to be reachable.
- Edge weights, self-loops, and parallel edges are out of scope (don't affect shortest *unweighted* distance).
- The graph fits in memory; $0 \le V \le 10^5$, $0 \le E \le 10^6$ (assume single-machine, in-process).

Test Case 1

- **Input**: `{1:[2,3], 2:[1,4], 3:[1,4], 4:[2,3,5], 5:[4]}, start=1, target=5`
- **Output**: 3 (1 → 2 → 4 → 5)

Test Case 2

- **Input**: `{1:[2], 2:[1], 3:[4], 4:[3]}, start=1, target=4`
- **Output**: 1 (disconnected)

Exercise 7: Number of connected components

Given `n` vertices labeled `0..n-1` and a list of undirected edges, return the **number of connected components** in an undirected graph.

Starter Code Template

```
import java.util.*;
public class CountComponents {
    public static int countComponents(int n, int[][] edges){
        // TODO
    }
    private static void dfs(int node, List<List<Integer>> adj, boolean[] visited){
```

```
        // TODO
    }
}
```

Assumptions and Constraints

- Vertices are integers `0..n-1; n ≥ 0`
- Edges are undirected; duplicate edges and self-loops may appear and should not break the count
- Isolated vertices (no edges) each count as their own component
- The graph fits in memory

Test Case 1

- **Input**: `n=6, edges=[[0,1],[1,2],[3,4]]`
- **Output**: 3

Test Case 2

- **Input**: `n=4, edges=[]` (no edges)
- **Output**: 4

Exercise 8: Analyze graph connectivity

Implement a `SimpleGraph` class that represents an undirected graph and provides methods to analyze its connectivity properties. The graph consists of `n` vertices numbered from `0` to `n-1`, and edges connecting pairs of vertices. The requirements are:

- Use an adjacency list representation to store the graph
- Implement `addEdge(u, v)` method to add undirected edges between vertices `u` and `v`
- Implement `isConnected()` method that returns `true` if all vertices are reachable from each other, `false` otherwise
- Implement `getConnectedComponents()` method that returns the number of separate connected components in the graph

Starter Code Template

```
import java.util.*;

public class SimpleGraph {

    // TODO: Implement graph representation and methods
```

```
    // Assumptions:
    // - Graph is undirected
    // - Vertices are numbered from 0 to n-1
    // - No duplicate edges
    // - No self-loops

    // TODO: Add your graph representation here

    // TODO: Implement addEdge method
    public void addEdge(int u, int v) {
        // Add edge between vertices u and v
    }

    // TODO: Implement isConnected method
    public boolean isConnected() {
        // Return true if all vertices are connected, false otherwise
        return false;
    }

    // TODO: Implement getConnectedComponents method
    public int getConnectedComponents() {
        // Return number of connected components
        return 0;
    }
}
```

Assumptions and Constraints

- The graph is undirected (edges have no direction)
- Vertices are numbered from `0` to `n-1`
- No duplicate edges in input
- No self-loops (vertex connected to itself)
- Graph may be connected or disconnected
- All vertices are integers in range `[0, n-1]`
- Time complexity should be efficient for typical use cases

Test Case 1

For a graph with 4 vertices and edges `[(0,1), (1,2), (2,3)]`:

- `isConnected()` should return `true` (all vertices form one connected component)
- `getConnectedComponents()` should return 1

Test Case 2

For a graph with 4 vertices and edges `[(0,1), (2,3)]`:

- `isConnected()` should return `false` (vertices 0,1 form one component; vertices 2,3 form another)
- `getConnectedComponents()` should return 2

Part 3

Practical Algorithms and Examples

This section provides a practical exploration of fundamental algorithms and design paradigms essential for efficient software development. We bridge the gap between theoretical complexity and real-world implementation by focusing on how these concepts are deployed in large-scale systems, including AI applications.

We begin with **Dynamic Programming** (**DP**) and **Recursion**, establishing the techniques for optimally decomposing complex problems. Sorting covers the theoretical and practical foundations of ordering data, including complexity analysis and production-ready hybrid algorithms. To address multi-core performance, we examine **Concurrency**, the challenges and solutions for running simultaneous tasks and managing thread synchronization. Finally, we integrate these principles in the final chapter, *DSA in Production*, demonstrating how efficient structures and algorithms serve as core architectural components in modern software systems.

You will gain the ability to design, analyze, and implement algorithms that are not only theoretically sound but also performant and scalable in production environments.

This part of the book includes the following chapters:

- *Chapter 8, Dynamic Programming*
- *Chapter 9, Recursion*
- *Chapter 10, Sorting*

- *Chapter 11, Concurrency*
- *Chapter 12, DSA in Production*

8

Dynamic Programming

Dynamic programming (**DP**) is a cornerstone of computer science, turning combinatorially explosive problems into tractable, polynomial-time solutions. At its core, a problem facing combinatorial explosion means that the search space, or the total number of potential states or combinations, increases exponentially with the input size `N`. By identifying optimal substructure and breaking a large optimization or counting task into smaller, overlapping subproblems, solving each once, and caching the results, DP eliminates redundant work and unlocks efficient algorithms. Understanding this fundamental concept is the key to tackling some of the hardest computational challenges in modern software.

In this chapter, we unpack the core ideas of DP, show why it is a vital algorithmic tool, and explore the major problem domains where it excels: sequences (such as Fibonacci and edit distance), graph problems (such as shortest paths in a DAG), interval problems, and beyond. By exploiting Java's collection classes (`ArrayList`, `HashMap`) alongside primitive arrays, we illustrate how to derive DP solutions that are both clear to read and efficient to run.

> **Note**
>
> When faced with combinatorially expansive growth, traditional brute-force or purely recursive methods are forced to explore redundant approaches repeatedly. This results in time complexities (such as `O(2N)` or `O(N!)`) that quickly exceed the computational limits of most computers. DP circumvents this by utilizing a space-time trade-off, solving each unique subproblem only once, and storing that result for subsequent use.

What is dynamic programming?

By definition, DP is a method for solving a problem by solving its subproblems once and storing the results for future use. The core idea behind DP is that when a problem can be divided into smaller, identical problems, and the optimal solution to the whole can be assembled from optimal solutions to the parts, we can avoid re-computation.

There are two structural pillars that must be present in a problem for DP to be applicable:

- **Overlapping subproblems**: If the recursive call tree of a problem encounters the same subproblem (the same input parameters) multiple times, a straightforward recursion will perform the same work repeatedly. DP mitigates this redundancy by caching intermediate results (memoization) or by filling a table in a bottom-up fashion (tabulation).
- **Optimal substructure**: This property guarantees that the optimal solution to the overall problem is composed of optimal solutions to its smaller subproblems. In simpler terms, the best way to solve the big problem must include the best way to solve its smaller parts. We can see this principle applied to pathfinding problems (*Figure 8.1*).

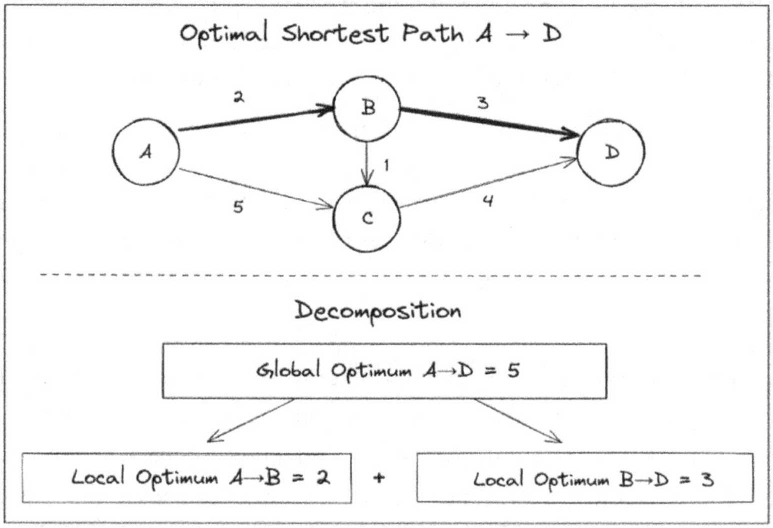

Figure 8.1: Optimal substructure: Path decomposition of the shortest route

We can categorize problems based on their internal structure, which determines the appropriate DP strategy. That is, whether the subproblems overlap or are independent:

- Overlapping subproblems: The same subproblem is encountered repeatedly across different branches of the solution space (e.g., Fibonacci series)
- Independent subproblems: The subproblems are distinct; solving one does not inherently require solving another (e.g., Merge Sort)

To visualize why DP is essential, we compare problems based on their subproblem structure in *Figure 8.2*:

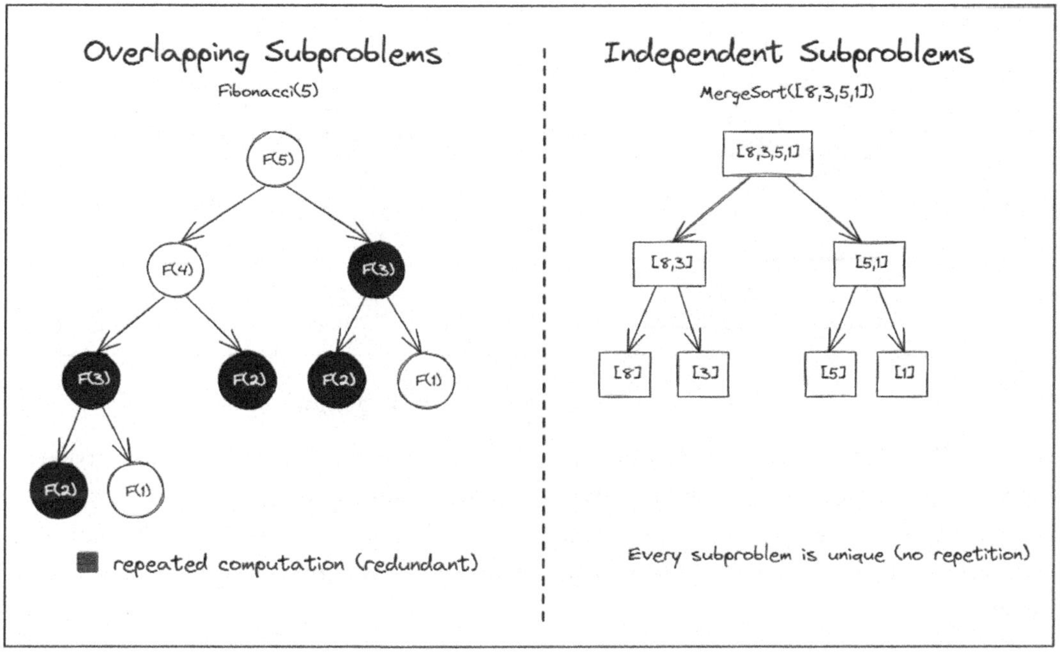

Figure 8.2: Overlapping vs. Independent Subproblems

The decision tree for identifying DP problems and the subsequent solving steps is captured in *Figure 8.3*.

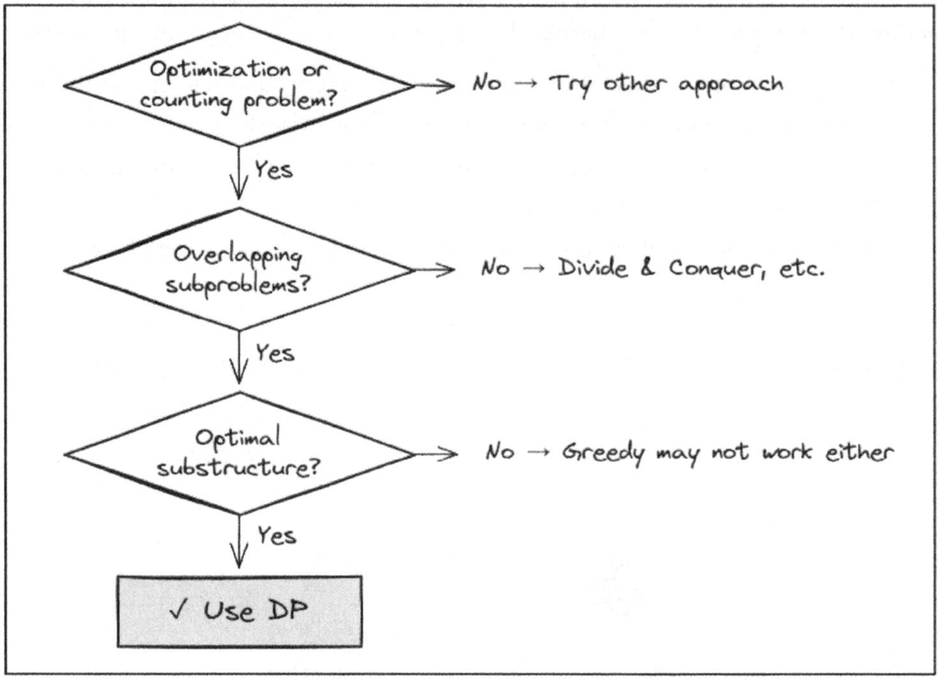

Figure 8.3: Applying DP: decision tree and steps

Later, we'll look at the classic Fibonacci sequence as an example. A simple recursive version repeatedly recomputes `fib(1)` and `fib(0)` many times, leading to an exponential time complexity. In contrast, a dynamic programming version stores these results in a lookup table (the cache) and reuses them, reducing the total number of evaluations from exponential to linear time.

Why DP Matters

Dynamic programming reduces the computational cost of a problem. It isn't a magical shortcut; it's a systematic approach that highlights two key structural traits: overlapping subproblems and optimal substructure. Recognizing these traits lets us chart a clear implementation path and transform an intractable, exponential-time problem into an efficient, polynomial-time solution.

Classic example: 0/1 knapsack problem

The objective of this problem is to maximize the total value of selected items without exceeding the weight limit. The subproblem is defined as `opt[i][w]`.

the best value achievable using the first `i` items with capacity `w`. The recurrence captures the two possibilities for each item:

```
opt[i][w] = max(
    opt[i-1][w],                        // skip item i
    opt[i-1][w-weight[i]] +
               value[i]                 // take item i (if w ≥ weight[i])
)
```

Either we skip it (`opt[i-1][w]`) or we take it, adding its value to the optimum for the remaining capacity (`opt[i-1][w-weight[i]] + value[i]`), provided the weight permits. This recurrence exhibits the two DP pillars:

- **Overlapping subproblems**: when solving `opt[i][w]`, the calculation frequently relies on the same intermediate results (e.g., `opt[i-1][w]`). These identical states are needed by many different higher-level subproblems, making memoization or tabulation necessary to avoid redundant computation.
- **Optimal substructure:** the global optimum must be composed of optimal solutions to its smaller subproblems. Specifically, the best solution for `opt[i][w]` must build upon the optimal solution of a smaller, related problem (either `opt[i-1][w]` or `opt[i-1][w-weight[i]]`).

For a comprehensive practice problem on this topic, refer to the Exercises section at the conclusion of this chapter.

Core concepts and techniques

In this section, we'll introduce recurrence and explore how to use DP to evaluate it exactly once and cache its outcome. We'll write down the recurrence, decide whether to apply memoization or tabulation, and then implement it by carefully handling base cases, encoding the state, and managing edge-case logic.

Recurrence relations

A recurrence relation is an equation that expresses the value of a function at a given index in terms of values at *smaller* indices. In DP, the recurrence is the *definition* of the subproblem and the glue that builds the global optimum. Formally, recurrence is expressed as:

```
F(n)  = f(F(n-1), F(n-2), …),
```

This has a few explicitly known base cases. Once the recurrence is known, we can compute any `F(n)` by repeatedly applying the rule until we hit a base case. The f function `f` is usually a simple arithmetic or logical operation (such as addition, max, or min), but it can be any well-defined operation. Let's look at some of the classic recurrence relations.

Classic example: Fibonacci sequence

The classic Fibonacci sequence is a prime example of a recurrence. Starting with the first two numbers of this sequence being 0 and 1, respectively, the entire sequence can be expressed as:

```
F(0)=0, F(1)=1, F(n)=F(n-1)+F(n-2) for n≥2
```

That is, the `n`-th Fibonacci number equals the sum of the two preceding numbers, which can be computed by pure recursion for any `n`-th Fibonacci number:

```
public int fib(int n) {
    if (n == 0) return 0;
    if (n == 1) return 1;
    return fib(n - 1) + fib(n - 2);
}
```

However, **recursion** is inefficient when performance matters, because:

- For `n=5`, `fib(5)` calls `fib(4)` and `fib(3)`.
- `fib(4)` again calls `fib(3)` and `fib(2)`.
- `fib(3)` is now computed twice (once by `fib(5)`, once by `fib(4)`).

The following recurrence tree depicts a Fibonacci sequence. Notice how `fib(3)`, `fib(2)`, and `fib(1)` appear repeatedly. DP would compute each once and then simply look it up:

```
fib(5)
├─ fib(4)
│  ├─ fib(3)
│  │  ├─ fib(2)
│  │  │  ├─ fib(1)
│  │  │  └─ fib(0)
│  │  └─ fib(1)
│  └─ fib(2)
│      ├─ fib(1)
│      └─ fib(0)
└─ fib(3)
```

```
├ fib(2)
│  ├ fib(1)
│  └ fib(0)
└ fib(1)
```

The same subproblems (e.g., `fib(3)`, `fib(2)`, ...) are recomputed exponentially many times. Time complexity is exponential ($O(2^N)$), whereas space complexity in call-stack depth is `O(n)`.

As we've already mentioned, DP takes advantage of overlapping subproblems by caching every value that's computed and reusing it whenever the same state reappears. This reduces the time complexity dramatically to `O(N)`. We can apply the recurrence for this problem in two common ways: a top-down method that combines recursion with memoization, or a highly efficient bottom-up iterative construction.

Bottom-up (iterative) approach

We may build the sequence from the ground up and use long (or `BigInteger` for very large `n`) to avoid overflow. Java's primitive integer overflows around the 47th Fibonacci number:

```
public long fib_dp(int n) {
    if (n == 0) return 0L;
    if (n == 1) return 1L;
    long[] dp = new long[n + 1];
    dp[0] = 0L;
    dp[1] = 1L;
    for (int i = 2; i <= n; i++) {
        dp[i] = dp[i - 1] + dp[i - 2];
    }
    return dp[n];
}
```

This requires a single loop in `O(n)` time, and `O(n)` space for an array of `n+1` elements. The space requirement goes down to `O(1)` if we just use 2 variables to keep track of the last 2 values in the sequence.

Top-Down (recursive + memoization) approach

Alternatively, we keep the recursive flavor but cache results. This version demonstrates the classic top-down, memoization pattern:

```
private final Map<Integer, Long> memo = new HashMap<>();
public long fibMemo(int n) {
```

```
        if (n == 0) return 0L;
        if (n == 1) return 1L;

        if (memo.containsKey(n))
            return memo.get(n);
        long value = fibMemo(n - 1) + fibMemo(n - 2);
        memo.put(n, value);
        return value;
    }
```

The recursion depth is at most n, but because we memoize every result, the overall time complexity is O(n) and the memory usage is also O(n) for cache. Bottom-up is often faster in practice because it eliminates recursion overhead and cache misses.

Fibonacci recurrence: Overlapping and optimal substructure

The Fibonacci recurrence, F(n)=F(n-1)+F(n-2), satisfies two key DP properties:

- Optimal Substructure: the best solution for F(n) is obtained by combining the optimal solutions for F(n-1) and F(n-2)
- Overlapping Subproblems: the same values of F(n) are recomputed many times in a recursive expansion

Because of these properties, a naive recursion runs in exponential time, whereas a DP formulation reuses the intermediate results and brings the running time down to linear.

Memoization vs. tabulation

As we see in the Fibonacci example, we may employ either top-down (**memoization**) or bottom-up (**tabulation**) techniques to solve it. Both approaches preserve intermediate results but differ in how they compute, where they store those results, and when each method is preferable. The following diagram (*Figure 8.4*) illustrates the structural difference between these two methods:

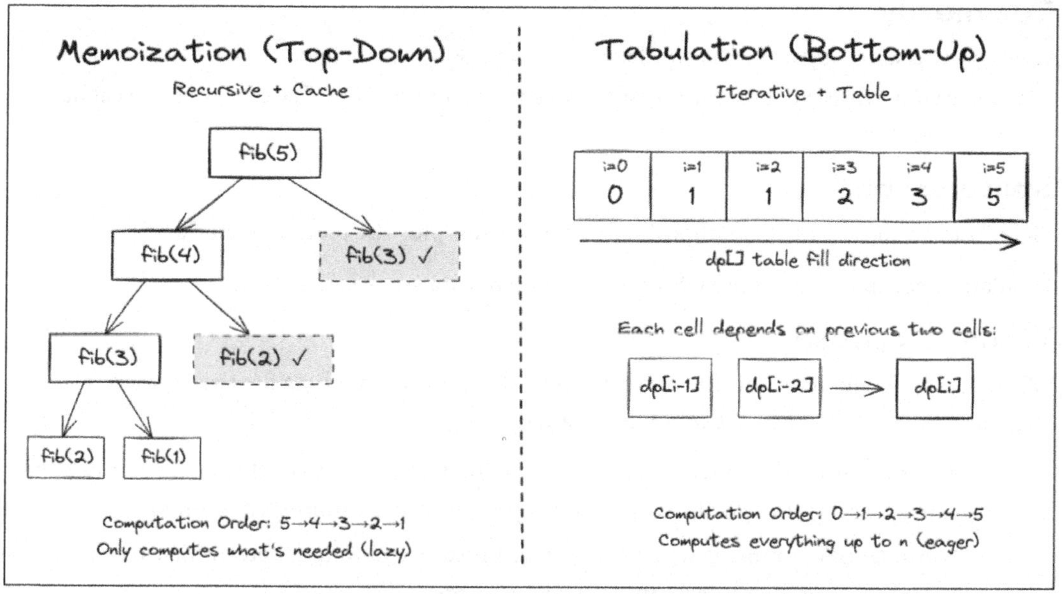

Figure 8.4: Fibonacci DP using memoization vs. tabulation

Both methods achieve the same asymptotic time bound of `O(N)`, but they differ in execution style, memory usage, and efficiency. As we saw, tabulation often eliminates recursion overhead and cache misses, making it generally faster in practice, especially when dealing with dense DP tables.

Execution style

Memoization is a top-down, recursive technique that checks a cache before computing a subproblem. If the value is already stored, it is returned. Otherwise, the routine recurses, saves the result, and returns it. We compute only the subproblems that are actually reached, or whatever is needed. Memoization is often referred to as the "lazy" approach.

Tabulation is bottom-up: a table (array, matrix, or higher dimensional array) is pre-allocated for all subproblems, and *iterative* loops fill it in a fixed order (smallest to largest or topological). Every entry is computed once, so no recursion is used and the algorithm typically enjoys better cache locality. Tabulation is often referred to as the "eager" approach.

Storage structure

Memoization uses a growing map or indexed array for discovered subproblems, whereas tabulation pre-allocates a fixed array or matrix containing all subproblem values from the outset; no extra hash tables are needed.

Complexity

Both give the same asymptotic bounds. For instance, Fibonacci runs in `O(n)`. Memoization adds recursion overhead; tabulation eliminates it, usually running faster, and using cache more efficiently.

Space usage

Memoization stores only the subproblems that are hit, plus the recursion stack.

Tabulation occupies a fixed table for all subproblems; no stack is used.

When to choose

When deciding which technique to use, we pick the method that best fits the problem's structure and performance requirements, namely:

- **Memoization**: we apply it when the recursion tree is sparse or the recurrence depends on irregular, state-specific values (e.g., dynamic programming on graphs)
- **Tabulation**: we apply it when every state must be evaluated, deterministic array access is needed, or predictable memory usage matters

Classic DP illustrations

DP addresses complex optimization problems by breaking them down into smaller, overlapping subproblems. This approach leverages memoization or tabulation to store intermediate results efficiently. By transforming inefficient exponential recursion into linear or polynomial solutions, DP provides high-performance algorithms for various applications. Key applications:

- **Optimization**: Find the minimum cost or maximum gain in scenarios like navigation (Shortest Path problem) and profit maximization (Knapsack problem)
- **Transformation**: Determine minimal steps required to convert one state to another, such as in the "Edit distance" problem

We will study these problems and their solutions in the following sections.

Problem: Continuous sum in an integer series

Given a positive integer array `arr` having `n` elements, `arr[0, 1, … n-1]`, find a contiguous segment `arr[i] + arr[i+1] + … + arr[r]` whose sum is maximal.

Intuition

This problem can be tackled with a brute-force approach, by enumerating every possible sum of consecutive integers and choosing the largest, namely, by ascertaining all possible pairs (l, r) and computing each sum:

$$\max_{0<l<r<n} \sum_{i=l}^{r} arr[\mathrm{i}]$$

The solution can be done by having three nested loops in $O(n^3)$, by re-summing each subarray from scratch:

```
int maxSumBruteForce03(int[] arr) {
    int n = arr.length;
    int globalMax = Integer.MIN_VALUE;
    for (int l = 0; l < n; ++l) {
        for (int r = l; r < n; ++r) {
            int currentSum = 0;
            for (int k = l; k <= r; ++k) {
                currentSum += arr[k];
            }
            globalMax = Math.max(globalMax, currentSum);
        }
    }
    return globalMax;
}
```

The above solution can be improved to $O(n^2)$, with the outer loop running in $O(n)$ and the inner, on average, $O(n/2)$:

```
int maxSumBruteForce02(int[] arr) {
    int n = arr.length;
    int max = Integer.MIN_VALUE;
    for (int l = 0; l < n; ++l) {
        int current = 0;
        for (int r = l; r < n; ++r) {
            current += arr[r];
            if (current > max) max = current;
        }
    }
```

```
    return max;
}
```

Neither of the above solutions is optimal. While they solve the problem, they are inefficient when performance matters.

Solution

The core idea behind DP is that we can build the best answer for the big problem *globally* by combining the best answers from its smaller parts *locally*. If we can keep surveying the local outcome while keeping track of the `globalMax` , then we can solve this problem in one `O(n)` pass.

The key observation is that the optimum for the prefix ending at index `i` can be obtained by looking only at the optimum for the prefix ending at `i-1`. We define `localMax` as the maximum sum of any subarray that ends at index i, where `0 ≤ i < arr.length`. The base case is as follows:

```
localMax = arr[0]
```

Consider we already know the max local sum for all sub-arrays that end at index `i-1`. When we look at position `i`, we have only two choices:

- Start a new sub-array that contains only `arr[i]`
- Extend the max sub-array that ended at `i-1` by including `arr[i]`

The larger of these two sums is the max sum for sub-arrays ending at `i`:

```
localMax = Math.max(arr[i], localMax + arr[i])
```

As we move across the entire series, we only need one variable to keep track of the previous local max instead of persisting all local max values in an array. We derive the following, in-place:

```
public int maxContinuousSum(int[] arr) {
    int localMax = arr[0];
    int globalMax = arr[0];

    for (int i = 1; i < arr.length; ++i) {
        localMax = Math.max(arr[i], localMax + arr[i]);
        globalMax = Math.max(globalMax, localMax);
    }
```

```
    return globalMax;
}
```

Observation

The above approach is the classic Kadane's algorithm running in `O(n)` time and `O(1)` space. In summary, if the optimal solution for a given position relies solely on the solution(s) of one or a few preceding positions, the problem is an ideal fit for dynamic programming.

Problem: Edit distance (levenshtein) in strings

Let `w1` and `w2` be two strings, find the minimum number of insertions, deletions, or replacements required to transform `w1` into `w2`. This problem calculates the Levenshtein distance (edit distance) between the two strings.

For example, to transform "`FLAW`" into "`LAWN`", we need a minimum of two edits:

- Edit 1: *delete* the `f` ("`FLAW`" ⟶ "`LAW`")
- Edit 2: *insert* an `n` at the end ("`LAW`"⟶ "`LAWN`")

Since these two edits are the most efficient way to convert the first word into the second, the **edit distance** is 2.

Formulation

Consider two words, `w1` and `w2`, with lengths `m` and `n` respectively. To find the edit distance between `w1` and `w2`, we use a distance matrix, `dp`, of size `(m+1) x (n+1)`. Rows encode prefixes of `w1` (including the empty prefix), whereas columns encode prefixes of `w2`. The entry in row `i` and column `j` is denoted `dp[i][j]` and stores the minimum number of single-character edits required to transform the first `i` characters of `w1` into the first `j` characters of `w2`.

For `0 ≤ i ≤ m` and `0 ≤ j ≤ n`, `dp[i][j]` represents the minimum edit distance between the first `i` characters of `w1` and the first `j` characters of `w2`:

```
dp[i][j] = min{
    edit distance between w1[0..i-1] and w[0..j-1]
}
```

The additional row and column for the empty strings (""), at `dp[0][0]`, provide the base cases for insertions and deletions. In reading the matrix, we define the following:

- `dp[0][0]`: distance between two empty strings; cost = 0

- First row dp[0][j]: cost of inserting the first j characters of w2 into an empty string (i.e., j insertions)
- First column dp[i][0]: cost of deleting the first i characters of w1 to obtain an empty string (i.e., i deletions)
- General cell dp[i][j]: minimum cost to transform w1[0..i-1] into w2[0..j-1] by evaluating insertions, deletions, or replacements

This cell relies on optimal substructure, building the solution from smaller subproblems. For our "FLAW" -> "LAWN" example, computing the final cell dp[4][4] compares the last characters ('W' and 'N') and pulls the minimum cost from three neighboring subproblems:

- dp[3][4] ("FLA" -> "LAWN"): represents a deletion
- dp[4][3] ("FLAW" -> "LAW"): represents an insertion
- dp[3][3] ("FLA" -> "LAW"): represents a substitution

Adding 1 to the cheapest option (or 0 if the characters match) yields the optimal choice. The value in the bottom-right corner, dp[m][n], is the edit distance between the full words w1 and w2.

Initialization

To understand the dp table, observe that the origin, dp[0][0], corresponds to both strings being empty. Converting an empty string to another empty string costs nothing, so the value is 0. In the table, the vertical axis (index i) represents the string "FLAW", while the horizontal axis (index j) represents "LAWN". The two boundary rows and columns are simple base cases:

- dp[0][j] = j, moving along the first row turns an empty string into the first j characters of "LAWN". This requires exactly j **insertions**; the insertion cost is j.
- dp[i][0] = i, moving down the first column turns the first i characters of "FLAW" into an empty string. This needs i **deletions**; the deletion cost is i.

Figure 8.5 shows the boundary values for "FLAW" vs "LAWN" in the edit distance matrix.

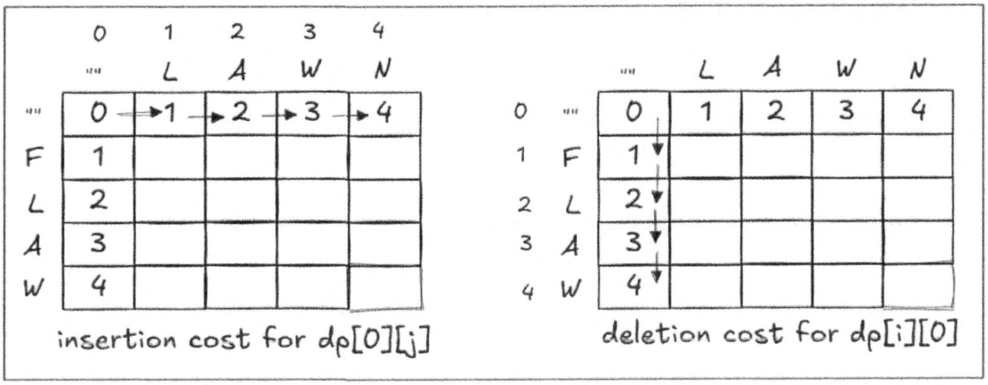

Figure 8.5: Boundary costs in the edit distance matrix

Solution

Each inner entry `dp[i][j]` stores the minimum cost required to convert the first `i` characters of string "`FLAW`" into the first `j` characters of string "LAWN". To compute the value for each cell beyond the boundary cases, we look at all the neighboring cells adjacent to each cell. To illustrate, let's compute `dp[1][1]`, the cost of converting '`F`' into '`L`'. We evaluate three paths:

- From `dp[0][1]`, we delete first:
  - Delete '`F`' from `w1` → ""
  - Now convert "" → '`L`', which costs 1 (insert '`L`')
  - Total: 1 (delete) + 1 (insert) = 2 edits
- From `dp[1][0]`, we insert first:
  - `L` to satisfy `w2` → `w2` side is done
  - Now convert '`F`' → "", which costs 1 (delete '`F`')
  - Total: 1 (insert) + 1 (delete) = 2 edits
- From `dp[0][0]`, we replace first:
  - Replace '`F`' with '`L`' → both characters are now consumed
  - What remains is converting "" → "", which is `dp[0][0] = 0`
  - Total: 1 (replace) + 0 = 1 edit

The cost of dp[1][1] is therefore the minimum of these paths:

```
dp[1][1] = min(dp[0][1] + 1, dp[1][0] + 1, dp[0][0] + 1)
         = min(2, 2, 1)
         = 1
```

Thus, replacing 'F' with 'L' requires the least amount of effort, hence the step to take among all others. Generally:

```
dp[i][j] = min(
    dp[i-1][j] + 1,          // delete
    dp[i][j-1] + 1,          // insert
    dp[i-1][j-1] + cost      // replace
)
```

The formula calculates the minimum edit distance by selecting the least expensive of three operations. The min() function guarantees that every table cell reflects the minimum operation count for the path evaluated thus far. Here cost = 0 if two characters are matched, or 1 otherwise. *Figure 8.6* shows the computational workflow for three possible neighbors of each cell, dp[i][j].

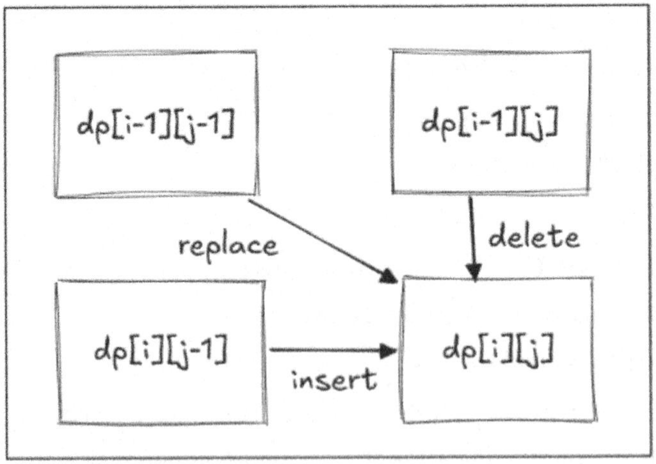

Figure 8.6: Cost workflow in the edit distance matrix

The above-described workflow can be generalized as follows:

- Diagonal (replacement): `dp[i-1][j-1] -> dp[i][j]`
    - +0 cost if `w1.charAt(i-1) == w2.charAt(j-1)`: there's no additional work needed. We simply carry over the cost from the previous state:
        - Total cost = cost(`dp[i-1][j-1]`)
    - +1 cost if `w1.charAt(i-1) != w2.charAt(j-1)`: there's a mismatch and we need to swap them
        - Total cost = cost(`dp[i-1][j-1]`) + 1
- Top-to-Bottom (deletion): `dp[i-1][j] -> dp[i][j]`
    - +1 cost for performing a deletion
    - Total cost = cost(`dp[i-1][j]`) + 1
- Left-to-Right (insertion): `dp[i][j-1] -> dp[i][j]`
    - +1 cost for performing an insertion
    - Total cost = cost(`dp[i][j-1]`) + 1

Extrapolating further, we derive the full edit distance matrix in *Figure 8.7*:

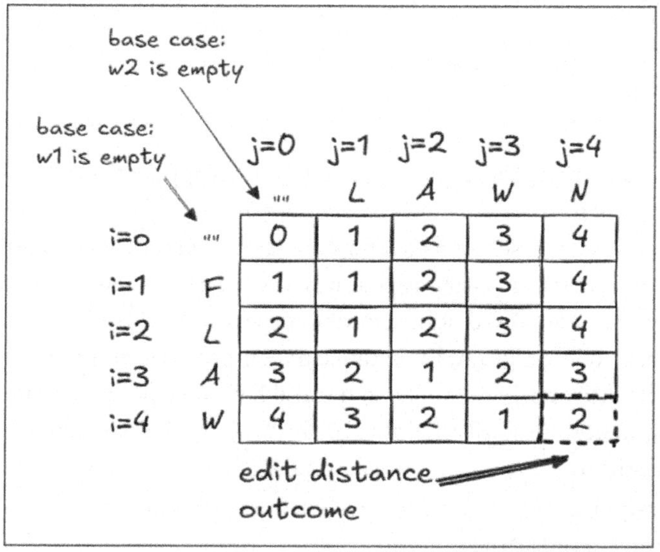

Figure 8.7: The edit distances for transforming "FLAW" into "LAWN"

The edit distance between the two words is in the bottom-right cell: dp[4][4] = 2. The standard routine for determining the edit distance between two strings is shown below:

```
public int getEditDistance(String w1, String w2) {
    int m = w1.length(), n = w2.length();
    int[][] dp = new int[m + 1][n + 1];

    for (int i = 0; i <= m; i++) dp[i][0] = i; // deletions
    for (int j = 0; j <= n; j++) dp[0][j] = j; // insertions

    for (int i = 1; i <= m; i++) {
        char c1 = w1.charAt(i - 1);
        for (int j = 1; j <= n; j++) {
            int cost = (c1 == w2.charAt(j - 1)) ? 0 : 1;
            dp[i][j] = Math.min(
                Math.min(dp[i - 1][j] + 1,
                dp[i][j - 1] + 1),
                dp[i - 1][j - 1] + cost
            );
        }
    }
    return dp[m][n];
}
```

Observation

The edit distance metric finds widespread use in practical applications. In spell checking, it guides the correction of misspelled words by ranking dictionary entries with the smallest distance. In bioinformatics, it serves as the basis for DNA sequence alignment, quantifying genetic similarity. Fuzzy string matching that powers search engines, autocomplete, and duplicate detection relies on low-distance matches to tolerate typos or variant spellings. Version control "diff" tools employ edit distance to compute the minimal set of edits required to transform one file into another. Finally, in natural language processing it offers a character-level measure of semantic similarity, helping to cluster or rank texts that are nearly identical. The prescribed algorithm using a two-dimensional DP matrix runs in O(m x n) time and space. This space requirement can be optimized using a one-dimensional DP, which keeps the same O(m x n) time but only O(n) memory.

Problem: Cheapest flight route with At-Most K stops

While the edit distance problem focuses on minimizing total transformations, this problem aims to identify the most cost-effective path to reach a specific objective.

Given a directed, weighted graph where each vertex represents a city, each edge represents a direct flight with an associated cost. For a specified source city `s`, destination city `t`, and a maximum number of layovers `K`, find the least cost itinerary that uses at most `K` stops (i.e., no more than `K+1` edges). If no such itinerary exists, return "no route".

Intuition

The graph is arbitrary: it may contain cycles, negative weights (but no negative cycles are reachable), and many vertices/edges. Conventional graph algorithms fall short on this problem:

- Dijkstra (or `A*`) efficiently finds the overall cheapest path but cannot restrict the number of hops, so it may return a route with more stops than allowed
- DFS or BFS explores every possible walk up to depth `K + 1`, which in the worst case is exponential in the graph size
- Bellman-Ford handles arbitrary weights but ignores the "at most K stops" constraint, relaxing all edges up to `V - 1` times and doing far more work than necessary

Dynamic programming resolves these issues by compressing the state to a pair (current city, stops used so far). Each such state represents the subproblem "what is the cheapest cost to reach this city after having taken these many edges?" Since many distinct routes can converge on the same state, subproblems overlap, making DP a natural fit that computes each state only once.

Solution: Bottom-Up DP

To compute the cheapest route that uses at most `K` stops, we use an optimal substructure approach. The global problem for finding the cheapest route to our final destination, using at most `K` stops, depends entirely on the optimal solutions of smaller subproblems. That is, the cheapest routes to all neighboring cities using at most `K-1` stops.

Mathematically, the relationship can be framed as:

$$dp[i][v] \; = \; \min_{(u,v)\in E}\big(dp[i-1][u] \; + \; weight(u,v)\big)$$

here `dp[i][v]` represents the cheapest price to reach city `v` using at most `i` flights, and `E` is the set of all available flights.

For example, if our destination is London with at most 2 stops, the algorithm looks at every city that has a direct outbound flight to London (e.g., Paris and New York). It then finds the minimum combined cost between:

- The cheapest way to reach Paris in at most 1 stop + flight from Paris to London
- The cheapest way to reach New York in at most 1 stop + flight from New York to London

To implement this layer-by-layer subproblem evaluation, we start by initializing a `dist` array of size `n` to `Integer.MAX_VALUE` and setting `dist[src]` to zero. Then, we repeat the relaxation process for `i` from 0 up to `K` (totaling `K+1` iterations), with each iteration allowing for one additional flight.

For each round, we first clone the current `dist` array to a new array `nextDist` using `Arrays.copyOf()`. This snapshot ensures that updates from the current iteration (representing `K` stops) do not influence other relaxations in the same round (which much build on the `K-1` stop results). We then traverse every flight in flights to extract `u` (source), `v` (destination), and `w` (weight/price). If the path through `u` is reachable (`dist[u] != Integer.MAX_VALUE`) and offers a cheaper price (`dist[u] + w < nextDist[v]`), we update `nextDist[v]`.

After all flights in the current round have been relaxed, we assign `dist = nextDist` and proceed to the next iteration. Once all rounds finish, the answer is `dist[dst]`; if it remains `Integer.MAX_VALUE`, no route satisfying the stop limit exists, and we return -1.

```
public int findCheapestPrice(int n, int[][] flights, int src, int dst, int K) {
    // Initialize distances with a large value (Infinity)
    int[] dist = new int[n];
    java.util.Arrays.fill(dist, Integer.MAX_VALUE);
    dist[src] = 0;

    // Perform K + 1 iterations (K stops means at most K + 1 edges)
    for (int i = 0; i <= K; i++) {
        // Create a copy of the current distances to avoid using
        // updated values from the same iteration
        int[] nextDist = java.util.Arrays.copyOf(dist, n);

        for (int[] flight : flights) {
            int u = flight[0]; // source
            int v = flight[1]; // destination
            int w = flight[2]; // weight/price

            // If source city is reachable, try relaxing
```

```
                    // the edge
                if (dist[u] != Integer.MAX_VALUE) {
                    if (dist[u] + w < nextDist[v]) {
                        nextDist[v] = dist[u] + w;
                    }
                }
            }
            // Update dist for the next iteration
            dist = nextDist;
        }
        return dist[dst] == Integer.MAX_VALUE ? -1 : dist[dst];
    }
```

This algorithm runs in `O((K+1)·E)`, where `E` is the number of flights (edges), and `O(V)` in space for storing distance arrays.

Solution: Top-Down DP

With this approach, we perform a memoized DFS starting from `src` with `remEdges` set to `K+1` (since `K` stops allow for `K+1` flights). We first organize the input into an adjacency list `adj` for efficient lookups. The recursive `dfs` function checks the memo table at each city to see if the minimum cost for the current `remEdges` has already been calculated.

If the city matches `dst`, the cost is `0`. If `remEdges` reaches `0` without hitting the destination, we return `INF`. Otherwise, the function iterates through each neighbor in `adj[city]`, recursively calculating the cost with `remEdges - 1` and updating best to capture the minimum total price. This result is stored in `memo[city][remEdges]`, ensuring each state is computed only once. Below is the complete Java code illustrating this approach.

```
import java.util.ArrayList;
import java.util.List;

public class Solution {

    /* ---------------------------------------------------------------
     *  Constant used to represent "infinity".
     *  A large value is chosen to avoid overflow when adding edge costs.
     * ---------------------------------------------------------------
     */
    private static final int INF = 1_000_000_000;
```

```
/*  memo[city][remEdges] - cached cheapest cost from `city`
 *  to the destination using at most `remEdges` flights.
*/
private Integer[][] memo;

/**
  * @param n        number of cities (vertices)
  * @param flights each flight is {from, to, cost}
  * @param src      source city index
  * @param dst      destination city index
  * @param K        maximum number of lay-overs (stops)
  * @return cheapest cost, or -1 if no route exists within stop limit
  */
public int findCheapestPrice(int n, int[][] flights,
                             int src, int dst, int K) {

    /* ----------------------------------------------------------
     *  1. Build adjacency list: adj[u] = list of (v, weight)
     * ----------------------------------------------------------
    */
    @SuppressWarnings("unchecked")
    List<int[]>[] adj = new ArrayList[n];
    for (int i = 0; i < n; i++) {
        adj[i] = new ArrayList<>();
    }
    for (int[] f : flights) {
        adj[f[0]].add(new int[]{f[1], f[2]});
    }

    /* ----------------------------------------------------------
     *  2. Allocate memo table.
     *     K stops → at most K+1 edges, so we need indices
     *     0 … K+1 inclusive.
     * ----------------------------------------------------------
    */
    memo = new Integer[n][K + 2];

    /* ----------------------------------------------------------
     *  3. Kick off the DFS from the source with K+1 edges available.
     * ----------------------------------------------------------
    */
```

```
        int result = dfs(src, dst, K + 1, adj);

        return result >= INF ? -1 : result;
    }

    /**
     * Recursive helper: cheapest cost from {@code city} to {@code dst}
     * using at most {@code remEdges} flights.
     */
    private int dfs(int city, int dst, int remEdges,
                    List<int[]>[] adj) {

        /* Base case - destination reached. */
        if (city == dst) {
            return 0;
        }
        /* Base case - no flights left. */
        if (remEdges == 0) {
            return INF;
        }
        /* Memoisation - return cached answer if available. */
        if (memo[city][remEdges] != null) {
            return memo[city][remEdges];
        }
        int best = INF;
        /* Explore all outgoing flights from the current city. */
        for (int[] neighbor : adj[city]) {
            int nextCity = neighbor[0];
            int weight = neighbor[1];

            /* Solve the sub-problem: cost from nextCity to dst with one
              fewer flight available. */
            int sub = dfs(nextCity, dst, remEdges - 1, adj);

            if (sub != INF) {
                best = Math.min(best, weight + sub);
            }
        }

        /* Cache and return the result. */
        memo[city][remEdges] = best;
```

```
        return best;
    }

    /* ------------------------------------------------------------
     *  Demo / test
     * ------------------------------------------------------------
     */
    public static void main(String[] args) {
        int n = 5;
        int[][] flights = {
            {0, 1, 100},
            {0, 2, 500},
            {1, 2, 100},
            {1, 3, 600},
            {2, 3, 200},
            {3, 4, 100},
            {0, 4, 1000}
        };
        int src = 0, dst = 4, K = 2;    // at most 2 lay-overs

        Solution sol = new Solution();
        int answer = sol.findCheapestPrice(n, flights, src, dst, K);

        System.out.println(answer == -1
                ? "no route"
                : "cheapest cost = $" + answer);
    }
}
```

The top-down memoised DFS runs in `O(V·K)` time in the worst case, because each state (`city`, `remEdges`) is solved once and then cached. Its space consumption is also `O(V·K)` for the memoization table, plus an additional recursion stack of depth at most `K`. Because the recursion explores only states that are reachable from the source, a sparse graph often yields far fewer explored states than the bottom-up Bellman–Ford variant, allowing the top-down approach to outperform it in practice.

Problem: Building a product pipeline with DP

A manufacturing plant produces a single consumer device. There are `N` distinct production steps, labeled `1 … N`. For each step `i`, we let:

- $\texttt{time}_i$: time required to finish step `i`.
- $\texttt{cost}_i$: cost incurred for performing step `i`.

The dependency structure is a **directed acyclic graph** (DAG). Namely, if step `j` is a prerequisite of step `i`, then `i` cannot start before `j` completes. No cycle exists, so every feasible production plan can be represented as a topological ordering of the steps. The final product is complete once a special step `F` has been finished.

Objectives

Determine the minimal total cost of all steps that must be performed to reach step `F`, subject to the prerequisite constraints. The total `costi` is simply the sum of the costi values of every step that appears in a valid execution path from the start of production to step F.

Intuition

Dynamic programming on directed acyclic graphs (DAGs) naturally captures the structure of a production pipeline. Every manufacturing step becomes a vertex; a directed edge `x → y` represents that step `x` must precede step `y`. The weight of the edge is the cost of executing `y` (or its duration if we are talking about time).

We add a dummy source vertex `S` with zero-cost edges to each step that has no prerequisites, modeling the ability to start any independent operation without extra expense. The final product corresponds to a unique destination vertex `F`.

In this graph, any path from `S` to `F` is a valid, precedence-respecting schedule, and the weight of the path equals the total cost of the selected steps. Thus, minimizing production cost is precisely the shortest-path problem on this DAG, solvable with DP.

Solution

Since the graph contains no cycles, we can sweep through its vertices in a topological sequence and relax each edge only once.

Topological ordering

Compute a topological sort of all nodes (for example, with DFS or Kahn's algorithm). In this ordering, every prerequisite precedes the step that depends on it.

Initialization

Set `dist[S] = 0` and `dist[v] = +∞` for all other v vertices v. The `dist` array records the lowest cost discovered so far to reach each vertex.

Edge relaxation

Process the vertices in topological order. For each vertex `v` and each outgoing edge `v → u` with weight `w`:

```
dist[u] = Math.min(dist[u], dist[v] + w);
```

If `dist[v]` is still infinite, the edge is ignored because `v` is not yet reachable.

Results

After all vertices are processed, `dist[F]` contains the minimal total cost to produce the final product. If `dist[F]` remains ∞, no valid production sequence exists (e.g. the graph is disconnected).

Because each edge is relaxed once and each vertex is visited once, the algorithm runs in `O(V + E)` time and uses `O(V)` additional space for the distance array (the adjacency list itself is part of the input).

The complete Java code is shown below.

```
public int minCost(
    int N,
    int[] costi,
    List<int[]> prerequisites,
    int F)
{
    // ---------- build graph ----------
    List<Integer>[] g = new ArrayList[N + 1];
    int[] indeg = new int[N + 1];
    for (int i = 0; i <= N; i++) g[i] = new ArrayList<>();

    for (int[] e : prerequisites) {
        int u = e[0] - 1, v = e[1] - 1;
        g[u].add(v);
        indeg[v]++;
    }
    int S = N;
    for (int v = 0; v < N; v++){
```

```
            if (indeg[v] == 0) {
                g[S].add(v);
                indeg[v]++;
            }
        }
        // ---------- topological order ----------
        Queue<Integer> q = new ArrayDeque<>();
        for (int v = 0; v <= N; v++)
            if (indeg[v] == 0) q.add(v);

        List<Integer> topo = new ArrayList<>();
        while (!q.isEmpty()) {
            int v = q.poll();
            topo.add(v);
            for (int nb : g[v]) if (--indeg[nb] == 0) q.add(nb);
        }

        // ---------- DP: shortest path in DAG ----------
        final int INF = Integer.MAX_VALUE / 4;
        int[] dist = new int[N + 1];
        Arrays.fill(dist, INF);
        dist[S] = 0;

        for (int v : topo) {
            if (dist[v] == INF) continue;
            for (int nb : g[v]) {
                int w = costi[nb];
                if (dist[v] + w < dist[nb]) {
                    dist[nb] = dist[v] + w;
                }
            }
        }
        int ans = dist[F - 1];
        return ans == INF ? -1 : ans;
    }
```

Setting `N = 5` and the cost of steps 1 through 5 as [10, 20, 30, 40, 50] we can check for the minimal production cost:

```
int N = 5;
int[] costi = {10, 20, 30, 40, 50};    // costs of steps 1…5
```

```
List<int[]> prereq = List.of(
    new int[]{1, 3},
    new int[]{1, 4},
    new int[]{2, 3},
    new int[]{3, 5},
    new int[]{4, 5}
);
int F = 5;    // final product is step 5

System.out.println("Minimal production cost: " + minCost(N, costi, prereq, F));
```

The above yields a dependency graph.

```
1 → 3
1 → 4
2 → 3
3 → 5
4 → 5
```

The dummy source `S` has zero-cost edges to every step that has no prerequisites (steps 1 and 2). Running the algorithm finds the cheapest path from `S` to the final step 5:

```
S → 1 (cost 10)
1 → 3 (cost 30)
3 → 5 (cost 50)
```

The total cost is $10 + 30 + 50 = 90$.

Generally, the dummy source `S` connects to every step with no prerequisites, making it possible to start any independent operation at zero cost. The graph is topologically sorted with Kahn's algorithm. In the DP pass, each vertex is relaxed once, and the edge weight is simply the cost of the destination vertex (`costi[nb]`). `dist[F-1]` yields the cheapest total cost, which becomes -1 if the final step is unreachable. Overall, the program runs in `O(V+E)` time and uses `O(V)` additional memory, which is optimal for shortest-path problems on DAGs.

DP practicals checklist

Dynamic programming is applicable to a broad spectrum of problems, from tree, and graph problems to pattern recognition tasks. Yet, when the input size grows, a naïve recurrence often becomes impractical. In such cases, we must rely on more advanced techniques such as knapsack reductions, convex hull tricks, divide-and-conquer optimizations, and other structure-exploiting methods, to keep the computation feasible. Keeping this in mind, the following checklist offers a practical, step-by-step guide for applying DP to any problem. This list is by no means prescriptive, but it can help when applying DP to a problem:

1. Is a recurrence possible?
   a. Does the problem naturally split into subproblems?
   b. Do the same subproblems appear multiple times?
   c. Can the global optimum be built from optimal subsolutions?
2. If the answer is "yes" for all three, DP is the way to go. Now you can go to Step 2.Define the state, e.g., indices, bitmasks, intervals, etc.
3. Write the recurrence, e.g., clear transition and base cases.
4. Implement the solution:
   a. Pick the style, i.e., memoization (top-down) for sparse recursion, or tabulation (bottom-up) for dense DP.
   b. Optimize space: keep only the previous row/column if possible.
   c. Look for structure: monotonicity, convexity → divide-and-conquer, Convex Hull Trick, etc.
   d. Verify small cases before scaling up.

These problem-solving steps are visually summarized in *Figure 8.8*:

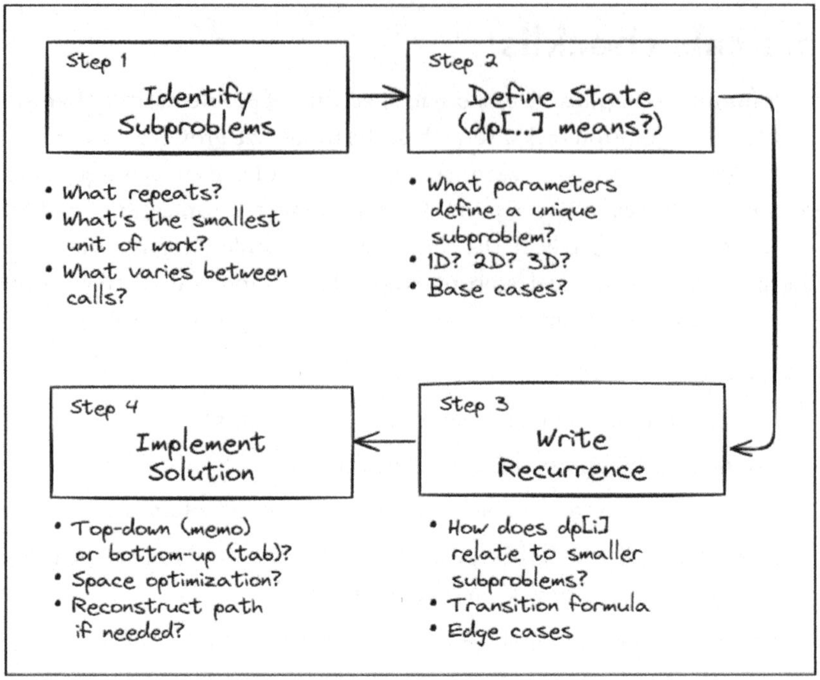

Figure 8.8: DP problem-solving flowchart

Summary

Dynamic programming is a powerful design paradigm that transforms computationally intractable problems into manageable, polynomial-time solutions. It achieves this by recognizing that a global optimal solution is built from smaller pieces (**Optimal Substructure**) which, in turn, share common, repetitive subproblems (**Overlapping Subproblems**). By storing these intermediate results and solving each state only once, DP efficiently converts sprawling, exponential search trees into linear or polynomial time passes. The ability to identify the correct state, establish the recurrence, and choose the right implementation style (**Memoization** or **Tabulation**) is the mastery required to apply this technique. *Figure 8.9* provides a summary diagram of dynamic programming techniques; this same reference model will reappear in *Chapter 12* to accompany several practical, real-world examples.

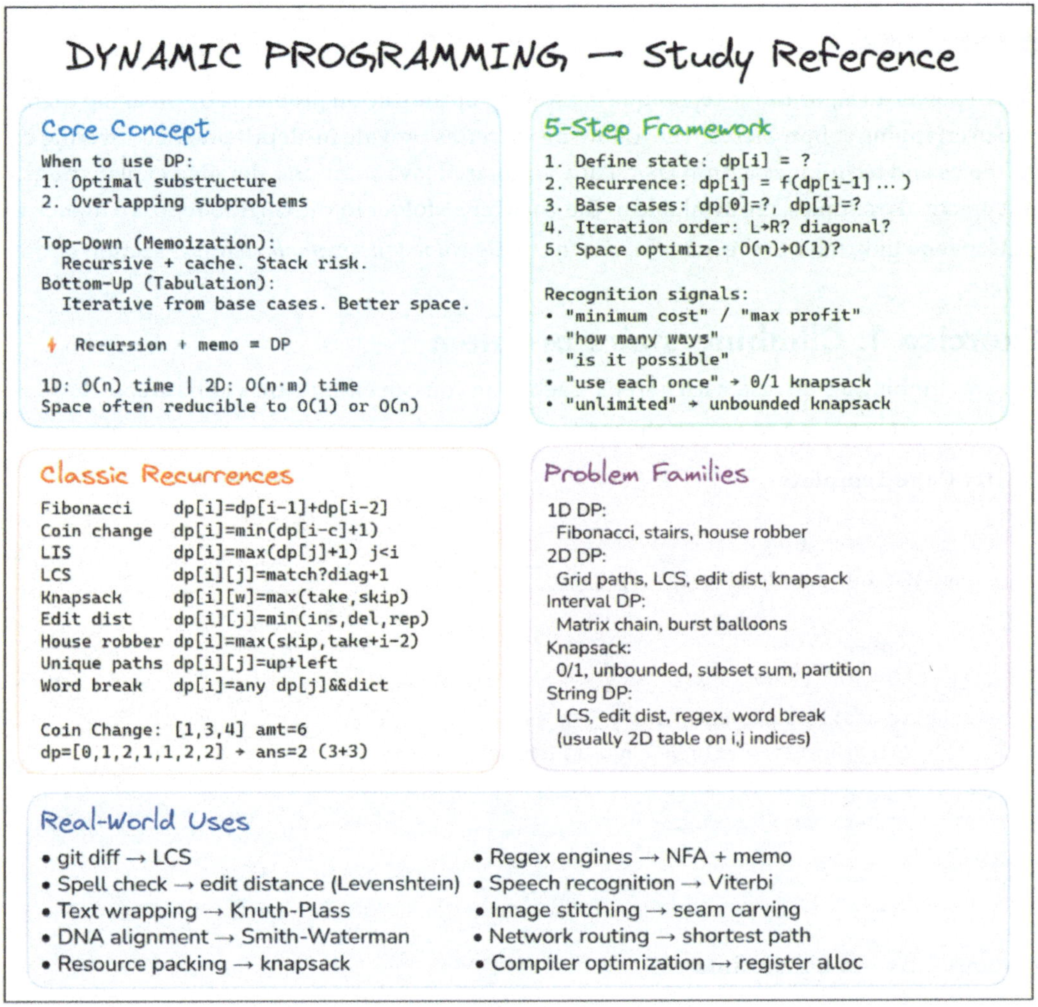

Figure 8.9: DP techniques and their use cases

Understanding DP is fundamentally about abstraction: translating a real-world constraint or problem into a clean recurrence relation. With these tools, you can tackle everything from the shortest paths in DAGs and calculating edit distance to complex resource allocation. However, mastering this systematic approach requires mastery of the underlying mechanism itself.

Next, let's turn our focus to the foundation that makes all of this possible: recursion.

Exercises

DP is a powerful algorithmic technique for solving optimization problems by breaking them into overlapping subproblems. The following exercises provide in-depth practice covering core DP topics and techniques within DSA. Fully annotated Java solutions, detailed explanations, and practical examples, are available in the `Chapter08` folder in the GitHub repo. To unlock the GitHub repo link, refer to the instructions in the *Download the example code files* section of the *Preface*.

Exercise 1: Climbing stairs problem

You are climbing a staircase with `n` steps. Each time you can climb either 1 or 2 steps. How many distinct ways can you reach the top?

Starter Code Template

```
public class ClimbingStairs {
    public int climbStairs(int n) {
        // TODO
        return 0;
    }
    public static void main(String[] args) {
        ClimbingStairs solver = new ClimbingStairs();
        // Test Case 1: small n
        // Test Case 2: larger n
    }
}
```

Assumptions and Constraints

- Input `n` is a non-negative integer (number of stairs)
- Each move climbs exactly 1 or 2 stairs
- Order matters: (1 + 2) and (2 + 1) count as distinct ways
- N = 0 returns 0; `n = 1` returns 1
- Result fits in a 32-bit `int`
- Time: `O(n)`, Space: `O(n)` with a dp array, reducible to `O(1)` with rolling variables
- Single-threaded, in-memory computation

Test Case 1: Small input

- **Input**: `n = 3`.
- **Expected Output**: 3.
- **Explanation**: The 3 distinct ways are (1 + 1 + 1), (1 + 2), (2 + 1). Validates the base recurrence `ways(3) = ways(2) + ways(1) = 2 + 1`.

Test Case 2: Larger input

- **Input**: `n = 5`.
- **Expected Output**: 8.
- **Explanation**: Following the Fibonacci progression, where `ways(4) = 5; ways(5) = ways(4) + ways(3) = 5 + 3 = 8;` etc. The loop accumulates correctly beyond the base cases.

Hints

The number of ways to reach step `n` equals the number of ways to reach step `n-1` (then take 1 step) plus the number of ways to reach step `n-2` (then take 2 steps). This is exactly the Fibonacci recurrence. Recognizing this pattern is the foundation for almost every one-dimensional DP problem.

- **Define** `dp[i]` = number of distinct ways to reach step `i`
- **Base cases**: `dp[1] = 1, dp[2] = 2`
- **Recurrence**: `dp[i] = dp[i-1] + dp[i-2]`
- You only need the last two values; space can be reduced to `O(1)`

Solution

The problem asks how many distinct ways you can climb `n` stairs taking 1 or 2 steps at a time. The key realization is that to arrive at step `i`, you must have come from either step `i-1` or step `i-2`. The number of ways to reach step `i` is the sum of the ways to reach the two preceding steps.

1. **Handle base cases**: For `n ≤ 2`, the answer equals `n` itself: 1 stair has 1 way, 2 stairs have 2 ways (1+1 or 2). These also seed the recurrence:

```
if (n <= 2) return n;
```

2. **Set up the DP array**: `dp[i]` holds the number of ways to reach step `i`. Initialize the two known values:

```
int[] dp = new int[n + 1];
dp[1] = 1;  // one way to reach step 1
dp[2] = 2;  // two ways to reach step 2
```

3. **Build up the recurrence**: Each step's answer is the sum of the previous two, which is a Fibonacci series in disguise. Iterating from 3 to `n` yields:

```
for (int i = 3; i <= n; i++) {
    dp[i] = dp[i - 1] + dp[i - 2];
}
```

4. **Step 4: Return the top**: `dp[n]` now holds the total ways to reach the final step, so we return the result stored in it:

```
return dp[n];
```

Evaluate dp[n] at n = 5:

```
dp[1] = 1
dp[2] = 2
dp[3] = dp[2] + dp[1] = 2 + 1 = 3
dp[4] = dp[3] + dp[2] = 3 + 2 = 5
dp[5] = dp[4] + dp[3] = 5 + 3 = 8    // answer
```

We optimize the time complexity from exponential to `O(n)` by utilizing tabulation. Each state `dp[i]` is computed exactly once in constant time by transitioning from its two immediate predecessors.

Because computing each step only requires the two immediate predecessors, the `O(n)` array can be collapsed into two rolling variables to achieve optimal `O(1)` space complexity. By initializing these variables to track just the last two calculated states, we can iteratively update them in a loop, successfully eliminating the full memory footprint while maintaining the linear `O(n)` runtime:

```
int prev2 = 1, prev1 = 2;
for (int i = 3; i <= n; i++) {
    int cur = prev1 + prev2;
```

```
        prev2 = prev1;
        prev1 = cur;
    }
    return prev1;
```

Complexity

- **Time O(n):** a single loop from 3 to n, with O(1) work (one addition) per iteration. While advanced mathematical approaches like matrix exponentiation can solve this sequence pattern in logarithmic O(log n) time, this iterative loop is highly optimal for a sequential DP framework.
- **Space:** O(n) for the array-based approach; optimized to O(1) via rolling state variables.

Exercise 2: Maximize sum without adjacent elements

You are given an array nums where each element represents a value at a position. Select a subset of these values such that no two selected positions are adjacent, and the total sum of selected values is maximized.

Consider the following:

- At each position, you have two choices: include this value or exclude it
- If you include the current element, then you must skip the previous one (i.e., add the best result up to two positions back)
- If you exclude the current element, carry forward the best result from the previous position

Hints:

- dp[i] = maximum sum achievable using elements from index 0 to i
- **Recurrence relation**:

```
dp[i] = max (dp[i-1], dp[i-2] + nums[i])
```

- **Base cases**:
    - dp[0] = nums[0]
    - dp[1] = max(nums[0], nums[1])
- **Stretch goal**: only keep track of the last two values to optimize space

Starter Code Template

```
public class MaxNonAdjacentSum {
    public int maxSum(int[] nums) {
        // TODO: Implement solution here
        return 0;
    }
}
```

Assumptions and Constraints

- `1 ≤ nums.length ≤ 100`
- `0 ≤ nums[i] ≤ 400`
- No adjacent selection: cannot select two elements that are next to each other in the array
- All intermediate values and results are guaranteed to fit within a standard 32-bit signed integer without overflow
- Optimal solution: There is always a unique maximum sum possible under the given constraints
- Solution can be optimized to `O(1)` space using only two variables instead of full array
- `O(n)` time complexity, where n is the length of the input array

Test Case 1

- **Input**: `[1, 2, 3, 1]`
- **Output**: 4
- **Explanation**: Choose elements at indices 0 and 2 (values 1 and 3). Total = 1 + 3 = 4. Cannot choose adjacent indices.

Test Case 2

- **Input**: `[2, 7, 9, 3, 1]`
- **Output**: 12
- **Explanation**: Choose elements at indices 0, 2, and 4 (values 2, 9, and 1). Total = 2 + 9 + 1 = 12. Cannot choose adjacent indices.

Exercise 3: Coin change

You're given an array of distinct coin denominations `coins` and an integer `amount`. Return the **fewest number of coins** needed to make up `amount`. If that amount **cannot** be made from any combination of the coins, return `-1`. You have an **unlimited** supply of each coin.

Examples

```
coins = [1, 5, 6, 9], amount = 11
->  2     // 5 + 6
coins = [2], amount = 3
->  -1    // 3 is odd, only even sums reachable
coins = [1, 2, 5], amount = 11
->  3     // 5 + 5 + 1
coins = [], amount = 0
->  0     // zero coins make zero
```

Starter Code Template

```
import java.util.*;
public class CoinChange {
    // Returns the fewest coins to make
    // amount, or -1 if impossible.
    public int coinChange(int[] coins, int amount) {
        // TODO
        return -1;
    }
}
```

Assumptions and Constraints

- Denominations are positive integers and distinct; amount ≥ 0
- Order of coins doesn't matter; we want the count, not the actual combination
- Amount == 0, return 0 (no coins needed), regardless of the coin set (even if `coins` is empty)
- If amount `> 0` and no combination sums to it, return -1
- The graph of subproblems fits in memory; `0 ≤ amount ≤ 10`^{4}`, 1 ≤ coins.length ≤ 12`
- Coin values may exceed `amount` (they're simply never usable for that amount)

Test Case 1

- **Input**: (`coins, amount`): `[1,5,6,9], 11`
- **Output**: 2

Test Case 2

- **Input**: (`coins, amount`): `[2], 3`
- **Output**: 1 (unreachable)

Test Case 3

- **Input**: (`coins, amount`): `[1, 2, 5], 11`
- **Output**: 3

Exercise 4: Longest common subsequence

Given two strings `text1` and `text2`, return the **length of their longest common subsequence (LCS)**. If there is no common subsequence, return `0`.

A **subsequence** is a sequence derived from a string by deleting some (possibly zero) characters **without changing the relative order** of the remaining characters. It does **not** need to be contiguous. A **common subsequence** is a subsequence of both strings.

Examples

- text1 = "abcde", text2 = "ace" -> 3 // "ace"
- text1 = "abc", text2 = "abc" -> 3 // "abc"
- text1 = "abc", text2 = "def" -> 0 // nothing in common

Starter Code Template

```
public class LongestCommonSubsequence {
    public int longestCommonSubsequence(String text1, String text2) {
        // TODO: 2-D DP. dp[i][j] = LCS of text1[0..i-1] and text2[0..j-1].
        return 0;
    }
}
```

Assumptions and Constraints

- Characters can be any (case-sensitive); `'A'` and `'a'` differ.
- Either string may be **empty**; LCS is `0`.
- We want the **length**, not the subsequence itself (reconstruction is an extension).

- Relative order must be preserved; characters need **not** be contiguous.
- The DP table fits in memory; `1 ≤ text1.length, text2.length ≤ 1000.`
- There may be **multiple** longest common subsequences; we only need the length (all are equal).

Test Case 1

- **Input**: (`text1`, `text2`): `"abcde"`, `"ace"`
- **Output**: 3 // (`a, c, e`)

Test Case 2

- **Input**: (`text1`, `text2`): `"abc"`, `"abc"`
- **Output**: 3

Test Case 3

- **Input**: (`text1`, `text2`): `"abc"`, `"def"`
- **Output**: `0` (disjoint)

Exercise 5: 0/1 knapsack

Given item `weights[]`, item `values[]`, and a knapsack capacity `W`, pick a subset of items so total weight ≤ `W` and total value is maximized. Each item may be used **at most once** (0/1).

Examples

- **Input**:
  - `weights = [2, 3, 4, 5]`
  - `values = [3, 4, 5, 6]`
  - `W = 8`
- **Optimal Output**: `10`
- **Explanation**: Choosing items at indices 1 and 3 maximizes total profit within the weight limit. Their combined weight is 3 + 5 = 8 ≤ 8, and their combined value is 4 + 6 = 10

Starter Code Template

```
public class Knapsack01 {
    // Returns the maximum value of items fitting within
    // capacity W (each item used at most once).
    public int knapsack(int[] weights, int[] values, int W) {
        // TODO: dp[i][w] = max value using the first i items with capacity w.
```

```
        return 0;
    }
}
```

Assumptions and Constraints

- Each item is used **at most once.**
- Weights, values, and `W` are **non-negative** integers.
- A subset may be empty, returning value `0` (e.g. if every item exceeds the budget).
- We want the **maximum value**, not the subset itself (reconstruction is an extension).
- The DP table fits in memory; $1 \le n \le 1000, 0 \le W \le 10^4$ (pseudo-polynomial in `W`).
- `weights.length == values.length`.

Test Case 1

- **Input**: (weights, values, W): `[2,3,4,5]`, `[3,4,5,6]`, `8`
- **Output**: `10` (items 1 and 3)

Test Case 2

- **Input**: (weights, values, W): `[1,2,3]`, `[10,20,30]`, `0`
- **Output**: `0` (no budget)

Test Case 3

- **Input**: (weights, values, W): `[5]`, `[10]`, `3`
- **Output**: `0` (item does not fit)

Exercise 6: Word break

Given a string `s` and a dictionary of strings `wordDict`, return `true` if `s` can be **segmented** into a space-separated sequence of one or more dictionary words. The same dictionary word may be **reused** multiple times in the segmentation.

Starter Code Template

```
import java.util.*;
public class WordBreak {
    // Returns true if s can be segmented into a sequence
    // of dictionary words.
    public boolean wordBreak(String s, List<String> wordDict) {
        // TODO: 1-D DP. dp[i] = can s[0..i-1] be segmented?
        return false;
```

```
    }
}
```

Assumptions and Constraints

- s and dictionary words consist of lowercase letters (clarify if asked).
- Dictionary words are **distinct**; the same word may be **reused** in the segmentation.
- An **empty** s is trivially segment-able, returning `true` (the empty prefix needs no words).
- We want a **boolean** (can it be segmented), not the segmentation itself or the count.
- The DP table fits in memory; `1 ≤ s.length ≤ 300, 1 ≤ wordDict.length ≤ 1000.`
- Dictionary may contain words longer than s (simply never match).

Test Case 1

- **Input**: `(s, wordDict)`: `"applepenapple", ["apple","pen"]`
- **Output**: `true`

Test Case 2

- **Input**: `(s, wordDict)`: `"catsandog", ["cats","dog","sand","and","cat"]`
- **Output**: `false`

Exercise 7: Longest increasing subsequence

Given an integer array `nums`, return the **length of the longest strictly increasing subsequence**. A **subsequence** is derived by deleting some (possibly zero) elements **without changing the order** of the remaining elements. It need **not** be contiguous.

Examples

- `nums = [10, 9, 2, 5, 3, 7, 101, 18]` -> 4 // [2, 3, 7, 101] (or [2,3,7,18])
- `nums = [0, 1, 0, 3, 2, 3]` -> 4 // [0, 1, 2, 3]
- `nums = [7, 7, 7, 7]` -> 1 // strictly increasing; equal values don't count

Starter Code Template

```
import java.util.Arrays;
public class LongestIncreasingSubsequence {
    public int lengthOfLIS(int[] nums) {
        // TODO
        return 0;
```

```
    }
}
```

Assumptions and Constraints

- Elements may be negative, zero, or positive; values may repeat.
- "Increasing" means **strictly** increasing (<).
- We want the **length**, not the subsequence itself (reconstruction is an extension).
- Empty array → returning `0`; single element → returning `1`.
- Fits in memory; `1 ≤ nums.length ≤ 2500` for the DP solution.

Test Case 1

- **Input (nums)**: [10,9,2,5,3,7,101,18]
- **Output**: 4 // [2,3,7,101]

Test Case 2

- **Input** (nums): `[7,7,7,7]`
- **Output**: 1 // strict

Hints

This problem can be solved using either a brute force approach with `O(n²)` time complexity or by implementing a binary search-based algorithm that operates in `O(n log n)` time.

Exercise 8: Target sum

Given an array of non-negative integers and a target sum, determine the number of ways to assign '+' or '-' signs to each element such that the resulting sum equals the target.

Starter Code Template

```
public class TargetSum {
    public int findTargetSumWays(int[] nums, int target) {
        // TODO: Implement space-optimized DP solution
        return 0;
    }
}
```

Assumptions and Constraints

- `1 ≤ nums.length ≤ 20`
- `0 ≤ nums[i] ≤ 1000`

- `0 ≤ sum(nums[i]) ≤ 1000`
- `-1000 ≤ target ≤ 1000`
- Each element must be assigned exactly one sign (+ or -).
- Values fit within a standard 32-bit signed integer.

Test Case 1

- **Input**: `nums = [1, 1, 1, 1, 1]`, `target = 3`
- **Output**: `5`
- **Explanation**: There are 5 ways to get a sum of 3, namely
  1. -1 + 1 + 1 + 1 + 1 = 3
  2. +1 - 1 + 1 + 1 + 1 = 3
  3. +1 + 1 - 1 + 1 + 1 = 3
  4. +1 + 1 + 1 - 1 + 1 = 3
  5. +1 + 1 + 1 + 1 - 1 = 3

Test Case 2

- **Input**: `nums = [1, 2]`, `target = 4`
- **Output**: `0`
- **Explanation**: Total sum is = 3. Even if all elements are positive, the maximum possible sum is 3. Since 4 > 3, it is impossible to reach the target.

Hints

- This problem can be transformed into a subset sum problem where we need to find subsets that sum to a specific value.
- If we partition the array into two subsets with sums `S1` and `S2`, where `S1 - S2 = target`, then `S1 = (target + total_sum) / 2`.
- The problem reduces to counting the number of subsets that sum to `(target + total_sum) / 2`.
- State representation: `dp[i][j]` represents the number of ways to achieve a subset sum `j` using the first `i` elements.

Complexity

Time is `O(n × sum)` and space `O(n × sum)`, using a 2-D table. Note that space can be reduced to `O(sum)` by utilizing a 1-D rolling array traversed backward.

9

Recursion

Recursion is a technique that solves a problem by repeatedly applying the same solution to progressively smaller versions of that problem. In addition, recursion is a fundamental design principle for solving complex problems by breaking them into smaller, similar subproblems. A classic illustration of recursion in production systems is a directory-tree walker used by backup and antivirus software. The routine processes the current directory and then recurses on each subdirectory it finds. This mirrors the way humans naturally explore folders ("look inside this folder, then inside every sub-folder, and so on"), and it implements a depth-first traversal of the file-system graph. Even when the directory depth grows to millions of levels, modern operating systems supply ample stack space, and many languages optimize tail calls so the recursion can run with essentially constant auxiliary space. Because it maps so naturally to hierarchical data, recursion is a foundational technique in a wide range of industry applications, from compilers and XML parsers to GUI layout engines and network protocol handlers. This chapter lays out the fundamentals of recursion, contrasts it with iterative approaches, and explains why recursion remains a core engine behind many real-world software systems.

Understanding recursion: patterns, mechanics, and pitfalls

Recursion provides a powerful alternative to brute-force iteration for solving complex problems by recursively breaking them down into manageable sub-problems. This approach yields highly efficient and clean code, particularly for working with nested data structures. We will explore the core principles of recursion: the function, the base case, and the recursive step, to master the mechanism and avoid errors like stack overflows.

Recursive patterns

The key ingredients that make a recursive solution work are:

- **Recursive Function**: a code routine that can be invoked by itself repeatedly. This self-reference is the hallmark of recursion. A recursive call tackles a smaller sub-problem that is structurally identical to the original.
- **Base case**: the specific condition that signals the end of recursion. It prevents infinite loops by ensuring the chain of calls stops before the program crashes. Think of it as the bottom of a ladder; once the recursion reaches this point, it stops calling itself and begins to "unwind," returning results back up the call stack.
- **Recursive case**: the rule that reduces the problem size and invokes the function again on a smaller instance. Drives the computation toward the base case. The following example shows the anatomy of a simple recursive function to count down a positive number, from n to 0.

```
int countdown(int n) {
    if (n == 0)            // base case
        return 0;
    else                   // recursive case
        return countdown(n-1) + 1;
}
```

Here, each call to countdown asks the same question for a smaller `n`. When `n` finally reaches 0, the recursion stops, and the results unwind back up the call chain. Without the base case, the function would keep invoking itself indefinitely, leading to a `java.lang.StackoverflowError`. This JVM-initiated error occurs because every method call requires a new stack frame for local variables and return addresses. When the thread's stack runs out of memory and cannot accommodate a new frame, this error is thrown. See the complete implementation in the `Countdown.java` file in the `Chapter09` folder on GitHub. To unlock the GitHub repo link, refer to the instructions in the *Download the example code files* section of the *Preface*.

Designing good base cases

A common mistake when writing recursive functions is choosing a base case that's too narrow, too broad, or missing entirely. Getting it wrong leads to bugs that are often hard to trace, such as infinite loops, skipped inputs, or unnecessarily complex code. Common pitfalls to watch for:

- Missing base case: e.g., omitting the `n == 0` check entirely. Without a termination condition, the function recurses indefinitely until the stack overflows. As frames are pushed, the JVM will eventually exhaust its fixed-size stack memory; a limit typically reached between 500 and 1000 frames under default configurations.

- Base case `n` never reached: e.g., decrementing n but checking for `n` equaling something else. For most inputs, the condition is never satisfied, so the recursion blows past it and never terminates.
- Too many base cases: e.g., handling `n == x`, `n == y`, and `n == z` as separate cases. This is usually a sign that the recurrence relation isn't clean and should be simplified.

Additional recursion pitfalls, including array bounds checking and wrong identity value in base case, are demonstrated in the `RecursionPitfalls.java` source file inside the `Chapter09` subfolder on GitHub. To unlock the GitHub repo link, refer to the instructions in the *Download the example code files* section of the *Preface*. A good rule of thumb is to start with the smallest valid input for your problem. For natural numbers, that's typically 0 or 1. For strings, the empty string. For trees, a null or empty node. For lists, the empty list. If your base case maps naturally to that smallest input, the recursive structure will almost always fall into place cleanly.

Example: Factorial

The factorial function defines the following:

- `n! = 1` if `n = 0` (base case).
- `n! = n × (n - 1)!` if `n> 0` (recursive case).

The implementation yields:

```
int factorial(int n) {
    if (n == 0)                    // base case
        return 1;
    return n * factorial(n - 1); // recursive case
}
```

The execution stack accumulates during the downward recursion, while the actual computations occur during the upward unwinding. This is crucial because it requires the system to maintain all intermediate stack frames in memory until the base case is finally reached and the recursive calls begin to resolve. This call flow is visually represented as follows:

```
factorial(4)
    4 * factorial(3)
        3 * factorial(2)
            2 * factorial(1)
                1 * factorial(0)
                    return 1        // base case hit, bubbling up
```

```
        return 1 * 1 = 1
      return 2 * 1 = 2
    return 3 * 2 = 6
  return 4 * 6 = 24
```

This code is annotated in the `Factorial.java` file in the `Chapter09` folder on GitHub. To unlock the GitHub repo link, refer to the instructions in the *Download the example code files* section of the *Preface*. We will observe more examples in a later section.

Recursion vs. iteration

Any recursive algorithm can be transformed into an iterative one by using a loop and an explicit stack data structure to manually manage function states. Conversely, every iterative loop can be converted into a recursive function, typically through passing local variables as arguments to the recursive calls. The following example illustrates this equivalence using the same logic in both patterns for calculating the sum of all elements in an integer array, from index 0 to index `i`.

Recursive approach:

```
int sum(int a[], int i) {
    return (i==0) ? a[0] : sum(a, i-1) + a[i];
}
```

Iterative approach:

```
int sum(int a[], int n) {
    int total=0;
    for (int i=0; i<n; i++)
        total+=a[i];
    return total;
}
```

Both achieve the same result, but the recursive version uses the stack to remember where to return after each sub-sum, while the iterative version keeps a running total in a local variable. *Figure 9.1* shows the recursive approach:

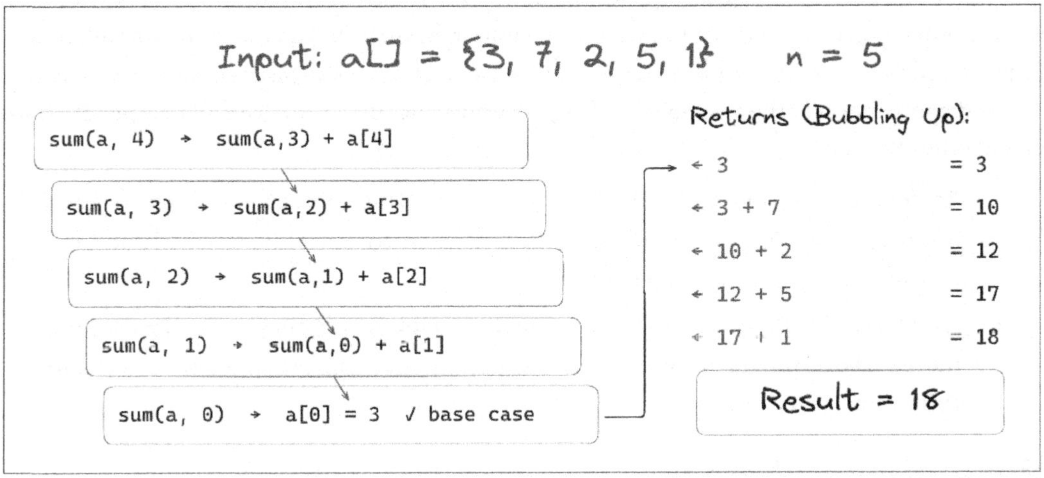

Figure 9.1: Recursive approach for summing all array elements in a[]

Figure 9.2 shows the iterative approach:

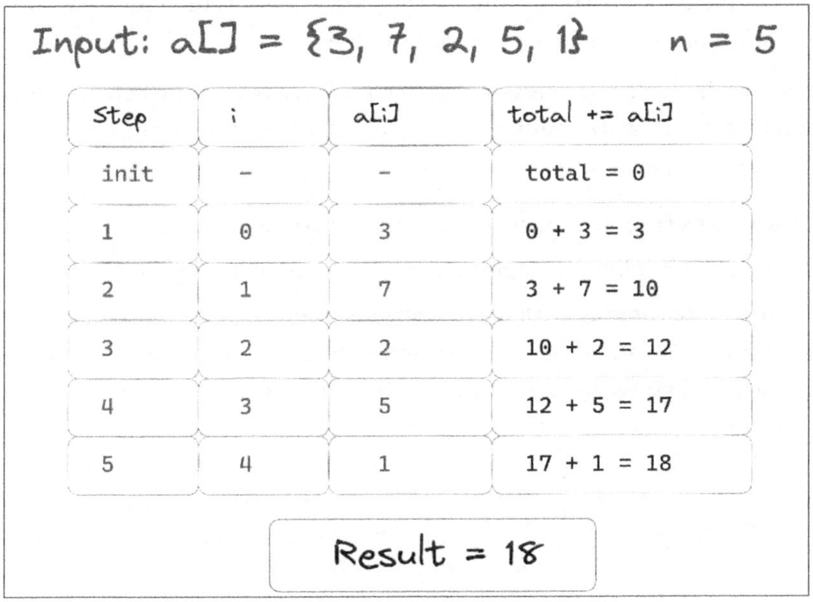

Figure 9.2: Iterative approach for summing all array elements in a[]

The annotated code demonstrating both recursive and iterative array summation is available in the `SumArray.java` file inside the `Chapter09` folder on GitHub. To unlock the GitHub repo link, refer to the instructions in the *Download the example code files* section of the *Preface*. A detailed comparison of the two approaches reveals distinct performance and complexity trade-offs as follows:

- **Recursive**: `O(n)` time and `O(n)` space (call stack): This approach offers cleaner, more intuitive code, but it consumes additional memory for each function call and can lead to a stack overflow with large input
- **Iterative**: `O(n)` time and `O(1)` space (single variable): This approach, while slightly more verbose, provides optimal space efficiency with constant memory usage and no risk of stack overflow

Recursion call stack

A stack frame (also called an activation frame or activation record) is a block of memory allocated on the call stack each time a function is invoked. It stores everything the function needs to execute and return correctly: the return address, the arguments, local variables, and optionally a frame pointer linking to the caller's frame.

When a function calls itself, the operating system pushes a stack frame onto the call stack. *Figure 9.3* depicts three stack frames for a recursive call chain from `main()` → `f(2)` → `f(1)` → `f(0)`, rewinding from `f(0)` → `f(1)` → `f(2)` → `main()`. Each frame contains three components:

- A **return address** indicating where execution resumes after the function returns.
- Local variables holding the arguments and temporaries for that invocation
- A **frame pointer** linking back to the previous frame. Arrows between frames visualize how each frame pointer references the one beneath it, forming a chain that the runtime or debugger can traverse to reconstruct the call history.

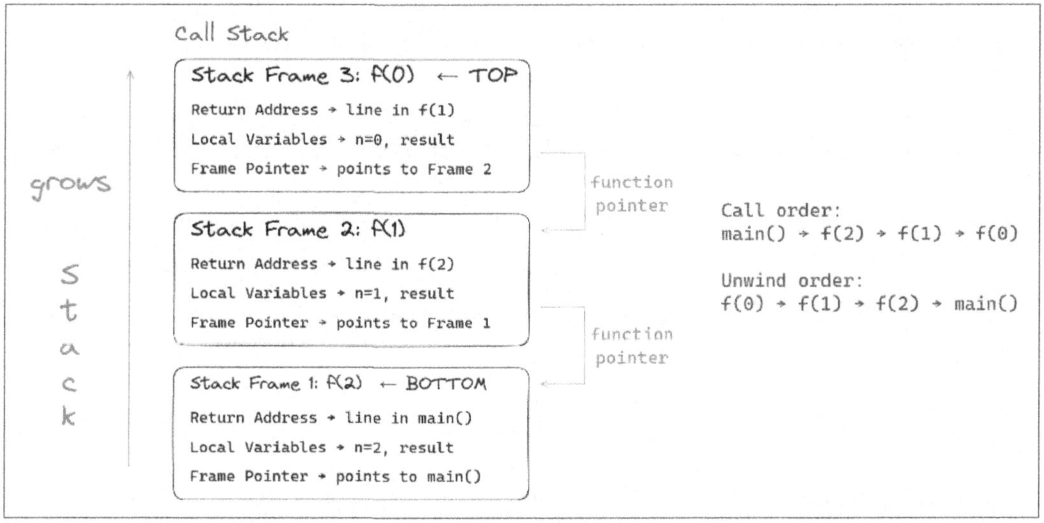

Figure 9.3: Recursive call stack

Each frame sits on the stack until its computation completes, after which the stack pointer moves back down, freeing that frame's memory.

The stack, therefore, automatically stores the state of each recursive call, and no manual data structures are needed unless the recursion is particularly deep, or you want to convert it to an iterative form. This mechanism is essential for three reasons: it **maintains context** so the program never loses track of where it left off in each call, it provides **memory isolation** so local variables don't interfere across recursive invocations, and it enables **automatic cleanup** since each frame is popped and its memory freed the moment the call returns, with no explicit deallocation required.

The implicit call stack: How recursion works

Recursion and an explicit stack are computationally equivalent; every recursive algorithm can be rewritten with a Deque. The difference is not what is computed, but in how memory is managed. The iterative approaches are functionally identical; they only differ in the mechanism of memory control. If you need to manipulate the stack, such as deep traversals, pausing execution, or checkpointing, you should move the stack management from the implicit JVM call stack to an explicit `Deque`. The following recursion shows that the JVM call stack is the stack:

```
// The JVM manages the stack for you.
// Each call = one hidden stack frame.
static int sumRecursive(int[] a, int i) {
```

```
    if (i == a.length) return 0;
    return a[i] + sumRecursive(a, i+1);
}
```

We replicate what the JVM does automatically, but with a `Deque<Integer>` allocated on the heap:

```
// You manage the stack with Deque.
// Each push = one visible work item.
static int sumExplicit(int[] a) {
    Deque<Integer> stk = new ArrayDeque<>();

  // PUSH phase: Load all indices onto stack
  for (int i = 0; i< a.length; i++)
    stk.push(a[i]);              // Deque.push()

  // POP phase: drain stack, accumulate sum
  int total = 0;
  while (!stk.isEmpty())
    total += stk.pop();          // Deque.pop()

  return total;
}
```

We prefer `ArrayDeque` over the legacy `java.util.Stack` for better performance and cleaner design. Unlike `Stack`, which is slowed down by unnecessary synchronization inherited from `Vector`, `ArrayDeque` is unsynchronized and array-backed, making it significantly faster for single-threaded tasks. Additionally, `ArrayDeque` maintains a strict LIFO contract, whereas `Stack` exposes inappropriate methods that allow middle-stack modifications.

Examples comparing implicit and explicit stacks in tree recursion are available in the `ImplicitExplicitStack.java` file in the `Chapter09` folder on GitHub. To unlock the GitHub repo link, refer to the instructions in the *Download the example code files* section of the *Preface*.

The challenge of naive recursion (overlapping subproblems)

Starting with 0 and 1, the Fibonacci sequence (0, 1, 1, 2, 3, ...) is a classic mathematical pattern used to demonstrate recurrence relations and optimize algorithms through dynamic programming. This series is defined by:

- `fib(0) = 0` (base case)

- `fib(1) = 1` (base case)
- `fib(n) = fib(n-1) + fib(n-2)` (recursive case)

This is implemented as follows, where `n` represents the `n`-th Fibonacci number in this series:

```
int fib(int n) {
   if (n<= 1)
      return n;
   return fib(n - 1) + fib(n - 2);
}
```

This solution is extremely slow, as the recursion branches at every level (*Figure 9.4*) for computing `fib(5)`.

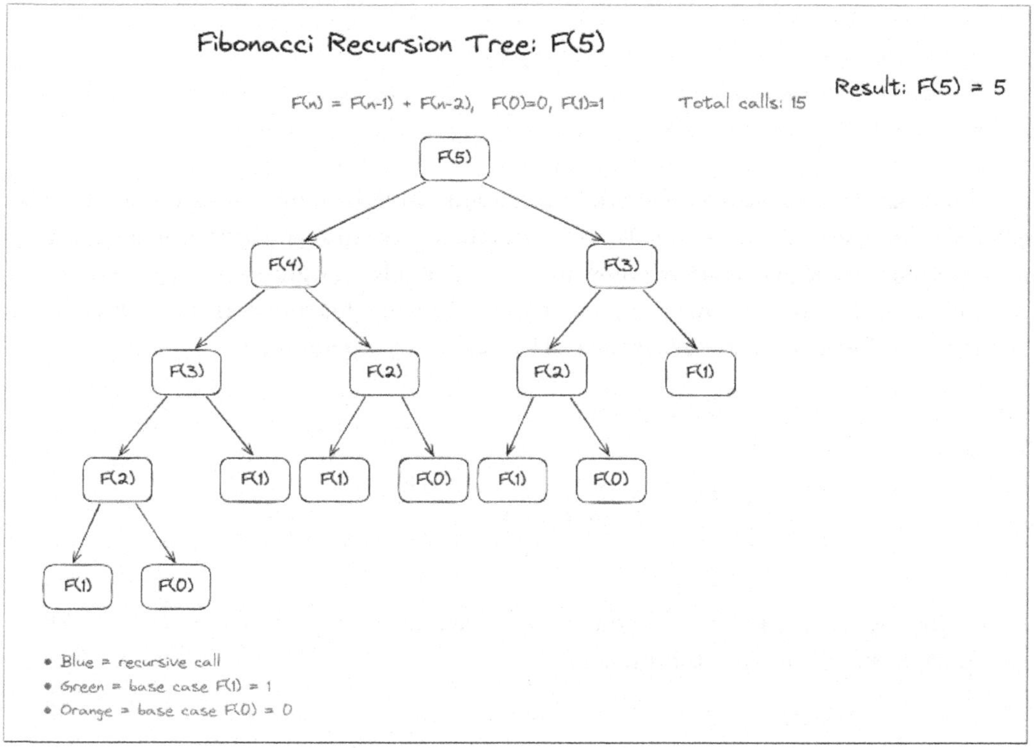

Figure 9.4: The recursion tree for computing Fib(5)

Generally, `fib(n)` makes roughly 2^n calls in exponential time. The problem is overlapping subproblems, namely `fib(3)` is computed twice, `fib(2)` three times, and so on. This is the classic motivation for memoization and dynamic programming covered in *Chapter 8*. For now, we recognize such a pattern as a red flag for performance.

Tail recursion

Tail recursion is a special form of recursion where the recursive call is the very last operation in the function: there's no pending work after it returns. This matters because the compiler can optimize it into a simple loop (called tail-call optimization or TCO), reusing the current stack frame instead of pushing a new one. The result is constant `O(1)` stack space instead of `O(n)`.

Examples

Using the factorial example, we can implement it naively as we had earlier:

```
int factorial(int n) {
   if (n == 0)                     // base case
      return 1;
   return n * factorial(n - 1); // recursive case with pending work
}
```

Standard recursion, like the basic factorial calculation, works by returning values up the call stack after the recursive call returns. This requires the system to keep all intermediate results in memory, which can lead to stack overflow for very deep calls. To optimize this, we use an accumulator to carry the running result down the call chain. This transforms the function into a tail-recursive form, where the recursive call is the very last operation:

```
int factorial(int n, int accumulator) {
   if (n == 0)
      return accumulator; // Base case, returning accumulated result
   return factorial(n - 1, n * accumulator); // tail position
}
```

The core logic is managed by a helper function that accepts an accumulator parameter. The main function simply initiates this process:

```
int fact(int n) {
  // The initial call sets the starting point (n)
  //and the initial accumulator value (1)
  return factorial_helper(n, 1);
}
```

Likely, we may convert the prior Fibonacci series to a tail-recursive form:

```
int fib(int n, int a = 0, int b = 1) {
   if (n == 0)
      return a;
   return fib(n - 1, b, a + b);
}
```

This runs in `O(n)` time and `O(1)` stack space (with TCO). Compare that to the naive version in `O(`2^n`)` time.

In the above tail-recursive version, the accumulated result is carried forward as a parameter with each call, so by the time the base case is reached, the final answer is already in hand. The stack doesn't need to unwind through previous frames to assemble it.

We provide another example, a Fibonacci demo, available in the GitHub repo in the `FibonacciDemo.java` file inside the `Chapter09` subfolder. To unlock the GitHub repo link, refer to the instructions in the *Download the example code files* section of the *Preface.* to further this algorithmic thinking. This code illustrates the shift from naive exponential recursion to linear time (`O(n)`) using iterative techniques. It demonstrates how this optimization relates to core dynamic programming concepts: tabulation (bottom-up) and memoization (top-down), offering a complete, optimized algorithmic approach.

One important note: tail-call optimization is language-dependent. Scheme, Haskell, Scala, and Kotlin guarantee TCO, meaning the compiler will reuse the current frame and keep stack usage constant. Python, Java, and JavaScript do not, so even a properly tail-recursive function in those languages will still allocate a new frame per call and risk a stack overflow on deep recursion. Therefore, for these languages, converting the logic into an explicit iterative loop, as shown in the factorial example, is the safer, and equally effective solution:

```
int factorial_iterative(int n) {
   int result = 1;
   for (int i = 2; i<= n; i++)
      result *= i;
   return result;
}
```

Measuring complexity

Recursion is a powerful problem-solving paradigm. Understanding its efficiency requires us to analyze how this technique scales. To do this, we use the Recursion Tree method to visually dissect the workload generated by recursive functions. We will use this method to systematically calculate the time complexity of recursive algorithms, starting with a classic example like Merge Sort, to see how the structure of recursion translates into Big O notation.

Analyzing merge sort

Merge Sort is a classic example of a Divide and Conquer algorithm. It works by repeatedly dividing the problem into individual elements and then merging those sorted pieces back together. The pseudocode below illustrates this approach:

```
solve(subproblem) {
  if base_case: return trivial
  left  = solve(first_half)
  right = solve(second_half)
  return merge(left, right)
}
```

Figure 9.5 shows how an array of `[38, 27, 43, 3, 9, 82]` is merge-sorted via this divide-and-conquer approach:

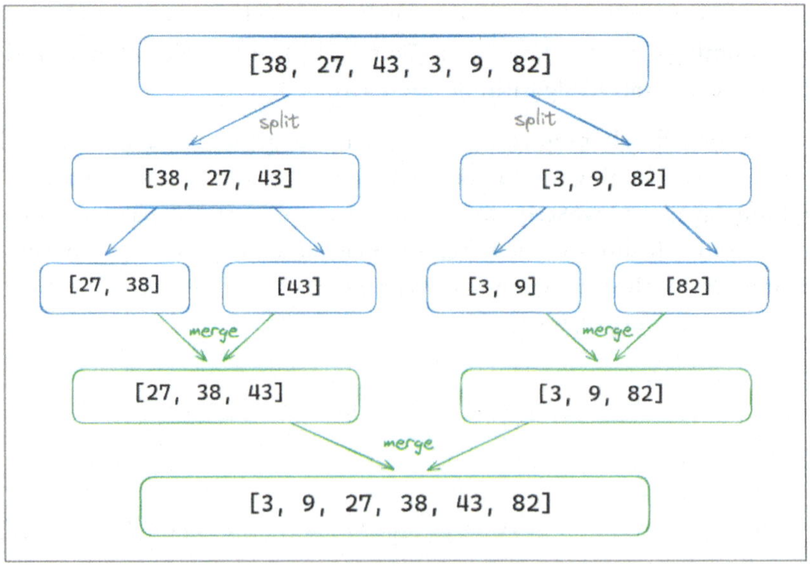

Figure 9.5: Merge sort

A practical treatment of the Merge Sort algorithm is available in the GitHub repo in the `Chapter09` subfolder inside the `MergeSortDemo.java` file. To unlock the GitHub repo link, refer to the instructions in the *Download the example code files* section of the *Preface*, showing how the

recurrence relation translates into work at different levels, and the detailed theoretical analysis in the comments.

Merge Sort has a time complexity of `O(n log n)` and a space complexity of `O(n)`. We can use the Recursion Tree method to visualize and calculate the distribution of work across the algorithm's execution.

Method: Recursion tree

In this method, we let `T(N)` be the total time (or work, or cost) required to solve a problem of size `N` or, specifically, the time to sort `N` elements. The recurrence relation for Merge Sort can be represented as a combination of recursive and non-recursive work:

```
T(N) = 2T(N/2) + f(N)
```

Recursive component: 2T(N/2)

As illustrated in *Figure 9.5*, this term represents the cost of delegating tasks to recursive subproblems:

- Multiplier (2): Indicates the algorithm branches into two separate recursive calls at each level. This number informs the width of the tree. At level `k`, the number of nodes grows to 2^k.
- Input Size (N/2): Signifies that each recursive call processes a dataset exactly half the size of the original ($N \rightarrow \frac{N}{2} \rightarrow \frac{N}{4} \rightarrow \frac{N}{2^{k-1}} \rightarrow \frac{N}{2^k} = 1$). This ½ multiplier informs the depth of the tree. To calculate k, we solve $\frac{N}{2^k} = 1$, which gives $k = \log_2 N$.The number of nodes at the bottom level is therefore $2^{\log_2 N} = N$.
- Total Cost of 2T(N/2): in a recursion tree, the recursive calls are what creates the levels and nodes. The total expansion cost for reaching a depth of $\log_2 N$ levels is `N x O(1)`. Since each leaf represents a base case of size 1 requiring `O(1)` work, the total recursive cost across all leaves is

$$N \times O(1) = \Theta(N)$$

We use Θ to show that the performance of merge sort is highly consistent. Both best-case and worst-case scenarios are identical.

Non-recursive component: f(N)

`f(N)` represents the local cost at each level of the tree, which includes splitting the data and merging the results:

- **Splitting O(1)**: Locating the middle index of the array: *mid = (low + high)/2*

- **Merging O(N)**: combining the two sorted halves from their recursive calls
- **Total**: Since merging dominates the constant-time split, `f(N)` is effectively `O(N)`, as seen in the next section

Recursive tree analysis of f(N)

The cost of merging at each level:

- **Level 0 (root)**: We do `f(N)` work as part of the initial merge on the whole array
- **Level 1**: We merge 2 subproblems, each of size `N/2`, for a total of `2 x f(N/2) = f(N)` work
- **Level 2**: We merge 4 subproblems, each of size `N/4`, for a total of `4 x f(N/4) = f(N)`
- **Level K**: At every level, the doubling of subproblems and the halving of their size cancel each other out, keeping the work constant at f(N)

The tree has an overall depth of $\log_2 N$ levels, each assuming `f(N)` work. Because $\Theta(N)$ work is done at every level, and there are $\log_2 N + 1$ total levels including the leaves, the overall time complexity is

$$\Theta(N) \times (\log_2 N + 1) = \Theta(N \log_2 N)$$

Like our recursive component analysis.

$$\Theta(N \log N)$$

is the exact and most precise way to describe the time complexity of Merge Sort.

Total cost of merge sort

The total complexity `T(N) = 2T(N/2) + N` is the sum of the work at all levels. In asymptotic notation, we keep the fastest-growing term in log base 2:

$$T(N) = \Theta(N \log N)$$

While the Recursion Tree method provides excellent visual insight into how algorithms scale, drawing it out for every problem is tedious. The *Master Theorem* serves as a powerful mathematical shortcut, offering a much faster and more efficient way to analyze complexity.

Method: the master theorem

Most recursive algorithms follow predictable patterns of splitting and merging. The Master Theorem is a mathematical formulation that generalizes these inherent patterns, providing a straightforward method for determining the complexity of recursive algorithms. Instead of relying on exhaustive manual visualization of recursion trees, this theorem allows us to quickly grasp the growth rate of a solution by analyzing the relationship between the recursive structure and the work done at each level. For consistency with the Master's Theorem framework, the original input size N is standardized here to lowercase n, defining the canonical recurrence relation as:

```
T(n) = aT(n/b) + f(n)
```

Here:

- `T(n)`: the total time required to solve a problem of size `n`.
- `a`: the number of subproblems ≥ 1. This is the factor by which the problem splits (e.g., splitting into two halves, `a=2`).
- `b`: the size reduction factor > 1. This tells us how much the problem size shrinks in each recursive call (e.g., splitting into two halves, `b=2`).
- `f(n)`: the combination cost. This is the amount of non-recursive work to divide the problem and merge all subproblems at the root.

Summarily, `T(n)` represents the cost of recursive calls (`aT(n/b)`) plus the cost of non-recursive work (`f(n)`).

Cost of recursive calls (aT(n/b))

This cost expands with each recursive call until it reaches the leaves. Each level of recursion multiplies the number of subproblems by a. When the call reaches the bottom level ($\log_b n$) where each node has a size of 1, the number of nodes at the terminal level becomes

$$a^{(\log_b n)} = n^{(\log_b a)}$$

This is due to the algebraic exponent swap rule. This is itemized level-wide as follows:

- Level 0 has $a^0 = 1$ node
- Level 1 has $a^1 = a$ nodes
- Level 2 has a^2 nodes
- Level $\log_b n$ has $a^{(\log_b n)}$ nodes which is equivalent to $n^{(\log_b a)}$ nodes per the above relation

In Master Theorem, we assume that each leaf node is too small and atomic to be split further, hence performing a constant amount of work, $\Theta(1)$. *Figure 9.6* shows this recursive fan-out cost for any divide-and-conquer algorithm bearing this nature.

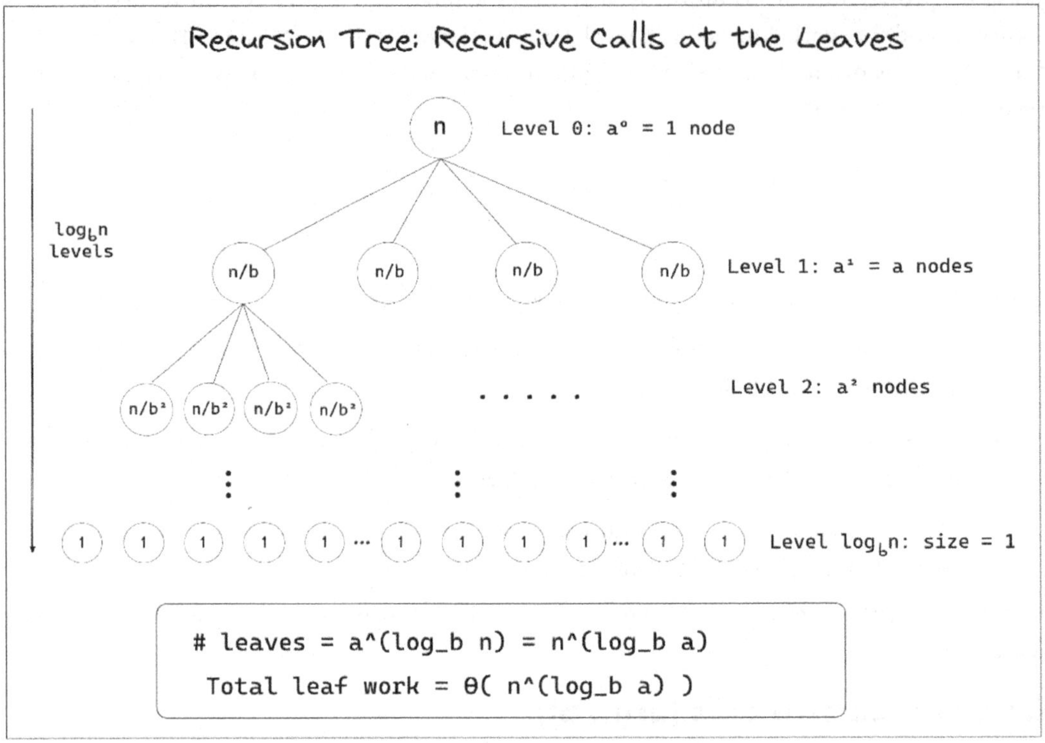

Figure 9.6: Recursive expansion cost in a recursion tree

If the number of subproblems (a) branches faster than the reduction of data (b), we end up with a massive number of leaves, and the fan-out cost will dominate the entire algorithm runtime. Conversely, if the branching factor (a) is smaller than the reduction factor (b), the recursive growth is minimal, shifting the performance bottleneck to the non-recursive cost of merging solutions at the root level.

Cost of non-recursive work (f(n))

`f(n)` represents the local overhead at the root for splitting and merging subproblems. At any level `k`, the workload is distributed across a^k subproblems, each incurring a cost of $f(n/b^k)$. This leads to a total level-wide cost of $a^k f(n/b^k)$.

Intuitively, the cost at each level often decreases as we branch deeper into the tree. This occurs because the overhead of managing a single massive problem at the root (`f(n)`) can be significantly more expensive than the collective cost of performing that same work on many smaller, fragmented subproblems. *Figure 9.7* provides a visual summary of the non-recursive overhead (`f(n)`) distributed across the levels of a recursion tree.

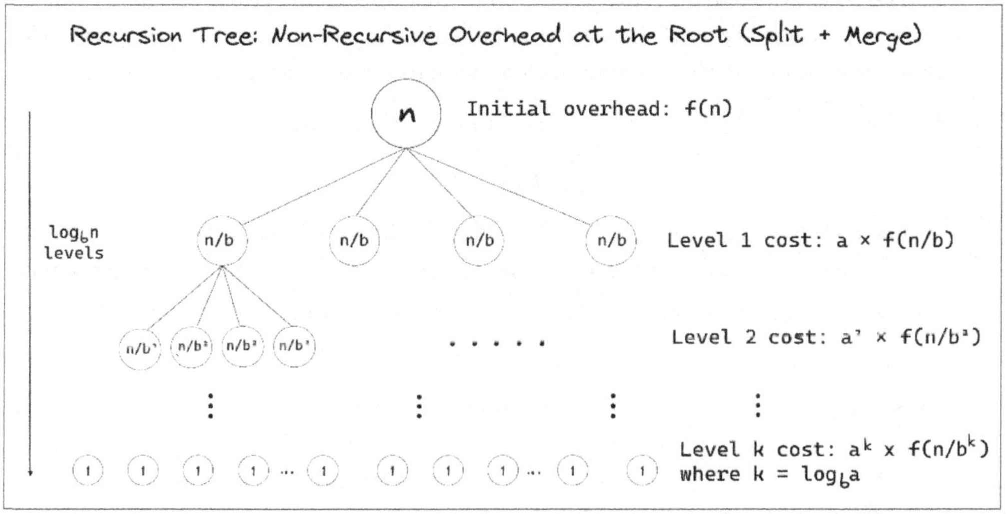

Figure 9.7: Non-recursive overhead in a recursion tree

The essence of the Master Theorem is determining which cost is dominant: recursion explosion at leaves vs split/merge overhead at root. The total complexity of T(n) is precisely: $\Theta(n^{\log_b a})$

if `f(n)` is smaller, meaning the work gets progressively heavier as we go down the tree, eventually landing all the weight on the leaves. Otherwise, the root does all the heavy lifting, meaning `f(n)` grows faster than the recursion.

Theorem summary

The Master Theorem's complexity is determined by comparing the non-recursive overhead `f(n)` and the total number of leaves in the recursion tree when a divide-and-conquer algorithm runs to completion is:

$$n^{\log_b a}$$

Where `a` is the degree of branching or the number of subproblems and `b` is the data reduction factor:

- In a **balanced** scenario when the root work and leaf work are asymptotically equal, we have

  $$f(n) = \Theta(n^{\log_b a})$$

  The total complexity is the work per level multiplied by the number of levels $\log_b n + 1$, which yields:

  $$\Theta(n^{\log_b a} \log n)$$

- In a leaf-heavy expansion case, the number of subproblems grows so rapidly that the leaves dominate the total time. Mathematically, this occurs when the root work f(n) grows polynomially slower than the leaf work function, meaning $f(n) = O(n^{\log_b a-\epsilon})$

  for some ϵ> 0. This leads to the leaf-dominant total time

$$T(n) = \Theta(n^{\log_b a})$$

- In a **root-heavy case**, the recursive growth is minimal, allowing the **root** overhead `f(n)` to become the dominant polynomial force. Mathematically, this occurs when the root work f(n) grows polynomially faster than the leaf work function, meaning

$$f(n) = \Omega(n^{\log_b a+\epsilon})$$

  for some $\epsilon > 0$, this leads to the root-dominant total time of

$$T(n) = \Theta(f(n))$$

Here are two detailed examples illustrating the step-by-step application of the Master Theorem.

Example 1: Merge sort

Having analyzed Merge Sort using the Recursion Tree method, we use the Master Theorem to formally determine its asymptotic complexity.

Step 1: Define the recurrence relation

As we studied earlier, the time complexity for Merge Sort is defined by the recurrence relation:

$$T(n) = 2T(n/2) + n$$

Step 2: Identify the parameters (a, b, and f(n))

We compare this relation to the general form.

$$T(n) = aT\left(\frac{n}{b}\right) + f(n)$$

This yields:

- a = 2 (the number of recursive subproblems)
- b = 2 (the factor by which the subproblem size is reduced)
- f(n) = n (the non-recursive work to merge the subproblems)

Step 3: Calculate the recursive value

The recursive formula with a = 2 is 2T(n/2).

The non-recursive force is:

$$f(n) = n$$

Step 4: Apply the master theorem

Since both recursive and non-recursive forces are asymptotically equal, this is the **balanced** scenario in the Theorem. We compare `f(n)` with:

$$n^{\log_b a}$$

This yields:

$$n^{\log_2 2} = n^1 = n$$

Since f(n) = n and $n^{\log_b a} = n$ both have the same asymptotic growth rate, yielding $f(n) = \Theta(n^{\log_b a})$

According to the **balanced** scenario in the Master Theorem, if

$$f(n) = \Theta(n^{\log_b a})$$

Then:

$$T(n) = \Theta(n^{\log_b a} \log n)$$

Step 5: Determine the complexity

Substituting our values we arrive at

$$T(n) = \Theta(n \cdot \log n) = \Theta(n \log n)$$

Example 2: Binary search

Binary Search is a linear search optimization that is often implemented recursively and can be analyzed using the Master Theorem. At each level, the algorithm makes exactly one recursive call to a subproblem of half the original size, plus a constant amount of work.

Step 1: Define the recurrence relation

The recurrence relation for Binary Search is

$$T(n) = T(n/2) + 1$$

Step 2: Identify the parameters (a, b, and f(n))

We compare this relation to the general form.

$$T(n) = aT\left(\frac{n}{b}\right) + f(n)$$

You note that:

- a = 1
- b = 2
- f(n) = 1

Step 3: Calculate the recursive value

The recursive formula with a = 1 is T(n/2).

The non-recursive force is:

$$f(n) = 1$$

Step 4: Apply the master theorem

We compare f(n) with $n^{\log_b a}$

To compute:

$$n^{\log_2 1} = n^0 = 1$$

Since f(n) = 1 and $n^{\log_b a} = 1$, both have the same asymptotic growth rate, yielding

$$f(n) = \Theta\left(n^{\log_b a}\right)$$

According to the **balanced** scenario in the Master Theorem, if $f(n) = \Theta(n^{\log_b a})$, then

$$T(n) = \Theta\left(n^{\log_b a} \log n\right)$$

Step 5: Determine the complexity

Substituting our values we arrive at

$$T(n) = \Theta(1 \cdot \log n) = \Theta(\log n)$$

Because $f(n) = \Theta(n^{\log_b a})$, the work done at the root matches the work done at the leaves.

Despite the problem size shrinking at each level, the recursive, and non-recursive forces are asymptotically equal and constant. This creates the balanced scenario of the Master Theorem, where the work performed remains essentially constant at every level of the recursion tree.

Recursion in data structures

In the previous chapters, we have seen recursion in hierarchical structures. Let's review a few of them. Recursion is excellent for defining hierarchical relationships (like trees) and deep, depth-first exploration. Although recursion is mathematically elegant, complex problems with overlapping subproblems, like Fibonacci, are inefficiently solved by brute-force recursion. A better approach is Dynamic Programming (DP), which is a direct optimization of recursive thinking. As we went through this in the earlier chapter, DP builds upon this recursive foundation to eliminate redundant computations, thereby providing the highly efficient, practical solutions required in advanced algorithms.

Binary tree depth-first search

This demo performs a pre-order recursion as DFS on an explicit `TreeNode` structure. Each recursive call to `dfs()` corresponds to visiting one node in the tree. The JVM call stack is the current path from root to the node being visited. This demo is available in the GitHub repo in the `BinaryTreeDFS.java` file inside the `Chapter09` subfolder. To unlock the GitHub repo link, refer to the instructions in the *Download the example code files* section of the *Preface*.

Quick sort depth-first search

In Quick Sort, the recursion tree isn't a physical data structure, but a conceptual one formed by the JVM call stack. Each `quickSort()` call is a node in that tree. Each node executes the partitioning logic on a specific subarray. The left child is the recursive call for smaller elements, and the right child is the call for larger elements. The base cases are the subarrays of size 0 or 1 that are already sorted. The algorithm essentially performs a DFS traversal across this virtual tree as it sorts. The demo is in placed in the GitHub repo inside the `QuickSortSFS.java` file in the `Chapter09` subfolder. To unlock the GitHub repo link, refer to the instructions in the *Download the example code files* section of the *Preface*.

Recursive BFS on a graph

Implementing BFS recursively is conceptually challenging because BFS relies on the FIFO behavior of a queue, which is inherently iterative. Recursion naturally implements LIFO via the call stack. Therefore, the recursive solution for BFS must be structured to explicitly manage the "level" of exploration, simulating the queue behavior. This is observed in the demo code placed in the GitHub repo inside the `RecursiveBFS.java` file inside the `Chapter09` subfolder. To unlock the GitHub repo link, refer to the instructions in the *Download the example code files* section of the *Preface*.

The graph is built using an adjacency list (`Map<Integer, Node>`). This is the physical structure we traverse. The recursion does not traverse the graph layer by layer (like a queue); instead, it follows depth first. The structure of the Node object and its neighbors list provides the raw data that the recursion operates on.

> **Note**
>
> Recursive BFS is structurally identical to implementing a queue using two stacks. This is because BFS requires FIFO ordering, while recursion inherently builds a LIFO call

> stack. To force this LIFO mechanism into a FIFO flow, recursive BFS must use the underlying execution call stack as the first stack and an explicit helper argument as the second stack to reverse the nodes into the correct processing order. For a practical exercise on this mechanism, please refer to the "Queue Using Two Stacks" problem in Chapter 3.

Summary

This chapter establishes recursion as a powerful design paradigm for solving complex problems by breaking them down into subproblems. At its core, recursion requires three components:

- A recursive function that calls itself
- A precise base case that defines the termination condition
- A recursive step that reduces the problem size toward that base case

This process is managed by the **call stack**, where each recursive call creates a new stack frame to maintain the context, which is subsequently "unwound" as the function returns.

While recursion is elegant for defining hierarchical structures, it inherently uses `O(n)` space on the call stack, which contrasts with the optimal `O(1)` space of iterative solutions. This trade-off is central to algorithm design. To manage the associated performance risks, we introduce optimization techniques like **Tail Recursion** (which can be optimized to `O(1)` space) and Dynamic Programming (**memoization**), which are essential for solving problems with overlapping subproblems efficiently.

Finally, the chapter equips the reader with tools to analyze the efficiency of recursive algorithms. Through the **Recursion Tree Method** and the **Master Theorem**, we learn to systematically analyze recurrence relations like `T(n) = aT(n/b) + f(n)`. This analysis reveals whether an algorithm's performance bottleneck is caused by the exponential growth of recursive calls or the overhead of splitting and merging work. By quantifying this balance, we can calculate an algorithm's true complexity, confirming that recursion is a foundational mechanism for many high-performance, real-world software systems. *Figure 9.8* provides a summary diagram of recursion techniques. The same reference will reappear in *Chapter 12* to support various practical case studies.

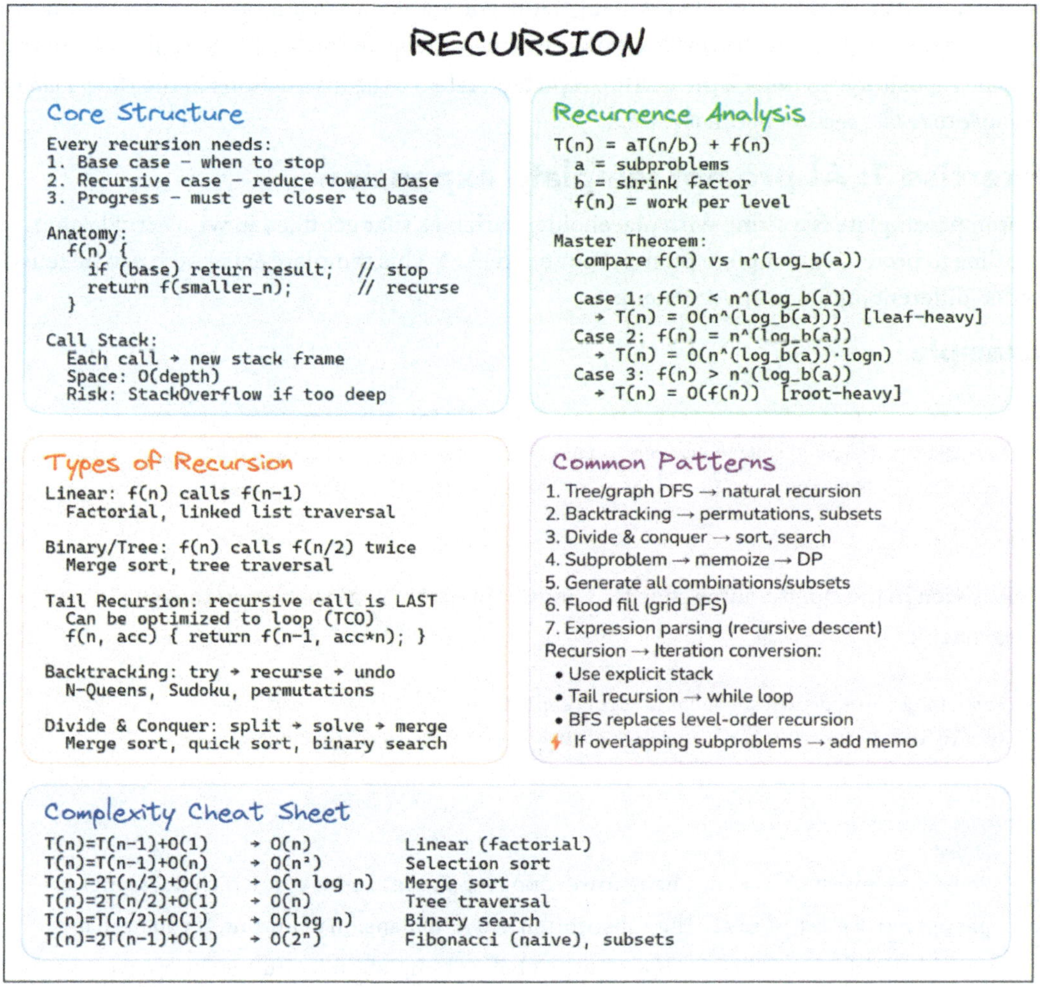

Figure 9.8: Summary of recursion techniques

Now that we can confidently design, visualize, and mathematically prove the efficiency of recursive operations, let's see them in action. We turn next to the study of sorting algorithms, where the trade-offs between recursion and iteration dictate how software handles massive datasets.

Exercises

The following exercises delve into fundamental recursive algorithms and problem-solving techniques that are essential for mastering algorithm design and analysis. Each exercise extends basic recursive thinking to introduce advanced concepts and methodologies critical for sophisticated algorithmic problem solving. Fully annotated Java solutions, practical examples, and algorithm explanations for these exercises are available in the `Chapter09` subfolder in the GitHub repository. To unlock the GitHub repo link, refer to the instructions in the *Download the example code files* section of the *Preface*.

Exercise 1: AI prompt template expansion

A prompt template is a string with placeholder variables that get filled in with actual values at runtime to produce a complete prompt sent to an LLM. This template exists so it can be reused across different inputs in an AI system.

Example

```
Template:  "You are a {{role}}. Please {{task}} for the user."
Variables: {role: "code reviewer", task: "review this pull request"}
Output:    "You are a code reviewer. Please review this pull request for the
user."
```

This is seen in the Open-Source code for LangChain (`http://github.com/langchain-ai/langchain`):

```
from langchain.prompts import PromptTemplate
template = PromptTemplate.from_template("Summarize this {document_type}:
{content}")
```

Note

Some systems, such as LangChain, use `PromptTemplate.format()`, which does single-pass `str.format()` / `f-string` substitution. No re-expansion of output. If you need a variable inside a variable, you pre-resolve it before template substitution. Recursive expansion introduces risks (infinite loops, injection attacks via user-controlled values expanding into more templates).

Problem

An AI system uses prompt templates with nested variable references. A template like `"{{greeting}}, please {{task}}"` may be designed to be recursively expanded because variables can themselves contain other variables. Given a template string and a variable map (where values may contain other `{{variables}}`), recursively expand all variables until no more remain. Detect infinite recursion.

For example, we may start with a prompt template as follows:

```
Map<String, String> vars = Map.of(
    "greeting", "Hello {{name}}",
    "name", "Agent {{version}}",
    "version", "3.5",
    "task", "summarize {{topic}}",
    "topic", "recursion"
);
expand("{{greeting}}, please {{task}}", vars)
// → "Hello Agent 3.5, please summarize recursion"
```

The template can be recursively expanded in the following trace:

```
Step 1: "{{greeting}}, please {{task}}"
Step 2: "Hello {{name}}, please summarize {{topic}}"
Step 3: "Hello Agent {{version}}, please summarize recursion"
Step 4: "Hello Agent 3.5, please summarize recursion"
```

Example:

```
Map<String, String> cyclic = Map.of(
    "a", "{{b}}",
    "b", "{{a}}"
);
expand("{{a}}", cyclic)
// → infinite loop without cycle detection
```

Starter Code Template

```
import java.util.*;

public class RecursiveTemplateExpander {
    public String expand(String template, Map<String, String> vars) {
        // Delegate to helper with cycle-detection set
    }
    private String expand(String template, Map<String, String> vars, Set<String>
seen) {
        // 1. Find next {{varName}} in template
        // 2. If not found → return template as-is (base case)
        // 3. If varName already in seen → throw cycle error
```

```
        // 4. Look up value, add to seen, recurse on value, remove from seen
        // 5. Replace placeholder with expanded value
        // 6. Recurse on remaining template (may have more variables)
    }
}
```

Assumptions and Constraints

- Placeholders use the `{{varName}}` format
- Variable map is static during expansion
- Single-threaded execution
- A variable can appear multiple times without conflict
- Templates fit in memory
- Circular references detected and rejected (throws exception)
- Undefined variables are preserved as raw placeholders
- Expansion is fully recursive (values are themselves templates)
- Backtracking on the seen set (same variable reusable in unrelated branches)
- No depth limit (stack overflow possible on deep non-circular chains)
- Unmatched {{ without }} treated as literal text

Test Case 1: Nested variable expansion

- **Input**:
  - **Template**: `"{{greeting}}, please {{task}}"`
  - **Variables**: `{greeting: "Hello {{name}}", name: "Agent {{version}}", version: "3.5", task: "summarize {{topic}}", topic: "recursion"}`
- **Output**: `"Hello Agent 3.5, please summarize recursion"`
- **Reason**: Validates depth (greeting → name → version = 3 levels) and breadth (greeting resolved first, then task resolved separately). Confirms backtracking works because both branches expand independently without interfering.

Test Case 2: Circular reference detection

- **Input**:
  - **Template**: `"{{a}}"`
  - **Variables**: `{a: "{{b}}", b: "{{c}}", c: "{{a}}"}`

- **Output**: Throws `IllegalStateException`: `"Circular reference: a"`
- **Reason:** Expansion follows a → b → c → a. When a is encountered the second time, it's already in the seen set from the current expansion chain. Confirms cycle detection works regardless of chain length (not just direct self-reference).

Solution

The algorithm processes a template string by finding one placeholder at a time, resolving it fully (including any nesting), substituting it back, and then looking for the next placeholder in the updated string. This creates two directions of recursion: depth (a variable's value contains more variables that need expanding) and breadth (after one placeholder is resolved, the remaining template may still contain others).

```
private String expand(String template, Map<String, String> vars, Set<String>
seen) {

    // Find one placeholder
    int start = template.indexOf("{{");
    int end = (start != -1) ? template.indexOf("}}", start) : -1;

    // No placeholder → done
    if (start == -1 || end == -1) {
        return template;
    }

    // Resolve it fully (DEPTH – recurse into the value's nested variables)
    String varName = template.substring(start + 2, end);
    if (seen.contains(varName)) {
        throw new IllegalStateException("Circular reference: " + varName);
    }
    String value = vars.getOrDefault(varName, "{{" + varName + "}}");
    seen.add(varName);
    String expanded = expand(value, vars, seen);  // ← depth recursion
    seen.remove(varName);

    // Substitute it back
    String result = template.substring(0, start) + expanded +
template.substring(end + 2);

    // Look for next placeholder in updated string (BREADTH – handle remaining
variables)
```

```
    return expand(result, vars, seen);            // ← breadth recursion
}
```

The method makes two distinct recursive calls that serve different purposes. The first, `expand(value, vars, seen)`, drives **depth**: it takes a variable's value and expands any nested variables within it, chaining as deep as necessary (e.g., "`greeting`" resolves to "`Hello {{name}}`", which resolves to "`Agent {{version}}`", which resolves to "`3.5`"). The second, `expand(result, vars, seen)`, drives **breadth**: after one placeholder is fully resolved and substituted back into the template, it recurses on the updated string to find and resolve the next placeholder (e.g., greeting is done, now find and resolve "`{{task}}`"). Together, depth ensures every variable is fully expanded regardless of nesting level, and breadth ensures every placeholder in the template is processed regardless of how many there are.

Cycle detection uses a `seen` set that acts like a call stack for variable resolution. If this variable is already being expanded somewhere up the call stack, we've hit a loop (e.g., `a → b → a`). Throw immediately rather than recursing forever:

```
if (seen.contains(varName)) {
    throw new IllegalStateException("Circular reference: " + varName);
}
```

When we start expanding a variable, we add it to the set. If we encounter it again during nested expansion, we know we've hit a circular reference and throw immediately. Once a variable is fully resolved, we remove it from the set. This backtracking ensures that the same variable can appear in unrelated parts of the template without triggering a false cycle.

```
// Add before expanding: marks "currently resolving this variable"
seen.add(varName);

// Recurse into value: if varName appears again deeper, seen.contains() catches it
String expanded = expand(value, vars, seen);

// Remove after fully resolved: varName can now appear without false cycle
seen.remove(varName);
```

The base case is simple: if the template contains no `{{...}}` pattern, return it as-is. Everything else is just "find, resolve, replace, repeat" until you hit that base case. The key insight is that resolving a single variable is itself the same problem (expand a template with variables), which is what makes recursion the natural fit.

> **Note**
>
> **Key insight**
>
> This is structurally identical to macro expansion in programming languages. The `expanding` set acts as cycle detection. If we encounter a variable we're already in the process of expanding, it's infinite recursion. Each variable is expanded at most once per path (not per call), giving us safe termination.

Exercise 2: Merge sort analysis

Merge-Sort is a classic **Divide-and-Conquer** algorithm. The total time T(n) to sort an array of size n is broken down into several phases. Derive the recurrence relations for Merge-Sort and solve using the Master Theorem.

For example:

- Array `[3, 1, 4, 1, 5, 9, 2, 6]` with n = 8 elements
- Recurrence: `T(8) = 2T(4) + 8, T(4) = 2T(2) + 4, T(2) = 2T(1) + 2, T(1) = 1`

Assumptions and Constraints

- Input array contains n elements where `n ≥ 1`
- Array elements are comparable integers
- Merge sort assumes an array can be divided into equal halves
- Master Theorem applies when `a ≥ 1`, `b> 1`, and `f(n)` is polynomial
- Time complexity should be `O(n log n)`

Hints:

- Recurrence: `T(n) = 2T(n/2) + O(n)`
- Master Theorem: With `a = 2`, `b = 2`, `f(n) = n`, we have $\log_b a$ `= 1`, so `T(n)` = `Θ(n log n)`

Rather than a code-based solution, this problem is resolved through logical, step-by-step analysis available in the GitHub repo inside the `MergeSortAnalysis.md` file inside the `Chapter09` subfolder. To unlock the GitHub repo link, refer to the instructions in the *Download the example code files* section of the *Preface*.

Exercise 3: Recursion to iteration conversion

Convert recursive Depth-First Search (DFS) on a graph to an iterative version using a stack. The iterative solution must output the same exact traversal order as a standard recursive DFS.

For example:

- Graph with vertices {0, 1, 2, 3} and edges (0,1), (0,2), (1,3)
- Recursive DFS traversal: 0 → 1 → 3 → 2

Starter Code Template

```
import java.util.*;
public class GraphDFS {
    // Recursive DFS (Provided as a reference for execution order mapping)
    public static List<Integer> recursiveDFS(List<List<Integer>> adj, int start, 
int n) {
        List<Integer> result = new ArrayList<>();
        dfs(adj, start, new boolean[n], result);
        return result;
    }

    private static void dfs(List<List<Integer>> adj, int curr, boolean[] visited, 
List<Integer> result) {
        visited[curr] = true;
        result.add(curr);
        for (int next : adj.get(curr)) {
            if (!visited[next]) dfs(adj, next, visited, result);
        }
    }

    /**
     * Iterative DFS implementation using a custom Deque stack.
     * Must produce the exact same traversal sequence as the recursive variant.
     */
    public static List<Integer> iterativeDFS(List<List<Integer>> adj, int start, 
int n) {
        List<Integer> result = new ArrayList<>();
        boolean[] visited = new boolean[n];
        Deque<Integer> stack = new ArrayDeque<>();

        // TODO: Step 1 - Initialize the stack with the starting node
```

```
        while (!stack.isEmpty()) {
            // TODO: Step 2 - Extract the current node from the stack

            // TODO: Step 3 - Apply visited conditions and append to result
collection

            // TODO: Step 4 - Fetch and push neighbors onto the stack
            // Hint: Pay close attention to insertion order to match recursive
behavior!
        }
        return result;
    }

}
```

Assumptions and Constraints

- Graph represented as an adjacency list
- Vertices are numbered from `0` to `n-1`
- No self-loops or parallel edges
- Stack implementation must handle duplicate vertices properly
- Traversal order should be the same as with the recursive version

Hints

- To ensure an iterative DFS using an explicit stack produces the exact same traversal order as a standard recursive DFS, you must push a node's neighbors onto the stack in reverse order

Exercise 4: String permutations

Write a recursive Java method that accepts a string of unique characters as an input and returns a list containing all possible arrangements (permutations) of those characters. For example, if the input string is "`abc`", the method should return a list containing: ["`abc`", "`acb`", "`bac`", "`bca`", "`cab`", "`cba`"]

Starter Code Template

```
import java.util.ArrayList;
import java.util.List;
public class PermutationGenerator {
```

```
    /**
     * Public wrapper method to generate permutations.
     * Time Complexity: O(n * n!)
     * Space Complexity: O(n) on the call stack
     */
    public static List<String> getPermutations(String str) {
        List<String> result = new ArrayList<>();

        // Edge case handling
        if (str == null) {
            return result;
        }

        generateRecursive("", str, result);
        return result;
    }

    /**
     * Private recursive helper method.
     * Students must implement this method to solve the problem.
     */
    private static void generateRecursive(String prefix, String remaining,
List<String> result) {
        // TODO: Implement the Base Case
        // Hint: What should you do when there are no more remaining characters to
process?

        // TODO: Implement the Recursive Step
        // Hint: Loop through the 'remaining' characters, pick one, isolate
        // the rest using substring(), and make a recursive call.
    }

    // Optional: Quick driver code to verify your behavior
    public static void main(String[] args) {
        // Expected output when complete: [abc, acb, bac, bca, cab, cba]
        System.out.println(getPermutations("abc"));
    }

}
```

Assumptions and Constraints

- The input string contains only unique, case-sensitive alphanumeric characters (e.g., 'a' and 'A' are treated as distinct)
- The length of the string, n, satisfies `0 <= n <= 8`
- If the input string reference is null, the method should return an empty list rather than throwing a `NullPointerException`
- The order of the permutations in the returned list does not matter

Test Case 1

- **Input**: `"xyz"`
- **Output**: `["xyz", "xzy", "yxz", "yzx", "zxy", "zyx"]` (any order is OK)

Test Case 2

- **Input**: `""` (empty string)
- **Output**: `[""]`

Exercise 5: Subset sum

Determine if a subset exists whose elements sum to a target. For example, for an input array `[3, 34, 4, 12, 5, 2]`, we can fetch its subset `[4,5]` to arrive at a target of 9.

Starter Code Template

```
public class SubsetSum {

     // Determines if a subset exists whose elements sum to
     // a target using pure recursion.
     */
    public static boolean hasSubsetSum(int[] arr, int target) {
        // Handle basic structural validation upfront
        if (target == 0) return true;
        if (arr == null || arr.length == 0) return false;

        return checkSubset(arr, 0, target);
    }

    private static boolean checkSubset(int[] arr, int index, int target) {
        // TODO: Step 1 - Implement Terminal Base Cases (Success / Failure
conditions)
```

```
        // TODO: Step 2 - Execute Pure Recursive Branching (Include vs. Exclude
strategy)

        return false; // Placeholder
    }
}
```

Assumptions and Constraints:

- Array contains only positive integers
- Target sum is a non-negative integer
- Each element can be used at most once
- Return `true` if a subset exists, `false` otherwise
- Input size should be manageable for a recursive approach
- The arrangement of elements in the input array does not affect the outcome; elements can be picked from any position to form the target sum

Test Case 1

- **Input**: `[8, 15, 3, 22]`; Target: 6.
- **Output**: `false`
- **Explanation**: The smallest number is `3`. The next smallest is `8` (which is already greater than the target `6`). No single element or combination equals `6`.

Test Case 2

- **Input**: `[12, 1, 61, 4, 33, 5]`; Target: 10
- **Output**: `true`
- **Explanation**: Elements {1, 4, 5} can be found at indices 1, 3, and 5 respectively, summing up to 10

Exercise 6: Arithmetic expression parser

Implement a recursive parser for arithmetic expressions. For example:

- **Expression:** `"3 + 4 * 2"`
- **Expected result**: `11` (following operator precedence)
- **Expression may contain parentheses:** `"(3 + 4) * 2"` = 14

Starter Code Template

```
public class RecursiveParser {
    /**
     * Evaluate an arithmetic expression string and return its integer value.
     * Supports +, -, *, / with standard precedence, and parentheses.
    *Example:"2+3*4"-> 14,   "(2+3)*4"-> 20,   "10/3"-> 3 (integer division)
     */
    public static int parse(String expression) {
        // TODO: hold the current index in a size-1 array so it is shared
        //       "by reference" across all recursive calls, then kick off the
        //       lowest-precedence parse.
        int[] pos = new int[]{0};
        return parseExpression(expression, pos);
    }

    // Lowest precedence: handles + and -
    private static int parseExpression(String str, int[] pos) {
         // TODO: parse the first term, then loop while the next char is + or -:
         //       consume the operator, parse the next term, fold it into result
        //       (left-associative). Break on anything else (e.g. ')').
        return 0;
    }

    // Middle precedence: handles * and /
    private static int parseTerm(String str, int[] pos) {
        // TODO: parse the first factor, then loop while the next char is * or /:
        //       consume the operator, parse the next factor, fold into result.
        //       Break on anything else (so +/- bubbles up to parseExpression).
        return 0;
    }

    // Highest precedence: handles numbers and parentheses
    private static int parseFactor(String str, int[] pos) {
        // TODO:
        //   - if current char is '(': consume it, recurse into parseExpression,
        //     consume the matching ')', return the inner result.
        //   - else: accumulate consecutive digits into a multi-digit number
        //     (result = result * 10 + digit) and return it.
        return 0;
    }
```

```
}
```

Assumptions and Constraints

- Input expression contains only digits, +, -, *, /, and parentheses
- No spaces in input expression
- Operators follow standard precedence rules (*, / before +, -)
- Parentheses can be nested
- Expression is valid and well-formed
- Return integer result (truncated division for integer division)

Test Case 1

- **Input**: "3+4*2"
- **Output**: 11

Test Case 2

- **Input**: "(3+4)*2"
- **Output**: 14

Exercise 7: Binary tree traversal

To comprehensively revisit binary tree data structures, we explore the three fundamental depth-first traversal strategies (pre-order, in-order, post-order). Implement a recursive solution for binary tree traversals for each of the strategies. Each tree node is defined as follows:

```
class TreeNode {
    int val;
    TreeNode left, right;
    TreeNode(int val) {
        this.val = val;
    }
}
```

Starter Code Template

```
import java.util.ArrayList;
import java.util.List;
```

```
public class BinaryTreeTraversals {

    public List<Integer> preorderTraversal(TreeNode root) {
            List<Integer> res = new ArrayList<>();
        if (root == null) return res;
        // TODO: Implement Preorder traversal logic (Root, Left, Right)
        return res;
    }

    public List<Integer> inorderTraversal(TreeNode root) {
            List<Integer> res = new ArrayList<>();
        if (root == null) return res;
        // TODO: Implement Inorder traversal logic (Left, Root, Right)
        return res;
    }

    public List<Integer> postorderTraversal(TreeNode root) {
            List<Integer> res = new ArrayList<>();
        if (root == null) return res;
        // TODO: Implement Postorder traversal logic (Left, Right, Root)
        return res;
    }
}
```

Assumptions and Constraints

- Binary tree nodes have integer values
- Tree may be empty (root = `null`)
- Each node has left and right child references
- Traversals should visit each node exactly once
- Result for each traversal strategy is to be persisted in `List<Integer>`
- Time complexity should be O(n) for all traversals

Test Case 1

- **Input:**

```
TreeNode root = new TreeNode(1,
    new TreeNode(2, new TreeNode(4),
    new TreeNode(5)),
```

```
        new TreeNode(3)
);
```

- **Output:**
    - Pre-order: `[1, 2, 4, 5, 3]`
    - In-order: `[4, 2, 5, 1, 3]`
    - Post-order: `[4, 5, 2, 3, 1]`

Test Case 2

- **Input:**

```
TreeNode root = new TreeNode(10,
    new TreeNode(20, new TreeNode(30), null),
    null
);
```

- **Output:**
    - Pre-order: `[10, 20, 30]`
    - In-order: `[30, 20, 10]`
    - Post-order: `[30, 20, 10]`

Exercise 8: Geometric series sum

Implement a recursive function that calculates the sum of the first n even powers:

$$S(n) = 2^0 + 2^1 + 2^2 + \cdots + 2^{(n-1)}$$

Starter Code Template

```
public class PowerSum {
    public static BigInteger sumConsecutivePowers(int n) {
        // TODO
    }
}
```

Assumptions and Constraints

- Must use recursion
- Employ `java.math.BigInteger` instead of `long` for this problem
- n must be a non-negative integer (n ≥ 0)

- For n = 0, the result must strictly be 0
- The result should handle large numbers (consider overflow for large n)

Test Case 1

- $S(4) = 2^0 + 2^1 + 2^2 + 2^3 = 1 + 2 + 4 + 8 = 15$

Test Case 2

- $S(5) = 2^5 - 1 = 32 - 1 = 31$

Hints

- `Math.pow()` can be slow for large `N`. You may consider processing the power directly at the bitwise layer.
- In Java, a signed 64-bit primitive `long` can store values up to 2^{63}-1. The formula S(n) = 2^n-1 hits this hardware capacity when `n = 62`.
- We may therefore consider `BigInteger` instead of `long` for overflow protection, which allows the recursion to compute values beyond `n = 62` without integer overflow.

10

Sorting

Sorting is a fundamental computer science problem because its solutions reveal core trade-offs in algorithm design, specifically the balance between time efficiency, space complexity, simplicity, and performance guarantees. Since nearly all major computing applications, including search engines, databases, and operating systems, rely on ordered data, a deep understanding of sorting is essential for assessing algorithmic efficiency and selecting the most efficient algorithm for a given task. In this chapter, we will build our knowledge from the ground up, exploring basic algorithms, advanced techniques, and real-world performance considerations.

What is sorting?

Sorting is an algorithm used to arrange a set of items based on a defined comparison criterion, resulting in a sequence where each element is ordered relative to the others. This action is fundamental because it unlocks vast algorithmic efficiencies. For instance, search operations improve from `O(n)` to `O(log n)` via binary search, and database queries use `ORDER BY` to retrieve data efficiently.

Because ordering is a prerequisite for optimized performance across nearly every computing domain, understanding sorting is key to reasoning about algorithmic efficiency and selecting the correct tool for performance constraints.

Sorting algorithm properties and trade-offs

The selection of an optimal sorting algorithm involves evaluating multiple criteria beyond simple time complexity. This analysis delves into the crucial concepts of sorting stability, the trade-off between in-place and out-of-place memory usage, and the nuances of time and space complexity. By examining these factors, including algorithm classification (comparison-based vs. non-comparison-based), we can determine the most effective approach for sorting data, balancing performance, stability, and memory efficiency for various applications.

Stability in sorting

The stability of a sorting algorithm refers to its ability to preserve the relative order of equal elements. The difference between stable and unstable sorting lies in how they handle duplicate elements:

- **Stable Sort**: Preserves the original relative order of equal elements. If two elements are the same, they stay in the same relative sequence after sorting.
- **Unstable Sort**: May change the relative order of equal elements.

For example, if sorting students by grade puts Bob and Diana both in the "A" category, a stable sort ensures that if Bob was listed before Diana originally, he will remain before her in the sorted output. *Figure 10.1* compares the sorting outcome using a stable vs. unstable sorting mechanism:

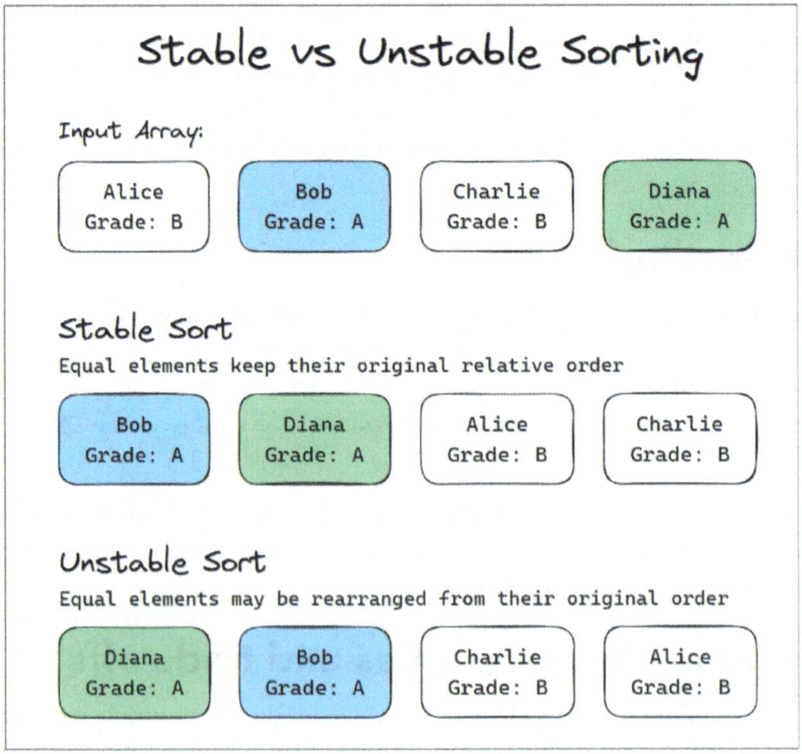

Figure 10.1: Comparison of stable and unstable sorting algorithms for student grades

Both sorts produce a correctly sorted result (A's before B's). The difference is that stable sort preserves the original order of equal elements, whereas unstable sort does not. Algorithms like Merge Sort and Insertion Sort are stable, whereas Quicksort and Heapsort are generally unstable.

Stability is important when sorting involves multiple criteria (multi-key sorting). Stable sorting algorithms are essential here because they allow us to establish a hierarchy of sorting rules. For instance, to sort by last name, and then maintain a secondary order by first name, we first sort by first name, and then perform a stable sort by last name to preserve the order of the secondary sort key. This stability is vital in database operations and any scenario where the relative order of secondary criteria must be maintained.

In-place vs. out-of-place sorting

Sorting algorithms are primarily evaluated not only by their time complexity `O(n log n)` but also by their space complexity, namely how much auxiliary memory they require beyond the input array. This distinction determines whether an algorithm is practical for massive datasets. We categorize sorting methods into two main classes: In-place and Out-of-place:

In-place

In-place sorting algorithms perform the entire sorting operation by rearranging elements within the original array, requiring only a small, constant amount of extra memory `O(1)` or `O(log n)`:

- **Characteristics**: They save memory by operating directly on the input array, making them highly space-efficient
- **Examples**: Quick Sort, Heap Sort, Insertion Sort
- **Trade-Off**: While highly memory-efficient, in-place algorithms often come with trade-offs, potentially sacrificing stability or implementation simplicity compared to other methods

Out-of-place

Out-of-place algorithms require additional memory proportional to the input size, `O(n)` or more, to store auxiliary data, such as a temporary array, to facilitate the sorting process:

- **Characteristics**: They are often conceptually simpler to implement correctly and can naturally be stable.
- **Examples**: Merge Sort (which requires an auxiliary array), Counting Sort (which requires a count array).
- **Trade-Off**: They use more memory, which can be prohibitive for very large datasets, although they offer increased ease of implementation and stability.

The choice between in-place and out-of-place sorting involves a critical trade-off: memory efficiency versus implementation simplicity and stability. For large-scale data processing, space efficiency is paramount; for smaller or critical applications, the ease of implementation offered by out-of-place methods can be advantageous.

Time complexity

Time complexity is used to evaluate the efficiency and performance of an algorithm. Rather than measuring the actual wall-clock time an algorithm takes, time complexity measures the rate of growth of the number of operations an algorithm performs as the size of the input data (`n`) increases. We must consider three key scenarios:

- **Best case**: The minimum work required (often when input is already sorted). Useful for understanding when an algorithm excels.
- **Average case**: Expected performance over random inputs. Most relevant for practical decisions.
- **Worst case**: Maximum work required. Critical for systems with latency guarantees.

Space complexity

Space complexity measures the total amount of auxiliary memory an algorithm requires beyond the space needed to store the input data (of size `n`). It is a critical factor in determining whether an algorithm is practical for systems dealing with massive datasets, as memory constraints often dictate algorithm selection. The various forms of space complexity reflect the memory demands of different sorting strategies:

- `O(1)`: Constant extra space (Heap Sort, Selection Sort)
- `O(log n)`: Stack space from recursion (Quick Sort's call stack)
- `O(n)`: Linear extra space (Merge Sort's auxiliary array, Counting Sort's count array)
- `O(n + k)`: Depends on data range (Counting Sort where `k` is the value range)

For large datasets that barely fit in memory, in-place algorithms are essential. For datasets that fit comfortably, the extra space of Merge Sort is a worthwhile trade for guaranteed `O(n log n)` and stability.

Selecting the optimal algorithm requires looking beyond theoretical Big O complexities and inherent properties. The following sections provide an in-depth analysis of two primary sorting categories.

Classification of sorting algorithms

Sorting algorithms are broadly divided based on their methodology:

- **Comparison-Based Sorting**: These algorithms determine the order by directly comparing pairs of elements (e.g., `a < b`). Most comparison-based sorts, such as Merge Sort, Quick Sort, and Heap Sort, are bounded by a worst-case time complexity of `O(n log n)`.
- **Non-Comparison-Based Sorting**: These algorithms exploit specific properties of the data itself (such as the integer values, digit representations, or data distribution) to sort without relying solely on pairwise comparisons. Examples include Counting Sort and Radix Sort, which achieve linear time complexity, `O(n)`, under specific conditions.

We will analyze the practical performance of three key categories of sorting algorithms: basic comparison sorts, advanced comparison sorts, and non-comparison sorts.

O(n^2) basic comparison sorts

O(n^2) sorting algorithms are simple, intuitive methods for organizing data. Bubble Sort and Insertion Sort are the most common examples. Bubble Sort repeatedly swaps adjacent elements to move the largest value to the end, while Insertion Sort builds a sorted list by placing each new item into its correct position. The following examples show these processes in action.

Bubble sort

Bubble Sort is one of the simplest sorting algorithms. The core idea is straightforward: repeatedly step through the list, comparing adjacent elements, and swapping them if they are in the wrong order. With each pass through the list, the largest unsorted element "bubbles up" to its correct, final position at the end of the unsorted portion. This mechanism is illustrated in *Figure 10.2* and the following code:

```
void bubbleSort(int[] arr) {
    int n = arr.length;
    for (int i = 0; i < n - 1; i++) {
        for (int j = 0; j < n - i - 1; j++) {
            if (arr[j] > arr[j + 1]) {
                // Swap elements
                int temp = arr[j];
                arr[j] = arr[j + 1];
                arr[j + 1] = temp;
```

```
            }
        }
    }
}
```

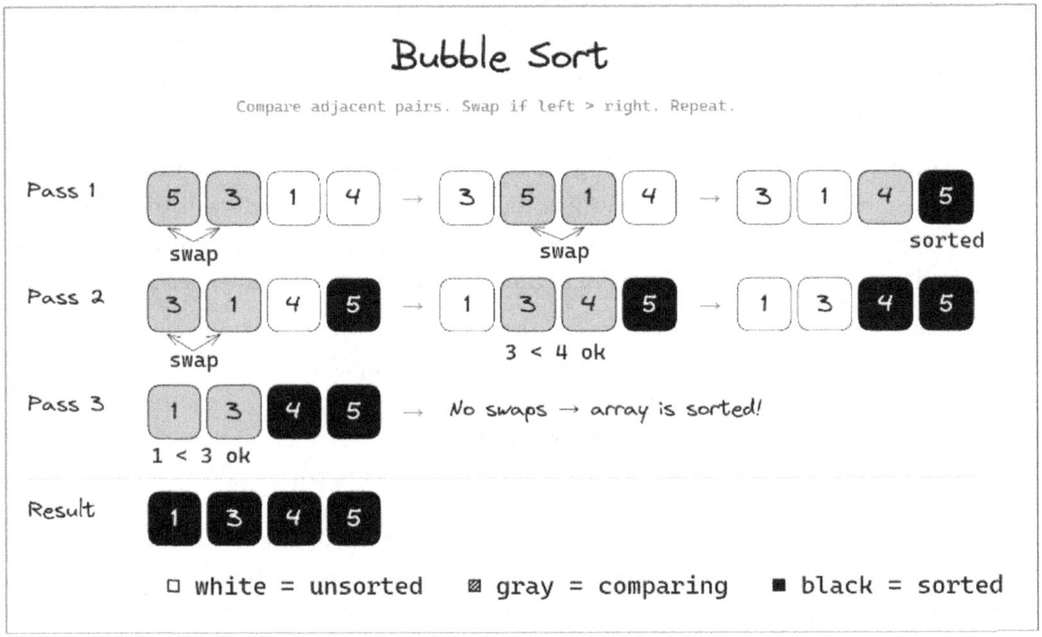

Figure 10.2: Bubble sort

Bubble Sort operates by using nested loops to compare and swap adjacent elements. Its time complexity is $O(n^2)$ in the average and worst cases. In the best-case scenario, if the list is already sorted, it can terminate in `O(n)` time by checking for zero swaps in a full pass. Furthermore, Bubble Sort is both stable and in-place.

While excellent for teaching the concept of iterative sorting, bubble sort is inefficient for large datasets.

Selection sort

Selection Sort works by repeatedly finding the minimum element and swapping it into place. It is an in-place algorithm that minimizes swaps (`n-1` swaps), but its time complexity is always `O(n`^{2}`)`. While easy to understand, it is generally too slow for production use compared to other methods. This process is shown in *Figure 10.3* and the following code:

```
void selectionSort(int[] arr) {
    int n = arr.length;
    for (int i = 0; i < n - 1; i++) {
        int minIdx = i;
        for (int j = i + 1; j < n; j++) {
            if (arr[j] < arr[minIdx]) {
                minIdx = j;
            }
        }
        // Swap elements
        int temp = arr[i];
        arr[i] = arr[minIdx];
        arr[minIdx] = temp;
    }
}
```

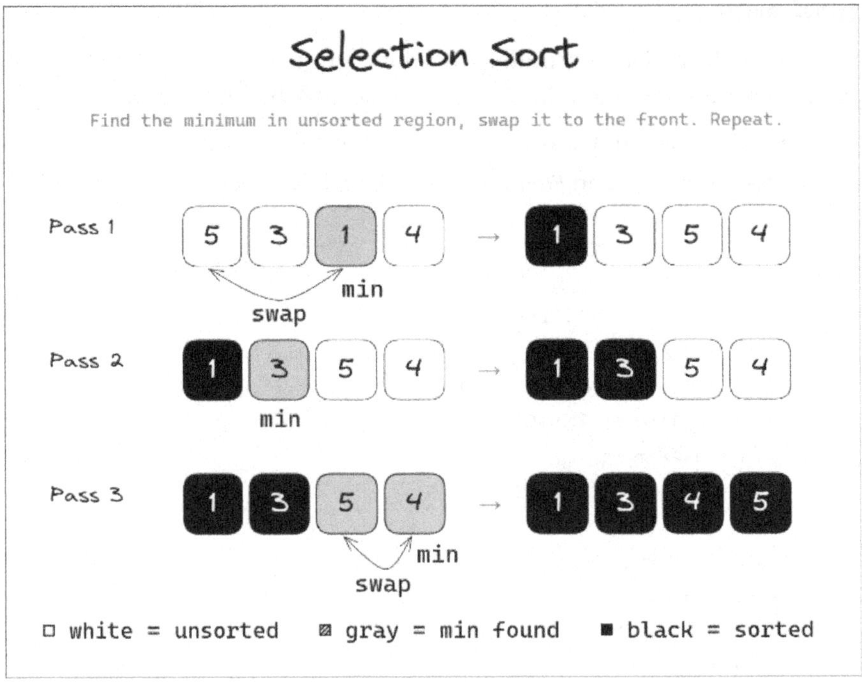

Figure 10.3: Selection sort

Selection sort is valuable for illustrating the concept of iterative refinement. Its primary advantage lies in minimizing element swaps, which is relevant in environments where write operations are extremely costly.

Time complexity is `O(n²)` for best, average, and worst cases because the nested loops always execute fully. Space complexity is `O(1)`, as it only requires a single temporary variable for swapping in place. Selection sort is unstable; namely, the swap can move equal elements past each other.

Insertion sort

Insertion Sort builds a sorted array one element at a time. The core idea is to take the next unsorted element and insert it into its correct position within the already sorted portion of the array.

To perform an insertion sort, iterate through the array starting at the second element and compare each to the sorted values on its left. Shift any larger preceding elements one position to the right to create a gap. Once the correct spot is reached, insert the current element into that space, repeating the process until the entire list is ordered. This process is captured in the following code and illustrated in *Figure 10.4*:

```
void insertionSort(int[] arr) {
    for (int i = 1; i < arr.length; i++) {
        int key = arr[i], j = i - 1;
        while (j >= 0&&arr[j]> key) {
            arr[j + 1] = arr[j--];
        }
        arr[j + 1] = key;
    }
}
```

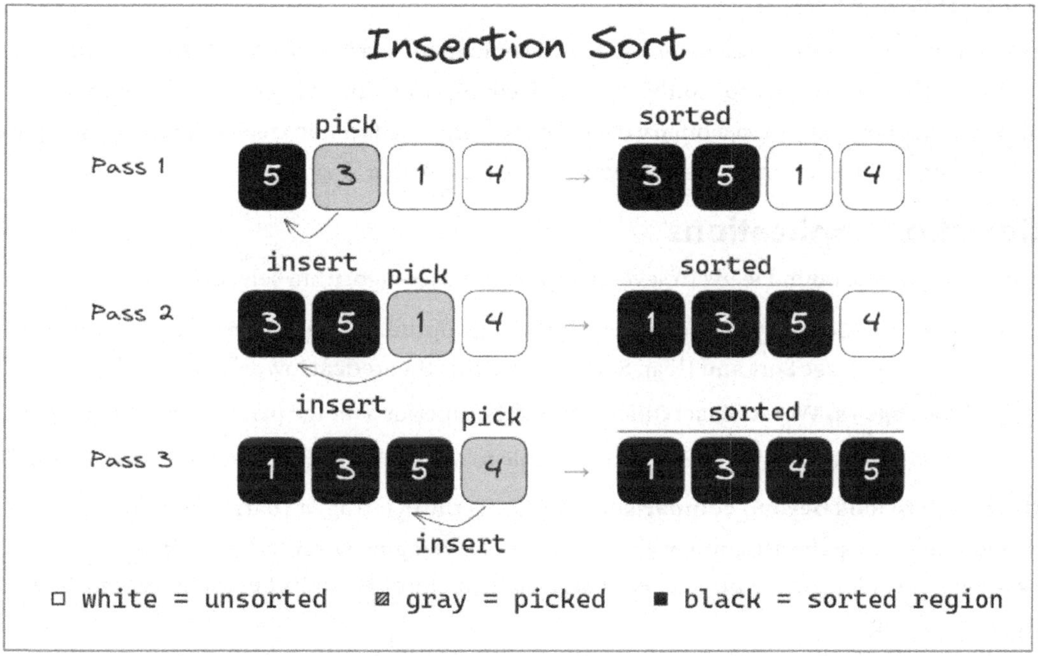

Figure 10.4: Insertion sort

Insertion sort mirrors how most people naturally organize a hand of playing cards. It is an in-place and stable algorithm, meaning it requires no extra memory and preserves the original relative order of duplicate values. While its complexity makes it slow for massive datasets, its adaptive nature makes it incredibly efficient for small lists or arrays that are already mostly sorted, often outperforming more complex algorithms in those specific cases. The complexity is `O(n²)` on average and worst, and `O(n)` for the best case with an already sorted input.

We have explored the mechanics of fundamental sorting algorithms like Bubble Sort and Insertion Sort, which provide a practical understanding of sorting mechanisms. However, to understand the true power of sorting algorithms, we must shift our focus to algorithmic limits as this perspective reveals why algorithms like the upcoming Merge Sort and Heap Sort are considered optimal, comparison-based solutions.

The Ω (n log n) limit

Before diving into the more advanced algorithms, it is important to understand the theoretical limits of sorting. This section establishes the theoretical lower bound for any sorting method that relies purely on pairwise comparisons to determine order. This bound dictates the absolute minimum amount of work required to sort any arbitrary set of `n` items.

The proof sketch

We examine the decision tree associated with comparison-based sorting. With `n` distinct elements, there are `n!` possible orderings. Each comparison operation essentially halves the set of remaining possibilities in a binary decision. Therefore, a decision tree with `n!` leaves requires at least $\log_2(n!)$ elements in height, which translates to $\Omega(n \log n)$.

Selection implications

This fundamental bound leads to several implications for algorithm selection:

- **Optimal Comparison Sorts**: Asymptotically optimal comparison-based algorithms, such as Merge Sort and Heap Sort, achieve this theoretical lower bound.
- **Average vs. Worst-Case**: Quick Sort offers superior average performance $O(n \log n)$; however, we must implement it carefully to avoid a poor $O(n^2)$ worst-case scenario.

If we were to look beyond comparison, bypassing the $\Omega(n \log n)$ barrier requires abandoning pure pairwise comparisons in favor of leveraging specific data structures. For example, by exploiting the properties of digits, algorithms like Radix Sort achieve $O(n)$ linear time complexity.

Because this lower bound applies to any algorithm using comparisons, it serves as a mathematical standard for measuring the performance of all subsequent sorting techniques. We will dive into three well-known comparison-based sorts next: Merge Sort, Quick Sort, and Heap Sort.

Advanced comparison sorts

Efficient sorting is a foundational pillar in computer science. This section introduces the mechanics of core sorting algorithms, focusing on Merge, Quick, and Heap comparison methods alongside the non-comparison Radix algorithm.

We will analyze the inner workings of each algorithm, from recursive division in Quick Sort to priority queue management in Heap Sort. The subsequent comparative analysis will facilitate a rigorous evaluation of the best time- and space-efficient sorting algorithm appropriate for your data set.

Merge sort

Merge Sort is a highly efficient, Divide, and Conquer sorting algorithm renowned for its consistent performance across all data distributions. The general approach involves recursively dividing the unsorted list into two halves until each sub-list contains only one element (which is inherently sorted). It then systematically merges these sorted sub-lists back together in a controlled, linear fashion to produce the final, fully sorted list. This methodical process ensures that the entire array is sorted by merging smaller, already-sorted segments, making it highly predictable and reliable. This process is shown below:

```
public class MergeSort {
    // The main function that initiates the recursive sorting process
    public static void mergeSort(int[] arr, int left, int right) {
        if (left < right) {
            int mid = left + (right - left) / 2;

            // Recursively sort the two halves
            mergeSort(arr, left, mid);
            mergeSort(arr, mid + 1, right);

            // Merge the sorted halves
            merge(arr, left, mid, right);
        }
    }

    // The core function that merges two sorted sub-arrays
    private static void merge(int[] arr, int left, int mid, int right) {
        int n1 = mid - left + 1;
        int n2 = right - mid;
```

```
        // Create temporary arrays
        int[] L = new int[n1];
        int[] R = new int[n2];

        // Copy data to temp arrays
        for (int i = 0; i < n1; i++) {
            L[i] = arr[left + i];
        }
        for (int j = 0; j < n2; j++) {
            R[j] = arr[mid + 1 + j];
        }

        // Merge the temporary arrays back into arr[left..right]
        int i = 0, j = 0, k = left;
        while (i <n1&&j< n2) {
            if (L[i] <= R[j]) {
                arr[k] = L[i];
                i++;
            } else {
                arr[k] = R[j];
                j++;
            }
            k++;
        }

        // Copy remaining elements of L[], if any
        while (i < n1) {
            arr[k] = L[i];
            i++;
            k++;
        }

        // Copy remaining elements of R[], if any
        while (j < n2) {
            arr[k] = R[j];
            j++;
            k++;
        }
    }
}
```

Algorithm walkthrough

Let's try to understand the above algorithm in detail:

- **Divide**: The `mergeSort` function recursively divides the input array into two halves until the base case (a single element) is reached.
- **Conquer**: Once the recursion hits the base case, the algorithm begins the merging process.
- **Combine (Merge)**: The core work happens in the merge function, where two adjacent, sorted sub-arrays are efficiently combined into a single, larger sorted array by comparing elements from both arrays sequentially and writing the smaller element into the final array.

The algorithm is shown in *Figure 10.5*.

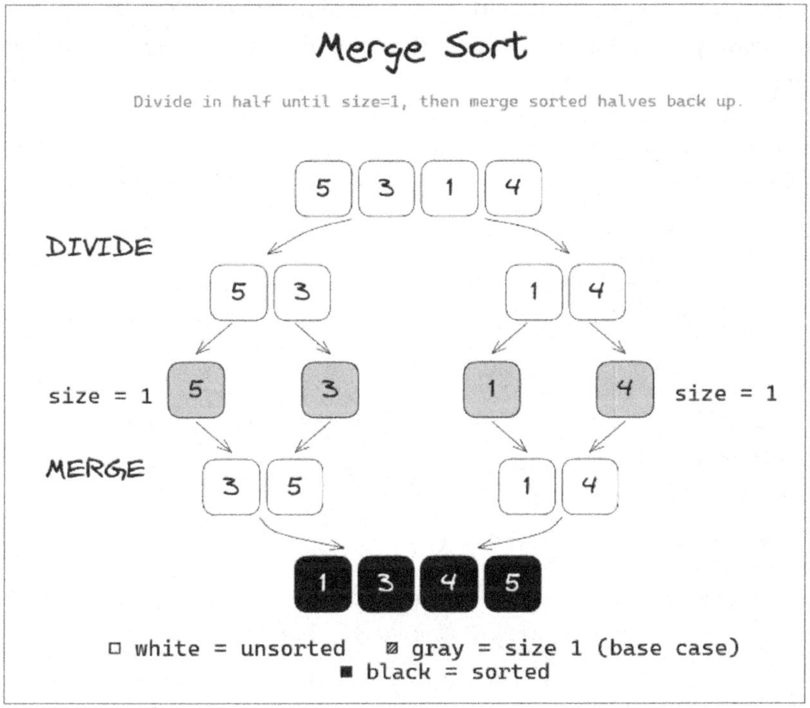

Figure 10.5: Merge sort

Merge Sort introduces the divide-and-conquer paradigm, involving breaking a problem into smaller subproblems, solving them independently, and combining the results. This pattern appears in many computing applications: binary search, FFT, closest pair, matrix multiplication, to name a few. In summary:

- **Time** : `O(n log n)`
- **Space**: `O(n)`
- **In-Place Status**: Out-of-Place, requiring auxiliary memory for the merging step.
- **Stability**: Stable; the relative order of equal elements is preserved.

We will look at another efficient, divide-and-conquer sorting algorithm called quick sort next.

Quick sort

Quick Sort is a highly efficient, divide-and-conquer sorting algorithm that relies on a partitioning strategy to yield excellent, average-case performance. The core idea is to select a pivot element and rearrange the array such that all elements smaller than the pivot are placed to its left, and all elements greater than the pivot are placed to its right. Once partitioned, the algorithm recursively sorts the sub-arrays to the left and right of the pivot. The algorithm is shown below:

```
void quickSort(int[] a, int low, int high) {
    if (low < high) {

        //PHASE 1: DIVIDE
        //The partition function separates the array and returns the pivot index
        int p = partition(a, low, high);

        //PHASE 2: CONQUER
        //Recursively sort the elements to the left/right of the pivot
        quickSort(a, low, p - 1);
        quickSort(a, p + 1, high);

        //PHASE 3: COMBINE (Implicit)
        //No code is needed here! Because the operations were done in-place,
        //the sub-arrays are already perfectly combined.

    }
}
int partition(int[] a, int low, int high) {
    int pivot = a[high], i = low - 1;
    for (int j = low; j < high; j++) {
        if (a[j] < pivot) {
            int t = a[++i];
```

```
                a[i] = a[j];
                a[j] = t;
            }
        }
        int t = a[i + 1];
        a[i + 1] = a[high];
        a[high] = t;
        return i + 1;
    }
```

The partition process

The partition function is the heart of the Quick Sort algorithm. It is responsible for partitioning the array around a chosen pivot. The choice of pivot significantly affects performance. Common strategies include:

- **First/Last Element**: Simplest to implement, but risks `O(n`^{2}`)` performance on already sorted data.
- **Random Pivot**: Selecting a random element ensures an expected `O(n log n)` performance, effectively eliminating adversarial worst-case scenarios.
- **Median-of-Three**: Selecting the median of the first, middle, and last elements offers a good balance between simplicity and performance, making it a common choice in library implementations.

Algorithm walkthrough

Let's try to understand the above algorithm in better detail:

- **Pivot Selection**: Select an element (the pivot) to act as the divider for a portion of the array.
- **Partition**: Rearrange the array such that all elements smaller than the pivot come before it, and all elements greater than the pivot come after it. The pivot is now in its final, correct sorted position.
- **Recurse**: Recursively apply the partitioning step to the sub-array of elements to the left of the pivot and the sub-array of elements to the right of the pivot.

Figure 10.6 shows the visual process of pivoting and partitioning the input.

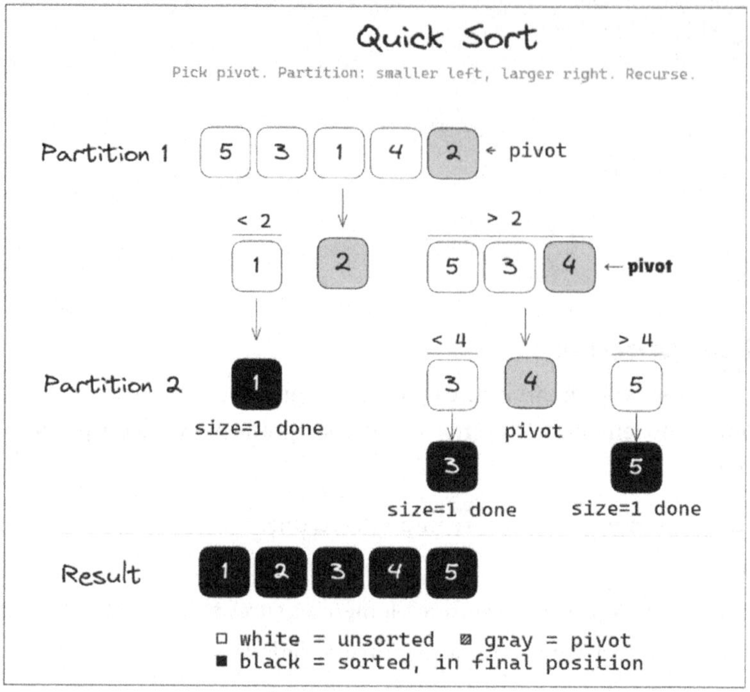

Figure 10.6: Quick sort

Quick sort is fast in practice due to effective partitioning. In summary:

- **Time**: `O(nlog n)` on average, with the worst case being `O(n²)` when the pivot selection consistently results in highly unbalanced partitions in an already sorted input.
- **Space**: `O(log n)` average for recursion stack, `O(n)` worst case.
- **In-Place Status**: In-place, requiring only space for the recursion stack.
- **Stability**: Unstable; the relative order of equal elements is not guaranteed to be preserved.

Pivot selection: Mitigating the $O(n^2)$ Worst-Case

There are two common pivot selection heuristics. For brevity, we will discuss one of them herein: randomized pivoting. To begin, we select a random index within the current subarray and swap that element with the first (or last) element before partitioning. This is shown in steps 1 and 2 in the snippet below:

```
import java.util.Random;
```

```
public class RandomizedQuickSort {
    private static final Random RANDOM = new Random();

    // Helper function to select and swap a random pivot into the first position
    private static void swap(int[] arr, int i, int j) {
        int temp = arr[i];
        arr[i] = arr[j];
        arr[j] = temp;
    }

    private static int partition(int[] arr, int low, int high) {
        // 1. Select a random pivot index
        int pivotIndex = low + RANDOM.nextInt(high - low + 1);

        // 2. Swap the random pivot to the 'low' position
        swap(arr, low, pivotIndex);

        // Standard partitioning logic follows...
        // ... (rest of the partitioning logic)
    }

    // ... rest of the quicksort implementation
}
```

While Quick Sort relies on partitioning to efficiently divide an array, Heap Sort utilizes a specific, powerful data structure: the Heap. The next section details this algorithm.

Heap sort

A heap is a specialized binary tree structure that satisfies the heap property, namely either a Max-Heap, where the parent is always larger than its children, or a Min-Heap, where the parent is always smaller than its children. Heap Sort leverages this property to sort the data in-place. This approach offers a reliable, `O(n log n)` performance guarantee over the potentially $O(n^2)$ worst case scenarios of quick sort. The algorithm is shown below:

```
public class HeapSort {
    // A helper function to maintain the max-heap property
    private static void heapify(int arr[], int n, int i) {
        int largest = i; // Initialize largest as root
        int left = 2 * i + 1; // Left child index
        int right = 2 * i + 2; // Right child index
```

```
        // Check if left child exists and is greater than root
        if (left <n&&arr[left]> arr[largest]) {
            largest = left;
        }

        // Check if right child exists and is greater than the largest
        if (right <n&&arr[right]> arr[largest]) {
            largest = right;
        }

        // If the largest element is not the root, swap them
        if (largest != i) {
            int temp = arr[i];
            arr[i] = arr[largest];
            arr[largest] = temp;

            // Recursively heapify the affected sub-tree
            heapify(arr, n, largest);
        }
    }

    // Main function to perform Heap Sort
    public static void heapSort(int arr[], int n) {
        // 1. Build the initial Max-Heap
        for (int i = n / 2 - 1; i >= 0; i--) {
            heapify(arr, n, i);
        }

        // 2. Extract elements one by one
        for (int i = n - 1; i > 0; i--) {
            // Move current root (largest element) to the end
            int temp = arr[0];
            arr[0] = arr[i];
            arr[i] = temp;

            // Call heapify on the reduced heap
            heapify(arr, i, 0);
        }
    }
}
```

Heapification and extraction: The two-phase approach

The entire process can be broken down into two distinct, yet interdependent, phases:

- **Building the Max-Heap (Heapification)**: The algorithm first analyzes the entire array and transforms it into a heap satisfying two requirements: the Max-Heap structure (the ordering rule) and the complete binary tree shape (the structural layout). This process establishes a guaranteed maximum element at the root. This process starts from the last non-leaf node and iteratively applies the heapify process up to the root. This setup phase is key because it guarantees that the largest element in the entire dataset will inevitably reside at the root (index 0). This preparation ensures that the subsequent retrieval of the maximum element is always instantaneous, maintaining the overall `O(n log n)` efficiency.
- **Repeated Extraction**: The sorting algorithm then repeatedly extracts the largest element (the root of the heap) and swaps it with the last element of the unsorted portion of the array, thus placing the largest element into its final, sorted position. After the swap, the heap property is broken at the root. To recover, the heapify procedure is called again on the new root, sinking the misplaced element down the heap structure until the Max-Heap property is restored for the remaining elements. This cycle continues until only one element remains unsorted.

Algorithm walkthrough

Let's try to understand the above algorithm in detail:

- **Heapify Initial Build**: The algorithm first transforms the entire array into a Max-Heap by starting from the middle and applying the heapify operation upwards. This establishes the root (the largest element) at the beginning of the array.
- **Extract Max**: The largest element (at index 0) is swapped with the last unsorted element, effectively placing the largest element in its final sorted position.
- **Re-Heapify**: The boundary of the unsorted portion is reduced by one, and the new largest element at the root is used to restore the Max-Heap property in the remaining elements, preparing the next largest element to be swapped into the correct position.
- **Repeat**: This process is repeated until the entire array is sorted.

Heap sort is highly efficient and reliable across all input cases. In summary:

- **Time**: `O(n log n)` in all input cases.
- **Space**: `O(1)` sorting in place.

- **In-Place Status**: In-place, with no significant auxiliary memory required.
- **Stability**: Unstable; the process of swapping elements to maintain the heap property generally results in a change to the relative order of equal elements.

In the next section we will look at two sort algorithms that transcend the Ω(n log n) barrier in performance. These algorithms do not rely on comparing the values of the elements to determine their order.

> Note
>
> **Transcending the lower bound**
>
> To "transcend" the `Ω(n log n)` barrier means to bypass it by changing the computational model. Comparison sorts are mathematically bound to `Ω(n log n)` time to resolve all input permutations. Non-comparison algorithms escape this binary decision tree model by abandoning pairwise comparisons entirely.

Non-comparison sorts

Unlike comparison sorts that rely on pairwise element comparisons, non-comparison sorts operate by exploiting the inherent structure of the data itself; specifically, the individual values or digits. Algorithms like counting sort and radix sort leverage the numerical properties of the data, allowing them to sort in linear time, `O(n)`, thereby bypassing the `Ω(nlogn)` limit imposed by comparison-based approaches.

Counting sort

Counting Sort is a highly efficient, non-comparison-based sorting algorithm designed specifically for sorting integers within a specific range. Unlike comparison sorts that rely on pairwise comparisons, Counting Sort operates by counting the frequency of each distinct element in the input array. It then uses these counts to determine the correct final position of each element.

The algorithm operates in the following steps:

- **Frequency Count**: The algorithm traverses the input array to record the frequency of each unique element in a temporary count array.
- **Cumulative Position Mapping**: The count array is transformed into a prefix sum array to determine the precise final index for each element.
- **Output Construction**: The input array is traversed again, placing each element into its designated spot in the sorted output array based on the cumulative mapping.

In essence, Counting Sort transforms the problem of sorting into a problem of simple counting and indexing, making it exceptionally fast for integer data.

```
public class CountingSort {

    public static void countingSort(int arr[], int n) {
        // 1. Find max to determine size of count array
        int max = arr[0];
        for (int i = 1; i < n; i++) {
            if (arr[i] > max) {
                max = arr[i];
            }
        }

        // Create count array to store element frequency
        int[] count = new int[max + 1];

        // Store the count of each element
        for (int i = 0; i < n; i++) {
            count[arr[i]]++;
        }

        // Modify count array to store position of elements
        for (int i = 1; i <= max; i++) {
            count[i] += count[i - 1];
        }

        // Build the output array
        int outputSize = n;
        int[] output = new int[outputSize];

        // Build output array by placing elements based on counts
        for (int i = n - 1; i >= 0; i--) {
            output[count[arr[i]] - 1] = arr[i];
            count[arr[i]]--;
        }

        // Copy output array to the original array
        for (int i = 0; i < n; i++) {
            arr[i] = output[i];
        }
```

```
    }

    public static void main(String[] args) {
        int arr[] = {170, 45, 75, 90, 800, 24, 2, 66};
        int n = arr.length;

        countingSort(arr, n);

        System.out.println("Sorted array:");
        for (int i = 0; i < n; i++) {
            System.out.print(arr[i] + " ");
        }
    }
}
```

The algorithm is visualized in *Figure 10.7*.

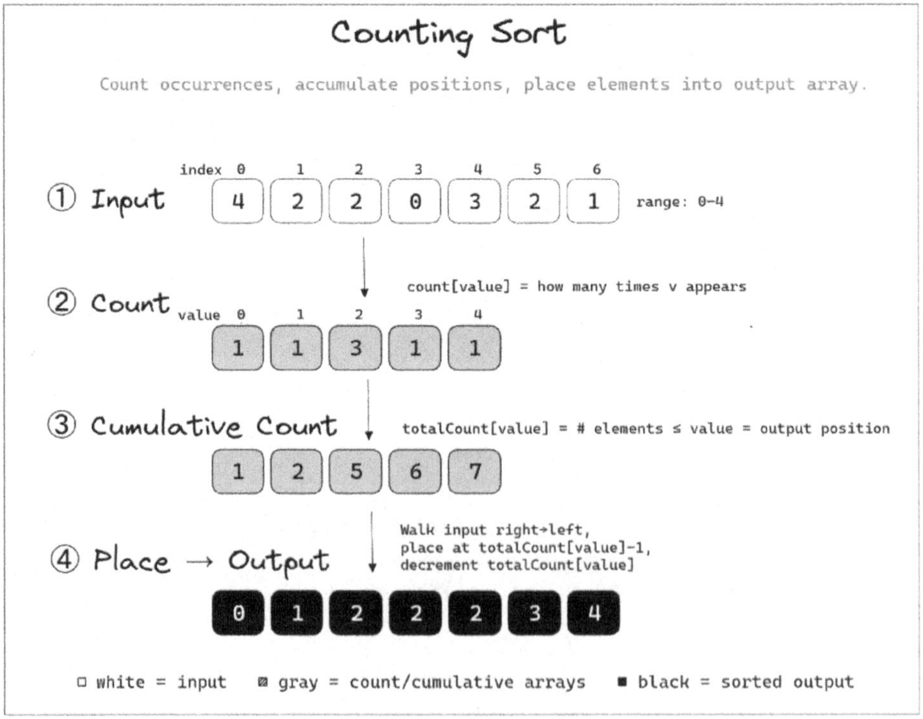

Figure 10.7: Counting sort

Counting Sort transforms the problem of sorting into a problem of simple counting and indexing integers, where the range of the numbers, `k`, is not significantly larger than the number of elements, `n`. In summary:

- **Time**: `O(n + k)`
- **Space**: `O(n + k)`, requiring auxiliary space for the stable sub-sort.
- **In-Place Status**: Out-of-place, requiring auxiliary space for the counting and output arrays.
- **Stability**: Stable, preserving the relative order of equal elements.

We will look at another non-comparison sorting algorithm that exploits the numerical properties of the array elements to achieve exceptional performance in sorting them.

Radix sort

Radix Sort achieves a sorting speed faster than the `Ω(n log n)` limit by sorting based on the individual digits of the numbers. This method is particularly powerful for large sets of positive integers, with a sort time of `O(n)`. This code illustrates an LSD Radix Sort, using a helper function to showcase the iterative process of digit isolation:

```
public class RadixSort {

    public static void radixSort(int[] arr) {
        if (arr == null || arr.length == 0) {
            return;
        }

        int max = arr[0];
        for (int value : arr) {
            if (value > max) {
                max = value;
            }
        }

        // Sort by each digit, from least to most significant.
        // exp is the place value: 1 (ones), 10 (tens), 100 (hundreds), ...
        for (long exp = 1; max / exp > 0; exp *= 10) {
            countingSortByDigit(arr, exp);
        }
    }
```

```
    // Stable counting sort on the digit at the given place value (exp).
    private static void countingSortByDigit(int[] arr, long exp) {
        int n = arr.length;
        int[] output = new int[n];
        int[] count = new int[10];

        // Tally how many elements fall into each digit bucket (0-9).
        for (int value : arr) {
            count[(int) ((value / exp) % 10)]++;
        }

        // Turn counts into prefix sums: count[d] now holds the index
        // (one past the last slot) where digit d's block ends.
        for (int i = 1; i < 10; i++) {
            count[i] += count[i - 1];
        }

        // Place elements into output in reverse to keep the sort stable.
        for (int i = n - 1; i >= 0; i--) {
            int digit = (int) ((arr[i] / exp) % 10);
            output[--count[digit]] = arr[i];
        }

        System.arraycopy(output, 0, arr, 0, n);
    }

    public static void main(String[] args) {
        int[] arr = { 4321, 12, 9, 654, 88, 3000, 1 };
        radixSort(arr);

        System.out.println("Sorted array:");
        for (int value : arr) {
            System.out.print(value + " ");
        }
    }
}
```

Algorithm walkthrough

Since Radix Sort relies on the iterative application of a stable sort, we will focus on the core idea involving the LSD step:

1. **Start**: Start with the entire list of numbers.
2. **LSD Sort (Ones Place)**: Sort the entire list based only on the unit digit.
3. **Next Digit Sort (Tens Place)**: Sort the result from Step 2 based only on the tens digit.
4. **Continue**: Repeat this process for the hundreds place, thousands place, and so on, until all digits have been sorted.

Figure 10.8 shows the radix sort approach.

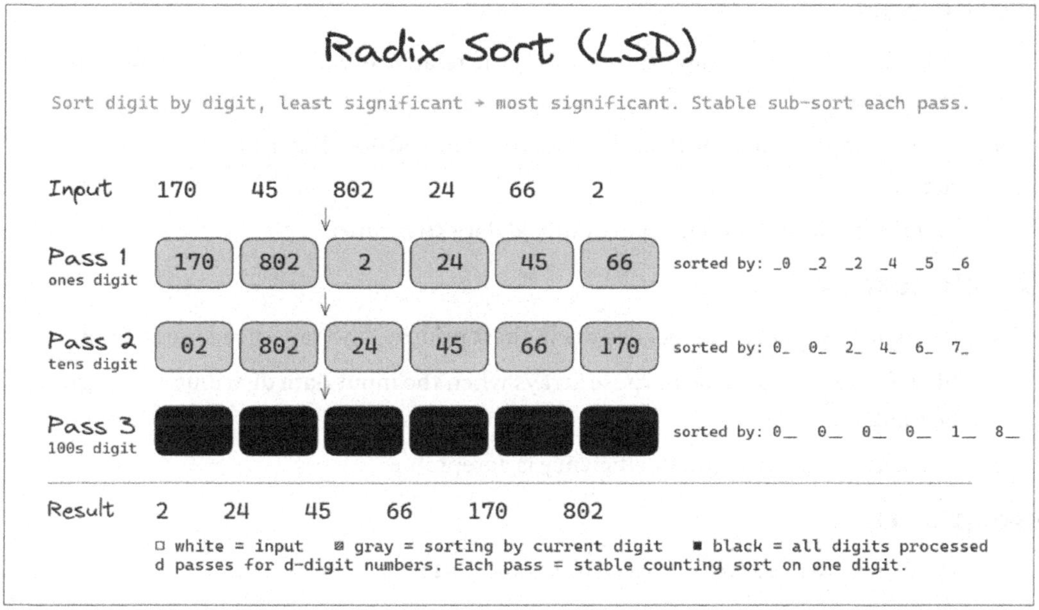

Figure 10.8: Radix sort

Radix sort excels at sorting large collections of integers or fixed-length strings when the number of digits (d) is small. For example, sorting 1 million 4-byte integers with base-256 requires only 4 passes, each of `O(n)` totaling `O(4n)`, which outperforms comparison-based sorts at `O(n log n) ≈ O(20n)`. In summary:

- **Time**: `O(d (n + b))`, where d = number of digits, n = elements, b = base (radix)
- **Space**: `O(n + b)`, requiring auxiliary space for the stable sub-sort.

- **In-Place Status**: Out-of-place, requiring auxiliary space for the counting sort mechanism.
- **Stability**: Stable; the process preserves the relative order of equal elements across digit passes.

When to use which sort

To effectively sort data, we must choose the right tool for the job. This analysis introduces several core sorting algorithms, each offering a unique approach to ordering. We will compare their performance characteristics, including time complexity, stability, and space efficiency, to guide our understanding of algorithmic trade-offs. In general:

Merge sort

- Use when stability is important, namely the relative order of equal elements must be preserved.
- Ideal for large, complex datasets where guaranteed `O(n log n)` performance is required.
- Suitable for multi-dimensional or linked data structures.

Quick sort

- Use when average-case speed is the highest priority, and raw speed is essential.
- Ideal for sorting general-purpose arrays when the input data distribution is expected to be random.
- Use when in-place memory efficiency is acceptable.

Heap sort

- Use when we need worst-case `O(n log n)` performance guarantee.
- Ideal for in-place sorting when memory usage must be minimized.
- Suitable for situations where the data structure itself can be efficiently managed via a priority queue.

Counting sort

- Use when sorting a large number of integers with a limited range `k`.
- Ideal for achieving linear time complexity `O(n + k)` when dealing with integer data.
- Effective when the range of values is small and known beforehand.

Radix sort

- Use exclusively when sorting integers and the range of the numbers is manageable.
- Ideal for extremely large sets of fixed-size integers where the number of digits is small relative to n.
- Utilize when sorting speed for integer data is essential, since maintaining the stable relative order of elements across consecutive digit passes is required to guarantee accuracy.

Table 10.1 quantifies performance and key characteristics of the aforementioned sorting mechanisms:

Algorithm	Best	Average	Worst	Space	Stable
Basic Sorts					
Bubble	`O(n)`	`O(n2)`	`O(n2)`	`O(1)`	Yes
Selection	`O(n2)`	`O(n2)`	`O(n2)`	`O(1)`	No
Insertion	`O(n)`	`O(n2)`	`O(n2)`	`O(1)`	Yes
Advanced Comparison Sorts					
Quick	`O(n log n)`	`O(n log n)`	`O(n2)`	`O(log n)`	No
Merge	`O(n log n)`	`O(n log n)`	`O(n log n)`	`O(n)`	Yes
Heap	`O(n log n)`	`O(n log n)`	`O(n log n)`	`O(1)`	No
Non-Comparison Sorts					
Counting	`O(n + k)`	`O(n + k)`	`O(n + k)`	`O(n + k)`	Yes
Radix	`O(d(n + b))`	`O(d(n + b))`	`O(d(n + b))`	`O(n + b)`	Yes

Table 10.1: Sorting algorithm performance and characteristics

In this table:

- n = number of elements
- d = number of digits

- b = base (radix)
- k = range of keys

Now that we understand the practical trade-offs of these algorithms, we move to hybrid sorts optimized for real-world performance.

Hybrid comparison-based sorts

We examine two popular hybrid sorts, dual-pivot Quicksort and Timsort, in this section. Dual-pivot Quicksort extends standard quicksort by partitioning data around two pivots into three sections, improving cache locality and reducing comparisons in practice. Timsort takes a different approach; it's a stable hybrid of merge sort and insertion sort that exploits naturally occurring runs in partially ordered data.

Dual-pivot quicksort

This algorithm was invented by Vladimir Yaroslavskiy in 2009 and adopted by Java 7 for primitive arrays. While traditional Quick Sort relies on a single pivot to divide the array into two partitions, Dual-Pivot Quick Sort introduces a refined strategy for partitioning, employing two pivots to divide the array into three distinct regions:

- **Left region**: elements x less than the first pivot P_1
- **Middle region**: Elements x between the two pivots: $P_1 \le x \le P_2$
- **Right region**: Elements x greater than the second pivot P_2

This approach aims to improve performance by reducing the number of recursive calls and improving cache locality.

The Two-pivot strategy

The core innovation lies in using two pivots (P_1 and P_2) to partition the array simultaneously. The algorithm then recursively calls itself on these three separate partitions. A key optimization is that for very small subarrays (typically under 47 elements), the recursion is halted, and the algorithm switches to a simpler, faster Insertion Sort. While generally faster, the worst-case complexity remains $O(n^2)$ on already sorted data.

A critical factor in avoiding the `O(n²)` worst-case complexity is the selection of the pivots. We employ two primary optimization techniques:

- **Randomized Pivoting**: By selecting the pivots randomly from the array, we ensure that the algorithm's behavior is independent of the input data order. This leads to an expected time complexity of `O(n log n)`, regardless of the input pattern.
- **Median-of-Three Selection**: For practical performance improvements, we can select the pivot by choosing the median of three elements (e.g., the first, middle, and last element of the current subarray) instead of just two arbitrary points. This generally leads to a more balanced partition, which exhibits good performance in practice.

Note

While the Median-of-Three strategy is the industrial standard for locating a single optimal divider, Dual-Pivot Quicksort naturally expands this sampling methodology. Instead of evaluating three elements to extract one median, production implementations sample five equidistant elements across the array. The algorithm sorts these five samples and extracts the second and fourth elements to serve as the highly balanced dual pivots, P_1 and P_2.

Example

Consider the array: `[5, 1, 8, 3, 7, 2, 9, 4, 6]` with P_1=3 and P_2=7. *Figure 10.10* shows the partitioning in action, where:

- **Left**: Elements less than 3 (e.g., `[1, 2]`)
- **Middle**: Elements between 3 and 7 (e.g., `[5, 4, 6]`)
- **Right**: Elements greater than 7 (e.g., `[8, 9]`)

This division allows the algorithm to process three sub-problems simultaneously, leading to more efficient recursive calls. *Figure 10.10* depicts this algorithm in action.

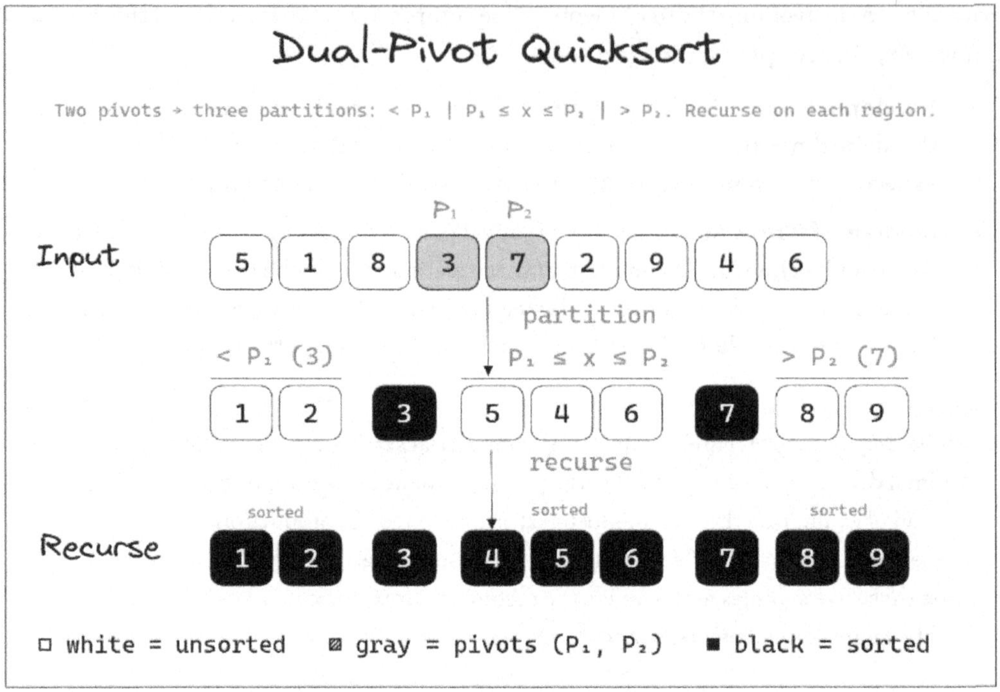

Figure 10.10: Dual-pivot quicksort

Partitioning reduces the total number of comparisons, particularly on large datasets. Dual-pivot quicksort often outperforms standard quicksort by better handling sorted or partially sorted data. In summary:

- **Time**: `O(n log n)` average, with `O(n²)` worst case being mitigated by pivot selection heuristics
- **Space**: `O(log n)` stack space
- **In-Place Status**: In-place
- **Stability**: Unstable; equal elements may be reordered

Timsort

Timsort is a sophisticated, hybrid sorting algorithm designed specifically to handle real-world data patterns. This hybrid algorithm was invented by Tim Peters in 2002 for Python, and later adopted by Java in 2009. Unlike algorithms that rely purely on a single comparison strategy, Timsort's core idea lies in its adaptability. By exploiting existing order in the input, this adaptive algorithm dynamically switches sorting techniques to maximize performance across diverse data distributions. Its hybrid strategy calls for:

- **Identifying natural runs**: Scan the array to identify existing, naturally sorted subsequences (runs) in ascending or descending order.
- **Extending short runs**: Use Insertion Sort to efficiently extend any short, naturally sorted run.
- **Merging runs**: Combine adjacent sorted runs using a modified merge process, managed by a merge stack to ensure balanced merging.
- **Adapting dynamically**: The algorithm dynamically switches between Insertion Sort for small segments and a modified Merge strategy for larger segments.

Example

Consider the array, `[2, 5, 8, 6, 3, 1, 4, 7, 9]`, that is split into 3 runs:

- **Run A (ascending)**: `[2,5,8]`
- **Run B (descending)**: `[6,3]`
- **Run C (ascending)**: `[1,4,7,9]`

The algorithm reverses Run B, utilizing Insertion Sort to extend any run whose size falls below a minimum threshold, while keeping both Run A and C as-is. Merging runs is done using a modified merge sort, by stacking runs incrementally to converge into the outcome. This hybrid approach is shown in *Figure 10.11*.

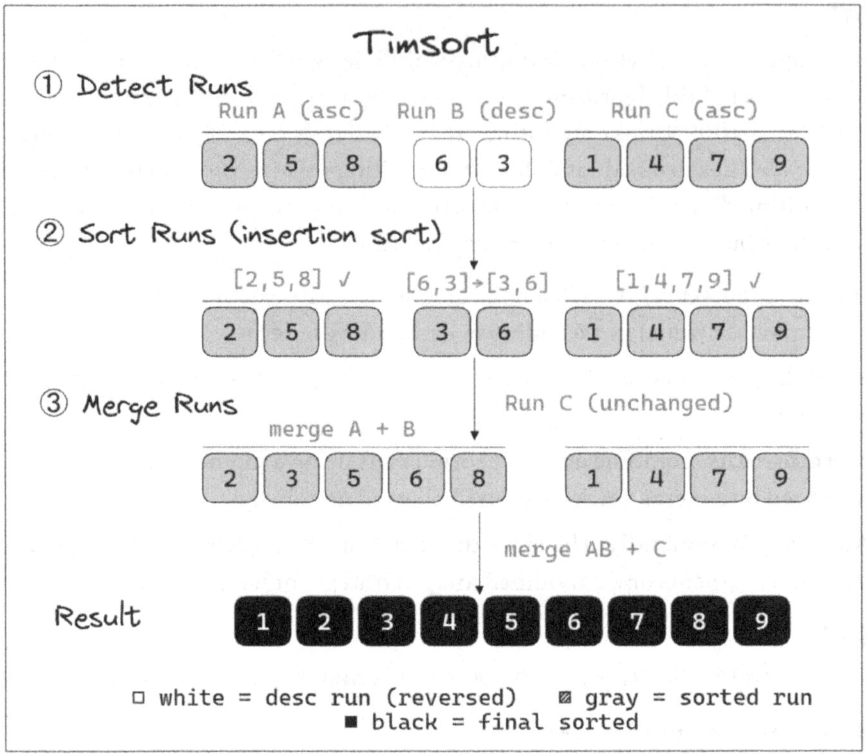

Figure 10.11: Timsort

Timsort adaptively combines the speed of Insertion Sort for small segments with the efficiency of Merge Sort for larger segments, resulting in a sorting mechanism that adapts dynamically to the structure of the input data. In summary:

- **Time**: `O(n)` on already sorted data, `O(n log n)` otherwise.
- **Space**: `O(n)` auxiliary space for the merge buffer.
- **In-Place Status**: Out-of-place, requiring auxiliary space as mentioned.
- **Stability**: Stable; equal elements maintain their relative order.

Moving from theory to practice, we will examine the built-in sorting methods in popular languages. Understanding the internal workings of algorithms like Timsort and Dual-Pivot QuickSort is essential knowledge for anyone building high-performance, real-world systems.

Engineered sorts in the real world

Many production sorting libraries are carefully engineered and tuned; no single algorithm is best for all inputs.

The following reference table shows many sorting facilities and their respective implementations and performance benchmarks. Some of the listed algorithms are beyond the scope of this text. For reference, both Introsort and PDQSort address the potential $O(n^2)$ worst-case performance of classic QuickSort. They achieve a guaranteed `O(n log n)` complexity by employing a robust strategy: Introsort monitors QuickSort's recursion depth and switches to HeapSort if a threshold is exceeded, while PDQSort tracks partition imbalance and falls back to HeapSort only if pivot selection choices fail repeatedly.

This strategy ensures efficient sorting regardless of the input structure.

Language Function	Algorithm	Stable	Space	Time (Avg | Worst)

`Java`
 	
`Arrays.sort(int[])`
	Dual-Pivot Quicksort	No	`O(log n)`	`O(n log n)`
				| $O(n^2)$

`Java`
 	
`Arrays.sort(Object []) `
	TimSort	Yes	`O(n)`	`O(n log n)`

`Java`
 	
`Collections.sort()`
	TimSort	Yes	`O(n)`	`O(n log n)`

`Python`
 	
`sorted() / list.sort()`
	TimSort	Yes	`O(n)`	`O(n log n)`

`JavaScript`
 	
`Array.sort()`
	TimSort (V8/Chrome)	Yes	`O(n)`	`O(n log n)`

`C++`
 	
`std::sort`
	Introsort (quicksort + heapsort)	No	`O(log n)`	`O(n log n)`

Language Function	Algorithm	Stable	Space	Time (Avg | Worst)
C++ `std::stable_sort`	TimSort variant (merge sort)	Yes	`O(n)`	`O(n log n)`
Go `sort.Sort`	Pattern-defeating Quicksort	No	`O(log n)`	`O(n log n)`

Table 10.3: Sorting facilities and their implementation

Summary

This chapter establishes the theoretical and practical foundations of sorting algorithms. We begin by understanding why sorting matters, from searching, and deduplication to data preprocessing, and introduce the critical concepts of stability, space complexity (in-place vs. out-of-place), and the distinction between comparison-based and non-comparison-based sorting algorithms. We then examine the progression from simple, inefficient methods (Bubble, Selection, Insertion) to highly optimized modern techniques, culminating in an understanding of the theoretical limits that define modern sorting performance and the real-world engineered sorting practices in production. In particular:

- **The Ω(n log n) Lower Bound**: Establishing the theoretical minimum number of comparisons required for any comparison-based sort.
- **Sorting Paradigms**: Differentiating between comparison-based methods and non-comparison-based methods.
- **Algorithm Families**: A deep dive into the mechanics, trade-offs, and performance profiles of comparison sorts (Merge Sort, Quick Sort, Heap Sort) and non-comparison sorts (Counting Sort, Radix Sort).
- **Hybridization**: Understanding how modern, production-ready algorithms (like Timsort) combine different techniques (Merge Sort and Insertion Sort) to achieve superior, real-world performance.

The central takeaway is that an optimal sorting solution depends entirely on the data type and constraints. Understanding the time complexity (best, average, and worst-case) and space requirements of each algorithm is essential for making informed engineering decisions, allowing us to select the right tool for the job, whether optimizing for speed, stability, or memory. *Figure 10.12* provides a summary diagram for sorting techniques. These concepts will be re-examined in *Chapter 12* within the context of practical examples.

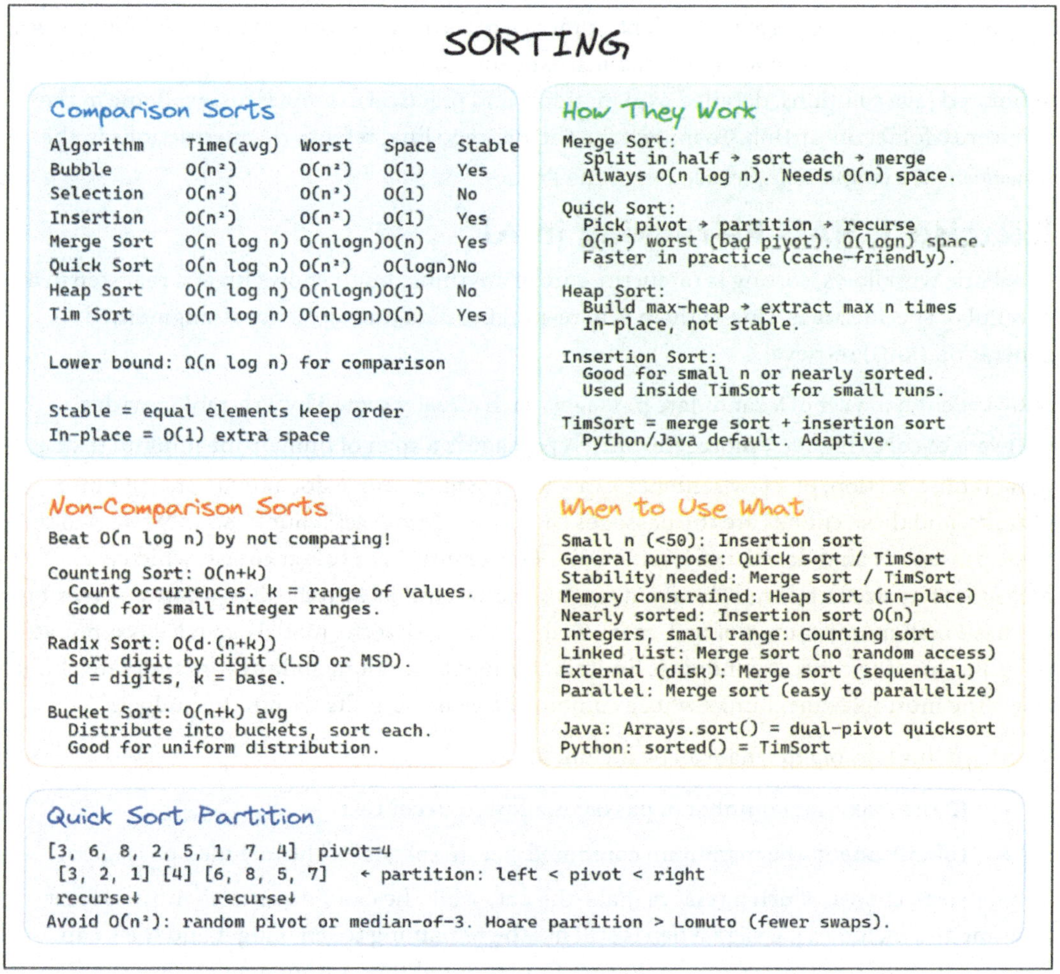

Figure 10.12: Summary diagram of sorting techniques

The completion of this study provides a robust library of sequential solutions, ranging from basic sorts to complex hybrid models. However, in real-world systems, efficiency is dictated by parallelism. The core challenge is not finding the optimal algorithm, but ensuring that the entire data process runs concurrently across multiple cores. The next chapter introduces parallel computation. We will expand our DSA knowledge base to understand how to restructure algorithms and data operations (be it sorting, hashing, or graph traversal) to utilize parallel hardware, focusing specifically on the mechanisms required for safe and efficient concurrent resource management.

Exercises

The following exercises provide in-depth practice covering core sorting topics and techniques within DSA. Every challenge offers practical exposure to specialized sorting patterns. Fully annotated Java solutions, detailed explanations, and practical examples are available in the `Chapter10` folder on GitHub. To unlock the GitHub repo link, refer to the instructions in the *Download the example code files* section of the *Preface*.

Exercise 1: RAG Re-ranking in AI

In agentic workflows, sorting is rarely the core of anything, but it shows up as a real step in a handful of specific areas. One of them is in re-ranking data during retrieval-augmented generation (RAG) retrieval.

A RAG agent has a set of `N` candidate passages, each already scored by a re-ranker with a `relevanceScore` (higher = more relevant). A passage is a span of human-meaningful text: a paragraph, a section, or a few sentences. In a RAG system, source documents are split into **chunks**, and these chunks are the passages the system retrieves; "chunk" simply refers to the same passage as an indexed, retrievable unit. Each chunk has a **token count**, which is a measure of its size in tokens. The agent feeds selected chunks into the LLM's **context window**: the fixed maximum amount of text, measured in tokens, that the model can take as input at once. Because the context window is limited, the agent cannot include every candidate; it must select the most relevant chunks whose combined token count fits within the budget.

Two hard limits apply to what can be included:

- **K**: the maximum number of passages allowed in context.
- **tokenBudget**: the maximum combined size, in tokens, of the included passages.

Your job is to choose which passages make the cut. Walk the candidates from most to least relevant and include a passage when it still fits the remaining token budget and the k cap hasn't been reached. A passage that doesn't fit is **skipped** (not a stopping point): a smaller, slightly-less-relevant passage further down may still fit.

Given this starter code:

```
public record Candidate(
    String chunkId,
    double relevanceScore, // higher = more relevant
    int tokenCount         // size of this chunk in tokens
) {}
```

You will implement:

```
public static List<Candidate> selectContext(
    List<Candidate> candidates,
    int k,
    int tokenBudget
)
```

This code returns the passages to place in context, such that:

- Rank by `relevanceScore` (descending)
- Limit the return to `k` chunks
- Ensure total `tokenCount` is £ `tokenBudget`
- Tie-break: Favor the chunk with the minimum `tokenCount`

Starter Code Template

```
import java.util.List;

public class ContextSelector {

    public record Candidate(
        String chunkId,
        double relevanceScore, // higher = more relevant
        int tokenCount         // size of this chunk in tokens
    ) {}

    /**
     * Select up to k candidates, ranked by relevanceScore descending
     * (tie-break: smaller tokenCount first), whose combined tokenCount
     * does not exceed tokenBudget. Returned in ranked order.
     */
    public static List<Candidate> selectContext(
            List<Candidate> candidates, int k, int tokenBudget) {
        // TODO: implement
        throw new UnsupportedOperationException("not implemented");
    }

    public static void main(String[] args) {
        List<Candidate> candidates = List.of(
            new Candidate("a", 0.42, 300),
```

```
            new Candidate("b", 0.91, 500),
            new Candidate("c", 0.91, 200),
            new Candidate("d", 0.88, 400)
        );
        System.out.println(selectContext(candidates, 2, 1000)); // expect c, b
    }
}
```

Assumptions and Constraints

- Each candidate's `relevanceScore` is precomputed by the re-ranker; we don't compute relevance
- Higher `relevanceScore` = more relevant (sort descending)
- Selection is greedy in ranked order: take a chunk if it fits the remaining budget and k isn't reached; a chunk that doesn't fit is skipped, not a stop signal
- Returned list stays in ranked order (most relevant first)
- chunkId values are unique
- `0 ≤ N ≤ 10_000, 0 ≤ k ≤ N, tokenBudget ≥ 0`, each `tokenCount ≥ 0`
- Rank by `relevanceScore` descending; tie-break by smaller `tokenCount`
- Return at most k chunks; sum of returned `tokenCount ≤ tokenBudget`
- Do not mutate the input list

Test Case 1: Tie-break + budget room

- **Input**:

```
candidates = [
  ("a", 0.42, 300),
  ("b", 0.91, 500),
  ("c", 0.91, 200),
  ("d", 0.88, 400) ], k = 2, tokenBudget = 1000
```

- **Output**: `["c", "b"]`
- **Explanation**: Since `b` and `c` have an equal relevance score of 0.91, we prioritize the chunk k with the smaller token count first. Because both choices fit within the remaining budget, we select the chunk with the smaller token count first to ensure we meet the limit k efficiently.

Test Case 2: Budget forces a skip

- **Input**:

```
candidates = [
  ("a", 0.95, 800),
  ("b", 0.90, 500),
  ("c", 0.80, 150) ], k = 3, tokenBudget = 1000
```

- **Output**: `["a", "c"]`
- **Explanation**: First, we attempt to take `a` (800) and `b` (500). Since their sum (1300) exceeds the budget limit (1000), we must skip this combination. Next, we try `a` (800) and `c` (150). Since their sum (950) fits within the budget, this combination is the valid solution.

Solution

The problem has two distinct concerns: **what order** candidates are considered (relevance) and **which ones survive** the caps (`k` and budget). Doing the sort first collapses the first concern into a clean pass, so the selection loop only worries about fitting. This is the load-bearing step: `O(N log N)` dominates the whole function.

```
List<Candidate> ranked = new ArrayList<>(candidates);
    ranked.sort(
        Comparator.comparingDouble(Candidate::relevanceScore).reversed()
            .thenComparingInt(Candidate::tokenCount)
    );
```

Specifically, `.reversed()` flips the **score** comparator to descending. But `thenComparingInt` builds a *fresh* comparator on `tokenCount` that is **not** reversed, so it stays ascending. This is the subtle area: on a score tie, the **smaller** chunk wins. A common bug here is assuming `.reversed()` flips the tie-break too; it only reverses the comparator it's chained onto.

The two caps are independent, so they're checked independently. Once `k` is hit, **no** later chunk can qualify regardless of size, so `break` (not `continue`) is correct and saves scanning the tail. Contrast with the budget check, which is a `skip` because a later smaller chunk *can* still qualify. Recognizing that one cap terminates the loop and the other doesn't is the insight that keeps this correct.

The first cap is k. We check it at the top of the candidate selection loop:

```
List<Candidate> selected = new ArrayList<>(Math.min(k, ranked.size()));
if (selected.size() == k) {
    break;    // k reached - nothing further can be added
}
```

Once k is hit, **no** later chunk can qualify regardless of size, so `break` (not `continue`) is correct and saves scanning the budgetary tail. Lastly, chunks that won't fit into the token budget are skipped:

```
if (usedTokens + c.tokenCount() <= tokenBudget) {
    selected.add(c);
    usedTokens += c.tokenCount();
}
// else: skip - keep scanning
```

This mechanism commits to each decision and moves on, trusting that locally-best choices add up to a good overall result. Namely, we walk candidates from most to least relevant and grab each one if it fits the remaining budget. Greedy is fast (one `O(N)` pass after sorting) and simple, but doesn't guarantee global optimality for every objective. However, it is optimal here because our goal is about including "the highest-relevance passages in priority order," which aligns with the greedy rule of always picking the next-best item.

Time complexity: O(N log N)

Where **N** = the number of candidate passages. The sort is the bottleneck, and `k` and `tokenBudget` **do not** reduce the asymptotic cost, even if `k = 1`. The solution still fully sorts all N candidates.

Exercise 2: Stability analysis

Implement and compare a stable sorting method (e.g., Merge Sort) and an unstable sorting method (e.g., Quick Sort) on an array of student records. The objective is to demonstrate how the relative order of elements with equal keys is preserved or disrupted.

The Student Record consists of

- Name (String)
- Grade (int – the sorting key)
- Id (int – unique identifier)

Input Data: [(Alice, 800, 101), (Bob, 500, 102), (Charlie, 800, 103), (Dana, 700, 104)]

Starter Code Template

```
import java.util.Arrays;

class Student {
    String name;
    int grade;
    int id;

    public Student(String name, int grade, int id) {
        this.name = name;
        this.grade = grade;
        this.id = id;
    }

    @Override
    public String toString() {
        return String.format("Name: %s, Grade: %d, ID: %d", name, grade, id);
    }
}

public class StabilityAnalysis {

    // --- Stable Sort Implementation (e.g., Merge Sort) ---
    public static void stableSort(Student[] students) {
        // TODO: Implement a stable sorting algorithm (e.g., Merge Sort)
    }

    // --- Unstable Sort Implementation (e.g., Quick Sort) ---
    public static void unstableSort(Student[] students) {
        // TODO: Implement an unstable sorting algorithm (e.g., Quick Sort)
    }

    public static void main(String[] args) {
        // Define the test data here
        Student[] students = { /* ... input data ... */ };

        System.out.println("--- Original Order ---");
```

```
        printArray(students);

        // Test Stable Sort
        Student[] stableStudents = Arrays.copyOf(students, students.length);
        stableSort(stableStudents);
        System.out.println("\n--- Stable Sort Order ---");
        printArray(stableStudents);

        // Test Unstable Sort
        Student[] unstableStudents = Arrays.copyOf(students, students.length);
        unstableSort(unstableStudents);
        System.out.println("\n--- Unstable Sort Order ---");
        printArray(unstableStudents);
    }

    private static void printArray(Student[] arr) {
        for (Student s : arr) {
            System.out.println(s);
        }
    }
}
```

Assumptions and Constraints

- Input will be an array of Student objects.
- All sorting must be performed based on the grade field.
- Implement at least one stable sort (e.g., Merge Sort) and one unstable sort (e.g., Quick Sort).
- The output must clearly demonstrate whether the relative order of students with identical grades is preserved (stable) or disrupted (unstable).

Test Case 1: Mixed Grades

This test case ensures that the sorting works correctly across different grade levels.

- **Input Array**: [`(Alice, 800, 101), (Bob, 500, 102), (Charlie, 800, 103), (Dana, 700, 104)`]
- **Output**: The stability of the sort should be observable in the output sequence

Test Case 2: Tie-Breaker Test (Critical Test)

This test is specifically designed to force the sort to resolve the relative order of elements with the same key.

- **Input**: [`(A, 800, 1), (B, 800, 2), (C, 500, 3)`]
- **Output**: When sorted by grade, the relative order of A and B (both grade 800) must be preserved in both the stable and unstable results

Exercise 3: Space complexity implementation

Implement and compare in-place and out-of-place sorting algorithms to understand their memory usage differences.

In-place sorting (like Quick Sort) sorts data by rearranging elements within the original array, using only a small, constant amount of extra memory. Out-of-place sorting (like Merge Sort) creates a new array to store sorted results, requiring additional memory proportional to the input size.

Your task is to implement both approaches and track how much extra memory they use during execution.

Starter Code Template

```
import java.util.Arrays;

class Student {
    String name;
    int grade;
    int id;

    public Student(String name, int grade, int id) {
        this.name = name;
        this.grade = grade;
        this.id = id;
    }

    @Override
    public String toString() {
        return String.format("Name: %s, Grade: %d, ID: %d", name, grade, id);
    }
}

public class SpaceComplexityAnalysis {
```

```
    // --- IN-PLACE SORT (Quick Sort) ---
    public static void inPlaceSort(Student[] students) {
        // TODO: Implement Quick Sort that modifies the original array
        // Track auxiliary space used (should be O(log n) for recursion stack)
    }

    // --- OUT-OF-PLACE SORT (Merge Sort) ---
    public static void outOfPlaceSort(Student[] students) {
        // TODO: Implement Merge Sort that creates new arrays
        // Track auxiliary space used (should be O(n) for temporary arrays)
    }

    public static void main(String[] args) {
        // Test data
        Student[] students = {
            new Student("Alice", 800, 101),
            new Student("Bob", 500, 102),
            new Student("Charlie", 800, 103),
            new Student("Dana", 700, 104)
        };

        System.out.println("--- Original Array ---");
        printArray(students);

        // Test In-Place Sort
        Student[] inPlaceStudents = Arrays.copyOf(students, students.length);
        System.out.println("\n--- In-Place Sort (Quick Sort) ---");
        inPlaceSort(inPlaceStudents);
        printArray(inPlaceStudents);

        // Test Out-Of-Place Sort
        Student[] outOfPlaceStudents = Arrays.copyOf(students, students.length);
        System.out.println("\n--- Out-Of-Place Sort (Merge Sort) ---");
        outOfPlaceSort(outOfPlaceStudents);
        printArray(outOfPlaceStudents);
    }

    private static void printArray(Student[] arr) {
        for (Student s : arr) {
            System.out.println(s);
        }
```

```
    }
}
```

Assumptions and Constraints

- Input is an array of Student objects sorted by the grade field
- Sorting Key: grade field (ascending order)
- Must track auxiliary space allocation during the sorting process
- Must be actual sorting algorithms, not just `Arrays.sort()`
- Compare space usage between in-place and out-of-place approaches

Test Case 1: Basic Sorting

- **Input**: `[(Alice, 800, 101), (Bob, 500, 102), (Charlie, 800, 103), (Dana, 700, 104)]`
- **Output**: Both algorithms should produce the same sorted order: `Bob(500), Dana(700), Alice(800), Charlie(800)`

Test Case 2: Larger Dataset

- **Input**: `[(A, 900, 1), (B, 600, 2), (C, 900, 3), (D, 800, 4), (E, 600, 5)]`
- **Expected Output**: `B(600), E(600), D(800), A(900), C(900)`

Exercise 4: Pivot selection strategies

Implement Quick Sort with three different ways to pick the pivot element and compare how each method performs on different types of data.

What is a pivot? In Quick Sort, we pick one element to divide the array into two parts—elements smaller than the pivot go to the left, elements larger go to the right.

Starter Code Template

```
import java.util.*;

public class PivotStrategyComparison {

    // Strategy 1: First element as pivot
    public static void quickSortFirstPivot(int[] arr, int low, int high) {
        if (low < high) {
            int pivotIndex = partitionFirst(arr, low, high);
            quickSortFirstPivot(arr, low, pivotIndex - 1);
            quickSortFirstPivot(arr, pivotIndex + 1, high);
```

```
        }
    }

    private static int partitionFirst(int[] arr, int low, int high) {
        int pivot = arr[low];  // First element as pivot
        int i = low + 1;
        int j = high;

        while (i <= j) {
            while (i <=j&&arr[i]<= pivot) i++;
            while (i <=j&&arr[j]> pivot) j--;
            if (i <= j) {
                swap(arr, i, j);
                i++;
                j--;
            }
        }
        swap(arr, low, j);
        return j;
    }

    // Strategy 2: Random element as pivot
    public static void quickSortRandomPivot(int[] arr, int low, int high) {
        if (low < high) {
            int pivotIndex = partitionRandom(arr, low, high);
            quickSortRandomPivot(arr, low, pivotIndex - 1);
            quickSortRandomPivot(arr, pivotIndex + 1, high);
        }
    }

    private static int partitionRandom(int[] arr, int low, int high) {
        // TODO: Complete this method
        // 1. Pick random pivot index between low and high
        // 2. Swap the random element with the first element
        // 3. Continue with standard partitioning logic using arr[low] as pivot
        return 0; // TODO: Return the correct pivot index
    }

    // Strategy 3: Median-of-three pivot
    public static void quickSortMedianPivot(int[] arr, int low, int high) {
        if (low < high) {
```

```
            int pivotIndex = partitionMedian(arr, low, high);
            quickSortMedianPivot(arr, low, pivotIndex - 1);
            quickSortMedianPivot(arr, pivotIndex + 1, high);
        }
    }

    private static int partitionMedian(int[] arr, int low, int high) {
        // TODO: Complete this method
        // 1. Find median of first, middle, and last elements
        // 2. Swap the median element with the first element
        // 3. Continue with standard partitioning logic using arr[low] as pivot
        return 0; // TODO: Return the correct pivot index
    }

    private static void swap(int[] arr, int i, int j) {
        int temp = arr[i];
        arr[i] = arr[j];
        arr[j] = temp;
    }

    public static void main(String[] args) {
        // Test with different datasets
        int[] sortedArray = {1, 2, 3, 4, 5, 6, 7, 8, 9, 10};
        int[] reverseArray = {10, 9, 8, 7, 6, 5, 4, 3, 2, 1};
        int[] randomArray = {5, 2, 8, 1, 9, 3, 7, 4, 6, 0};

        System.out.println("Testing with sorted array: " +
Arrays.toString(sortedArray));

        // TODO: Test all three strategies on each dataset and measure performance
        // Hint: Use System.nanoTime() to measure execution time
    }
}
```

Assumptions and Constraints

- Input is an array of integers with sizes between 5 and 100 elements
- All implementations must be comparison-based Quick Sort algorithms
- Pivot Strategies:
    - First element as pivot (Strategy 1)

    - Random element as pivot (Strategy 2)
    - Median-of-three elements as pivot (Strategy 3)
- Use `System.nanoTime()` to measure execution time
- Test on sorted, reverse-sorted, and random datasets
- Display execution times for each strategy and dataset combination
- Only use standard Java libraries (`java.util.*`)

Test Case 1

- **Input**:
    - **Sorted array**: `[1, 2, 3, 4, 5]`
    - **Reverse-sorted array**: `[5, 4, 3, 2, 1]`
    - **Random array**: `[3, 1, 4, 2, 5]`
- **Output**:
    - Show execution times for each strategy on each dataset
    - Demonstrate how pivot selection affects performance on edge cases

Test Case 2

- **Input**:
    - **Sorted array**: `[1, 2, 3, 4, 5, 6, 7, 8, 9, 10]`
    - **Reverse-sorted array**: `[10, 9, 8, 7, 6, 5, 4, 3, 2, 1]`
    - **Random array**: `[7, 2, 9, 1, 5, 8, 3, 10, 4, 6]`
- **Output**:
    - Show execution times for each strategy on each dataset
    - Analyze which pivot strategy performs best on different data patterns
    - Demonstrate the advantage of median-of-three on sorted/reverse-sorted data

Exercise 5: Hybrid algorithm design

Create a hybrid sorting algorithm that switches between Insertion Sort and Quick Sort based on input size. Determine the optimal threshold where switching occurs and justify your choice through performance testing.

Why Hybrid?

- Insertion Sort has low overhead and is efficient for small datasets (typically ≤ 10 elements)

- Quick Sort has better asymptotic complexity `O(n log n)` for large datasets
- A hybrid approach can achieve better overall performance by choosing the right algorithm for each input size

Starter Code Template

```
import java.util.*;

public class HybridSortingAlgorithm {

    // Hybrid sorting algorithm that switches between Insertion Sort and Quick
Sort
    public static void hybridSort(int[] arr, int low, int high) {
        // TODO: Implement the hybrid sorting logic
        // If array size is small (threshold), use Insertion Sort
        // If array size is large, use Quick Sort
    }

    // Insertion Sort implementation (used for small arrays)
    private static void insertionSort(int[] arr, int low, int high) {
        // TODO: Implement Insertion Sort
        // This should sort elements from index low to high
    }

    // Quick Sort implementation (used for large arrays)
    public static void quickSort(int[] arr, int low, int high) {
        if (low < high) {
            int pivotIndex = partition(arr, low, high);
            quickSort(arr, low, pivotIndex - 1);
            quickSort(arr, pivotIndex + 1, high);
        }
    }

    private static int partition(int[] arr, int low, int high) {
        int pivot = arr[high];  // Using last element as pivot
        int i = low - 1;

        for (int j = low; j < high; j++) {
            if (arr[j] <= pivot) {
                i++;
                swap(arr, i, j);
```

```
            }
        }
        swap(arr, i + 1, high);
        return i + 1;
    }

    private static void swap(int[] arr, int i, int j) {
        int temp = arr[i];
        arr[i] = arr[j];
        arr[j] = temp;
    }

    public static void main(String[] args) {
        // Test with different array sizes
        int[] smallArray = {5, 2, 8, 1, 9};
        int[] mediumArray = {64, 34, 25, 12, 22, 11, 90, 88, 76, 50, 42};
        int[] largeArray = {64, 34, 25, 12, 22, 11, 90, 88, 76, 50, 42, 33, 21,
10, 5, 1, 3, 7, 9, 2};

        System.out.println("=== Testing Hybrid Sorting ===");
        System.out.println("Small Array: " + Arrays.toString(smallArray));
        hybridSort(smallArray, 0, smallArray.length - 1);
        System.out.println("Sorted: " + Arrays.toString(smallArray));

        System.out.println("\nMedium Array: " + Arrays.toString(mediumArray));
        hybridSort(mediumArray, 0, mediumArray.length - 1);
        System.out.println("Sorted: " + Arrays.toString(mediumArray));

        System.out.println("\nLarge Array: " + Arrays.toString(largeArray));
        hybridSort(largeArray, 0, largeArray.length - 1);
        System.out.println("Sorted: " + Arrays.toString(largeArray));

        // TODO: Add performance testing to determine optimal threshold
    }
}
```

Assumptions and Constraints

- Input is an array of integers with sizes ranging from 1 to 1000 elements
- Algorithm must automatically switch between Insertion Sort (for small arrays) and Quick Sort (for large arrays)

- Must determine optimal threshold value through performance testing
- Implementation Requirements:
    - Insertion Sort must be implemented for small subarrays (size ≤ threshold)
    - Quick Sort must be implemented for large subarrays (size > threshold)
- Use `System.nanoTime()` to measure execution time
- Test with arrays of different sizes to validate threshold selection
- Display performance comparison and optimal threshold determination

Test Case 1

- **Input**:
    - **Small array**: `[5, 2, 8, 1, 9]` (size = 5)
    - **Medium array**: `[64, 34, 25, 12, 22, 11, 90, 88, 76, 50, 42]` (size = 11)
    - **Large array**: `[64, 34, 25, 12, 22, 11, 90, 88, 76, 50, 42, 33, 21, 10, 5, 1, 3, 7, 9, 2]` (size = 20)
- **Output**:
    - Hybrid algorithm should use Insertion Sort for small arrays (size ≤ threshold)
    - Hybrid algorithm should use Quick Sort for large arrays (size > threshold)
    - Demonstrate that the algorithm works correctly for different input sizes

Test Case 2

- **Input**:
    - Generate multiple arrays of varying sizes (5, 10, 15, 20, 25, 30, 50, 100 elements)
    - Each array contains random integers between 1-1000
    - Test different threshold values (1, 5, 10, 15, 20, 25, 30)
- **Output**:
    - Performance comparison for different threshold values
    - Identification of optimal threshold that minimizes total execution time
    - Analysis showing when hybrid approach outperforms using only one algorithm

Exercise 6: Find the K-th largest element in an array

Given an integer array `nums` and an integer `k`, return the `k`-th largest element in the array. Note that it is the `k`-th largest element in the sorted order, not the `k`-th distinct element.

Starter Code Template

```
import java.util.*;

public class KthLargestElement {

    // Method 1: Using Sorting (Simple but not optimal)
    public static int findKthLargestSorting(int[] nums, int k) {
        // TODO: Implement sorting approach
        // Time: O(n log n), Space: O(1)
        return 0;
    }

    // Method 2: Using Min-Heap (Optimal for this problem)
    public static int findKthLargestHeap(int[] nums, int k) {
        // TODO: Implement heap approach
        // Time: O(n log k), Space: O(k)
        return 0;
    }

    // Method 3: Using QuickSelect (Most Optimal)
    public static int findKthLargestQuickSelect(int[] nums, int k) {
        // TODO: Implement QuickSelect algorithm
        // Time: O(n) average, O(n²) worst case, Space: O(1)
        return 0;
    }

    public static void main(String[] args) {
        // Test cases
        int[] nums1 = {3, 2, 1, 5, 6, 4};
        int k1 = 2;
        System.out.println("Test 1:");
        System.out.println("Array: " + Arrays.toString(nums1));
        System.out.println("k = " + k1);
        System.out.println("Sorting approach: " + findKthLargestSorting(nums1,
k1));
        System.out.println("Heap approach: " + findKthLargestHeap(nums1, k1));
        System.out.println("QuickSelect approach: " +
findKthLargestQuickSelect(nums1, k1));

        int[] nums2 = {3, 2, 3, 1, 2, 4, 5, 5, 6};
```

```
        int k2 = 4;
        System.out.println("\nTest 2:");
        System.out.println("Array: " + Arrays.toString(nums2));
        System.out.println("k = " + k2);
        System.out.println("Sorting approach: " + findKthLargestSorting(nums2,
k2));
        System.out.println("Heap approach: " + findKthLargestHeap(nums2, k2));
        System.out.println("QuickSelect approach: " +
findKthLargestQuickSelect(nums2, k2));
    }
}
```

Assumptions and Constraints

- $1 \leq$ `k` $\leq$ `nums.length` $\leq 10^5$
- $-10^4 \leq$ `nums[i]` $\leq 10^4$

Test Case 1

- **Input**: nums = `[3,2,1,5,6,4], k = 2`
- **Output**: 5
- **Explanation**: The sorted array is [1,2,3,4,5,6], so the 2nd largest element is 5.

Test Case 2

- **Input**: nums = `[3,2,3,1,2,4,5,5,6], k = 4`
- **Output**: 4
- **Explanation**: The sorted array is [1,2,2,3,3,4,5,5,6], so the 4th largest element is 4.

Exercise 7: Top K frequent elements

Given an integer array `nums` and an integer `k`, return the `k` most frequent elements. The answer can be in any order.

Starter Code Template

```
import java.util.*;

public class TopKFrequentElements {

    // Method 1: Using HashMap + Sorting
    public static List<Integer> topKFrequentSorting(int[] nums, int k) {
        // TODO: Implement approach using HashMap + sorting
```

```
        // Time: O(n log n), Space: O(n)
        return new ArrayList<>();
    }

    // Method 2: Using HashMap + Min-Heap (Optimal)
    public static List<Integer> topKFrequentHeap(int[] nums, int k) {
        // TODO: Implement approach using HashMap + Min-Heap
        // Time: O(n log k), Space: O(n)
        return new ArrayList<>();
    }

    // Method 3: Using Bucket Sort (Most Optimal)
    public static List<Integer> topKFrequentBucketSort(int[] nums, int k) {
        // TODO: Implement approach using Bucket Sort
        // Time: O(n), Space: O(n)
        return new ArrayList<>();
    }

    public static void main(String[] args) {
        // Test cases
        int[] nums1 = {1, 1, 1, 2, 2, 3};
        int k1 = 2;
        System.out.println("Test 1:");
        System.out.println("Array: " + Arrays.toString(nums1));
        System.out.println("k = " + k1);
        System.out.println("Sorting approach: " + topKFrequentSorting(nums1, k1));
        System.out.println("Heap approach: " + topKFrequentHeap(nums1, k1));
        System.out.println("Bucket Sort approach: " +
topKFrequentBucketSort(nums1, k1));

        int[] nums2 = {1};
        int k2 = 1;
        System.out.println("\nTest 2:");
        System.out.println("Array: " + Arrays.toString(nums2));
        System.out.println("k = " + k2);
        System.out.println("Sorting approach: " + topKFrequentSorting(nums2, k2));
        System.out.println("Heap approach: " + topKFrequentHeap(nums2, k2));
        System.out.println("Bucket Sort approach: " +
topKFrequentBucketSort(nums2, k2));
    }
}
```

Assumptions and Constraints

- $1 \le$ `k` $\le$ `nums.length` $\le 10^5$
- $-10^4 \le$ `nums[i]` $\le 10^4$
- `k` is in the range [1, the number of unique elements in the array`]
- The answer is guaranteed to be unique

Test Case 1

- **Input**: `nums = [1,1,1,2,2,3], k = 2`
- **Output**: `[1,2]`

Test Case 2

- **Input**: `nums = [1], k = 1`
- **Output**: `[1]`

Exercise 8: Merge intervals

Given an array of intervals where `intervals[i] = [start`$_i$`, end`$_i$`]`, merge all overlapping intervals and return an array of the non-overlapping intervals that cover all the intervals in the input.

Starter Code Template

```
import java.util.*;

public class MergeIntervals {

    // Method 1: Sort and Merge
    public static int[][] merge(int[][] intervals) {
        // TODO: Implement the merge intervals algorithm
        // Steps:
        // 1. Sort intervals by start time
        // 2. Iterate through sorted intervals and merge overlapping ones
        // 3. Return merged intervals
        return new int[0][0]; // Placeholder - replace with actual implementation
    }

    // Helper method to print intervals
    private static void printIntervals(int[][] intervals) {
        System.out.print("[");
        for (int i = 0; i < intervals.length; i++) {
```

```
            System.out.print("[" + intervals[i][0] + "," + intervals[i][1] + "]");
            if (i < intervals.length - 1) System.out.print(",");
        }
        System.out.println("]");
    }

    public static void main(String[] args) {
        // Test cases
        int[][] intervals1 = {{1,3},{2,6},{8,10},{9,12}};
        System.out.println("Test 1:");
        System.out.print("Input: ");
        printIntervals(intervals1);
        int[][] result1 = merge(intervals1);
        System.out.print("Output: ");
        printIntervals(result1);

        System.out.println();

        int[][] intervals2 = {{1,4},{4,5}};
        System.out.println("Test 2:");
        System.out.print("Input: ");
        printIntervals(intervals2);
        int[][] result2 = merge(intervals2);
        System.out.print("Output: ");
        printIntervals(result2);*
```

Assumptions and Constraints

- $1 \leq$ `intervals.length` $\leq 10^4$
- `intervals[i].length` $== 2$
- $0 \leq$ `start_i` $\leq$ `end_i` $\leq 10^4$

Test Case 1

- **Input**: `intervals` = `[[1,3],[2,6],[8,10],[9,12]]`
- **Output**: `[[1,6],[8,12]]`
- **Explanation**: Since intervals [1,3] and [2,6] overlap, merge them into [1,6].

Test Case 2

- **Input**: `intervals` = `[[1,4],[4,5]]`

- **Output**: `[[1,5]]`
- **Explanation**: Intervals [1,4] and [4,5] are considered overlapping.

11

Concurrency

Building correct, performant systems with brute-force approaches and ad-hoc execution strategies is unsustainable. Concurrency bugs are invisible until they compound under production load. Race conditions surface only at scale. Naive, single-threaded systems pass all tests on local machines and collapse silently when real traffic arrives. Advanced data structures and algorithms exist to raise the abstraction level: replacing naive implementations with proven patterns that encode efficient computation and thread safety directly into the structure of your code.

This chapter provides practical steps for applying the right concurrent data structures and algorithms to mitigate these system challenges. We will delve into the common pitfalls and complexities associated with parallel computing, including:

- **Protecting Shared State**: Preventing data corruption from simultaneous modifications
- **Coordinating Execution**: Sequencing independent threads without blocking progress
- **Eliminating Race Conditions**: Replacing vulnerable check-then-act sequences with atomic operations
- **Managing Memory Visibility**: Ensuring multi-core processors see memory updates instantly
- **Maximizing Resource Utilization**: Scaling throughput without introducing deadlock or starvation

Through a combination of foundations and practical examples, this chapter aims to equip readers with the necessary knowledge and skills to design data structures and algorithms that not only meet logical correctness criteria but also demonstrate exceptional performance under concurrent load.

Introduction to threads and concurrent execution

A thread is a separate flow of execution within a program that can run concurrently with other threads. Each thread has its own program counter, stack, and local variables, allowing multiple tasks to be executed simultaneously without interfering with each other's operations. This independence enables efficient utilization of multi-core processors and improves overall system throughput.

The following example demonstrates that each thread maintains its own execution flow while sharing the same program structure, illustrating how threads can run concurrently without interfering with each other's operations, even when accessing shared variables:

```
// Simple thread demonstration showing independent execution
public class SimpleThreadDemo {
    private static int sharedCounter = 0;

    public static void main(String[] args) throws InterruptedException {
        Thread thread1 = new Thread(() -> {
            for (int i = 0; i < 3; i++) {
                System.out.println("Thread-1: " + i);
                sharedCounter++;
            }
        });
        Thread thread2 = new Thread(() -> {
            for (int i = 0; i < 3; i++) {
                System.out.println("Thread-2: " + i);
                sharedCounter++;
            }
        });
        thread1.start();
        thread2.start();
        thread1.join();
        thread2.join();

        System.out.println("Final counter: " + sharedCounter);
    }
}
```

Creating a Thread object in Java involves instantiating the Thread class with a Runnable task, which puts the thread in an initial state.

```
// Creation: Thread objects created but not running
Thread thread1 = new Thread(() -> { /* task 1 */ });
Thread thread2 = new Thread(() -> { /* task 2 */ });
```

The thread holds a reference to the code that will execute when the start() method is called, but the thread doesn't begin running until you explicitly invoke start(); that is:

```
// Start: Threads begin execution (concurrent)
thread1.start();
thread2.start();
```

The start() method creates a new thread of execution and begins concurrent processing, which is fundamentally different from calling run() directly. When run() is called directly, the code executes in the current thread rather than creating a new one, making start() essential for true concurrent execution. The thread's run() method executes concurrently with other threads, and the timing of execution depends on the thread scheduler and system resources.

The join() method makes the calling thread (typically the main thread) block and wait until the target thread completes its execution, ensuring proper sequencing of operations. This synchronization mechanism is crucial for coordinating thread execution and guaranteeing that dependent operations occur in the correct order.

```
// Join: Main thread waits for completion
thread1.join();
thread2.join();
```

Thread interruption is a cooperative mechanism that allows one thread to signal another thread to stop what it's doing, typically used for graceful shutdown of long-running operations. When a thread is interrupted, it should handle the InterruptedException appropriately and restore the interrupt status to maintain proper thread lifecycle management. While not shown in the above example, interruption can be handled as follows:

```
Thread interruptibleThread = new Thread(() -> {
    try {
        while (!Thread.currentThread().isInterrupted()) {
            // Do work
            Thread.sleep(1000); // This throws InterruptedException
```

```
        }
    } catch (InterruptedException e) {
        System.out.println("Thread interrupted!");
        Thread.currentThread().interrupt(); // Restore interrupt status
    }
});

interruptibleThread.start();
interruptibleThread.interrupt(); // Interrupt the thread
```

The SimpleThreadDemo shows a shared resource counter: `sharedCounter`. The `sharedCounter++` operation involves multiple steps that can be interleaved between threads, causing the final value to be incorrect despite appearing to work correctly. This is the classic race condition where multiple threads access and modify a shared resource without proper synchronization, leading to unpredictable results. We will map out these concurrency concepts in the ensuing sections.

A complete demo showing independent local variables, their stack frames, and concurrent executions is available in the `ThreadIsolationDemo.java` file in the `Chapter11` folder on GitHub. To unlock the GitHub repo link, refer to the instructions in the *Download the example code files* section of the *Preface*.

Shared state

In concurrent programming, threads operate independently with separate execution flows, stacks, and local variables, enabling efficient multi-core utilization and improved system throughput. However, when threads access shared variables concurrently, as demonstrated in the counter increment example, they can interfere with each other's operations, creating race conditions and synchronization challenges that require careful management of shared state through atomic operations and synchronization mechanisms to ensure data integrity and program correctness. Shared state in concurrent programming refers to data structures or variables that are accessed by multiple threads simultaneously. Managing shared state effectively is key to ensuring thread safety and preventing synchronization issues. When multiple threads share mutable state, it can lead to unpredictable behavior and synchronization problems.

A race condition occurs when a program's output depends on the unpredictable order in which multiple threads access and modify shared data. In the context of write-write races, it specifically means that multiple threads attempt to write to the same shared memory location concurrently, and the result depends on which thread's write operation "wins" the race, rather than being a predictable, correct result.

The issue arises because what appears to be a single logical operation (like updating a shared value) is actually composed of three non-atomic steps: **Read**, **Modify**, and **Write**. Consider the classic, unsynchronized R/W operations:

- Thread A reads the shared balance (e.g., balance = $100)
- Thread B reads the shared balance (also sees balance = $100)
- Thread A withdraws $30, modifies balance, and writes $70 into balance
- Thread B withdraws $30, modifies balance, and writes $70 into balance

In this scenario (*Figure 11.1*), two independent threads execute at different times, but because the operations interleaved, the final balance is $70 instead of the expected $40. The intended operation was lost because Thread B overwrote the correct result from Thread A without knowing the intermediate write had occurred.

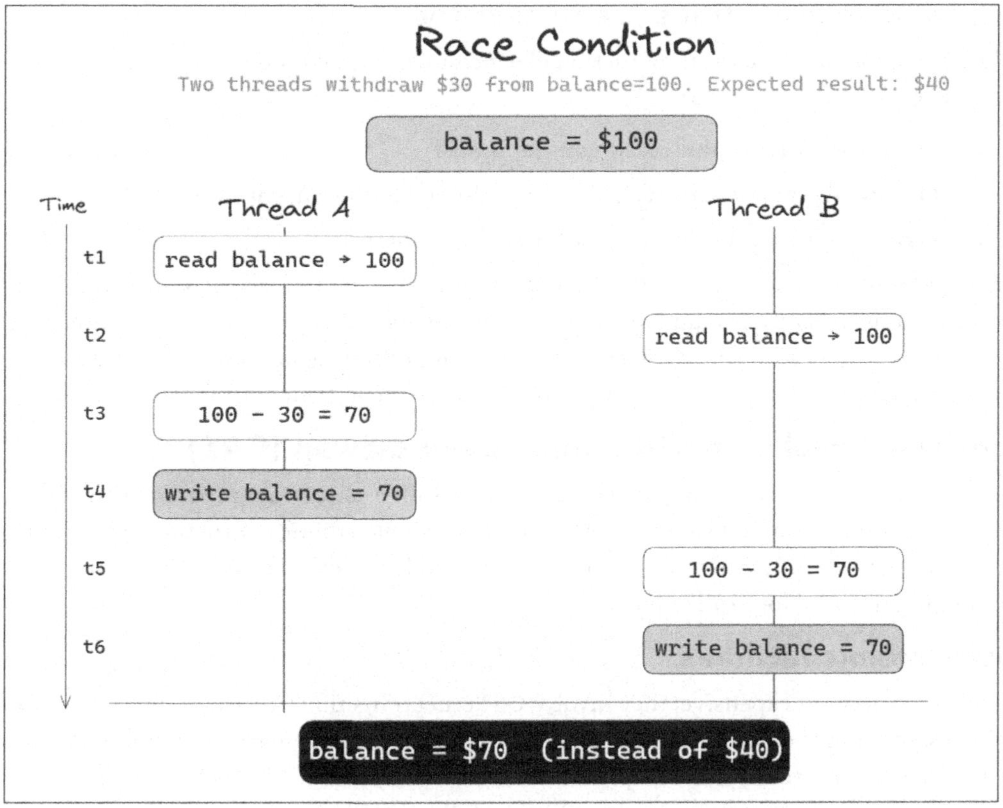

Figure 11.1: Race condition in concurrent bank withdrawals

The demo is in the `RaceConditionDemo.java` file in the `Chapter11` file on GitHub. To unlock the GitHub repo link, refer to the instructions in the *Download the example code files* section of the *Preface*. This demo presents a write-write race condition in a multi-threaded Java environment and shows how to fix it using `java.util.concurrent.atomic.AtomicInteger`. A race condition occurs when the final result depends on the unpredictable timing of thread execution. A simple increment (read-modify-write) is not atomic and can lead to lost updates when executed concurrently. We will look at this single, indivisible hardware instruction in the next section.

Atomic operations and hardware-level guarantees

In concurrent programming, atomic operations are crucial for ensuring thread safety and preventing synchronization issues. Java provides a set of atomic classes through the `java.util.concurrent.atomic` package, which enables lock-free concurrent programming by offering hardware-level atomic operations.

Why atomic operations are necessary

When a program performs a simple action like incrementing a counter, it is not atomic. Instead, it involves three steps:

- **Read**: The current value of the counter is read
- **Modify**: The new value is calculated by adding 1 to the current value
- **Write**: The new value is written back to the counter

If a thread switch occurs between these steps, another thread can read the stale value, leading to a race condition and a lost update. Atomic variables solve this problem by guaranteeing that the entire Read-Modify-Write cycle executes as one indivisible operation at the CPU level. Atomic operations are indivisible operations that complete in their entirety or not at all.

Hardware-level atomicity: Compare-and-Swap (CAS)

The shift from traditional locking mechanisms to lock-free concurrent programming is enabled by Compare-And-Swap (CAS). It is implemented as a single atomic instruction in modern CPUs and succeeds only when the expected value exactly matches the current value, eliminating the need for explicit locks.

Java's atomic facilities

Locks are correct but expensive; they involve OS kernel transitions, thread parking, and context switches. For simple operations (increment a counter, swap a reference), hardware provides atomic instructions (CAS) that complete in a single CPU cycle without locking. The `java.util.concurrent.atomic` package has the following facilities:

- `AtomicInteger`, `AtomicLong`: Enables atomic integer/long operations such as increment, request count, decrement, compare-and-set, and get-and-set
- AtomicReference: Offers equivalent functionality for object references

`AtomicLong.incrementAndGet()` is significantly faster than synchronized for moderately contended counters. `AtomicReference.set()` provides immediate visibility to all threads without explicit synchronization. The `AtomicExamples` demo, which is placed in the `AtomicExamples.java` file in the `Chapter11` folder on GitHub (to unlock the GitHub repo link, refer to the instructions in the *Download the example code files* section of the *Preface*), contrasts the non-atomic `unsafeCount` increment, which is susceptible to race conditions, against the thread-safe `safeCount` using `AtomicInteger.incrementAndGet()`.

Hardware-level guarantee

The power of CAS lies in its hardware-level implementation where modern processors guarantee that the compare-and-swap operation executes atomically. This means:

- **Atomic Operation**: The entire compare-and-swap sequence cannot be interrupted
- **Memory Consistency**: Hardware ensures proper memory ordering
- **No Blocking**: Threads spin or retry rather than block
- **Scalability**: High performance under concurrent access

This approach enables lock-free data structures like `ConcurrentHashMap`, `AtomicReference`, and other high-performance concurrent collections that outperform traditional synchronized alternatives in highly concurrent scenarios.

The CAS demo, placed in the `CasDemo.java` file in the `Chapter11` folder on GitHub (to unlock the GitHub repo link, refer to the instructions in the *Download the example code files* section of the *Preface*) showcases `AtomicInteger`'s `compareAndSet()` method and highlights the key advantage of CAS: lock-free, non-blocking thread safety through hardware guarantees. *Figure 11.2* shows the atomic operations in CAS.

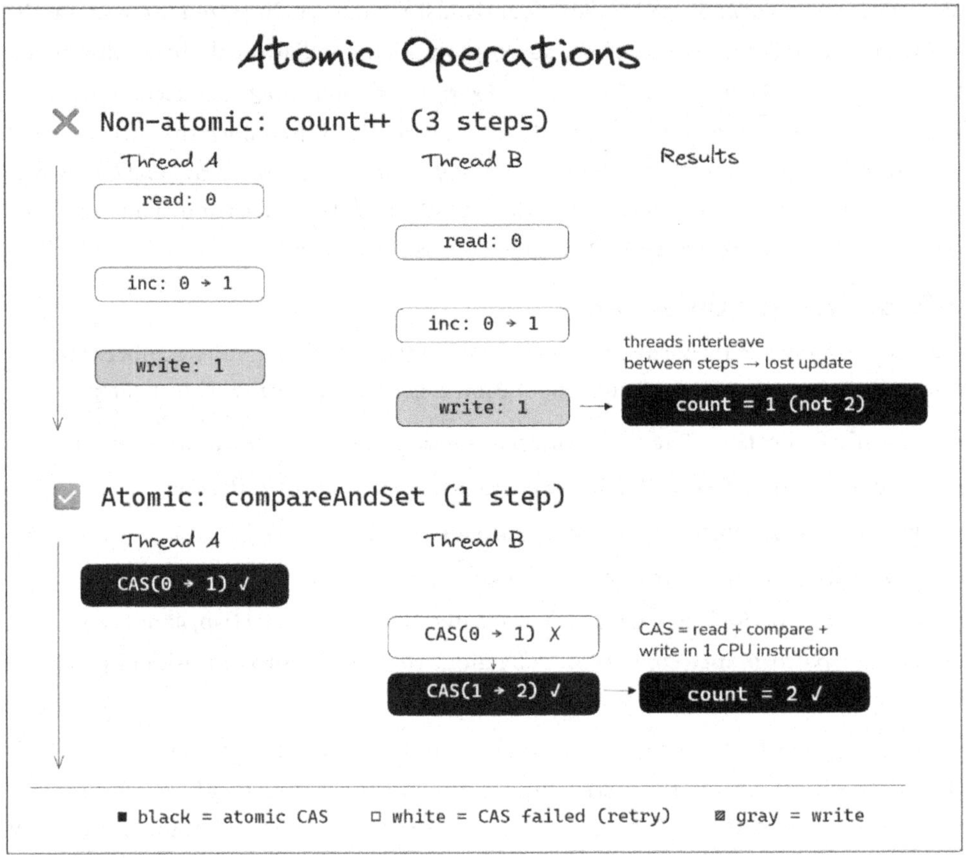

Figure 11.2: Atomic operations in CAS

Ensuring thread safety often dictates the implementation of explicit locking mechanisms. The subsequent section elucidates the foundational principles of mutual exclusion, exploring locks and semaphores as primary instruments for resource synchronization.

Mutual exclusion

Mutual Exclusion (Mutex) is a fundamental concept in concurrent programming that ensures only one thread can access a critical section of code or shared resource at any given time. Mutexes synchronize multi-threaded environments, preventing race conditions and guaranteeing data integrity.

The primary synchronization mechanisms in Java include the `synchronized` keyword, `ReentrantLock`, and `Condition` objects for advanced thread coordination.

Synchronization

The synchronized keyword provides automatic mutual exclusion by using Java's built-in monitor locks. When a thread enters a synchronized block or method, it acquires the lock associated with the object, and other threads attempting to enter any synchronized method or block of the same object must wait until the lock is released:

```
public class SynchronizedExample {
    private int counter = 0;

    // Synchronized method - ensures only one thread can execute at a time
    public synchronized void increment() {
        counter++; // This block is atomic due to synchronization
    }

    // Synchronized block - locks on specific object
    public void safeIncrement() {
        synchronized(this) { // Lock acquired on current object
            counter++; // Critical section
        } // Lock automatically released when block exits
    }

    // Synchronized block with different lock object
    private final Object lock = new Object();
    public void anotherMethod() {
        synchronized(lock) { // Lock acquired on specific object
            // Critical section
            counter++;
        } // Lock released automatically
    }
}
```

While the synchronized block is excellent for ensuring thread safety, improper nested locking can introduce a critical failure point known as deadlock.

Deadlock

Deadlock occurs when two or more threads are blocked indefinitely, each waiting for the other to release a resource that it needs to proceed. It is not a system failure; it is a logical programming error where the threads enter a permanent standstill. The classic **Dining Philosophers Problem** perfectly illustrates this: if every philosopher (thread) acquires their left fork (Resource A) and then stops, waiting indefinitely for their right fork (Resource B), all participants cease execution because they are each waiting for a resource that remains perpetually unavailable. *Figure 11.3* shows when two contending threads enter into a deadlock situation:

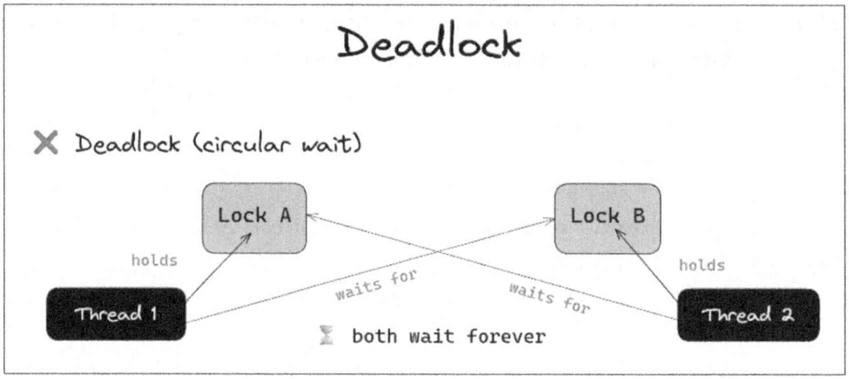

Figure 11.3: Deadlock between Thread 1 and 2

Mastering synchronization is not merely about using the `synchronized` keyword; it is about recognizing the inherent constraints of shared resources. The `synchronized` keyword guarantees mutual exclusion by acquiring a monitor lock, locking the method or object instance as a whole. While reliable, this approach is coarse-grained because it locks all related operations together. To gain the fine-grained control necessary for high-performance systems, we must move beyond this blanket protection. We require a mechanism that allows us to manage locks individually. For this, we will transition to the `java.util.concurrent.locks.Lock` interface, utilizing the `ReentrantLock` class to achieve targeted, explicit locking.

Lock interface

Locking via `ReentrantLock` is a more complex mechanism than the `synchronized` approach. Locking provides features like timed waits, non-blocking attempts, and the ability to interrupt waiting threads, allowing a thread to acquire the same lock multiple times (reentrant behavior). The below code shows the use of the Lock interface with `ReentrantLock` for mutex:

```
import java.util.concurrent.locks.ReentrantLock;
import java.util.concurrent.locks.Lock;
import java.util.concurrent.TimeUnit;

public class LockExample {
    private final Lock lock = new ReentrantLock(); // ReentrantLock
    private int counter = 0;
```

```java
// Example 1: Basic Lock usage with try-finally (recommended pattern)
public void basicLockUsage() {
    lock.lock(); // Acquire the lock
    try {
        counter++; // Critical section
    } finally {
        lock.unlock(); // Always release lock in finally block
    }
}

// Example 2: Timed wait - attempt to acquire lock with timeout
public boolean tryLockWithTimeout() {
    try {
        // Attempt to acquire lock within 1 second
        if (lock.tryLock(1, TimeUnit.SECONDS)) {
            try {
                counter++;
                return true;
            } finally {
                lock.unlock(); // Release lock
            }
        }
    } catch (InterruptedException e) {
        Thread.currentThread().interrupt(); // Restore status
    }
    return false; // Lock acquisition failed or interrupted
}

// Example 3: Non-blocking attempt - returns immediately
public boolean tryNonBlockingLock() {
    if (lock.tryLock()) { // Non-blocking attempt
        try {
            counter++;
            return true;
        } finally {
            lock.unlock();
        }
    }
    return false; // Lock not available immediately
}
```

```
    // Example 4: Reentrant - same thread acquiring lock many times
    public void reentrantExample() {
        lock.lock(); // First acquisition
        try {
            // Same thread can acquire the lock again (reentrant)
            lock.lock(); // Second acquisition - allowed!
            try {
                counter++;
            } finally {
                lock.unlock(); // Must match number of acquisitions
            }
        } finally {
            lock.unlock(); // Release first acquisition
        }
    }
}
```

Figure 11.4 shows the practical use of the synchronized vs reentrant locking mechanisms: synchronized is implicit, auto-release, whereas reentrant lock requires explicit lock/unlock and timed release.

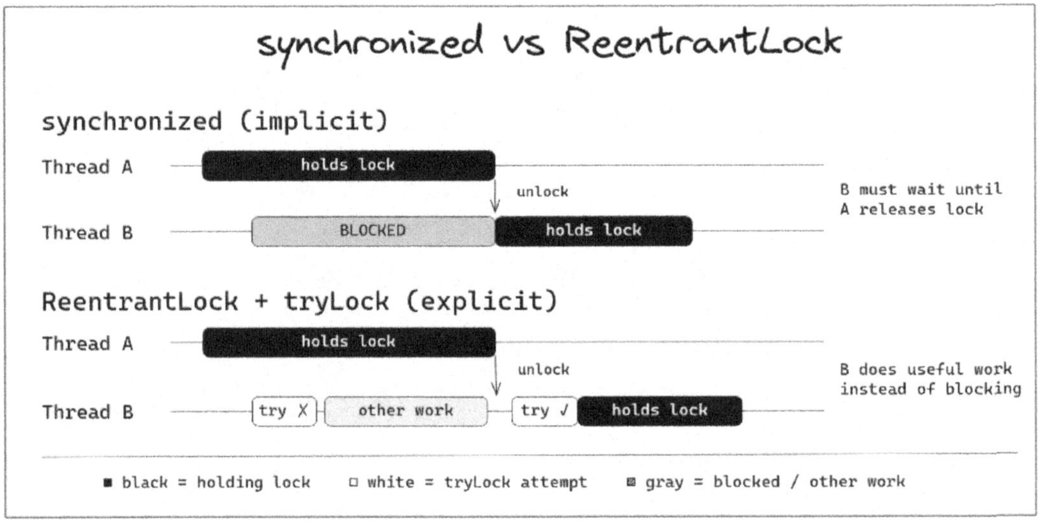

Figure 11.4: Synchronized vs Reentrant Lock

Condition

The `Condition` interface works in conjunction with `Lock` objects to enable threads to wait for specific conditions to become `true`, offering more flexible signaling mechanisms than traditional synchronized monitors. `Condition` objects are created using `lock.newCondition()` and must be used with explicit `Lock` objects for proper synchronization. Threads can wait for conditions using `condition.await()` and notify waiting threads with `condition.signalAll()` when the condition is met, allowing for complex coordination patterns beyond simple object monitor waiting. The following code shows a simple orchestration of the described mechanism:

```
import java.util.concurrent.locks.Condition;
import java.util.concurrent.locks.Lock;
import java.util.concurrent.locks.ReentrantLock;

public class ConditionExample {
    private final Lock lock = new ReentrantLock();
    private final Condition condition = lock.newCondition();
    private boolean isReady = false;

    // Thread waiting for condition
    public void waitForReady() throws InterruptedException {
        lock.lock(); // Acquire lock
        try {
            while (!isReady) {
                condition.await(); // Wait until condition is true
            }
            // Continue when condition is met
        } finally {
            lock.unlock(); // Release lock
        }
    }

    // Thread signaling condition
    public void setReady() {
        lock.lock(); // Acquire lock
        try {
            isReady = true;
            condition.signalAll(); // Notify all waiting threads
        } finally {
```

```
            lock.unlock(); // Release lock
        }
    }
}
```

This Java demo, placed in the `MutualExclusionDemo.java` file in the `Chapter11` folder on GitHub (To unlock the GitHub repo link, refer to the instructions in the *Download the example code files* section of the *Preface*), provides a practical comparison of mutual exclusion mechanisms with three key approaches to thread synchronization: the traditional `synchronized` keyword for automatic lock management, the Lock interface with `ReentrantLock` for explicit control and advanced features like timed waits, and `Condition` objects for sophisticated thread coordination.

Semaphore

A semaphore is a signaling mechanism using a counter; it allows multiple threads to access a limited number of resources and does not have strict ownership. Here's a simple example of using a `java.util.concurrent.Semaphore`:

```
public class SemaphoreExample {
    public static void main(String[] args) throws InterruptedException {
        Semaphore semaphore = new Semaphore(2);

        for (int i = 0; i < 5; i++) {
            Thread thread = new Thread(() -> {
                try {
                    System.out.println("Thread " +
                            Thread.currentThread().getName() +
                            " is waiting for access...");
                    semaphore.acquire();
                    System.out.println("Thread " +
                            Thread.currentThread().getName() +
                            " has accessed the shared resource.");

                    // Simulate some work...
                    try {
                        Thread.sleep(1000);
                    } catch (InterruptedException e) {
                        // Properly handle interruption
                        Thread.currentThread().interrupt(); // Restore interrupt
status
```

```
                    System.out.println("Thread interrupted during work");
                    return; // Exit thread gracefully
                }
            } finally {
                semaphore.release();
            }
        });
        thread.start();
    }

    Thread.sleep(5000);
  }
}
```

In this example, we create a `Semaphore` with 2 permits. This means that only 2 threads can access the shared resource at any given time. The remaining 3 threads will have to wait until one of the currently accessing threads releases its permit. A mutex, on the other hand, is a binary locking mechanism with strict ownership; only the thread that locks it can unlock it to ensure exclusive access. *Figure 11.5* shows the functional difference between mutex and semaphore.

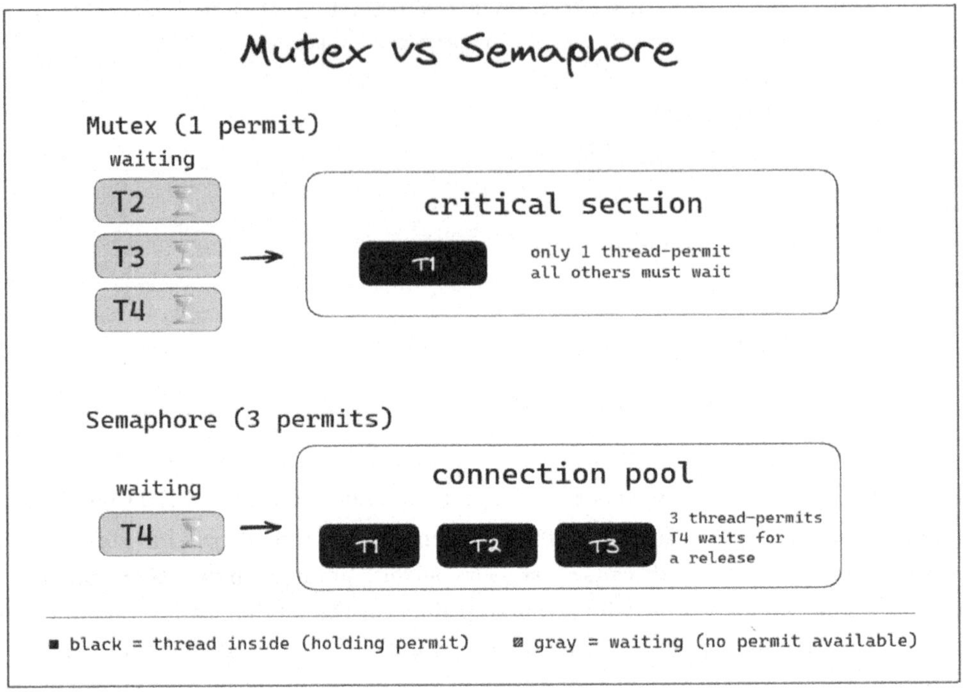

Figure 11.5: Mutex vs semaphore

Lock-free data structures and memory models

This chapter focuses on foundational concurrency concepts and modern lock-free data structures using atomic CAS operations, providing essential coverage of how multiple threads interact with shared memory and nodes. The rest of this material skips advanced topics like hazard pointers, memory barriers, and non-blocking memory reclamation. These specialized areas go beyond the scope of foundational concurrency and data structures. Next, we will look at the challenges of managing memory when multiple threads access nodes.

Memory visibility

Memory visibility refers to the guarantee that changes made by one thread are visible to other threads in a timely manner. Without proper memory visibility, threads may operate on cached copies of variables rather than the most recent values, leading to inconsistent program behavior.

The `volatile` keyword in Java provides memory visibility guarantees by ensuring that reads and writes to volatile variables are always performed directly from main memory, bypassing thread-local caches. This prevents the compiler and CPU from reordering operations around volatile accesses.

```
public class VolatileExample {
    // Volatile ensures visibility across threads
    private volatile boolean flag = false;
    private volatile int counter = 0;

    // Thread 1 - writer
    public void setFlag() {
        counter = 10;          // Write to volatile variable
        flag = true;           // Write to volatile variable
                               // both are visible immediately
    }

    // Thread 2 - reader
    public void checkFlag() {
        if (flag) {            // Read volatile variable
                               // guaranteed to see latest value
            // Visible due to volatile
            System.out.println("Counter value: " + counter);
        }
    }
}
```

Stacks and queues

Lock-free stacks and queues eliminate operating system-level thread blocking by using hardware-supported atomic machine instructions to manage state transitions directly in shared memory. The `AtomicReference` example from the previous section demonstrates this approach, where a stack's top pointer is encapsulated within an `AtomicReference` for safe concurrent access. During push operations, CAS is applied to atomically update the top pointer by linking the new node to the existing head. For pop operations, the current head is read, the new head (next node) is determined, and CAS is used to update the top pointer, ensuring that all operations complete as indivisible units without blocking other threads.

```
import java.util.concurrent.atomic.AtomicReference;

public class LockFreeStack<T> {
    // Node class for stack elements
    private static class Node<T> {
```

```
        final T data;
        volatile Node<T> next;

        Node(T data) {
            this.data = data;
        }
    }

    // Head pointer using AtomicReference
    private final AtomicReference<Node<T>> head = new AtomicReference<>();

    // Push operation - Lock-free using CAS
    public void push(T data) {
        Node<T> newNode = new Node<>(data);
        Node<T> currentHead;

        do {
            currentHead = head.get(); // Read current head
            newNode.next = currentHead; // Link new node to current head
        } while (!head.compareAndSet(currentHead, newNode));
    }

    // Pop operation - Lock-free using CAS
    public T pop() {
        Node<T> currentHead;
        Node<T> newHead;

        do {
            currentHead = head.get(); // Read current head
            if (currentHead == null) {
                return null; // Stack is empty
            }
            newHead = currentHead.next; // New head will be next node
        } while (!head.compareAndSet(currentHead, newHead));

        return currentHead.data; // Return popped data
    }
}
```

Figure 11.6 shows two threads pushing to the same stack without explicit locks, via CAS.

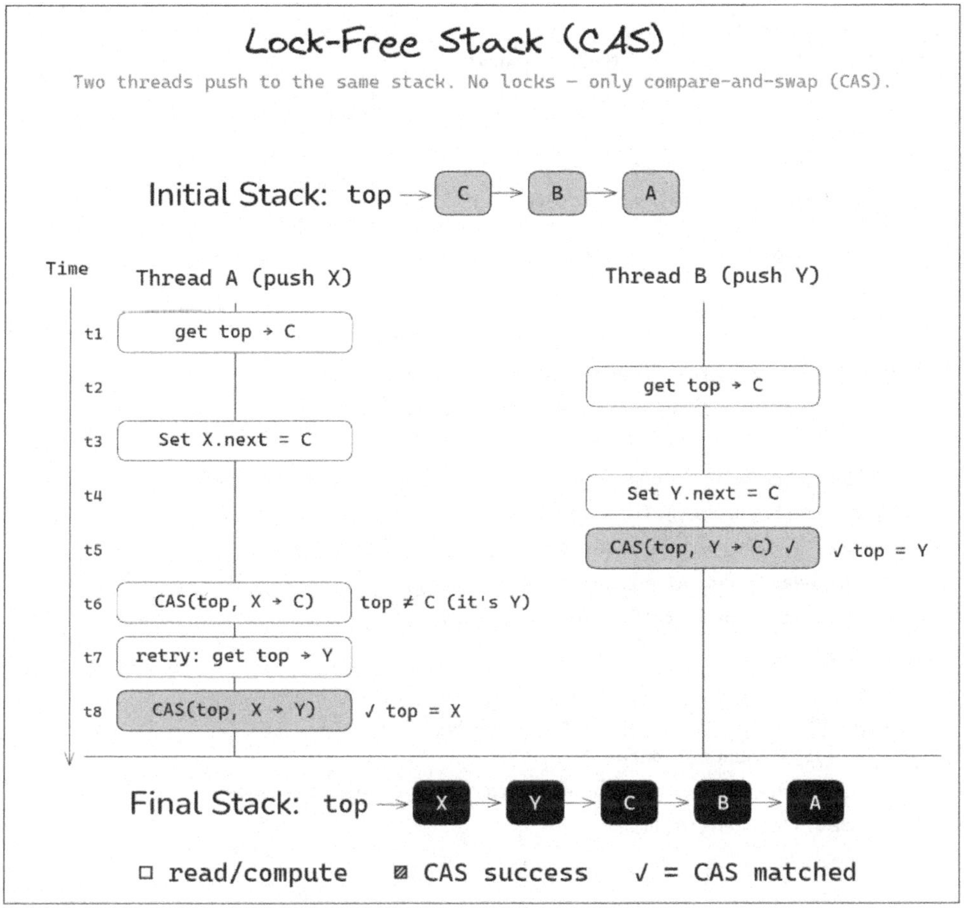

Figure 11.6: Lock-free stack with CAS

The next implementation is about another lock-free structure: queue and its enqueue mechanism. It uses `AtomicReference` to handle thread-safe updates to object references via CAS, while a dedicated `Node` class encapsulates an atomic next pointer for safe concurrent traversal. Operational edge cases are minimized through the use of a sentinel dummy node to streamline queue management. At the execution level, non-blocking CAS operations leverage `compareAndSet()` to guarantee atomic state updates, while a surrounding do-while loop serves as a retry mechanism to handle hardware-level contention during failed CAS attempts.

```
import java.util.concurrent.atomic.AtomicReference;
public class LockFreeQueue<T> {
    // Node class with atomic next pointer
```

```
    private static class Node<T> {
        final T data;
        final AtomicReference<Node<T>> next;

        Node(T data) {
            this.data = data;
            this.next = new AtomicReference<>();
        }
    }

    // Head and tail pointers using AtomicReference
    private final AtomicReference<Node<T>> head;
    private final AtomicReference<Node<T>> tail;

    // Constructor with dummy node
    public LockFreeQueue() {
        Node<T> dummy = new Node<>(null);
        this.head = new AtomicReference<>(dummy);
        this.tail = new AtomicReference<>(dummy);
    }

    // Enqueue operation - lock-free using CAS
    public void enqueue(T data) {
        Node<T> newNode = new Node<>(data);  // Create new node
        Node<T> currentTail;

        do {
            // Read current tail (step 1: Read)
            currentTail = tail.get();
            // Read next node
            Node<T> currentTailNext = currentTail.next.get();

            if (currentTailNext == null) {  // If tail points to last node
                // Try to link new node
                if (currentTail.next.compareAndSet(null, newNode)) {
                    break;  // Success - exit loop
                }
            } else {
                // Advance tail
                tail.compareAndSet(currentTail, currentTailNext);
            }
```

```
        } while (true);
        // Update tail to new node
        tail.compareAndSet(currentTail, newNode);
    }
}
```

We omit the dequeue mechanism here, as it uses a lock-free CAS approach similar to the enqueue method described above.

Arrays and lists

Implementing concurrent access to dynamic collections requires careful consideration of synchronization mechanisms, memory consistency, and performance overhead, as traditional `ArrayList` and arrays are not thread-safe and can lead to `ConcurrentModificationException` or a corrupted state when accessed concurrently.

As we explore the three fundamental approaches to handling thread-safe collections, we'll examine how each strategy addresses these challenges in different ways:

- The coarse-grained locking approach provides simple but performance-limiting synchronization through shared locks.
- The copy-on-write pattern offers lock-free reads at the cost of expensive writes.
- The lock-free data structures like `ConcurrentLinkedDeque` eliminate blocking overhead through atomic operations.

As we see next, each approach represents a different trade-off between safety, performance and complexity.

Option A: Coarse-grained thread safety via synchronized wrappers

```
import java.util.*;

// Synchronized wrapper creates a coarse-grained lock
List<String> syncList = Collections.synchronizedList(new ArrayList<>());

// Every operation grabs the same lock – safe but serialized
syncList.add("a");
syncList.get(0);

// Iteration STILL requires manual synchronization
synchronized (syncList) {
    for (String s : syncList) {
```

```
        System.out.println(s);
    }
}
```

Coarse-grained locking provides a simple implementation that is easy to understand, but it introduces a major performance bottleneck because all operations share a single lock. This shared lock forces serialization across threads, severely limiting the system's scalability. Additionally, it lacks full automation, meaning that operations like collection iteration still require manual synchronization to ensure thread safety.

Option B: Trade-offs of copy-on-write arrays

Iterating a list while another thread modifies it throws `ConcurrentModificationException`, or worse, produces garbage silently. `CopyOnWriteArrayList` solves this by creating a fresh copy of the underlying array on every write. Reads and iterations always see a consistent snapshot without locking. The trade-off is obvious: writes are `O(n)` because they copy the entire array. This is acceptable only when writes are rare and reads are frequent: exactly the pattern for event listener registries, subscriber lists, and configuration lists that change only on deployment.

```
import java.util.concurrent.CopyOnWriteArrayList;

// Every write copies the entire internal array → O(n) per write
// Reads never block and never throw ConcurrentModificationException
CopyOnWriteArrayList<String> cowList = new CopyOnWriteArrayList<>();

cowList.add("a");        // copies entire array
cowList.add("b");        // copies again

// Reads are lock-free – iterate safely without synchronization
for (String s : cowList) {
    System.out.println(s);  // reads a snapshot, never blocks
}
```

In concurrent Java development, safety, read speed, and write complexity represent a fundamental architectural trade-off. The basic `ArrayList` is unsafe for multi-threaded use. While explicit locking mechanisms enforce safety by serializing all operations, the `CopyOnWriteArrayList` resolves the read-write contention by incurring an `O(n)` write cost due to full copying. *Figure 11.7* maps the trade-offs required in multi-threaded programming. When concurrent read speed is paramount (e.g., monitoring), `CopyOnWriteArrayList` is ideal. For scenarios requiring guaranteed data integrity at the cost of performance, explicit locking mechanisms must be employed. The basic `ArrayList` should not be used in a multithreaded environment without explicit synchronization.

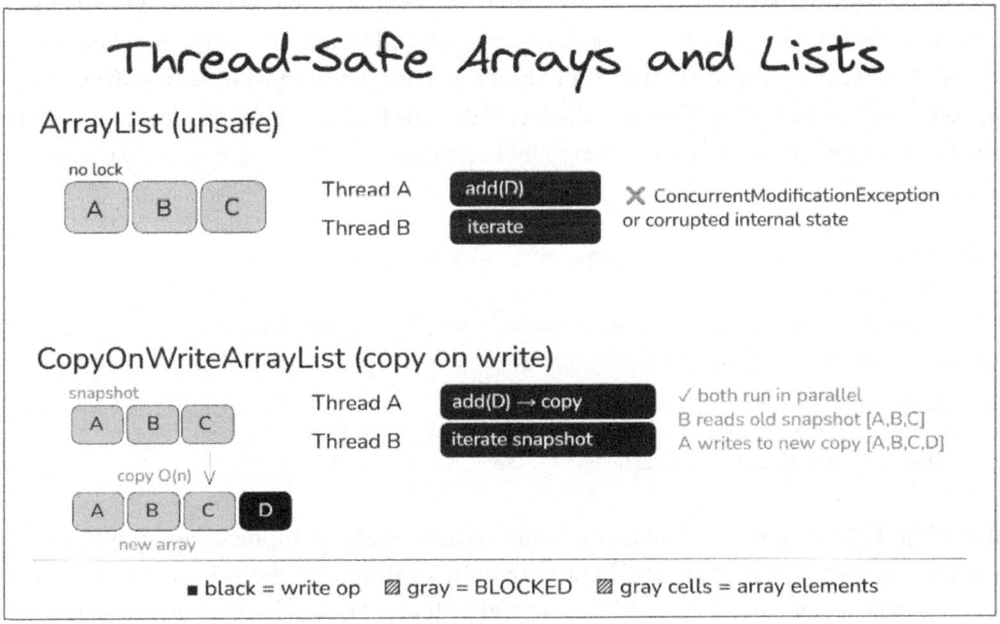

Figure 11.7: ArrayList vs CopyOnWriteArrayList

Option C: Lock-free general-purpose deques

```
import java.util.concurrent.ConcurrentLinkedDeque;
// Lock-free doubly-linked list using CAS
ConcurrentLinkedDeque<String> deque = new ConcurrentLinkedDeque<>();
deque.addFirst("a");
deque.addLast("b");
String head = deque.pollFirst();  // Lock-free removal
```

`ConcurrentLinkedDeque` is an efficient, general-purpose collection that utilizes lock-free CAS operations to achieve high thread safety with minimal blocking. While ideal for standard concurrent queue operations, it lacks a constant-time size method, requiring a full traversal to determine element counts.

Concurrent hash tables

Concurrent hash tables coordinate simultaneous insertions and deletions while executing seamless rehashing operations and resolving key collisions under highly-contended, multi-threaded access. A regular `HashMap` accessed by multiple threads corrupts silently: you get infinite loops, lost entries, or stale reads with no exception thrown. `Collections.synchronizedMap()` fixes correctness but serializes all access through a single lock, destroying throughput. `ConcurrentHashMap` uses fine-grained locking (segment-level in Java 7, node-level CAS in Java 8+) so reads never block and writes only contend when hitting the same bucket. The `computeIfAbsent` method is particularly important as it makes check-then-act atomic, eliminating the race where two threads both see a missing key and both try to initialize it. We see the use of this in shared lookup tables that can be accessed by many threads.

```
// Thread-safe topic mapping. Reads never block, whereas writes
// are fine-grained
ConcurrentHashMap<String, String> dataMap = new ConcurrentHashMap<>();
dataMap.put("data_key", "data_value");

// Atomic compute-if-absent. No double-initialization race
dataMap.computeIfAbsent("example_data", key -> createData(key));
```

A demo highlighting how to avoid race conditions in concurrent applications by replacing unsafe, multi-step "check-then-act" logic with built-in atomic methods is available in the `ConcurrentHashMapExample.java` file in `Chapter11` folder (To unlock the GitHub repo link, refer to the instructions in the *Download the example code files* section of the *Preface*). It shows that while individual map operations are thread-safe, compound actions require these built-in atomic methods to eliminate race conditions and optimize performance via lazy evaluation.

Lock-free striped word counter

This highly concurrent architecture eliminates thread contention by combining lock-free read-modify-write (RMW) operations, lock-striping, and cell-striping patterns into a unified, non-blocking counter. The details of these operations are beyond the scope of this book.

```
// Thread-safe word counter – no locks needed
ConcurrentHashMap<String, LongAdder> wordCounts =
new ConcurrentHashMap<>();

public void countWord(String word) {
    // computeIfAbsent is atomic
    // LongAdder.increment() is lock-free
    // Zero contention between words, min contention on same word
```

```
    wordCounts.computeIfAbsent(word, k -> new LongAdder()).increment();
}
```

This thread-safe word counter achieves high-throughput, lock-free concurrency by pairing `ConcurrentHashMap` with `LongAdder`. The `computeIfAbsent` method atomically initializes missing keys without blocking other threads, eliminating race conditions during map modification. Rather than contending for a single global lock, threads scale independently because `ConcurrentHashMap` isolates updates across separate buckets, while `LongAdder` strips internal counter cells to minimize CPU cache contention on identical keys.

Figure 11.8 shows how a `ConcurrentHashMap` improves performance over a single-lock synchronized map by using multiple bucket-level locks for parallel writes and lock-free volatile reads.

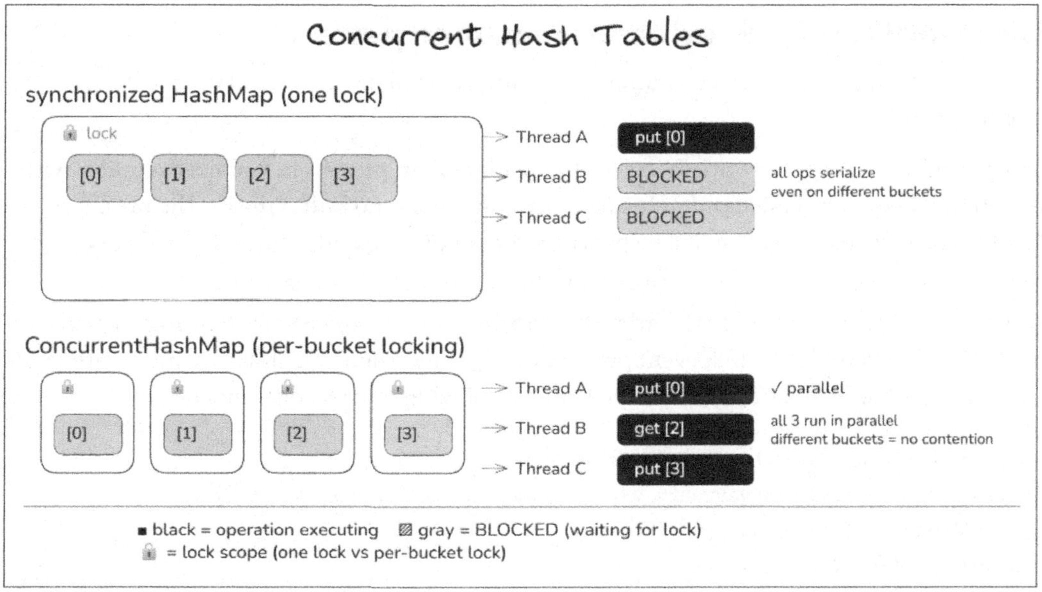

Figure 11.8: Concurrent hash tables

Collision resolution

To handle multiple keys mapping to the same index, `ConcurrentHashMap` employs separate chaining, organizing each bucket into a linked list that automatically converts into a balanced red-black tree once a specific threshold is breached to prevent performance degradation. Multi-threaded safety is guaranteed during these structural updates through a hybrid synchronization model: non-blocking CAS operations insert the initial node atomically, while fine-grained, bucket-level locking secures only the target bin during deeper traversals or tree conversions, allowing concurrent threads to modify adjacent buckets completely unhindered.

Safe and managed concurrency

Effective concurrency management goes beyond basic thread safety to include coordinated workflows, resource optimization, and asynchronous operation handling. We'll explore essential patterns for managing concurrent access, from producer-consumer flows with bounded buffering to thread pool management and asynchronous composition. Key topics include coordinating tasks with `CountDownLatch` and Semaphore, handling per-thread context with `ThreadLocal`, and optimizing read-heavy workloads with `ReadWriteLock`. These patterns provide practical solutions for building safe, reliable concurrent applications that efficiently manage resources while maintaining system stability and performance.

BlockingQueue: Producer-consumer pattern

Concurrency topic: Producer-consumer decoupling, backpressure, thread coordination, bounded buffers.

When producers generate work faster than consumers can process it, you need a buffer with flow control. An unbounded buffer leads to out of memory; no buffer means the producer blocks on every item. `BlockingQueue` provides the middle ground: a bounded buffer where `put()` blocks when full (backpressure on producer) and `take()` blocks when empty (consumer waits for work). This naturally throttles the system without explicit rate limiting. This pattern underlies, for example, a Kafka event processing pipeline where multiple stream events arrive in bursts, get buffered, and are consumed at a sustainable rate by consumers.

```
// Bounded queue; applied backpressure when full
BlockingQueue<DataChangeEvent> queue = new LinkedBlockingQueue<>(1000);
// Producer (stream handler) blocks if queue is full
queue.put(event);
// Consumer blocks if queue is empty
DataChangeEvent event = queue.take();
// Consumer to publish received events downstream at a sustainable rate.
```

Executors: Thread pool management

Concurrency topic: Thread lifecycle management, resource pooling, task scheduling.

Creating threads is expensive. Each thread may consume ~1MB of stack memory and incur OS scheduling overhead. In a system that handles thousands of concurrent requests, creating a new thread per request would exhaust memory quickly. Executors solve this by maintaining a pool of reusable threads. The pool assigns submitted tasks to available threads. This decouples what you want to run from how it gets scheduled, letting you tune concurrency (pool size) independently from business logic. This pattern appears in many concurrent services such as lambda processing of streams and scheduled jobs, to name a few.

```
// Fixed thread pool – bounded concurrency for parallel consumer data fetches
ExecutorService pool = Executors.newFixedThreadPool(5);
Future<ConsumerConfig> future = pool.submit(() ->
getConsumerConfig("customer"));
ConsumerConfig config = future.get(); // blocks until complete
pool.shutdown();
// ScheduledExecutor – periodic tasks without manual timer management
ScheduledExecutorService scheduler = Executors.newScheduledThreadPool(1);
scheduler.scheduleAtFixedRate(() ->
indexDealCounts(), 0, 1, TimeUnit.MINUTES);
```

ThreadLocal: Per-thread context

The safest way to handle mutable state in a concurrent system is to not share it at all. `ThreadLocal` gives each thread its own independent copy of a variable; that is, no synchronization is needed because no other thread can see it. This is perfect for request-scoped context in thread-pool-based servers. Each service request runs on a pool thread, sets context at the start, reads it during processing, and clears it at the end.

The pitfall: in thread pools, threads are reused. If you forget to `clear()` the `ThreadLocal`, the next request on that thread inherits stale state from the previous request: a common source of data leakage bugs in long-running services.

```
// Per-request context: each thread has its own independent copy
private static final ThreadLocal<RequestContext> CONTEXT =

ThreadLocal.withInitial(RequestContext::new);
public static void set(RequestContext ctx) { CONTEXT.set(ctx); }
public static RequestContext get() { return CONTEXT.get(); }

// MUST call in finally block – thread reuse leaks state
public static void clear() { CONTEXT.remove(); }
```

CompletableFuture: Async composition

Blocking on I/O wastes threads. While one thread waits for a database response, it could be doing useful work. `CompletableFuture` represents a value that will be available eventually, and lets you chain transformations and combinations without blocking. This is the Java equivalent of JavaScript's `Promise.all() + .then()`, involving asynchronous request fetches that can run in parallel. Without `CompletableFuture`, you'd fetch them sequentially or manage raw threads manually that are error-prone.

```
// Parallel fetch of independent dependencies, then combine
CompletableFuture<DataProfile> profileFuture = CompletableFuture.supplyAsync(() ->
fetchDataProfile(profileData));
CompletableFuture<DataType> typeFuture = CompletableFuture.supplyAsync(() ->
fetchDataType(typeData));

// Wait for both, then aggregate data. No thread blocked while waiting
CompletableFuture<CombinedData> combined = profileFuture.thenCombine(typeFuture,
  (profileData, typeData) -> aggregateData(profileData, typeData));
```

ReadWriteLock: Read-heavy workloads

Many data structures are read far more often than written. A mutex serializes all access, causing readers to block each other unnecessarily. `ReadWriteLock` allows unlimited concurrent readers but exclusive writer access. When a writer acquires the lock, all readers wait; when only readers hold it, they proceed in parallel. This is optimal for in-memory caches that are read on every request but updated infrequently, such as configuration caches, schema registries, or feature flag stores that refresh on a schedule or in response to a deployment event.

```
// Schema cache: many concurrent reads, rare exclusive writes
ReadWriteLock lock = new ReentrantReadWriteLock();
Map<String, JsonSchema> schemaCache = new HashMap<>();

// Read path: multiple threads enter simultaneously. Note readLock.lock()
// means "acquire a read lock", which is a shared lock. Multiple threads
// can hold the read lock concurrently. The read lock only blocks when a
// writer holds the write lock.
lock.readLock().lock();
try { return schemaCache.get(objectType); }
finally { lock.readLock().unlock(); }

// Write path: exclusive, blocks all readers
lock.writeLock().lock();
try { schemaCache.put(objectType, newSchema); }
finally { lock.writeLock().unlock(); }
```

CountDownLatch: Wait for N tasks

Sometimes you need to fan out work to N threads and wait for all of them to finish before proceeding. Using `Thread.join()` is unfeasible when tasks are submitted to an executor pool, and tracking N futures manually is verbose. `CountDownLatch` is a simple counter: each task decrements it on completion, and the waiting thread blocks until it reaches zero. This mechanism cannot be reset or undone once triggered.

This applies to any fan-out-then-aggregate pattern: waiting for all aggregation queries to complete, fetching configs from all tenants before rendering a summary, or collecting results from parallel API calls before returning a combined response.

```
// Wait for all tenant configs to load before rendering summary
CountDownLatch latch = new CountDownLatch(tenants.size());
for (String tenant : tenants) {
    pool.submit(() -> {
        try { loadConfig(tenant); }
        finally { latch.countDown(); } // always decrement
                                       // even on failure
    });
}
latch.await(30, TimeUnit.SECONDS); // timeout prevents infinite hang
renderSummary();
```

Semaphore: Concurrency limitation

A thread pool controls how many threads exist; a semaphore controls how many threads can access a specific resource simultaneously. This distinction matters when the bottleneck isn't CPU but an external dependency with rate limits on service level. For example, if you fire 50 concurrent requests at a service that allows 5, you get throttled and all 50 fail. A semaphore with 5 permits ensures at most 5 in-flight calls, while the remaining calls queue up and proceed as permits are released.

```
// Limit concurrent calls to a shared resource to avoid throttling
Semaphore concurrencyLimit = new Semaphore(5);
concurrencyLimit.acquire(); // blocks if 5 already in-flight
try {
    return client.call(request);
} finally {
    concurrencyLimit.release(); // MUST release in finally
}
```

Concurrency in java collections framework

To handle advanced concurrent programming, the Java Collections Framework includes many specialized, thread-safe implementations. We will review several built-in solutions to efficiently manage common concurrent operations without needing explicit locks.

ConcurrentSkipListMap: Sorted concurrent map

Unlike `ConcurrentHashMap`, which provides hash-based lookup, `ConcurrentSkipListMap` maintains sorted order with logarithmic time complexity for all operations. This is ideal for scenarios requiring sorted iteration, range queries, or maintaining ordered data in concurrent environments. Alternative approaches would require manual sorting or synchronized collections, which are significantly less efficient.

```
import java.util.concurrent.ConcurrentSkipListMap;

// Thread-safe sorted map with O(log n) operations
ConcurrentSkipListMap<String, Integer> sortedMap = new ConcurrentSkipListMap<>();
sortedMap.put("key1", 100);
sortedMap.put("key2", 200);

// Safe iteration without explicit synchronization
for (Map.Entry<String, Integer> entry : sortedMap.entrySet()) {
    System.out.println(entry.getKey() + ": " + entry.getValue());
}

// Range operations work atomically
SortedMap<String, Integer> subMap = sortedMap.headMap("key2");
```

ConcurrentSkipListSet: Sorted concurrent set

`ConcurrentSkipListSet` provides a thread-safe alternative to `TreeSet` with concurrent access capabilities. The sorted nature allows for efficient range operations and ordered iteration without the performance overhead of synchronized collections. This is particularly useful in concurrent applications requiring ordered data structures with atomic operations.

```
import java.util.concurrent.ConcurrentSkipListSet;

// Thread-safe sorted set implementation
ConcurrentSkipListSet<String> sortedSet = new ConcurrentSkipListSet<>();
sortedSet.add("item1");
```

```
sortedSet.add("item2");

// Safe iteration with sorted order
for (String item : sortedSet) {
    System.out.println(item);
}

// Range operations
SortedSet<String> subset = sortedSet.headSet("item2");
```

CopyOnWriteArraySet: Read-heavy workloads

This library is optimized for scenarios where reads vastly outnumber writes. Each modification creates a new copy of the underlying array, making reads extremely fast and lock-free. This is ideal for maintaining lists of listeners, configurations, or other data structures where the primary operation is reading rather than updating.

```
import java.util.concurrent.CopyOnWriteArraySet;

// Optimized for read-heavy scenarios with infrequent writes
CopyOnWriteArraySet<String> set = new CopyOnWriteArraySet<>();
set.add("item1");
set.add("item2");

// Read operations are lock-free and highly efficient
boolean contains = set.contains("item1"); // No locking required
int size = set.size(); // No locking required

// Iteration is safe and consistent
for (String item : set) {
    System.out.println(item);
}
```

BlockingDeque: Double-ended queue

`BlockingDeque` provides a complete thread-safe double-ended queue implementation with blocking operations. This is essential for producer-consumer patterns where data needs to be added or removed from both ends of the queue. The blocking operations eliminate the need for manual thread coordination and provide clean integration with thread pools.

```
import java.util.concurrent.BlockingDeque;
import java.util.concurrent.LinkedBlockingDeque;
```

```
import java.util.concurrent.TimeUnit;


// Thread-safe deque with blocking operations
BlockingDeque<String> deque = new LinkedBlockingDeque<>(100);

// Producer - blocks when queue is full
deque.putFirst("item1");
deque.offerLast("item2");

// Consumer - blocks when queue is empty
String item1 = deque.takeFirst(); // Blocks until item available
String item2 = deque.pollLast(1, TimeUnit.SECONDS); // Times out after 1 second
```

TransferQueue: With transfer operations

`TransferQueue` extends the capabilities of standard `BlockingQueue` by providing direct transfer operations that can immediately deliver items to waiting consumers. This eliminates the need for intermediate queue storage when a consumer is ready, reducing latency and improving performance in scenarios where immediate processing is critical.

```
import java.util.concurrent.TransferQueue;
import java.util.concurrent.LinkedTransferQueue;
import java.util.concurrent.TimeUnit;


// Advanced blocking queue with transfer operations
TransferQueue<String> transferQueue = new LinkedTransferQueue<>();

// Direct transfer - blocks until consumer is ready
transferQueue.transfer("item1"); // Blocks until consumer takes item

// Timed transfer - blocks up to specified time
boolean transferred = transferQueue.tryTransfer("item2", 1, TimeUnit.SECONDS);

// Regular put operations
transferQueue.put("item3"); // Non-blocking, adds to queue
import java.util.concurrent.TransferQueue;
import java.util.concurrent.LinkedTransferQueue;

// Advanced blocking queue with transfer operations
```

```
TransferQueue<String> transferQueue = new LinkedTransferQueue<>();

// Direct transfer - blocks until consumer is ready
transferQueue.transfer("item1"); // Blocks until consumer takes item

// Timed transfer - blocks up to specified time
boolean transferred = transferQueue.tryTransfer("item2", 1, TimeUnit.SECONDS);

// Regular put operations
transferQueue.put("item3"); // Non-blocking, adds to queue
```

PriorityBlockingQueue: Concurrent priority queue

`PriorityBlockingQueue` combines the benefits of priority queues with thread safety and blocking operations. This is particularly useful in task scheduling, event processing, or any scenario where elements need to be processed based on priority while maintaining concurrent access. The blocking operations integrate seamlessly with thread pools and other concurrent constructs.

```
import java.util.concurrent.PriorityBlockingQueue;
import java.util.Comparator;

// Thread-safe priority queue with blocking operations
PriorityBlockingQueue<Integer> priorityQueue = new PriorityBlockingQueue<>(100,
    Comparator.naturalOrder());

// Add elements
priorityQueue.put(5);
priorityQueue.put(1);
priorityQueue.put(3);

// Take elements in priority order
Integer first = priorityQueue.take(); // Returns 1 (lowest priority)
Integer second = priorityQueue.poll(); // Returns 3
```

ConcurrentLinkedQueue: Lock-free queue

`ConcurrentLinkedQueue` provides a lock-free implementation that scales well under high contention. Unlike synchronized collections, it uses atomic operations to achieve thread safety without blocking threads. This makes it ideal for high-throughput scenarios where minimizing thread contention is critical.

```
import java.util.concurrent.ConcurrentLinkedQueue;

// Lock-free queue implementation with high throughput
ConcurrentLinkedQueue<String> queue = new ConcurrentLinkedQueue<>();
queue.offer("item1");
queue.offer("item2");

// Thread-safe removal
String item = queue.poll(); // Non-blocking, returns null if empty
String item2 = queue.remove(); // Throws exception if empty

// Size estimation (not accurate in concurrent environments)
int estimatedSize = queue.size(); // Approximate size
```

ArrayBlockingQueue: Fixed-size queue

`ArrayBlockingQueue` provides bounded queue behavior with predictable memory usage and controlled resource allocation. The fixed-size constraint prevents unbounded memory growth while maintaining thread safety. This is essential for systems where memory constraints exist and queue capacity needs to be controlled.

```
import java.util.concurrent.ArrayBlockingQueue;

// Fixed-size blocking queue with bounded capacity
ArrayBlockingQueue<String> boundedQueue = new ArrayBlockingQueue<>(100);

// Producer - blocks when queue is full
boundedQueue.put("item1");
boundedQueue.offer("item2", 1, TimeUnit.SECONDS); // Times out after 1 second

// Consumer - blocks when queue is empty
String item = boundedQueue.take(); // Blocks until item available
String item2 = boundedQueue.poll(1, TimeUnit.SECONDS); // Times out after 1 second
```

There are more concurrency libraries in JCF beyond the above. These JCF implementations provide comprehensive solutions for concurrent programming scenarios, each optimized for specific use cases while maintaining thread safety and performance characteristics that manual implementations cannot match.

Summary

This chapter covers fundamental concurrency concepts essential for data structures and algorithms, including shared state management, race conditions, and atomic operations.

We explore advanced data structures and algorithms specifically designed for concurrent environments, such as lock-free implementations, concurrent collections, and performance optimization techniques. The chapter examines synchronization mechanisms like synchronized wrappers, copy-on-write arrays, and lock-free data structures including `ConcurrentLinkedDeque`, along with essential patterns such as `BlockingQueue`, `Executor` services, `ThreadLocal`, and `CompletableFuture`. Readers learn to identify and fix common concurrency bugs, understand synchronization trade-offs, and apply practical solutions for managing shared resources in multi-threaded environments. This knowledge is crucial for implementing concurrent data structures and understanding how synchronization overhead affects algorithmic complexity and performance. *Figure 11.9* presents a summary diagram of concurrency concepts in programming. These principles will be revisited in *Chapter 12* through practical examples.

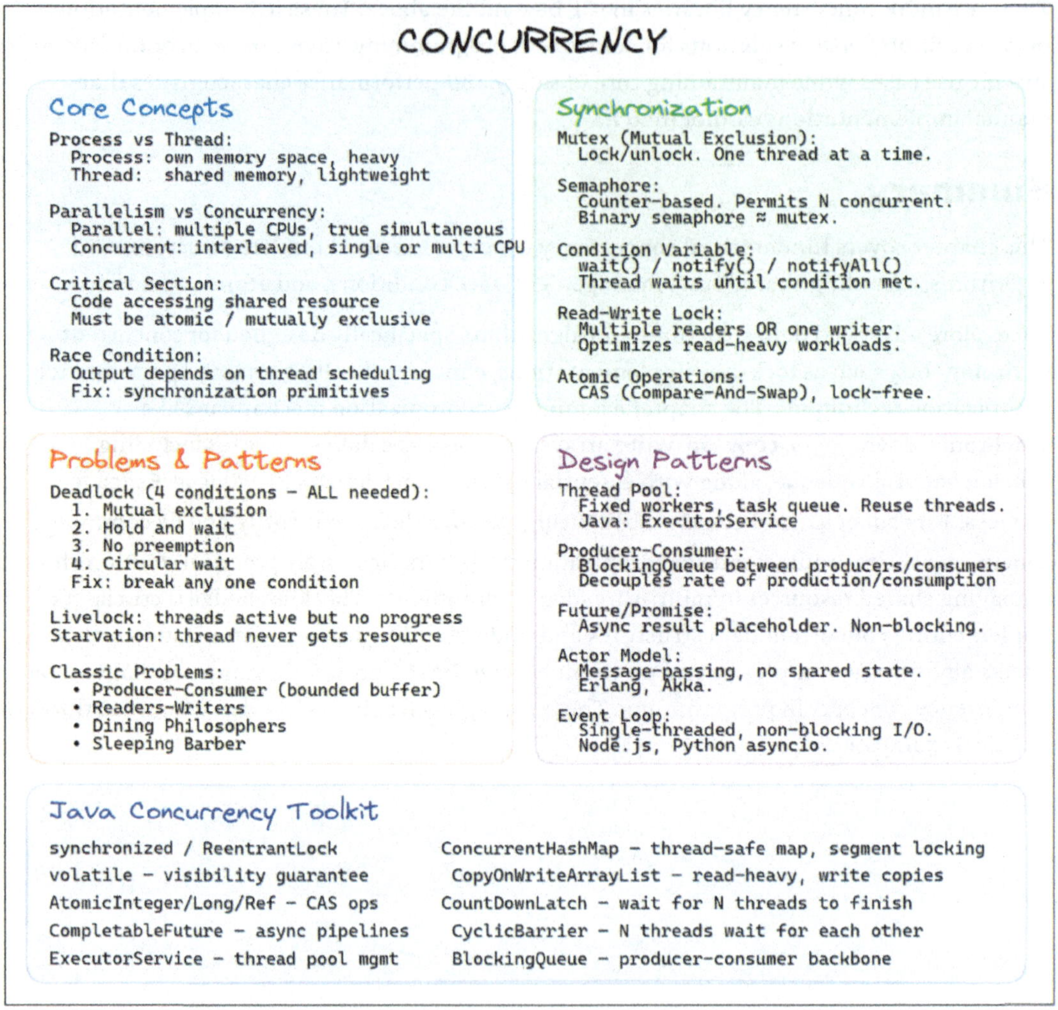

Figure 11.9: Summary diagram for concurrency use cases

In the next chapter, we wrap up this book by moving beyond the theoretical realm of complexity analysis. Instead, we will explore how practical DSA patterns are deployed in real-world applications to optimize performance, ensure scalability, and drive the success of modern software systems. This final chapter synthesizes the theoretical foundations and practical implementations discussed throughout the book, providing readers with the comprehensive toolkit needed to build robust, high-performance concurrent applications that can handle real-world demands.

Exercises

These exercises are highly relevant to data structures and algorithms because many algorithms and data structures must be implemented in concurrent environments to achieve optimal performance and scalability. Some of these exercises present common but subtle concurrency bugs that demonstrate the complexities of safe multi-threaded programming.

They highlight specific pitfalls in concurrent development, from memory visibility issues and race conditions to deadlock scenarios and resource management problems that directly impact algorithm efficiency and correctness.

Fully annotated Java solutions are available in the `Chapter11` folder on GitHub. To unlock the GitHub repo link, refer to the instructions in the *Download the example code files* section of the *Preface*.

Exercise 1: Shared model registry in AI

An AI agent system maintains a model registry mapping model names to endpoints. Many request-handling threads read the registry concurrently (on every incoming request to route to the right model). Updates are rare; only when a new model is deployed or decommissioned. A regular `synchronized` block would serialize all reads unnecessarily, degrading throughput.

Problem

Implement a thread-safe `ModelRegistry` for an AI agent system that maps model names to their service endpoints. Request-handling threads read the registry constantly to route incoming requests to the correct model, while updates (registering a newly deployed model, deregistering a decommissioned one) are rare. Because reads vastly outnumber writes, a plain `synchronized` block would needlessly serialize concurrent readers and degrade throughput. Use a `ReadWriteLock` so that multiple threads can read simultaneously without blocking each other, while writes acquire exclusive access that briefly blocks all readers and other writers. Support lookup (`getEndpoint`), listing (`listModels`), registration (`register`), removal (`deregister`), and an atomic check-then-act (`registerIfAbsent`).

Starter Code Template

```
import java.util.*;
import java.util.concurrent.locks.*;

/**
 * Thread-safe model registry optimized for read-heavy access.
 * ReadWriteLock allows concurrent reads; writes are exclusive.
```

```
 */
public class ModelRegistry {

    private final Map<String, String> models = new HashMap<>();
    private final ReadWriteLock lock = new ReentrantReadWriteLock();
    private final Lock readLock = lock.readLock();
    private final Lock writeLock = lock.writeLock();

    // Read: concurrent, blocks only during an active write
    public Optional<String> getEndpoint(String modelName) {
        // TODO: acquire readLock, look up endpoint, unlock in finally
    }

    // Read: return a defensive copy of all model names
    public Set<String> listModels() {
        // TODO: acquire readLock, copy keySet, unlock in finally
    }

    // Write: exclusive - insert or overwrite
    public void register(String modelName, String endpoint) {
        // TODO: acquire writeLock, put, unlock in finally
    }

    // Write: exclusive - remove, return whether it existed
    public boolean deregister(String modelName) {
        // TODO: acquire writeLock, remove, unlock in finally
    }

    // Write: atomic check-then-act, register only if absent
    public boolean registerIfAbsent(String modelName, String endpoint) {
        // TODO: acquire writeLock, check + put under one lock, unlock in finally
    }

    public static void main(String[] args) {
        // Test Case 1: concurrent reads see registered endpoints
        // Test Case 2: registerIfAbsent rejects duplicate
    }
}
```

Assumptions and Constraints

- Read-heavy workload: frequent concurrent reads, rare writes
- Model names are unique, non-null strings; one endpoint per name (re-registering overwrites)
- In-memory only; state lost on restart
- Reads and writes may come from any thread
- Concurrent reads must not block each other; writes are exclusive
- Check-then-act operations (`registerIfAbsent`) must be atomic
- `listModels` returns a defensive copy, not a live view
- Every `lock()` paired with `unlock()` in a `finally` block
- No persistence; no validation beyond null safety

Test Case 1: Concurrent reads return correct endpoints

- **Input**:
  - `register("claude-3.5", "https://...messages")`
  - Launch 8 threads, each calling `getEndpoint("claude-3.5")` repeatedly.
- **Expected Output**: Every read returns `Optional.of("https://...messages")`: no exceptions, no contention between readers, no torn reads during concurrent access
- **Verification**: All 8 threads complete; every result is the registered endpoint.

Test Case 2: `registerIfAbsent` **prevents duplicate overwrite**

- **Input**:
  - `registerIfAbsent("gpt-4", "https://endpoint-A")` → first call
  - `registerIfAbsent("gpt-4", "https://endpoint-B")` → second call
- **Expected Output**:
  - First call returns `true` (inserted).
  - Second call returns `false` (already present, not overwritten).
  - `getEndpoint("gpt-4")` returns `Optional.of("https://endpoint-A")`
- **Verification**: Endpoint remains the first value; the atomic check-then-act blocked the duplicate.

Solution

The registry wraps a plain `HashMap` (which is not thread-safe on its own) and guards every access with a `ReentrantReadWriteLock`. The lock hands out two separate locks from the same underlying state: one for readers and one for writers.

```
private final Map<String, String> models = new HashMap<>();
private final ReadWriteLock lock = new ReentrantReadWriteLock();
private final Lock readLock = lock.readLock();
private final Lock writeLock = lock.writeLock();
```

The key property: many threads can hold the read lock at once, but the write lock is exclusive; it waits for all readers to finish, then blocks everyone until it releases.

Read operations acquire the read lock. Because read locks don't conflict with each other, eight threads calling getEndpoint run truly concurrently, only ever pausing if a writer is mid-update:

```
public Optional<String> getEndpoint(String modelName) {
    readLock.lock();
    try {
        return Optional.ofNullable(models.get(modelName));
    } finally {
        readLock.unlock(); // always release, even on exception
    }
}
```

The `try/finally` is non-negotiable: if `get()` ever threw, an unreleased read lock would block all future writers forever. The same discipline applies to `listModels`, which additionally returns a defensive copy so a caller can't mutate internal state or iterate a snapshot while a writer changes it underneath them:

```
return new HashSet<>(models.keySet());
```

Write operations acquire the exclusive write lock. While held, no reader can enter, which is acceptable precisely because writes are rare (a deployment event), so the brief reader stall is a worthwhile trade:

```
public void register(String modelName, String endpoint) {
    writeLock.lock();
    try {
        models.put(modelName, endpoint);
```

```
    } finally {
        writeLock.unlock();
    }
}
```

The subtle case is `registerIfAbsent`, a compound check-then-act. If the check and the insert used separate lock acquisitions, two threads could both pass the check and both insert: a TOCTOU race. Holding the write lock across both steps makes the operation atomic:

```
public boolean registerIfAbsent(String modelName, String endpoint) {
    writeLock.lock();
    try {
        if (models.containsKey(modelName)) return false; // check
        models.put(modelName, endpoint);              // act - same lock
        return true;
    } finally {
        writeLock.unlock();
    }
}
```

The core idea: reads share access for throughput, writes take exclusive access for safety, and any operation that both inspects and modifies state must hold the write lock for its entire duration.

Time complexity

Per operation, excluding lock wait time:

- `getEndpoint`: `O(1)` per `HashMap.get`
- `register`: `O(1)` per `HashMap.put`
- `deregister`: `O(1)` per `HashMap.remove`
- `registerIfAbsent`: `O(1)` per `containsKey` + `put`; both amount to cumulative `O(1)`
- `listModels`: `O(n)` per copying all n keys into a new `HashSetSolution`

All map operations are `O(1)` average (`HashMap`), and the lock acquire/release adds `O(1)` overhead. `listModels` is the only non-constant operation because the defensive copy must touch every entry.

Space complexity

- Registry storage: `O(n)` per `n` model-name → endpoint entries
- Lock: `O(1)` per fixed-size lock state, independent of `n`
- `listModels` result: `O(n)` per defensive copy of all keys

Final notes

For scenarios involving a single map where atomic operations are performed on individual keys, `ConcurrentHashMap` provides a superior default choice compared to `ReadWriteLock`. `ReadWriteLock` becomes more valuable when operations need to ensure consistency across multiple keys or when coordinating changes across the entire map alongside other related operations, such as atomically updating a model's endpoint while simultaneously modifying a separate routing-weights structure, ensuring that readers never encounter partially applied changes.

Exercise 2: Concurrent counter

Implement a **thread-safe** counter that many threads increment and decrement concurrently. Support `increment()`, `decrement()`, `add(delta)`, and `get()`. Under heavy concurrent use, the final value must be exactly correct. No updates may be lost.

Implement it using shared variables and atomic updates (not by serializing every operation behind a single global lock, if you can avoid it).

Example

- 8 threads each call `increment()` 5,000 times
- Final result must be exactly 80,000 (never less)
- Non-thread-safe counter (`count++`) would return less than 80,000 due to race conditions

Starter Code Template

```
import java.util.concurrent.atomic.*;

public class ConcurrentCounter {

    // TODO: choose a thread-safe shared representation.

    /** Atomically add 1; return the value after the increment. */
    public long increment() { return 0; }
```

```
    /** Atomically subtract 1; return the value after the decrement. */
    public long decrement() { return 0; }

    /** Atomically add an arbitrary delta; return the value after the add. */
    public long add(long delta) { return 0; }

    /** Current value (consistent snapshot). */
    public long get() { return 0; }

    // A correctness harness lives in main(): spin up N threads, sum the work,
    // assert the final value equals the expected total. (See reference below.)
    public static void main(String[] args) throws InterruptedException { }
}
```

Assumptions and Constraints

- Many threads call all methods concurrently; no external synchronization by the caller.
- The count is a 64-bit signed value; assume it won't overflow `long` for this exercise.
- In-memory only; no persistence.
- Correctness is non-negotiable; after that, **prefer the highest-throughput correct design**.
- No reliance on `volatile` alone for compound updates (see common mistakes).

Exercise 3: Coarse-grained locking on a linked list

Implement a **thread-safe** sorted set backed by a singly-linked list, supporting `add`, `remove`, and `contains`, callable concurrently from many threads. Use a **coarse-grained** locking strategy: a single lock that guards the entire list, so every operation is mutually exclusive.

Keep the list sorted and reject duplicates (set semantics). Correctness first; then be ready to discuss the throughput cost of this approach and how finer-grained locking would improve it.

What "coarse-grained" means: one lock for the global structure. The opposite: fine-grained (lock-coupling) locks individual nodes so threads working on different regions can proceed in parallel.

Example

Create a thread-safe sorted set that:

- 8 threads each add 1,000 distinct integers concurrently
- Final size = 8,000 with no duplicates

- Fully sorted order maintained
- No lost links in the data structure
- `add()` returns false for duplicates
- `remove()` returns true for successful removal
- `contains()` works correctly

Starter Code Template

```
import java.util.*;
import java.util.concurrent.locks.*;

public class CoarseGrainedList<T extends Comparable<T>> {

    private static class Node<T> {
        final T value;
        Node<T> next;
        Node(T value) { this.value = value; }
    }

    private final Node<T> head = new Node<>(null);    // sentinel
    private final Lock lock = new ReentrantLock();    // one lock guards everything

    /** Insert keeping sorted order; false if already present. */
    public boolean add(T value) {
        // TODO: lock, walk to position, splice in, unlock in finally
        return false;
    }

    /** Remove value; true if it was present. */
    public boolean remove(T value) {
        // TODO: lock, find, unlink, unlock in finally
        return false;
    }

    /** Membership test (also under the lock). */
    public boolean contains(T value) {
        // TODO: lock, walk, unlock in finally
        return false;
    }
```

```
    public static void main(String[] args) throws InterruptedException {
        // Test 1: sorted insertion order
        // Test 4: concurrent adds from N threads -> correct size, sorted, no dups
    }
}
```

Assumptions and Constraints

- Many threads call `add`/`remove`/`contains` concurrently with no external synchronization.
- Elements are `Comparable` and unique (set semantics; re-adding returns `false`).
- Sorted ascending order is an invariant the structure must always preserve.
- In-memory only; no persistence.
- Correctness is non-negotiable; a single lock serializing all access is the *expected* design here.
- Every `lock()` must be paired with `unlock()` in a `finally` block.
- A sentinel head node is allowed (and encouraged) to simplify front-of-list edge cases.

Exercise 4: Optimistic locking on a linked list

Implement an optimistic locking mechanism for a concurrent linked list that supports the following operations:

- Lock-free traversal during read operations
- Selective locking only at commit point for write operations
- Validation to detect concurrent modifications
- Retry mechanism when validation fails
- Thread-safe operations that handle concurrent access properly

Note that optimistic locking represents a concurrency approach that operates under the assumption that conflicts are infrequent. This is the standard textbook (Herlihy and Shavit) optimistic list. It is not fully lock-free; it does take two short locks to commit. The optimism is that the expensive part (the traversal) runs lock-free and we only pay for locks + validation at the commit point.

Starter Code Template

```
import java.util.concurrent.atomic.AtomicReference;
import java.util.concurrent.locks.ReentrantLock;

public class OptimisticLinkedList<T> {
```

```
    private static class Node<T> {
        final T data;
        final AtomicReference<Node<T>> next;

        Node(T data) {
            this.data = data;
            this.next = new AtomicReference<>();
        }
    }

    private final AtomicReference<Node<T>> head;

    public OptimisticLinkedList() {
        this.head = new AtomicReference<>(new Node<>(null)); // Dummy head
    }

    // Read operation - lock-free traversal
    public boolean contains(T data) {
        // TODO: Implement lock-free traversal
        // Return true if data exists in list
        return false;
    }

    // Write operation - optimistic locking
    public boolean add(T data) {
        // TODO: Implement optimistic add with four-step pattern
        // 1. Traverse (lock-free)
        // 2. Lock target nodes
        // 3. Validate
        // 4. Act or Retry
        return false;
    }

    // Write operation - optimistic locking
    public boolean remove(T data) {
        // TODO: Implement optimistic remove with four-step pattern
        // 1. Traverse (lock-free)
        // 2. Lock target nodes
        // 3. Validate
        // 4. Act or Retry
```

```
            return false;
        }

        // Helper method to print list (for testing)
        public void printList() {
            Node<T> current = head.get().next.get();
            while (current != null) {
                System.out.print(current.data + " ");
                current = current.next.get();
            }
            System.out.println();
        }
    }
```

Test Case 1: Basic Operations

```
// Operations: add(3), add(1), add(2), add(1)
// Expected: contains(3) = true, contains(1) = true, contains(2) = true,
contains(4) = false
// Expected: add(1) returns false (duplicate)
```

Test Case 2: Concurrent Access

```
// Thread A: add(100)
// Thread B: add(200)
// Thread C: remove(100)
// Expected: Final list contains 200 and 100 (both added, then 100 removed
```

Exercise 5: The hidden bug in lazy initialization

Imagine you're building a system where multiple threads need to access an expensive resource (like a database connection pool or a complex configuration object). You want to create this resource only when it's first needed, not when your program starts. This is called "lazy initialization."

Here's what a developer might write:

```
public class BrokenInitializer {
    private ExpensiveResource resource;
    public ExpensiveResource getResource() {
        if (resource == null) {
            synchronized (this) {
```

```
                if (resource == null) {
                    resource = new ExpensiveResource();
                }
            }
        }
        return resource;
    }
}
```

Even though this code looks correct, there's a subtle but serious bug that can cause crashes:

- **The Bug**: The Java compiler and processor can rearrange the steps of object creation in ways that make the resource appear "ready" before it's actually fully constructed.
- **The Consequence**: When one thread tries to use the resource, it might read a reference that points to an object that's only partially built, causing a `NullPointerException` crash.

This bug can be incredibly hard to detect because it might work correctly most of the time, only failing under specific timing conditions, and it can crash your application in production without warning. This is a classic example of why understanding the Java memory model is crucial for writing reliable concurrent code.

Your next step: fix the above referenced `BrokenInitializer` code. The solution is available in the `FixedInitializer.java` file in `Chapter11` folder on GitHub. To unlock the GitHub repo link, refer to the instructions in the *Download the example code files* section of the *Preface*.

Exercise 6: The inventory race condition

Imagine you're building an online store where customers can buy products. You need to keep track of how many items are available in stock. Here's what a developer might write:

```
public class InventoryManager {
    private final ConcurrentHashMap<String, Integer> stock = new
ConcurrentHashMap<>();
    public void purchase(String itemId) {
        if(stock.containsKey(itemId)&&stock.get(itemId)> 0) {
            stock.put(itemId, stock.get(itemId) - 1);
        }
    }
}
```

This code looks correct at first glance, but there's a hidden problem that can cause serious issues. Namely, the operation is not atomic; it's actually two separate steps that can be interrupted:

- **Check** if item exists and has stock (> 0)
- **Act** by reducing the stock by 1

During high-demand situations (like flash sales), multiple customers might see that an item has stock and try to buy it simultaneously. All of them can pass the "check" step, but only one can successfully reduce the stock. This leads to negative inventory counts, like having -3 items in stock!

Example

Let's say you have 3 items in stock:

- Customer A checks and sees 3 items available
- Customer B checks and sees 3 items available (before A's purchase is complete)
- Customer C checks and sees 3 items available (before A and B's purchases are complete)
- All three customers proceed with their purchases
- Result: Stock goes to -3 (impossible!)

Hints

Always be careful with "check-then-act" patterns in multi-threaded code. If you need to check a condition and then act on it, make sure the entire operation is atomic. Otherwise, you might end up with inconsistent data that causes unexpected behavior in your application.

Now, it is your chance to fix this code. The solution is in the `FixedInventoryManager.java` file in the `Chapter11` folder on GitHub. To unlock the GitHub repo link, refer to the instructions in the *Download the example code files* section of the *Preface*.

Exercise 7: The banking deadlock

Imagine you're building a banking system where customers can transfer money between their accounts. Here's what a developer might write:

```
public class AccountTransfer {
    public void transfer(Account from, Account to, int amount) {
        synchronized (from) {
            synchronized (to) {
                from.withdraw(amount);
                to.deposit(amount);
```

```
            }
        }
    }
}
```

This code looks fine, but it can cause a serious problem called a deadlock. When multiple threads try to transfer money at the same time, they might lock accounts in different orders. The Consequence:

- Thread A locks Account X, then tries to lock Account Y
- Thread B locks Account Y, then tries to lock Account X
- Both threads wait forever for each other's locks
- The entire banking system freezes!

When you have multiple locks in your code, always acquire them in a consistent, predetermined order. This prevents deadlocks and keeps your multi-threaded applications running smoothly.

Now it is your chance to fix the above code. The solution is in the `FixedAccountTransfer.java` file in the `Chapter11` folder on GitHub. To unlock the GitHub repo link, refer to the instructions in the *Download the example code files* section of the *Preface*.

Exercise 8: The memory leak in ThreadLocal storage

Imagine you're building a web application that handles many user requests. Here's what a developer might write:

```
public class RequestContextHolder {
    private static final ThreadLocal<UserContext> context = new ThreadLocal<>();
    public void handle(Request req) {
        context.set(new UserContext(req));
        process(req);
    }
}
```

This code looks fine, but there's a hidden problem that causes memory leaks: `ThreadLocal` variables don't get automatically cleaned up when a thread is reused. The consequence:

- Web servers use thread pools (reusing the same threads for many requests)
- Each thread stores user data in `ThreadLocal`
- When the thread processes a new request, it still has the old user data
- This causes memory leaks and data contamination between users

Example

Let's say you have a thread pool of 10 threads:

Request 1 (User Alice):

- Thread 1 processes request for Alice
- Thread 1 stores Alice's data in `ThreadLocal`
- Thread 1 finishes and goes back to pool

Request 2 (User Bob):

- Thread 1 gets reused for Bob's request
- Thread 1 still has Alice's data from previous request
- Bob's request accidentally uses Alice's data!

`ThreadLocal` variables are like personal storage spaces that belong to each thread. If you don't clean up after yourself, that storage space stays filled with old data even when the thread is reused for other tasks.

Now, it is your turn to fix the above code. The solution can be found in the `FixedRequestContextHolder.java` file in the `Chapter11` folder on GitHub. To unlock the GitHub repo link, refer to the instructions in the *Download the example code files* section of the *Preface*.

12

DSA in Production

Data structures and algorithms (DSA) are not mere academic concepts; they are the fundamental architectural tools that determine whether a modern software system succeeds or fails. In this chapter, we move beyond the theoretical realm of complexity analysis. Instead, we will explore how practical DSA patterns are deployed in practice to steer the success, performance envelope, and scalability of modern software systems.

The following sections are organized in a systematic flow that mirrors the functional components of any robust modern software stack. We will see how DSA patterns are deployed and utilized to solve core problems in computing.

Foundational linear structures

Linear data structures govern sequential relationships and ordered operations. Arrays and linked lists are such linear structures that act as the foundational principles of data management, providing reliable mechanisms for controlling the flow of information, managing system state, and handling asynchronous processes in modern applications. This section demonstrates that these simple, linear concepts are powerful enough to handle the most complex, critical functions in large-scale software.

Key applications

- **Memory allocators**: Free lists in malloc implementations. Memory allocators use linked lists to manage available memory blocks, with each free block pointing to the next available chunk. This allows for efficient allocation and deallocation by maintaining a pool of reusable memory, enabling fast lookup and return of memory chunks during malloc/free operations.
- **LRU caches**: O(1) eviction when combined with LRU caches (HashMap) combine hash maps with doubly linked lists to achieve O(1) time complexity for both get and put

operations. The hash map provides constant-time lookup while the linked list maintains access order, allowing efficient eviction of least recently used items at the tail of the list.

- **Blockchain**: Each block points to the previous (singly linked list with hashes). Blockchains implement a linked list structure where each block contains a cryptographic hash of the previous block, creating an immutable chain. This design ensures data integrity and tamper evidence, as modifying any block would require recalculating all subsequent blocks in the chain.

See *Figure 12.1* for the summary diagram comparing these structures.

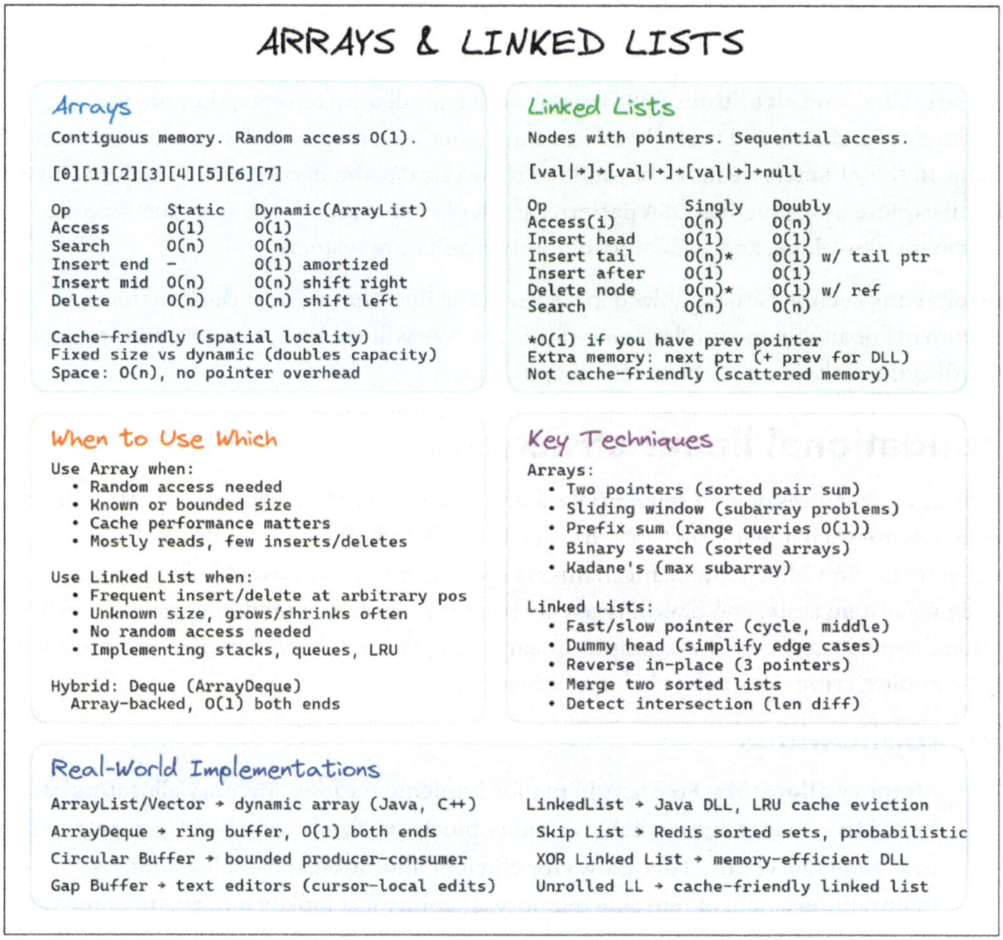

Figure 12.1: Arrays vs linked lists

Control flow and state management

Both stacks (Last-In, First-Out) and queues (First-In, First-Out) manage the order and flow of discrete events, making them vital for communication, state history, and navigating complex data relationships.

Key applications

- **Asynchronous Communication (Message Brokers)**: Systems like Kafka utilize queue data structures to manage the flow of messages between independent distributed services. This guarantees message ordering, persistence, and critical system decoupling by acting as a reliable, buffered intermediary for producers and consumers.
- **Traversal Algorithms (BFS)**: Breadth-First Search utilizes a queue to achieve level-order traversal. This specific traversal method is essential for identifying the shortest path in unweighted graphs and analyzing connectivity by systematically visiting all nodes at the current depth before proceeding to the next.
- **History Management (Undo/Redo)**: The stack structure is the canonical pattern for managing history. User actions are pushed onto the stack (and a separate stack for 'redo'). The LIFO nature allows the system to perfectly track and sequentially revert or reapply the previous states of the application.
- **Program Execution (The Call Stack)**: The call stack is the core operational component of any program. It manages the entire function execution lifecycle, tracking function calls, local variables, and return addresses via push/pop operations. This mechanism is not only critical for enabling recursion but is also the source of the debugging stack trace, detailing the precise sequence of function calls leading to an error.

See *Figure 12.2* for the summary diagram comparing these structures.

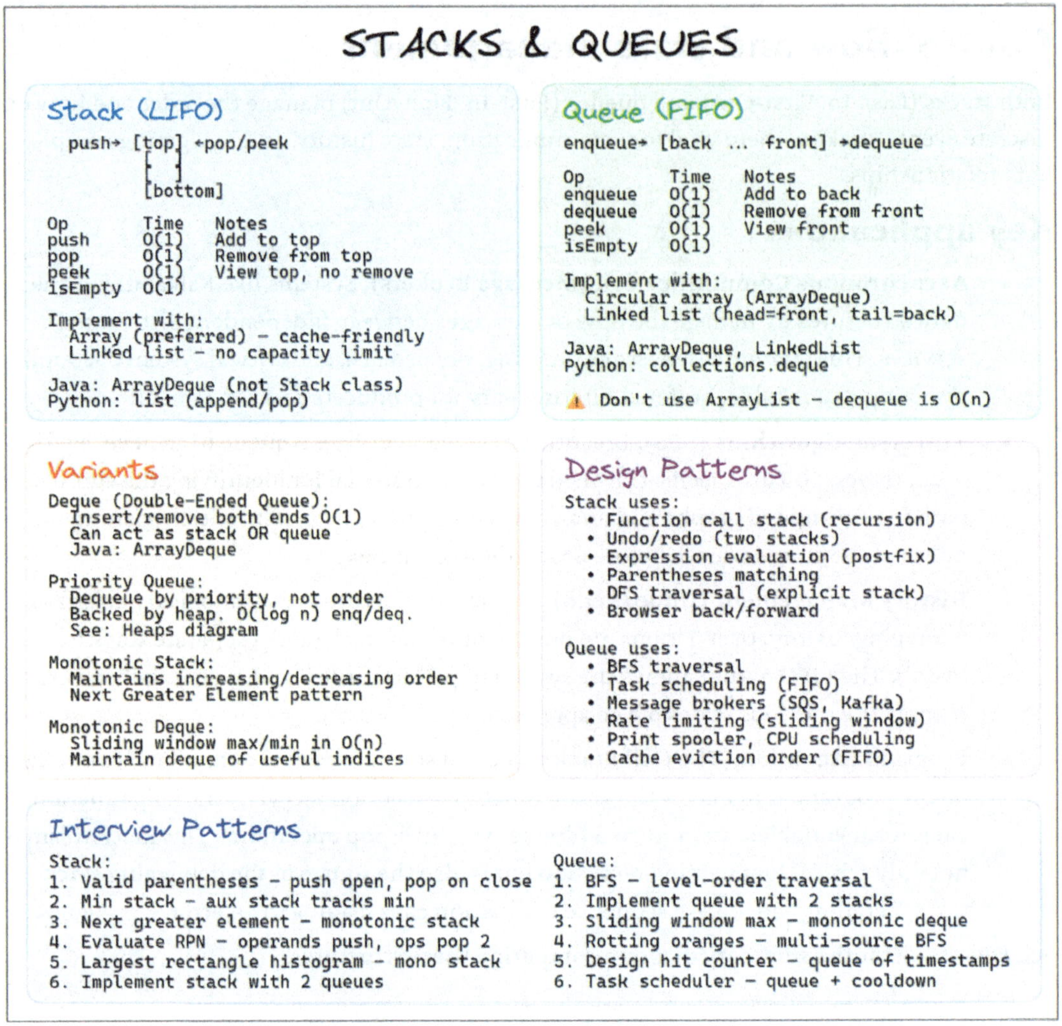

Figure 12.2: Stacks vs. Queues

Indexing and retrieval

Hash Tables (Maps) are data structures that map a unique key to a corresponding value. This pattern is the bedrock of modern computing, providing near-instantaneous lookup capabilities. By converting a key into a specific location (a hash), these structures enable O(1) performance: a massive advantage over linear searches. The examples show how the consistent, lightning-fast nature of hash mapping is utilized across the most critical, high-throughput components of modern software architecture.

Key applications

- **Database indexing**: Database indexing uses hash tables to enable O(1) key-value lookups in systems like DynamoDB and Redis, directly mapping keys to memory locations or disk addresses for instantaneous data retrieval, regardless of database size
- **Caching**: LRU caches combine hash maps with doubly-linked lists to achieve O(1) time complexity for both get and put operations, using hash maps for constant-time lookup and linked lists to maintain access order for efficient eviction
- **Deduplication**: Deduplication in streaming pipelines uses hash-based data structures to identify and eliminate duplicate events in real-time processing, preventing redundant operations and ensuring data integrity in high-throughput environments
- **Load balancers**: Load balancers use consistent hashing to distribute requests across servers while maintaining optimal distribution even when server capacity changes, minimizing request redistribution when servers are added or removed for stable load distribution

See *Figure 12.3* for the summary diagram for HashMap.

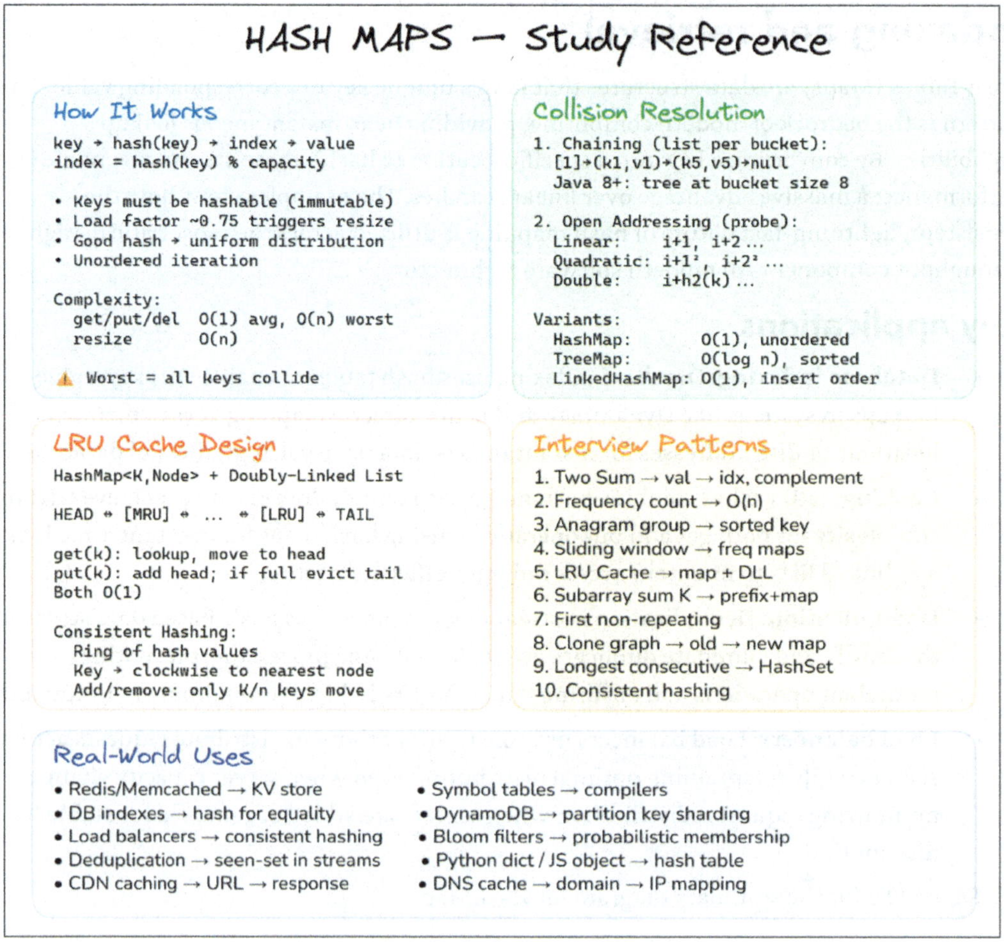

Figure 12.3: HashMap and its use cases and patterns

Organization and hierarchy

Trees model inherent hierarchical relationships, structuring data through defined parent-child connections. This pattern is fundamental whenever data requires organization or navigation across multiple levels of depth. We demonstrate its pervasive use across technology: From B-trees providing essential O(log n) indexing in databases, to Tries optimizing prefix matching for instant autocompletion, and the DOM defining the nested layout of all web content, trees provide the essential blueprint for structured data management.

Key applications

- **Databases**: Relational databases use B-trees and B+ trees for efficient indexing, providing O(log n) search, insertion, and deletion operations. B+ trees store all data in leaf nodes, enabling efficient range queries and sequential access while maintaining optimal tree balance for consistent performance across large datasets.
- **File systems**: File systems organize data using tree hierarchies, with ext4 employing extent trees for efficient file storage management. Extent trees group contiguous blocks together, reducing metadata overhead and improving performance for large file operations while maintaining intuitive directory structures for user navigation.
- **Document Object Model (DOM) rendering**: Web browsers parse HTML into tree structures (DOM), where React implements a virtual DOM using tree reconciliation. React compares virtual DOM trees with previous states to efficiently calculate minimal changes needed to update the actual DOM, reducing expensive browser reflows and repaints.
- **Autocomplete**: Autocomplete uses trie (prefix tree) data structures for fast prefix matching and word completion. Tries store strings as paths in a tree, enabling efficient real-time suggestions where time complexity is proportional to prefix length rather than total dictionary size.

See *Figure 12.4* for the summary diagram for trees.

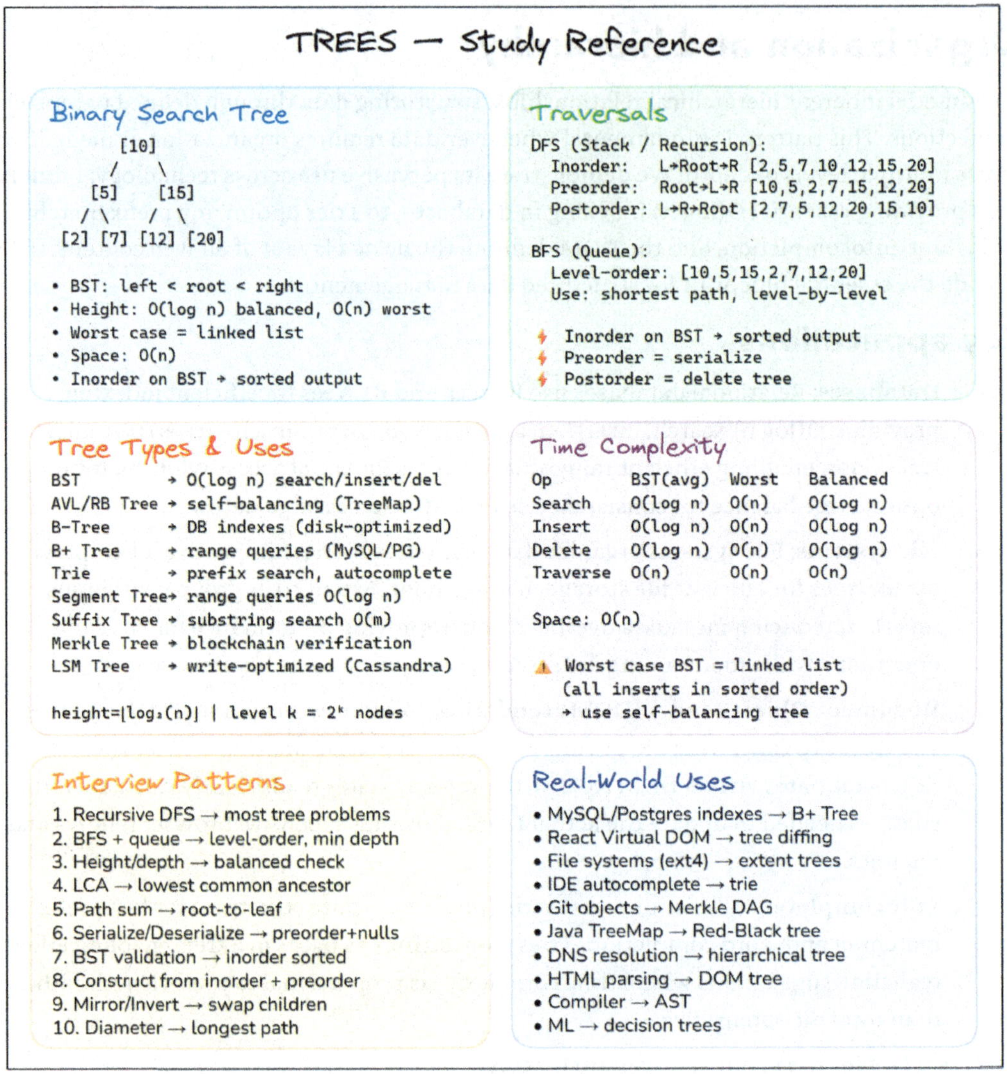

Figure 12.4: Trees and their use cases

Priority and scheduling

Priority Queues and Heaps allow systems to process data based on importance rather than chronological order. The underlying Heap structure maintains constant access to the highest (or lowest) priority element. This capability is essential for any service that requires managed prioritization, powering functions like operating system process schedulers, enforcing network rate limits (e.g., token buckets), managing time-sensitive event queues, and solving complex Top-K problems (e.g., finding the top search results).

Key applications

- **Task scheduling**: Task scheduling systems use priority queues and heaps to manage process execution, prioritizing tasks based on criteria like priority levels or resource requirements. OS schedulers and cron jobs maintain queues of ready processes, selecting the highest-priority task for execution while ensuring efficient CPU utilization and fair resource allocation.
- **Rate limiting**: Rate limiting systems implement token bucket and leaky bucket algorithms using queue and counter-based structures to control request throughput. Token bucket allows bursty traffic within limits while maintaining average rate, preventing system overload while maintaining acceptable performance for distributed applications.
- **Event-driven systems**: Event-driven systems use priority queues and heaps to process events in timestamp order, enabling timer-based and delayed queue functionality. These systems maintain event queues sorted by execution time, ensuring efficient processing of scheduled tasks and time-sensitive events for applications requiring precise timing.
- **Top-K problems**: Top-K problems use min-heaps and selection algorithms to efficiently find the K most relevant items from large datasets. These systems maintain priority queues of size K, keeping the smallest elements at the top and replacing them with better candidates, making them essential for search engines, recommendation systems, and machine learning applications.

See *Figure 12.5* for the summary diagram comparing these structures.

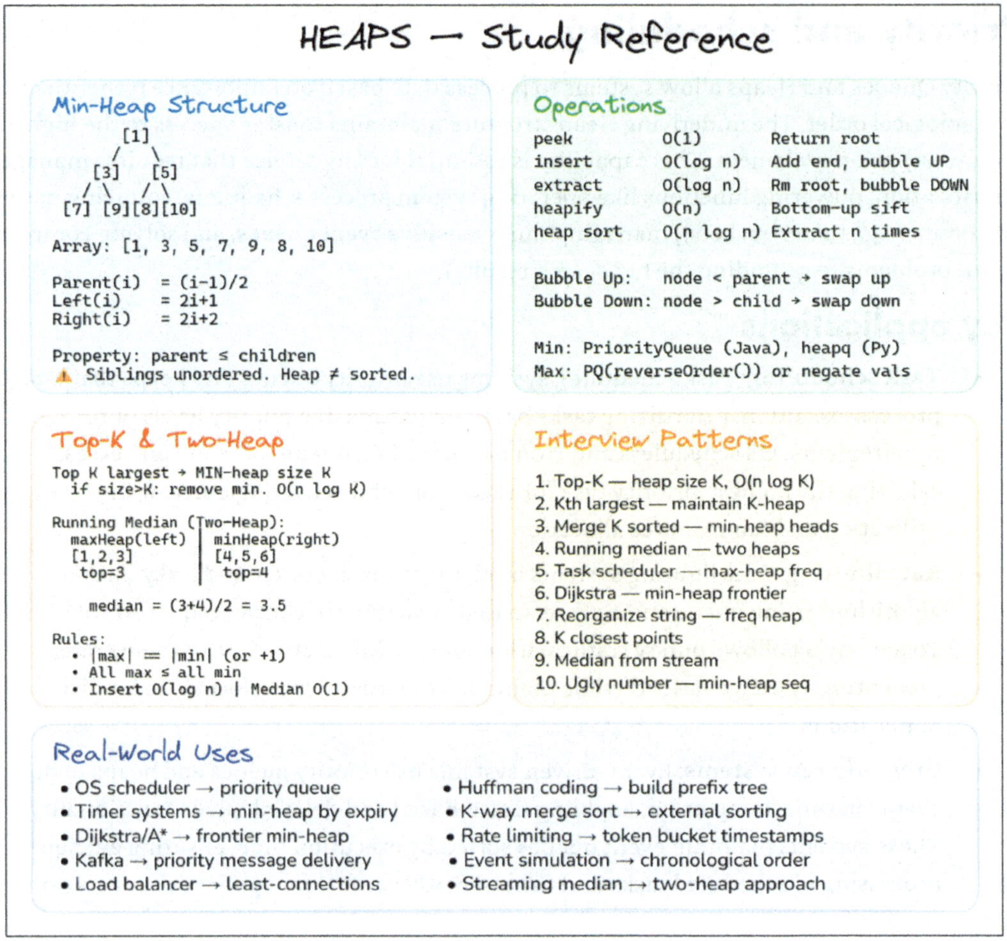

Figure 12.5: Heaps and their use cases

Graph theory and relational modeling

Graphs model relationships (nodes connected by edges), enabling the analysis of non-linear connectivity. This pattern is essential for solving problems involving paths and dependencies. We demonstrate its ubiquity in critical systems: Calculating optimal routes using Dijkstra's/A* algorithms; mapping the vast connections of social networks; and establishing strict dependency order using Topological Sort in package managers. Graphs are thus the definitive tool for analyzing connectivity, flow, and relational complexity.

Key applications

- **Social networks (BFS/DFS)**: They use BFS to find shortest paths (degrees of separation) and DFS to explore deeper community patterns, enabling sophisticated friend recommendations by analyzing the complex social graph.
- **Maps/routing (Dijkstra's/A*)**: This type of application calculates optimal routes by treating road networks as weighted graphs. A* improves Dijkstra's efficiency by using heuristics to guide the search, making real-time, large-scale GPS navigation possible.
- **Dependency Resolution (Topological Sort)**: Package managers use topological sorting on DAGs to determine the correct installation order for complex dependencies. This ensures that all required components are installed in the necessary sequence, maintaining consistent software states.
- **Service Meshes (Graph Representation)**: They represent microservice communication as a graph. This structure enables critical functions like distributed tracing and circuit breaking, allowing services to monitor dependencies and automatically handle service failures.
- **Garbage Collection (Reachability Analysis)**: It uses graph traversal starting from root objects. By treating the memory heap as a graph, the GC identifies all reachable objects and automatically reclaims those that are no longer in use, preventing memory leaks.

See *Figure 12.6* for the summary diagram of graphs.

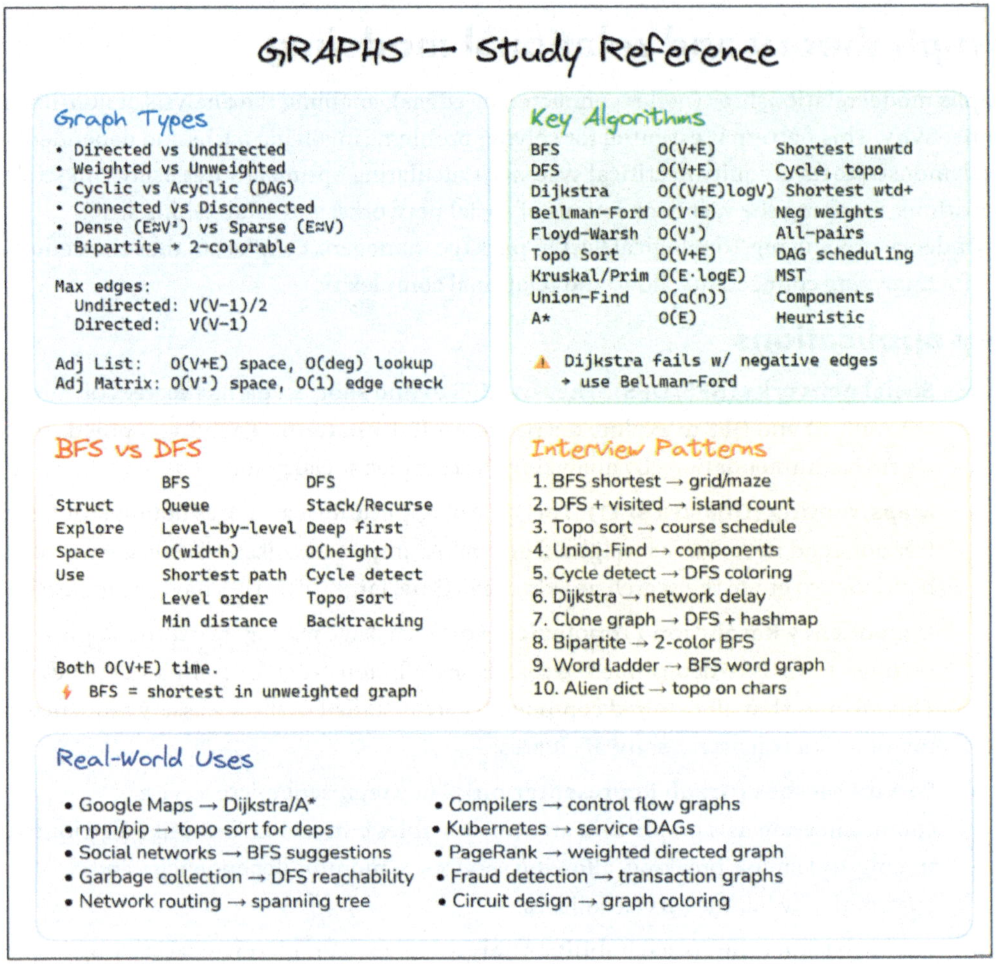

Figure 12.6: Graphs and their use cases

Memoization and optimization

Dynamic Programming (DP) is an optimization methodology that solves complex problems by breaking them down into overlapping subproblems. It achieves massive performance gains by storing and reusing the results of these subproblems (memoization), preventing redundant calculations. This technique is vital wherever finding an optimal solution is key. Key applications include Longest Common Subsequence (LCS) for diff algorithms, optimizing Knapsack-style resource allocation, and calculating sequence similarities in bioinformatics. DP is the definitive technique for achieving computational efficiency in complex, interlocking decision spaces.

Key applications

- **Diff algorithms**: Diff algorithms use longest common subsequence (LCS) to identify differences between document versions, enabling smart merge operations and collaborative editing by highlighting only modified sections while preserving unchanged content
- **Text wrapping**: The Knuth-Plass algorithm optimizes text wrapping by considering entire paragraphs rather than individual lines, using dynamic programming to minimize "badness" and produce visually pleasing layouts with optimal spacing and line lengths
- **Resource allocation**: Cloud resource allocation uses knapsack-style optimization to efficiently pack virtual machines onto physical servers, maximizing resource utilization while respecting constraints and minimizing the total number of required servers
- **Sequence alignment**: Sequence alignment algorithms compare DNA, RNA, or protein sequences using dynamic programming to calculate similarity scores, enabling evolutionary analysis, functional domain identification, and genetic variation studies in bioinformatics research

See *Figure 12.7* for the summary diagram of dynamic programming techniques.

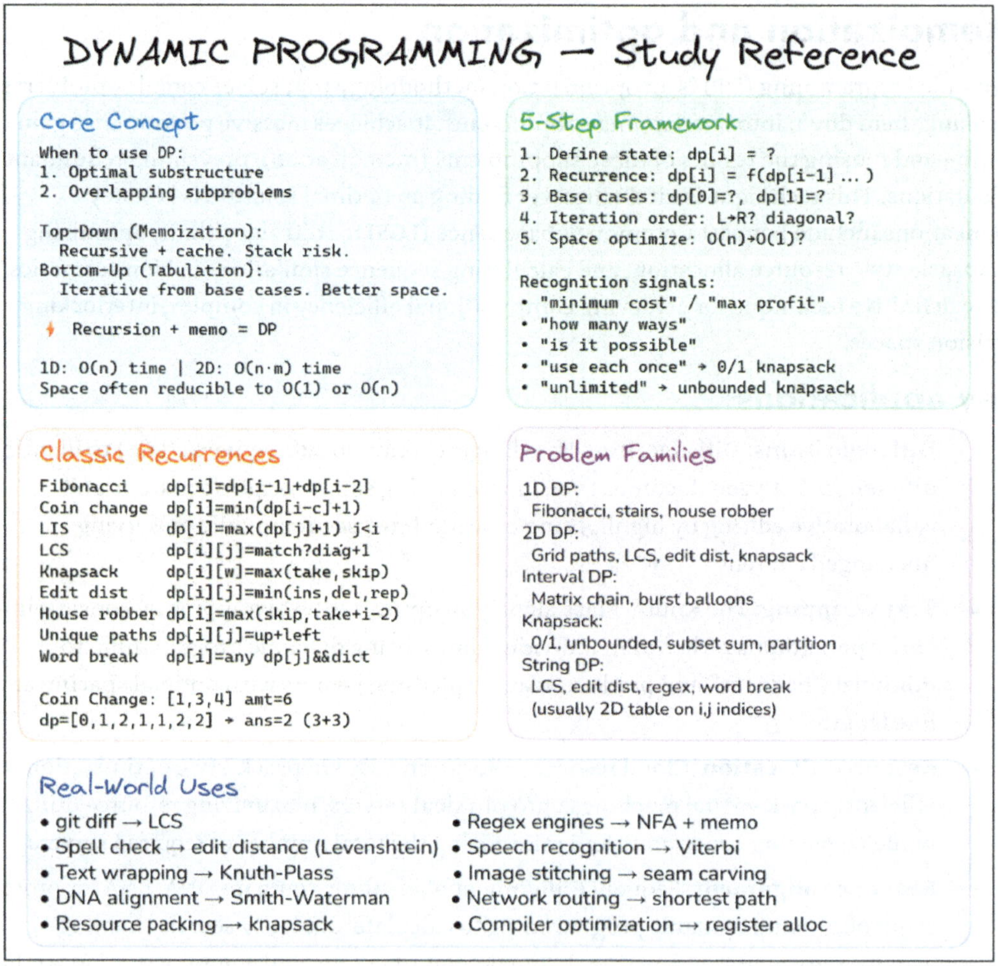

Figure 12.7: Dynamic programming use cases

Operational patterns: recursion

Recursion is the process of defining a function in terms of itself. It is the primary computational mechanism for systematically traversing nested or connected data. This pattern is essential for analyzing complexity in deeply nested structures. We demonstrate its critical application in core systems: traversing file system directory trees, parsing the nested grammar of source code for compiler design, and executing foundational graph algorithms like BFS/DFS. Recursion provides the necessary self-referential loop to explore every node within a complex structure.

Key applications

- **File System Traversal**: Recursion is used to map hierarchical directory structures. By recursively calling the search function on every subdirectory, the system can explore complex file paths efficiently, which is core to backup and archival utilities.
- **Compiler Design**: Compilers use recursive parsing (like recursive descent) to analyze source code's grammar. This technique validates the nested structure of code blocks (loops, functions), building a precise Abstract Syntax Tree (AST) to understand the program's meaning.
- **Tree and Graph Traversal (DFS)**: This fundamental graph algorithm is naturally recursive. It systematically explores connected structures like social networks or file hierarchies by recursively exploring paths, making it a key tool for finding paths and analyzing connectivity. (BFS, by contrast, is naturally iterative and utilizes a queue structure).
- **Divide and Conquer Algorithms**: Recursion powers algorithms like Merge Sort and Quick Sort. They solve large problems by recursively dividing the input into smaller, self-similar subproblems, drastically simplifying complex problem-solving and ensuring efficient processing of large data sets.

See *Figure 12.8* for the summary diagram involving recursion.

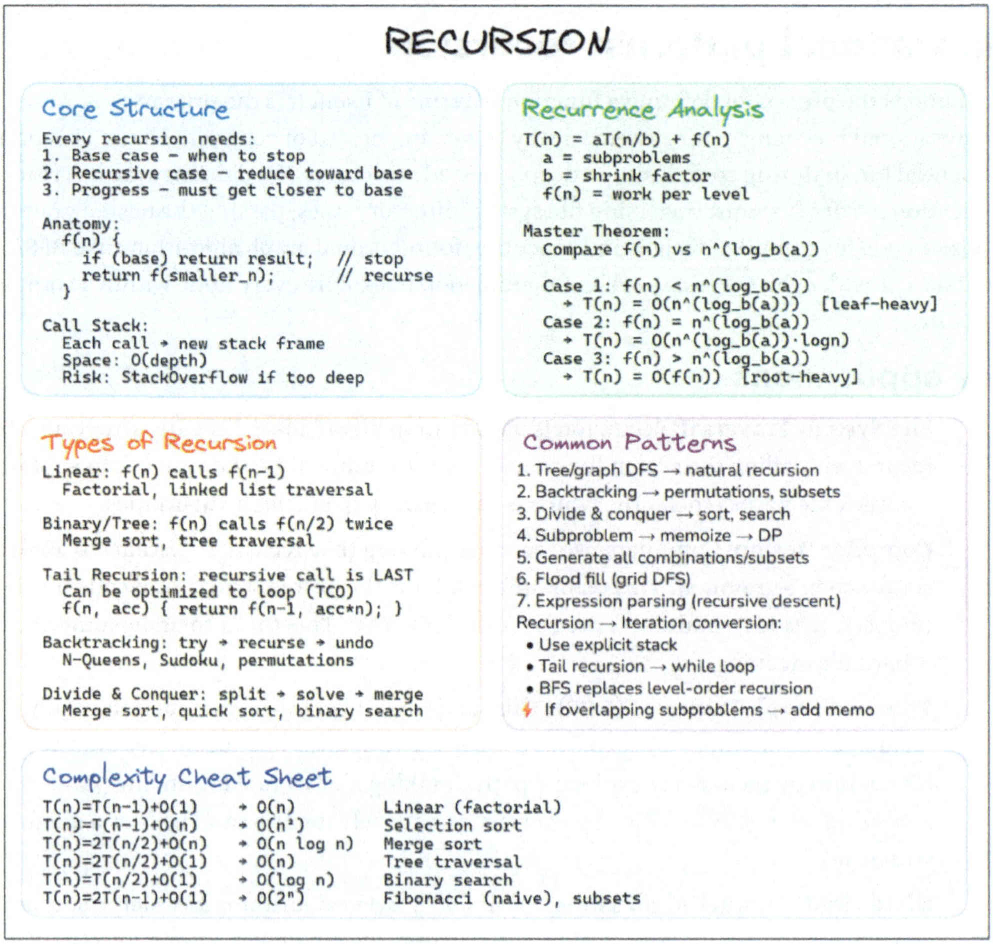

Figure 12.8: Recursion use cases

Algorithmic ordering

Sorting is the process of ordering data into a specific sequence. This is an essential pattern because many advanced operations are impossible without ordered input. We highlight its pervasive usage: Database systems mandate sorting for efficient query execution (e.g., ORDER BY and Merge Joins). GUI rendering uses Z-order sorting to define visual stacking priority. Furthermore, in large distributed systems, time-sorting is essential to reconstruct a true, accurate chronological event timeline. Sorting is the core mechanism for converting raw, unordered data into reliable, processable streams.

Key applications

- **Database Query Execution (ORDER BY, Merge Joins, Index Construction)**: Database sorting is crucial for optimized query execution. ORDER BY forces the engine to sort result sets, while Merge Joins require both tables to be sorted by the join key for efficient, linear matching. Furthermore, indexing relies on sorted keys (like B+ trees). These sorting functions ensure rapid, accurate data retrieval and optimized merging of large datasets.
- **Rendering (Z-Order Sorting for Overlapping UI Elements)**: Z-order sorting is essential in GUIs and rendering engines to determine the stacking order of overlapping elements. The engine sorts all components based on their defined depth (Z-index). This order dictates the drawing sequence; the element drawn last appears on top, preventing visual bugs and maintaining the correct, layered visual representation of the interface.
- **Log Analysis (Time-Sorting Distributed Logs for Debugging)**: In distributed cloud environments, logs from many sources must be reassembled and time-sorted for effective debugging. Time-sorting reconstructs the true chronological sequence of events across all nodes, allowing engineers to follow a single, coherent timeline. This is vital for pinpointing the exact moment and cause of a system failure in high-volume, distributed systems.
- **Leaderboards (Ranked Scoreboards in Gaming)**: Leaderboards require continuous, efficient sorting of scores. The system must instantly insert new scores and maintain the rank order across potentially millions of users. Optimized structures (often using heaps or balanced trees) are used to ensure the ranking is consistently accurate and displayed in real time, which is crucial for the integrity and real-time nature of the gaming experience.

See *Figure 12.9* for the summary diagram for sorting use cases.

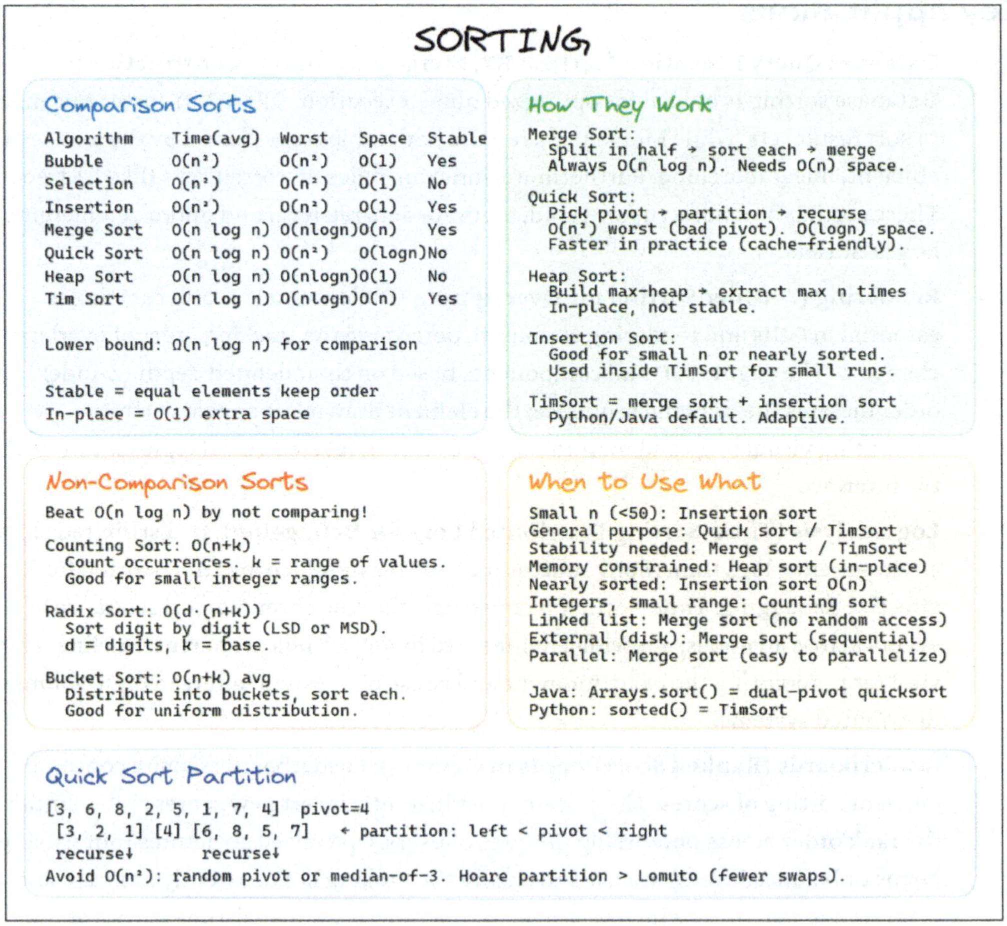

Figure 12.9: Sorting use cases

Concurrent system dynamics

Concurrency is the capability of a system to manage multiple tasks simultaneously. This pattern is essential for achieving high throughput and resilience. We illustrate its mandatory role in critical systems: Web APIs use it for processing concurrent user sessions; Database Transactions implement concurrency control (e.g., locking) to ensure data atomicity during simultaneous writes; and real-time data streaming requires it to reliably ingest variable, high-volume data spikes. By managing parallel operations, concurrency ensures that complex, modern applications remain stable, responsive, and dependable under massive, simultaneous load.

Key applications

- **Web API Endpoints (Concurrent Requests)**: High-traffic APIs must handle thousands of simultaneous requests. Concurrency is needed to prevent load spikes from affecting user experience, requiring thread pooling and isolation to process multiple user transactions reliably at once.
- **Database Transactions (ACID Compliance)**: Banking and financial systems require concurrency control (like locking) to manage simultaneous transactions. This ensures that all operations are atomic and isolated, maintaining data integrity even when multiple users modify the same data set simultaneously.
- **Real-Time Data Streaming (IoT/Clickstreams)**: Processing high-volume, asynchronous data streams requires concurrency. Systems must concurrently ingest and process data from numerous sources (like IoT sensors), using message queues to handle variable data volume spikes reliably.
- **Multi-threaded UI Operations (GUI Responsiveness)**: Concurrency prevents applications from freezing. By offloading long-running tasks to background threads, the primary UI thread remains free, ensuring the application remains responsive and interactive regardless of the intensive operations running behind the scenes.

See *Figure 12.10* for the summary diagram of concurrency use cases.

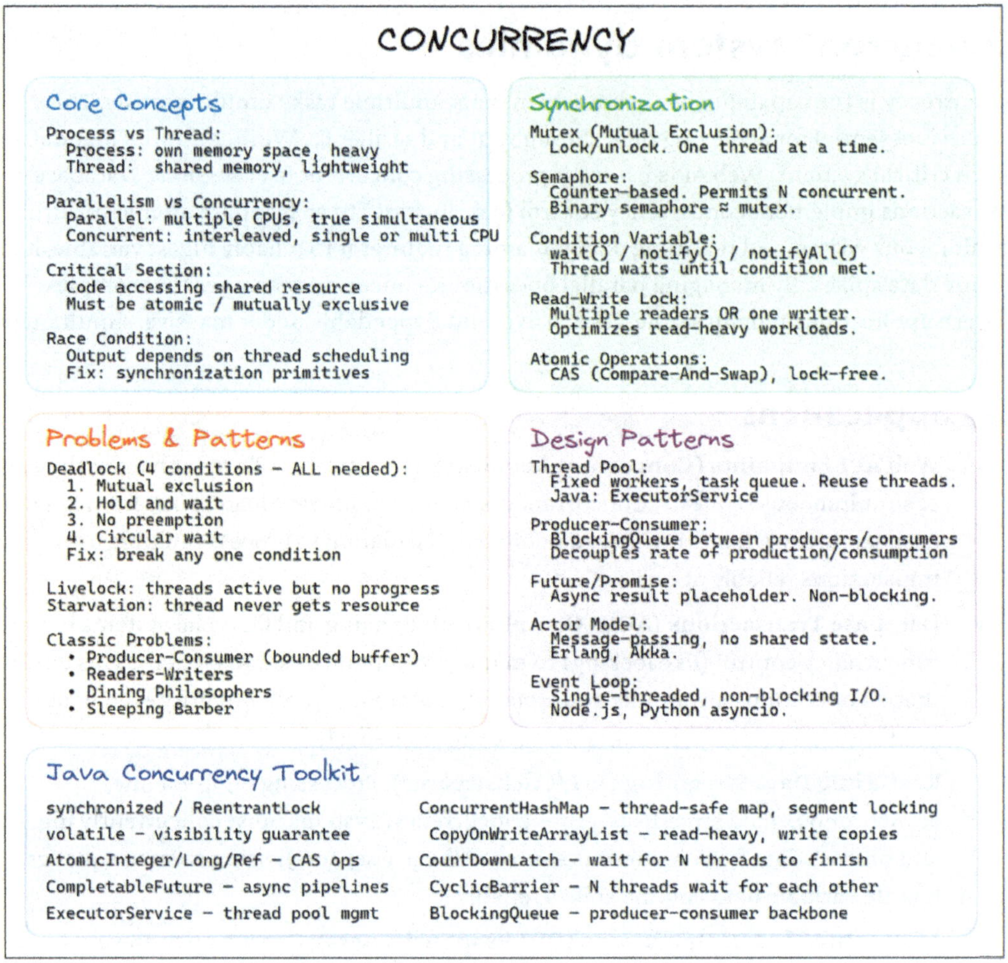

Figure 12.10: Concurrency use cases

13

Unlock Your Exclusive Benefits

Your copy of this book includes the following exclusive benefits:

DRM-Free PDF Version

Download DRM-free PDF and ePub copies of this book.

7-Day Packt Library Access

Get 7-day unlimited access to 8,000+ books and videos. No credit card required.

Available for first-time Packt+ trial users only.

Next-Gen Reader Access

Read this book on Packt Reader with progress sync, dark mode and note-taking.

Follow the guide below to unlock them. The process takes only a few minutes and needs to be completed once.

Unlock this Book's Free Benefits in 3 Easy Steps

Step 1

Keep your purchase invoice ready for *Step 3*. If you have a physical copy, scan it using your phone and save it as a PDF, JPG, or PNG.

For more help on finding your invoice, visit `https://www.packtpub.com/en-us/unlock?step=1`.

Note

If you bought this book directly from Packt, no invoice is required. After *Step 2*, you can access your exclusive content right away.

Step 2

Scan the QR code or go to `packtpub.com/unlock`.

On the page that opens (similar to *Figure 13.1* on desktop), search for this book by name and select the correct edition.

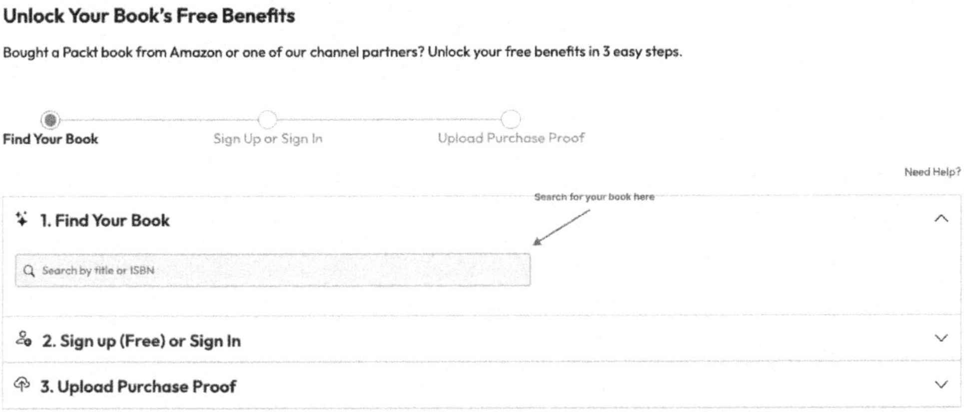

Figure 13.1: Packt unlock landing page on desktop

Step 3

After selecting your book, sign in to your Packt account or create one for free. Then upload your invoice (PDF, PNG, or JPG, up to 10 MB). Follow the on-screen instructions to finish the process.

Need Help

If you get stuck and need help, visit `https://www.packtpub.com/unlock-benefits/help` for a detailed FAQ on how to find your invoices and more. This QR code will take you to the help page.

Note

If you are still facing issues, reach out to `customercare@packt.com`.

Other Books You May Enjoy

If you enjoyed this book, you may be interested in these other books by Packt:

Kotlin for Java Developers

José Dimas Luján Castillo, Ron Veen

ISBN: 9781835884836

- Write Kotlin programs using variables, functions, and control flow
- Model real-world data with classes, properties, and constructors
- Handle missing data safely with nullable types and safe calls
- Simplify logic using lambdas and extension functions
- Work with Kotlin collections and sequences to process data efficiently
- Use Kotlin with Java, Gradle, and Maven for seamless project builds
- Write non-blocking code using coroutines and Async flows
- Create custom DSL for your projects

Java Coding Problems

Anghel Leonard

ISBN: 9781837633944

- Adopt the latest JDK 21 features in your applications
- Explore Records, Record Patterns, Record serialization and so on
- Work with Sealed Classes and Interfaces for increasing encapsulation
- Learn how to exploit Context-Specific Deserialization Filters
- Solve problems relating to collections and esoteric data structures
- Learn advanced techniques for extending the Java functional API
- Explore the brand-new Socket API and Simple Web Server
- Tackle modern Garbage Collectors and Dynamic CDS Archives

Packt is searching for authors like you

If you're interested in becoming an author for Packt, please visit `authors.packt.com` and apply today. We have worked with thousands of developers and tech professionals, just like you, to help them share their insight with the global tech community. You can make a general application, apply for a specific hot topic that we are recruiting an author for, or submit your own idea.

Share your thoughts

Now you've finished *Essential Data Structures and Algorithms in Java*, we'd love to hear your thoughts! Scan the QR code below to go straight to the Amazon review page for this book and share your feedback or leave a review on the site that you purchased it from.

`https://packt.link/r/1835883710`

Your review is important to us and the tech community and will help us make sure we're delivering excellent quality content.

Index

A

AI context **16**
ArrayBlockingQueue
- fixed-size queue 444, 445

ArrayDeque **243**
ArrayList **29**
AtomicLong.incrementAndGet() **417**
Autocomplete **469**
abstract data type (ADT) **27 - 29, 148**
- binary tree ADT 149, 150
- n-ary tree ADT 148

adjacency **218**
adjacency list **14, 228 - 230, 233**
adjacency matrix **230 - 233**
adjacent **218**
advanced comparison sorts **363**
- heap sort 369 – 372
- merge sort 363 – 365
- quick sort 366 – 368

advanced heaps **200**
- binomial heaps 200
- d-ary heaps 201
- fibonacci heaps 200
- pairing heaps 201

agentic lifecycle **17**
- context 19
- input gateway 18
- knowledge retrieval 19
- memory 19
- reasoning 21
- routing and verification 24 – 26
- task selection and execution 22

algorithmic blueprint **16**
algorithmic ordering **478**
- key applications 479

algorithmic performance **32**
algorithms **31**
- analysis 32 – 35
- significance 31

amortized analysis **55**
applications, data structures **5**
- data warehousing 7, 8
- file systems 6

array-based heap **191**
array-based queue **97 - 99**
array-based stack **85, 90**
- versus linked-based stack 88 – 90

arrays **11, 48, 49, 431**
- compression 53, 54
- efficiency 51, 52
- expansion 53, 54
- expansion cost, assessing 57 – 60
- operations 49 – 52
- ordered arrays 61, 64, 65
- resizing 53 – 57
- unordered arrays 61, 62

arrays, versus linked lists **69**
- access 69
- flexibility 69
- high-frequency logging 69
- operations 69

asymptotic analysis **37**
asynchronous communication (message brokers) **465**
atomic operations **416**
- hardware-level guarantee 417, 418
- Java's atomic facilities 416

B

B+ tree **8**
B-tree **8, 15**
Big O analysis

algebraic rules 41, 42

Big O notation **38**
examples 38, 39
significance 38
time complexities 40

Binary Search **331**
complexity, determining 332
master theorem, applying 332
parameters, identifying 331
recurrence relation, defining 331
recursive value, calculating 332

BlockingDeque
double-ended queue 441

BlockingQueue
Producer-Consumer pattern 436

base cases **314**
designing 314, 315

binary search trees (BST) **8, 144, 145**
Java representation 146

binary tree **142, 143**
depth-first search 333
Java representation 143, 144

binary tree ADT **149, 150**

binomial heaps **200**

blockchain **464**

bloom filters **9, 15**

breadth-first traversal **156, 239, 240**
complexity 158, 159
iterative methods 157
versus depth-first traversal 159, 160, 241

bubble sort **357, 358**

C

Compare-And-Swap (CAS) **416**

CompletableFuture
async composition 437, 438

ConcurrentHashMap **245**

ConcurrentLinkedDeque **433**

ConcurrentLinkedQueue **68**
lock-free queue 444

ConcurrentSkipListMap
sorted concurrent map 440

ConcurrentSkipListSet
sorted concurrent set 440

Copy-on-Write arrays
trade-offs 432

CopyOnWriteArraySet
read-heavy workloads 441

CountDownLatch **439**

caching **467**

cheapest flight route with At-Most K stops problem **287**
intuition 287
solution 287 – 289, 292

closed addressing **120**

coarse-grained thread safety
via synchronized wrappers 431, 432

code transformation **24**

collision resolution techniques **119**
closed addressing 120
open addressing 119
separate chaining 120, 121

comparator
for custom tree sorting 163, 164

comparison-based sorting **357**

compiler design **477**

complexity **36**

concurrency bags **411**

concurrency, in java collections framework **440**
ArrayBlockingQueue 444, 445
BlockingDeque 441
ConcurrentHashMap 440
ConcurrentLinkedQueue 444
ConcurrentSkipListSet 440
CopyOnWriteArraySet 441
PriorityBlockingQueue 443
TransferQueue 442

concurrent execution **412 - 414**
atomic operations 416
hardware-level atomicity 416
Mutual Exclusion (Mutex) 418
semaphore 424, 425
shared state 414 – 416

concurrent hash tables **433, 434**
collision resolution 435

lock-Free striped word counter 434, 435

concurrent system dynamics **481**
key applications 481

context **19**

continuous sum in integer series problem **278**
intuition 279, 280
observation 281
solution 280

control flow **465**
key applications 465

conversation window **20**

counting sort **372 - 375, 378**

create, read, update, and delete (CRUD) operations **52**

D

DSA bridge **15**

Deque **29**

Diff algorithms **475**

Dijkstra's algorithm **243**

Document Object Model (DOM) rendering **469**

Dual-Pivot quicksort **380**

Dynamic Programming (DP) **270 - 272, 475**
example 272
practicals checklist 297
significance 272

DynamicArrayQueue **97 - 99**

DynamicArrayStack **85**

d-ary heaps **201**

data structures **5**
applications 5
linear data structures 9 – 11
non-linear data structures 9, 13
recursion 332, 333
significance 5

data warehousing **7, 8**

database indexing **467**

database query execution **479**

database transactions **481**

databases **469**

deduplication **467**

degree **218**

dependency resolution (topological sort) **473**

depth-first search
binary tree 333
quick sort 333

depth-first traversal **151, 236 - 238**
complexity 156
iterative methods 153 – 155
recursive methods 151
versus breadth-first traversal 159, 160, 241

directed acyclic graph (DAG) **293**

directed graph **219, 220**

divide and conquer algorithms **477**

E

edges **218, 225, 226**

edit distance (levenshtein) in strings problem **281**
formulation 281, 282
initialization 282
observation 286
solution 283 – 286

event-driven systems **471**

executors
thread pool management 436

F

Fibonacci recurrence **276**

Fibonacci sequence example **274, 275**
bottom-up approach 275
optimal substructure 276
overlapping 276
top-down approach 275

factorial function
example 315, 316

fibonacci heaps **200**

file system traversal **477**

file systems **6, 469**

first-in first-out (FIFO) **12**
foundational linear structures **463**
key applications 463
frame pointer **318**

G

Google Guava Graphs Explained Wiki
reference link 242
garbage collection (reachability analysis) **473**
general (n-ary) trees **146**
Java representation 147
graph **14, 217, 228, 473**
abstract data type (ADT) 234, 235
adjacency list 228 – 230
adjacency matrix 230, 231
components 223
directed graph 219, 220
edge 225, 226
in Java Collections Framework (JCF) 242
key applications 473
performance characteristics 232
recursive BFS 333
undirected graph 219
vertex 223 – 225
vertex-to-edge 226 – 228
weighted graph 220 – 222
graph representation
selecting 233
graph-based structures **14**

H

HashMap **29**
HashSet **29**
for unweighted graphs 242
hardware-level atomicity **416**
hash **115**
hash function **115**
hash maps **14**
hash tables **9**
hash-based structures **14**
hashing **115**
amortizes to O(1) 117, 118
core map operations 121
example 122
properties 116
heap **13, 95, 190**
applications 199, 200
array-based heap 191
implementations 191
in Java Collections Framework (JCF) 201
max heap 192
min heap 192
O(delete) 198
O(insert) 198
operations 193, 194
shape property 190
tree-based heap 192
heap sort **369 – 372, 378**
extraction 371
heapification 371
heapify-down **197**
heapify-up **195, 196**
hierarchical structures **13**
history management (undo/redo) **465**
hybrid comparison-based sorts **380**
Dual-Pivot quicksort 380
Timsort 383, 384
Two-Pivot strategy 380 – 382
hybrid structures **15**

I

immutability **223**
implicit call stack **319, 320**
in-place sorting algorithms **355**
indexing and retrieval **467**
key applications 467
input gateway **18**
session and registry lookup 18
insertion sort **360, 361**
iteration
versus recursion 316 – 318
iterative BFS **158**

J

Java Collection Framework (JCF) 29, 30, 160
- trees 161

K

knowledge retrieval 19 - 21

L

LRU caches 463
LinkedHashMap 68
LinkedHashSet 245
LinkedList 29
LinkedListQueue 99, 100
LinkedListStack 86, 87
last-in first-out (LIFO) 12
leaderboards 479
linear data structures 9 - 11
- arrays 11
- linked lists 11
- queue 12
- stack 12

linear probing 119
link-based queue 99, 100
linked lists 6, 11, 65
- ConcurrentLinkedQueue 68
- efficiency 66
- LinkedHashMap 68
- operations 66

linked lists, versus arrays
- access 69
- flexibility 69
- high-frequency logging 69
- operations 69

linked-based stack 90
- versus array-based stack 88 – 90

list-based stack 86, 87
lists 431
load balancers 467
lock-free data structures and memory models 426
- arrays and lists 431
- concurrent hash tables 433, 434
- memory visibility 426
- stacks and queues 427 – 431

lock-free general-purpose deques 433
lock-free method 91
log analysis 479

M

Mutual Exclusion (Mutex) 418
- Condition interface 423, 424
- deadlock 419, 420
- lock interface 420 – 422
- synchronization 419

map 109, 110
- abstract data type (ADT) 112 – 114
- address book example 110
- concrete implementations 114
- parking garage ticketing system example 111, 112

maps/routing (Dijkstra's/A*) 473
master theorem 326, 327
- cost of non-recursive work 328
- cost of recursive calls 327, 328
- summary 329, 330

matrix 14
max heap 192
memoization 276, 475
- key applications 475

memoization, versus tabulation 276
- complexity 278
- execution style 277
- space usage 278
- storage structure 277
- usage scenario 278

memory 19
memory allocators 463
memory recall 19
merge sort 363 - 365, 378
- analyzing 324, 325
- complexity, determining 331
- master theorem, applying 331
- parameters, identifying 330
- recurrence relation, defining 330
- recursive value, calculating 330

min heap 192

multi-threaded UI operations **481**

music streaming service
- features 48

N

NavigableMap interface
- operations 162
- range operations 163

n-ary tree ADT **148**

naive recursion
- challenge 320 – 322

non-comparison-based sorting **357, 372**
- counting sort 372 – 375
- Radix sort 375 – 377

non-linear data structures **9, 13**
- graph-based structures 14
- hash-based structures 14
- hierarchical structures 13
- hybrid structures 15
- set-based structures 15

O

O(n2) sorting algorithms **357**

open addressing **119**
- linear probing 119
- quadratic probing 119

optimization **475**
- key applications 475

ordered arrays **61, 64, 65**

organization and hierarchy **469**
- key applications 469

out-of-place sorting algorithms **355**

P

Plain Old Java Objects (POJOs) **224**

PriorityBlockingQueue
- concurrent priority queue 443

PriorityQueue **29, 243**
- as heap 203

pairing heaps **201**

path **218**

priority and scheduling **471**
- key applications 471

priority queue **95, 183 - 185**
- abstract data type (ADT) 187
- complexity of unsorted array, versus sorted array 189
- flight seat assignments example 185
- implementing, with sorted array 189
- implementing, with unsorted array 188
- top K elements example 185, 186

product pipeline with DP **293**
- edge relaxation 294
- initialization 294
- intuition 293
- objectives 293
- results 294 – 296
- solution 293
- topological ordering 293

program execution (call stack) **465**

Q

quadratic probing **119**

queue **12, 68, 93**
- abstract data type (ADT) 95, 96
- array-based queue 97 – 99
- concrete implementations 96
- deferred processing and prioritization example 95
- dequeue operation 94
- enqueue operation 94
- link-based queue 99
- print spooler queue example 94

quick sort **366 - 368, 378**
- depth-first search 333
- partition process 367
- pivot selection 368

R

Radix sort **375 - 379**

ReadWriteLock
- read-heavy workloads 438

Reasoning phase **21**
rate limiting **471**
re-entrant lock **91**
real-time data streaming **481**
recurrence relations **273**
recursion **274, 313, 477**
complexity, measuring 323
in data structures 332, 333
key applications 477
tail recursion 322
versus iteration 316 – 318
recursion call stack **318, 319**
recursion tree **325**
analysis, of f(N) 326
non-recursive component 325
recursive component 325
total cost of merge sort 326
recursive BFS **158**
on graph 333
recursive case **314**
recursive function **314**
recursive methods, depth-first traversal
in-order traversal (left, node, right) 152
post-order traversal (left, right, node) 153
pre-order traversal (node, left, right) 151
recursive patterns **314**
recursive traversal **156**
registry lookup **18**
relational modeling **473**
key applications 473
rendering **479**
resource allocation **475**
return address **318**

S

safe and managed concurrency **436**
BlockingQueue 436
CompletableFuture 437, 438
CountDownLatch 439
executors 436
ReadWriteLock 438
semaphore 439
ThreadLocal 437
selection sort **359, 360**
semaphore **424, 425, 439**
separate chaining **120, 121**
sequence alignment **475**
service meshes (graph representation) **473**
session **18**
set-based structures **15**
sets **15**
shared state **414 - 416**
sharedCounter++ operation **414**
social networks (BFS/DFS) **473**
sorted array
priority queues, implementing 189
sorted set **15**
sorting algorithm **353**
advanced comparison sorts 363
bubble sort 357, 358
comparison-based sorting 357
facilities 385, 386
hybrid comparison-based sorts 380
implementations 385, 386
in-place sorting algorithms 355
insertion sort 360, 361
non-comparison sorts 372
non-comparison-based sorting 357
out-of-place sorting algorithms 355
proof sketch 362
selection implications 362
selection sort 359, 360
space complexity 356
stability 354, 355
time complexity 356
stack **12, 80**
abstract data type (ADT) 84
array-based stack 85
browser back-button navigation example 81, 82
concrete implementations 85
DFS implementation 244

elements, adding 81
elements, removing 81
example 90
list-based stack 86, 87
memory 90
pop operation 80
push operation 80
word processor undo/redo mechanismexample 83

state management **465**
key applications 465

T

ThreadLocal
per-thread context 437

Timsort **383**
example 383, 384

Top-K problems **471**

TransferQueue
transfer operations 442

TreeMap **29**
for sorted key-value storage 161
ordered map operations 244

TreeSet **29**
for sorted unique elements 162
with heap-like functionality 204

Two-Pivot strategy **380**
example 381, 382

tabulation **276**

tabulation, versus memoization **276**
complexity 278
execution style 277
space usage 278
storage structure 277
usage scenario 278

tail recursion **322**
examples 322, 323

task orchestration **23**

task prioritization **22**

task scheduling **471**

text wrapping **475**

thread **412 - 414**

thread-safe deque **91 - 93**

traversal **150, 151, 235, 236**
breadth-first traversal 239, 240
depth-first traversal 236 – 238

traversal algorithms (BFS) **465**

tree **13, 141**
binary tree 142, 143
general (n-ary) tree 146
in Java Collection Framework (JCF) 160, 161

tree and graph traversal (DFS) **477**

tree-based heap **192**

tries **9, 19**

U

undirected graph **219**

unordered arrays **61, 62**
drone log buffer example 63, 64
high-throughput service logger example 64

unsorted array
priority queues, implementing 188

V

vectors **61**

vertex **223 - 225**

vertex-to-edge **226 - 228**

vertices **218**

W

Web API endpoints **481**

weighted graph **220 - 222**